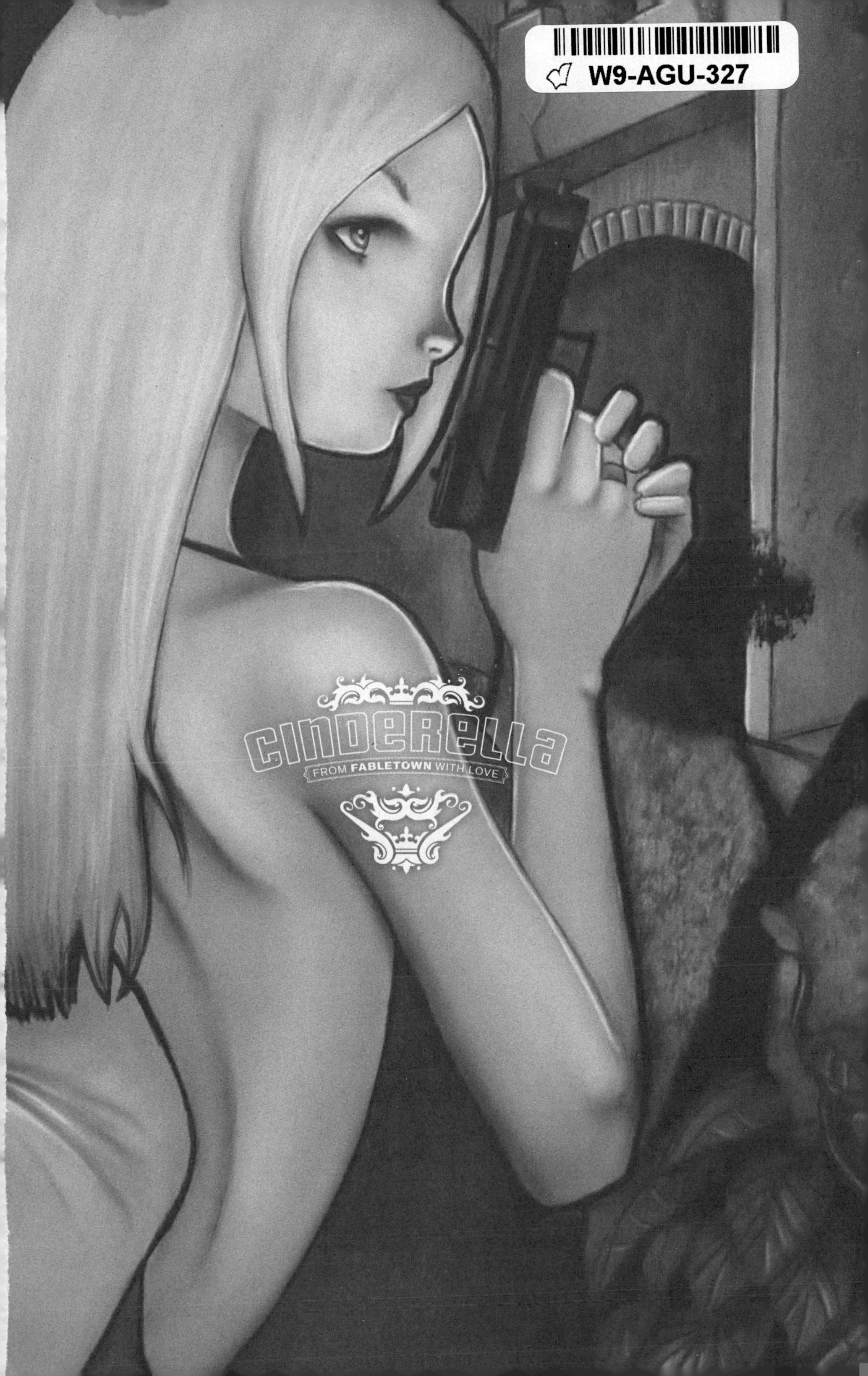
CINDERELLA
FROM FABLETOWN WITH LOVE

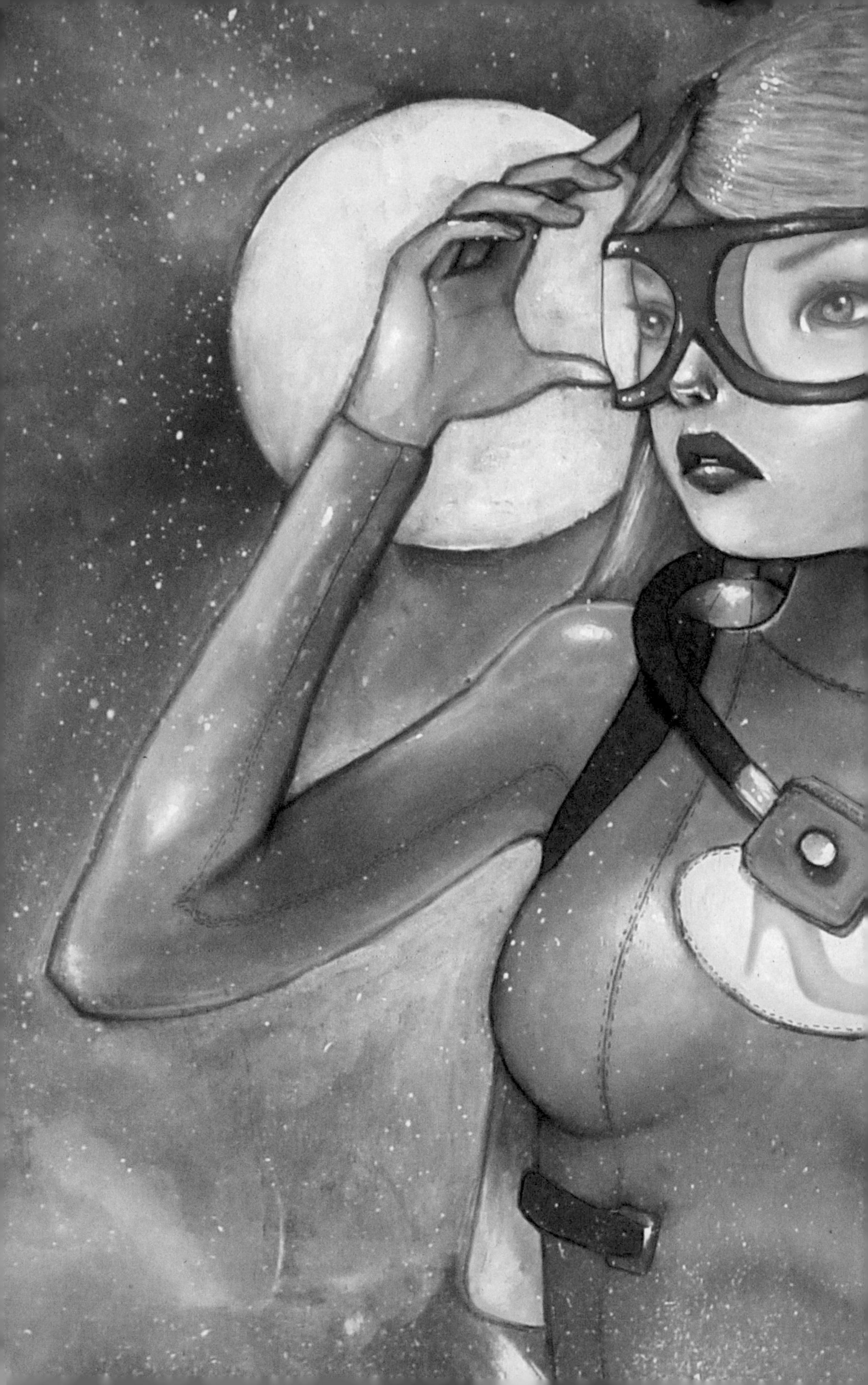

CINDERELLA

FROM **FABLETOWN** WITH LOVE

Chris Roberson Writer

Shawn McManus Artist

Lee Loughridge Colorist

Todd Klein Letterer

Bill Willingham Consultant

Chrissie Zullo Original Series Covers

FABLES created by Bill Willingham

Karen Berger, SVP – Executive Editor
Shelly Bond, Editor – Original Series
Angela Rufino, Associate Editor – Original Series
Bob Harras, Group Editor – Collected Editions
Scott Nybakken, Editor
Robbin Brosterman, Design Director – Books
Louis Prandi, Art Director

DC COMICS
Diane Nelson, President
Dan DiDio and Jim Lee, Co-Publishers
Geoff Johns, Chief Creative Officer
Patrick Caldon, EVP – Finance and Administration
John Rood, EVP – Sales, Marketing and Business Development
Amy Genkins, SVP – Business and Legal Affairs
Steve Rotterdam, SVP – Sales and Marketing
John Cunningham, VP – Marketing
Terri Cunningham, VP – Managing Editor
Alison Gill, VP – Manufacturing
David Hyde, VP – Publicity
Sue Pohja, VP – Book Trade Sales
Alysse Soll, VP – Advertising and Custom Publishing
Bob Wayne, VP – Sales
Mark Chiarello, Art Director

Cover illustration by Chrissie Zullo.

SUSTAINABLE
FORESTRY
INITIATIVE

Certified Fiber Sourcing
www.sfiprogram.org

Fiber used in this product line meets the
sourcing requirements of the SFI program.
www.sfiprogram.org PWC-SFICOC-260

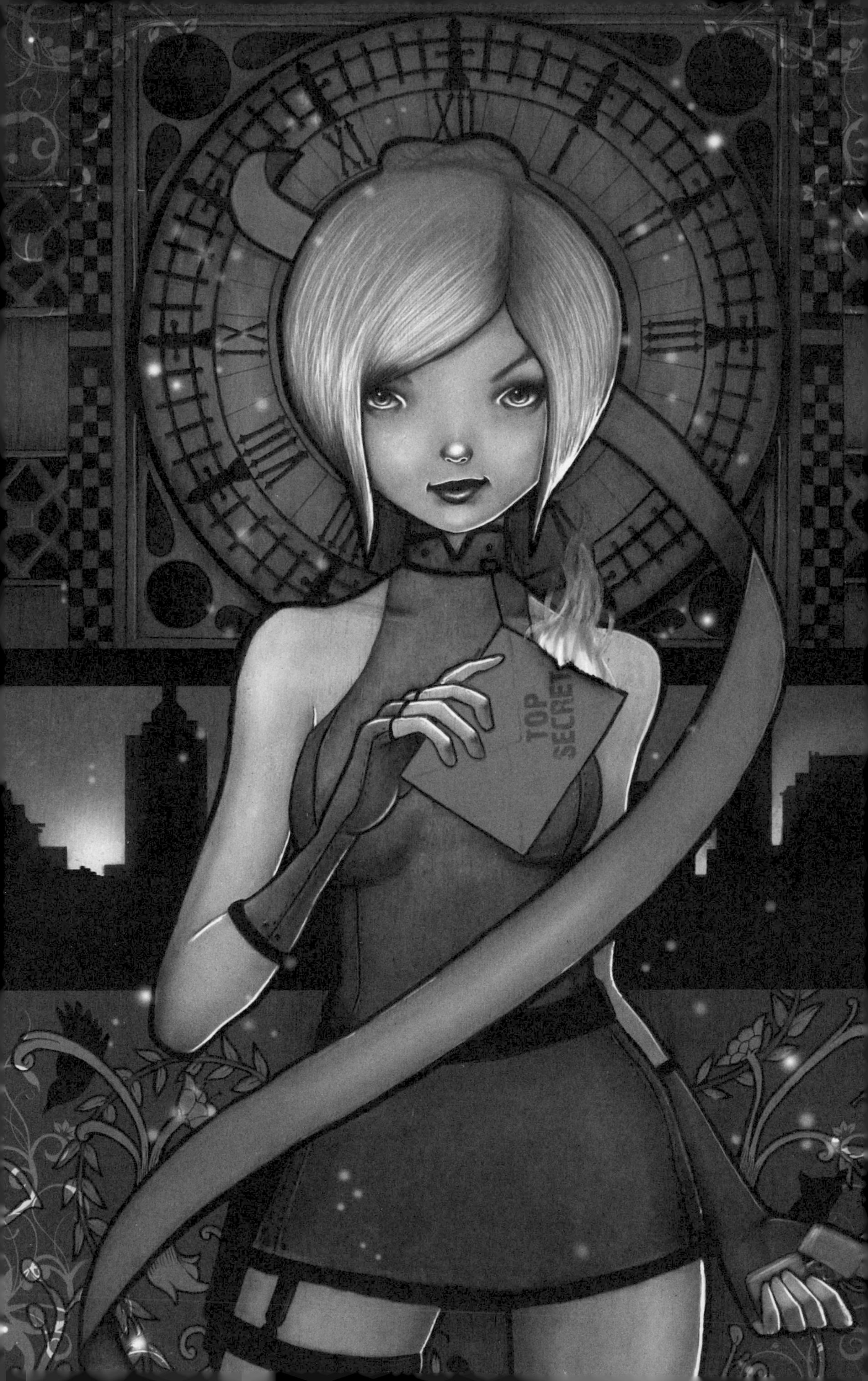
TOP SECRET

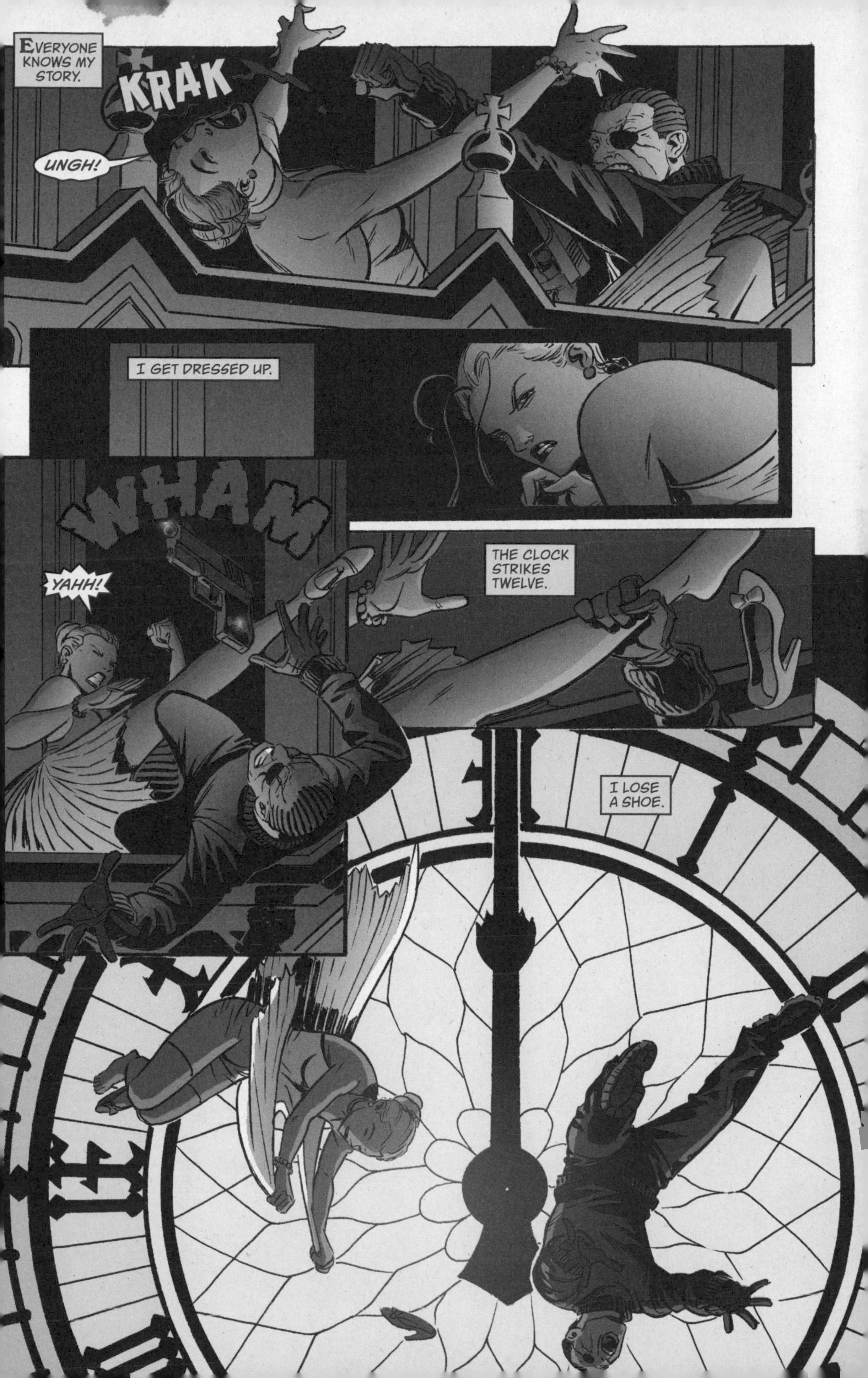

EVERYONE KNOWS MY STORY.
KRAK
UNGH!
I GET DRESSED UP.
WHAM
YAHH!
THE CLOCK STRIKES TWELVE.
I LOSE A SHOE.

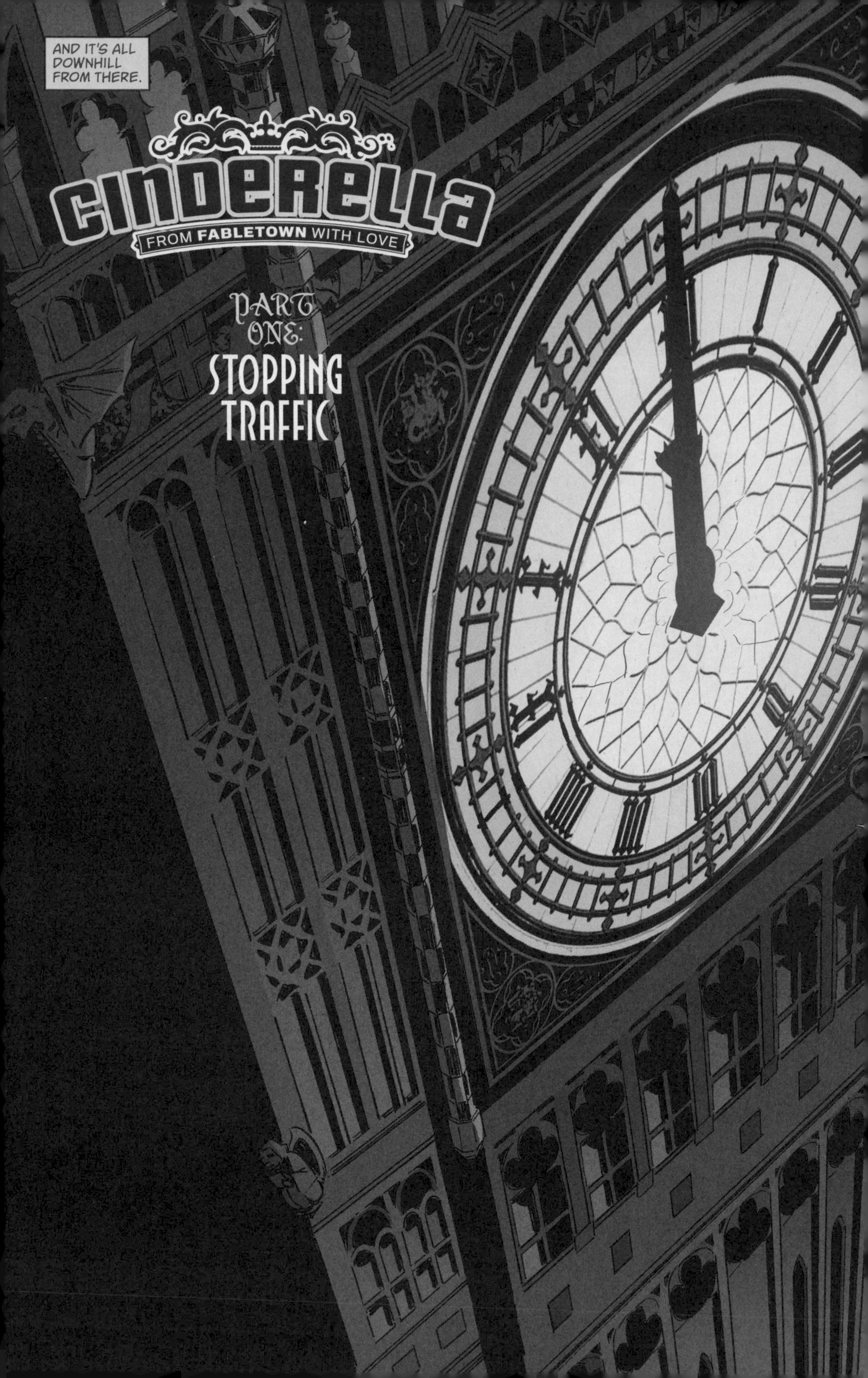

AND IT'S ALL DOWNHILL FROM THERE.
CINDERELLA
FROM FABLETOWN WITH LOVE
PART ONE:
STOPPING TRAFFIC

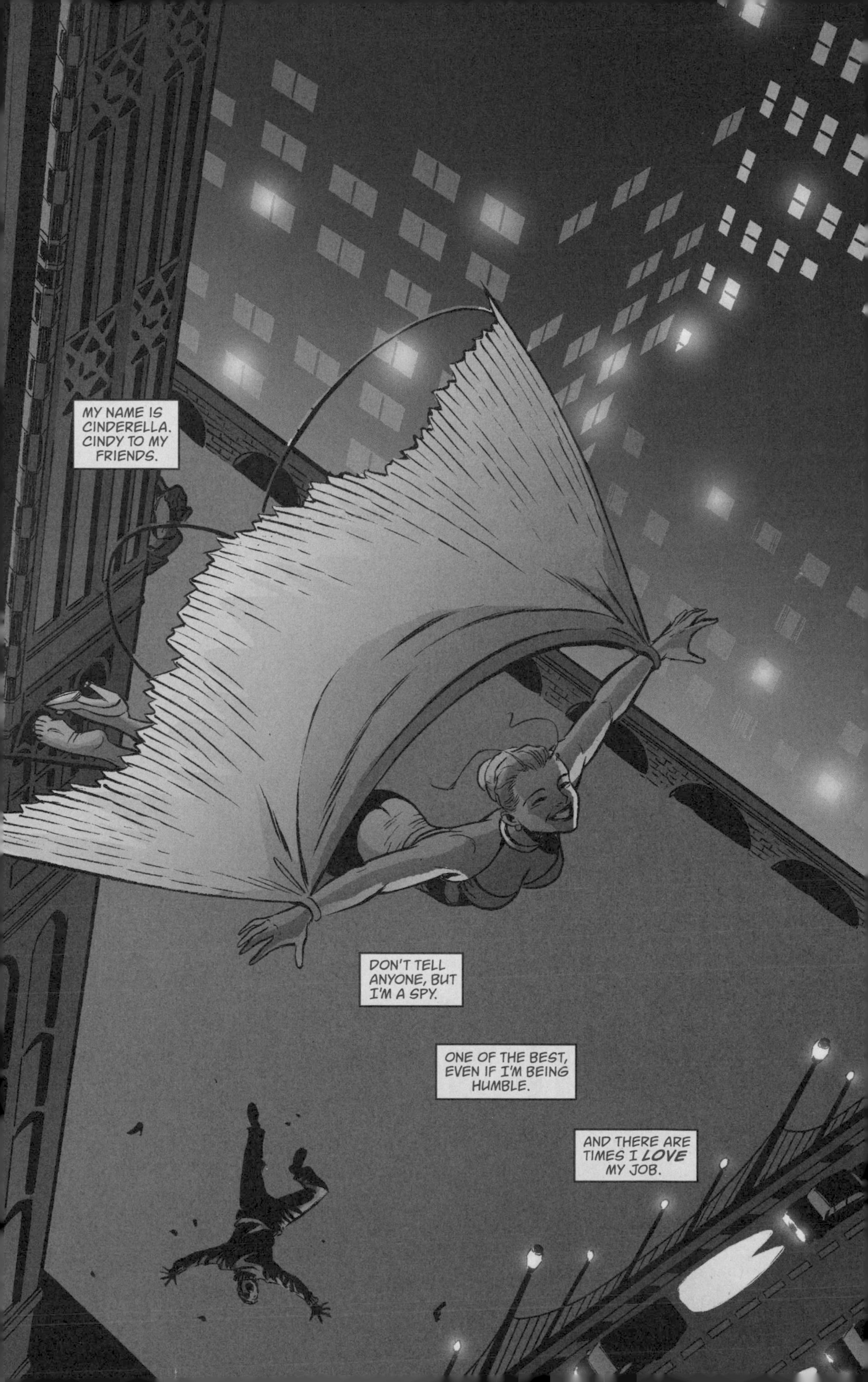
MY NAME IS CINDERELLA. CINDY TO MY FRIENDS.
DON'T TELL ANYONE, BUT I'M A SPY.
ONE OF THE BEST, EVEN IF I'M BEING HUMBLE.
AND THERE ARE TIMES I LOVE MY JOB.

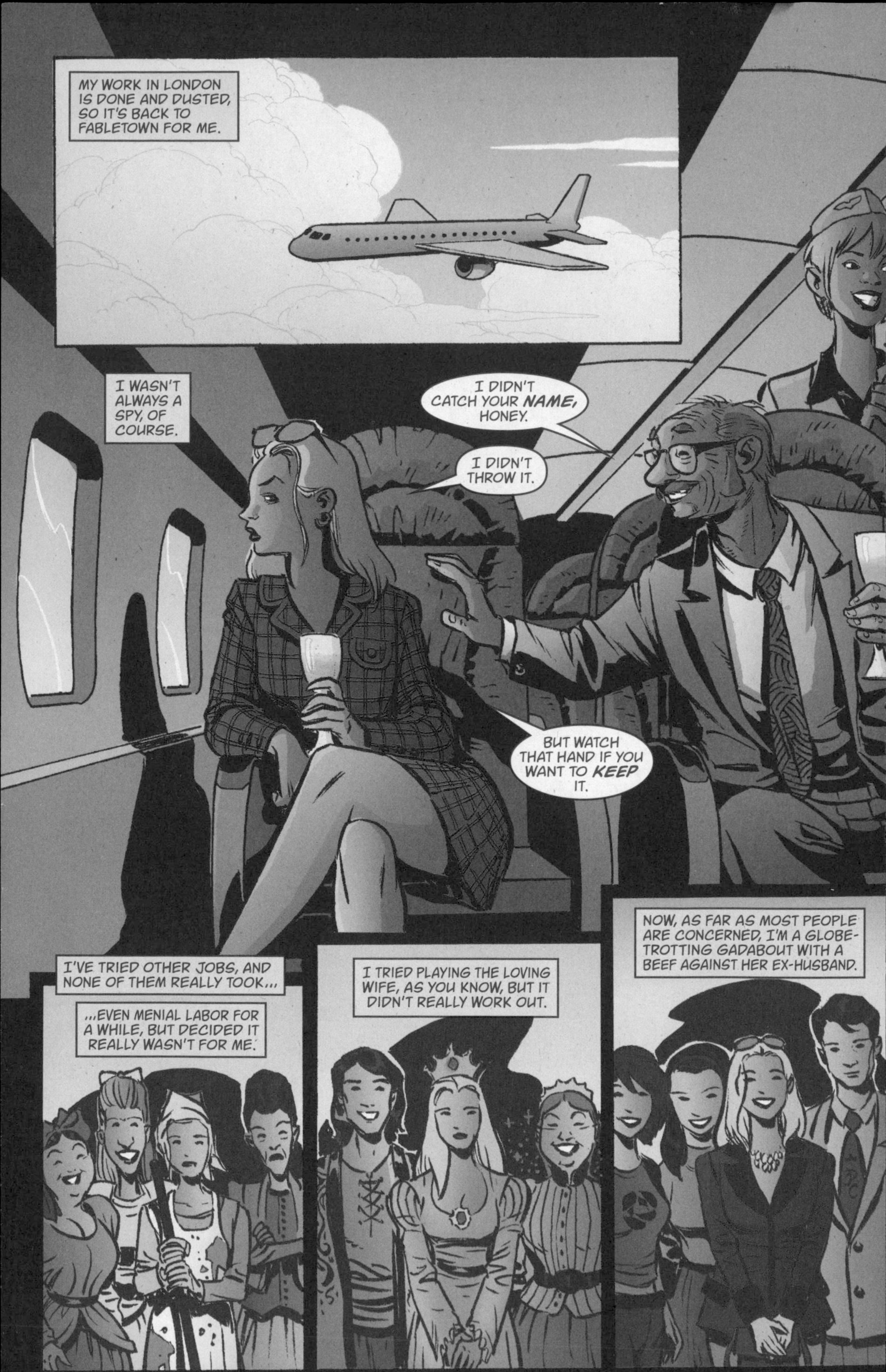
MY WORK IN LONDON IS DONE AND DUSTED, SO IT'S BACK TO FABLETOWN FOR ME.
I WASN'T ALWAYS A SPY, OF COURSE.
I DIDN'T CATCH YOUR NAME, HONEY.
I DIDN'T THROW IT.
BUT WATCH THAT HAND IF YOU WANT TO KEEP IT.
I'VE TRIED OTHER JOBS, AND NONE OF THEM REALLY TOOK...
...EVEN MENIAL LABOR FOR A WHILE, BUT DECIDED IT REALLY WASN'T FOR ME.
I TRIED PLAYING THE LOVING WIFE, AS YOU KNOW, BUT IT DIDN'T REALLY WORK OUT.
NOW, AS FAR AS MOST PEOPLE ARE CONCERNED, I'M A GLOBE-TROTTING GADABOUT WITH A BEEF AGAINST HER EX-HUSBAND.

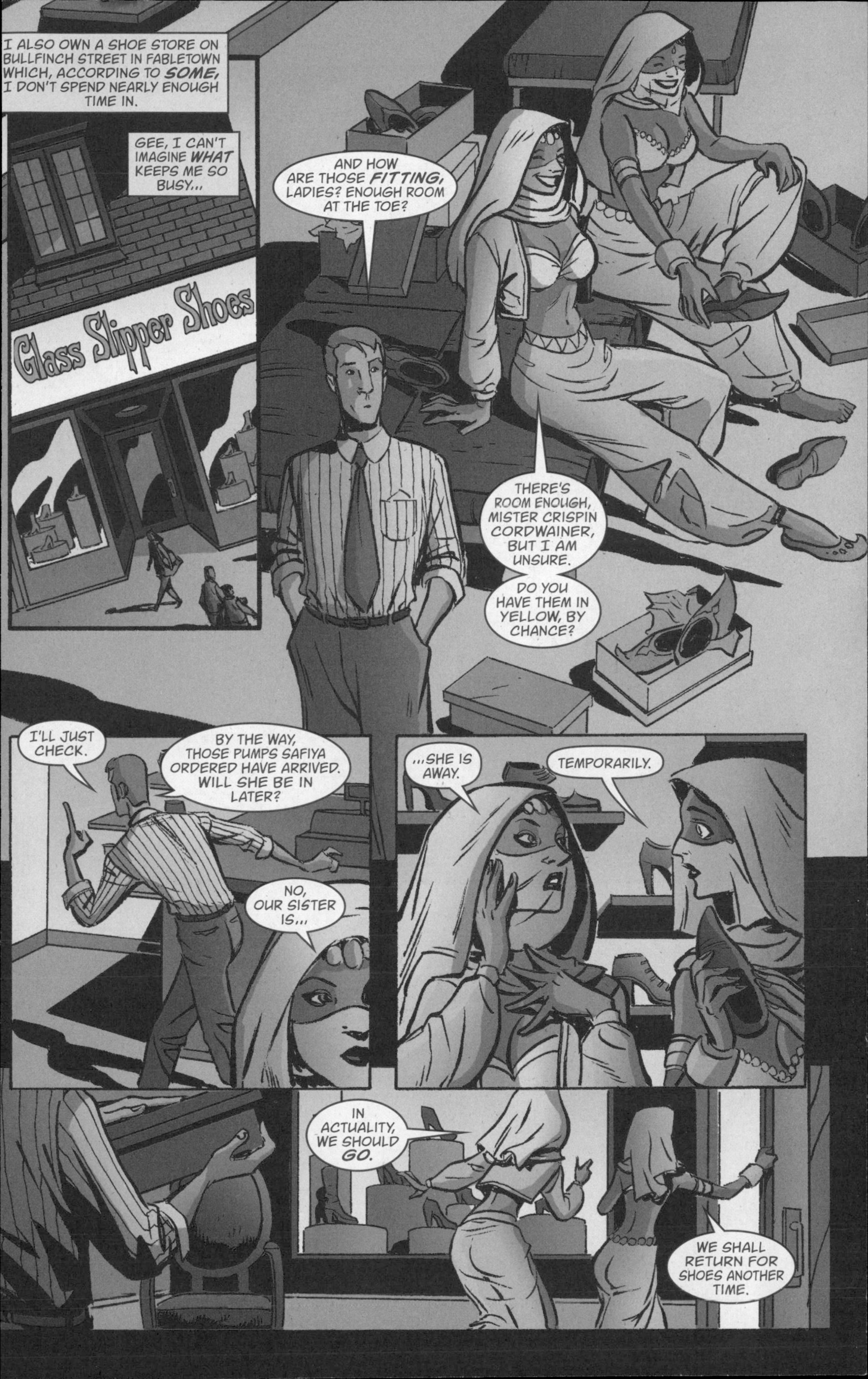
I ALSO OWN A SHOE STORE ON BULLFINCH STREET IN FABLETOWN WHICH, ACCORDING TO **SOME**, I DON'T SPEND NEARLY ENOUGH TIME IN.
GEE, I CAN'T IMAGINE **WHAT** KEEPS ME SO BUSY...
Glass Slipper Shoes
AND HOW ARE THOSE ***FITTING***, LADIES? ENOUGH ROOM AT THE TOE?
THERE'S ROOM ENOUGH, MISTER CRISPIN CORDWAINER, BUT I AM UNSURE.
DO YOU HAVE THEM IN YELLOW, BY CHANCE?
I'LL JUST CHECK.
BY THE WAY, THOSE PUMPS SAFIYA ORDERED HAVE ARRIVED. WILL SHE BE IN LATER?
NO, OUR SISTER IS...
...SHE IS AWAY.
TEMPORARILY.
IN ACTUALITY, WE SHOULD **GO**.
WE SHALL RETURN FOR SHOES ANOTHER TIME.

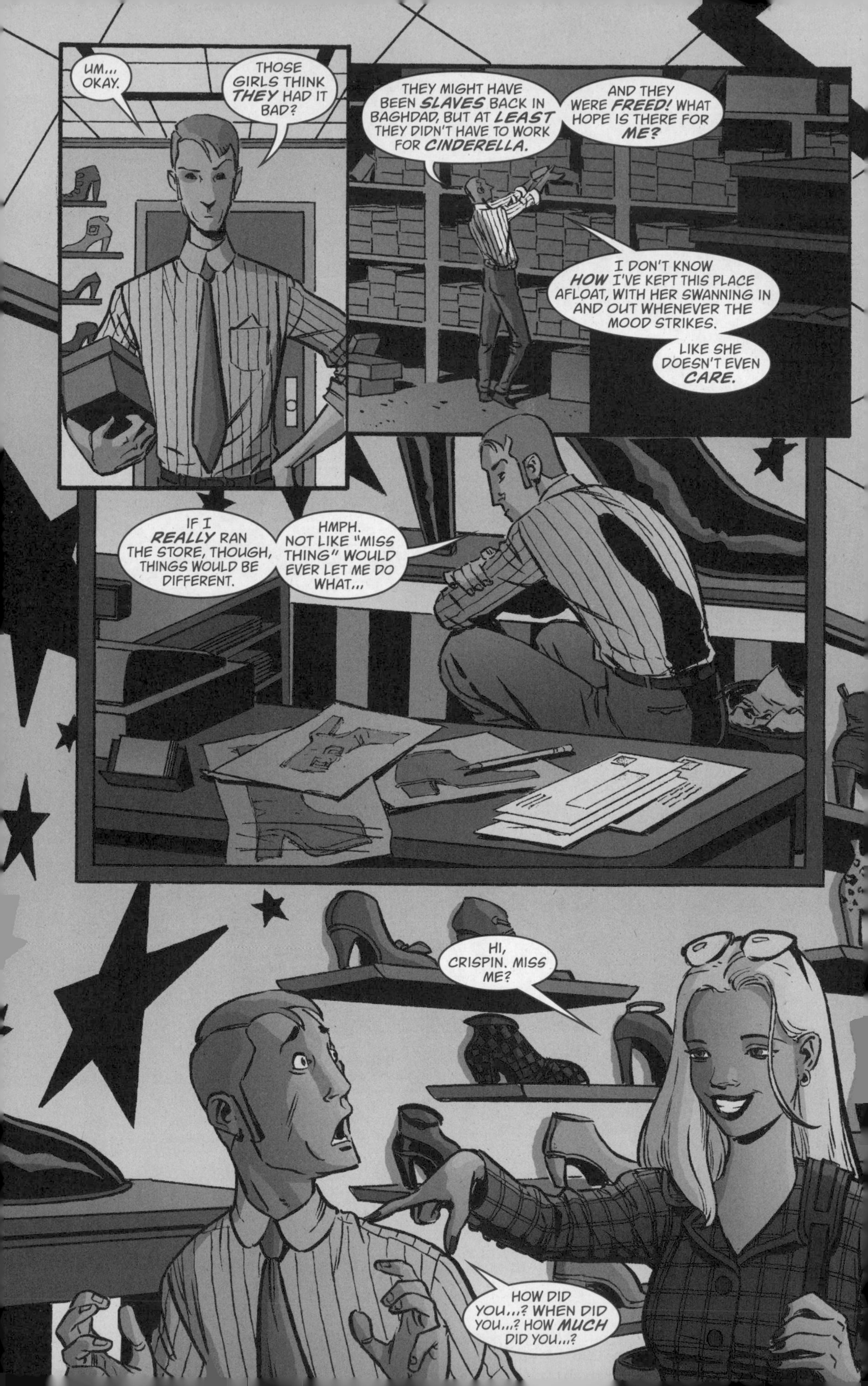
UM... OKAY.
THOSE GIRLS THINK THEY HAD IT BAD?
THEY MIGHT HAVE BEEN SLAVES BACK IN BAGHDAD, BUT AT LEAST THEY DIDN'T HAVE TO WORK FOR CINDERELLA.
AND THEY WERE FREED! WHAT HOPE IS THERE FOR ME?
I DON'T KNOW HOW I'VE KEPT THIS PLACE AFLOAT, WITH HER SWANNING IN AND OUT WHENEVER THE MOOD STRIKES.
LIKE SHE DOESN'T EVEN CARE.
IF I REALLY RAN THE STORE, THOUGH, THINGS WOULD BE DIFFERENT.
HMPH. NOT LIKE "MISS THING" WOULD EVER LET ME DO WHAT...
HI, CRISPIN. MISS ME?
HOW DID YOU...? WHEN DID YOU...? HOW MUCH DID YOU...?

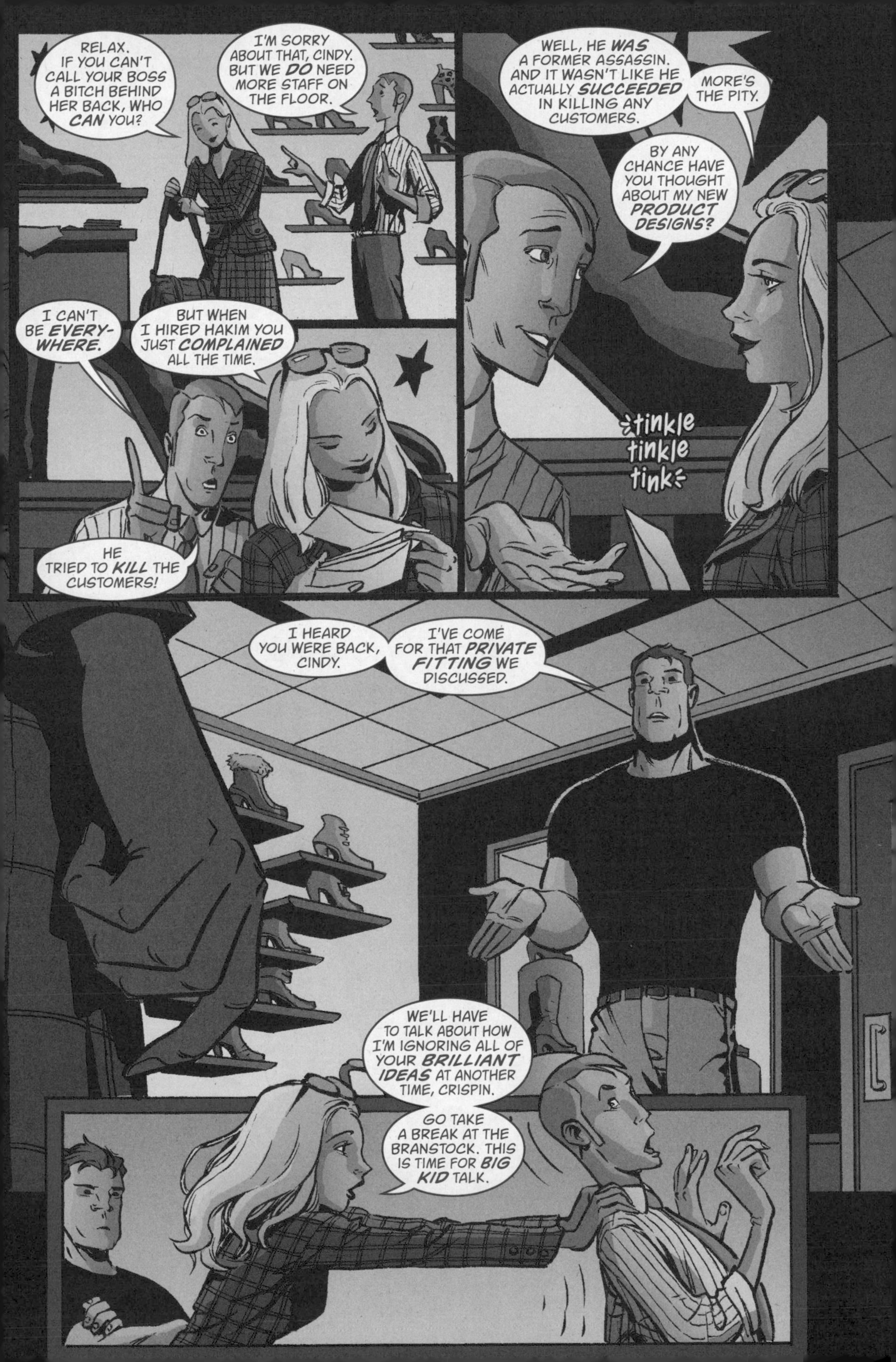
RELAX. IF YOU CAN'T CALL YOUR BOSS A BITCH BEHIND HER BACK, WHO CAN YOU?
I'M SORRY ABOUT THAT, CINDY. BUT WE DO NEED MORE STAFF ON THE FLOOR.
I CAN'T BE EVERY-WHERE.
BUT WHEN I HIRED HAKIM YOU JUST COMPLAINED ALL THE TIME.
HE TRIED TO KILL THE CUSTOMERS!
WELL, HE WAS A FORMER ASSASSIN. AND IT WASN'T LIKE HE ACTUALLY SUCCEEDED IN KILLING ANY CUSTOMERS.
MORE'S THE PITY.
BY ANY CHANCE HAVE YOU THOUGHT ABOUT MY NEW PRODUCT DESIGNS?
tinkle tinkle tink
I HEARD YOU WERE BACK, CINDY.
I'VE COME FOR THAT PRIVATE FITTING WE DISCUSSED.
WE'LL HAVE TO TALK ABOUT HOW I'M IGNORING ALL OF YOUR BRILLIANT IDEAS AT ANOTHER TIME, CRISPIN.
GO TAKE A BREAK AT THE BRANSTOCK. THIS IS TIME FOR BIG KID TALK.

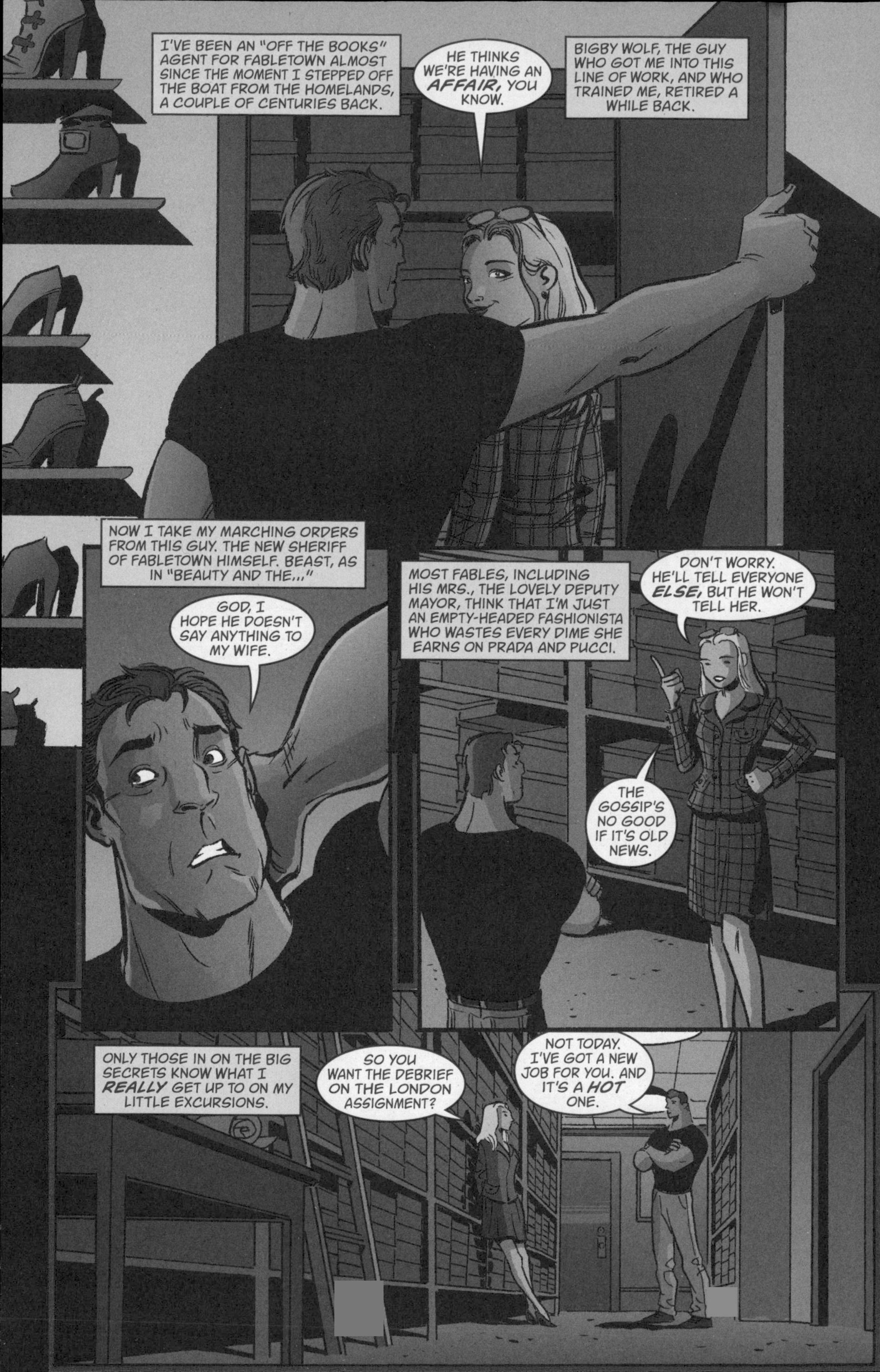

I'VE BEEN AN "OFF THE BOOKS" AGENT FOR FABLETOWN ALMOST SINCE THE MOMENT I STEPPED OFF THE BOAT FROM THE HOMELANDS, A COUPLE OF CENTURIES BACK.
HE THINKS WE'RE HAVING AN AFFAIR, YOU KNOW.
BIGBY WOLF, THE GUY WHO GOT ME INTO THIS LINE OF WORK, AND WHO TRAINED ME, RETIRED A WHILE BACK.
NOW I TAKE MY MARCHING ORDERS FROM THIS GUY. THE NEW SHERIFF OF FABLETOWN HIMSELF. BEAST, AS IN "BEAUTY AND THE..."
GOD, I HOPE HE DOESN'T SAY ANYTHING TO MY WIFE.
MOST FABLES, INCLUDING HIS MRS., THE LOVELY DEPUTY MAYOR, THINK THAT I'M JUST AN EMPTY-HEADED FASHIONISTA WHO WASTES EVERY DIME SHE EARNS ON PRADA AND PUCCI.
DON'T WORRY. HE'LL TELL EVERYONE ELSE, BUT HE WON'T TELL HER.
THE GOSSIP'S NO GOOD IF IT'S OLD NEWS.
ONLY THOSE IN ON THE BIG SECRETS KNOW WHAT I REALLY GET UP TO ON MY LITTLE EXCURSIONS.
SO YOU WANT THE DEBRIEF ON THE LONDON ASSIGNMENT?
NOT TODAY. I'VE GOT A NEW JOB FOR YOU. AND IT'S A HOT ONE.

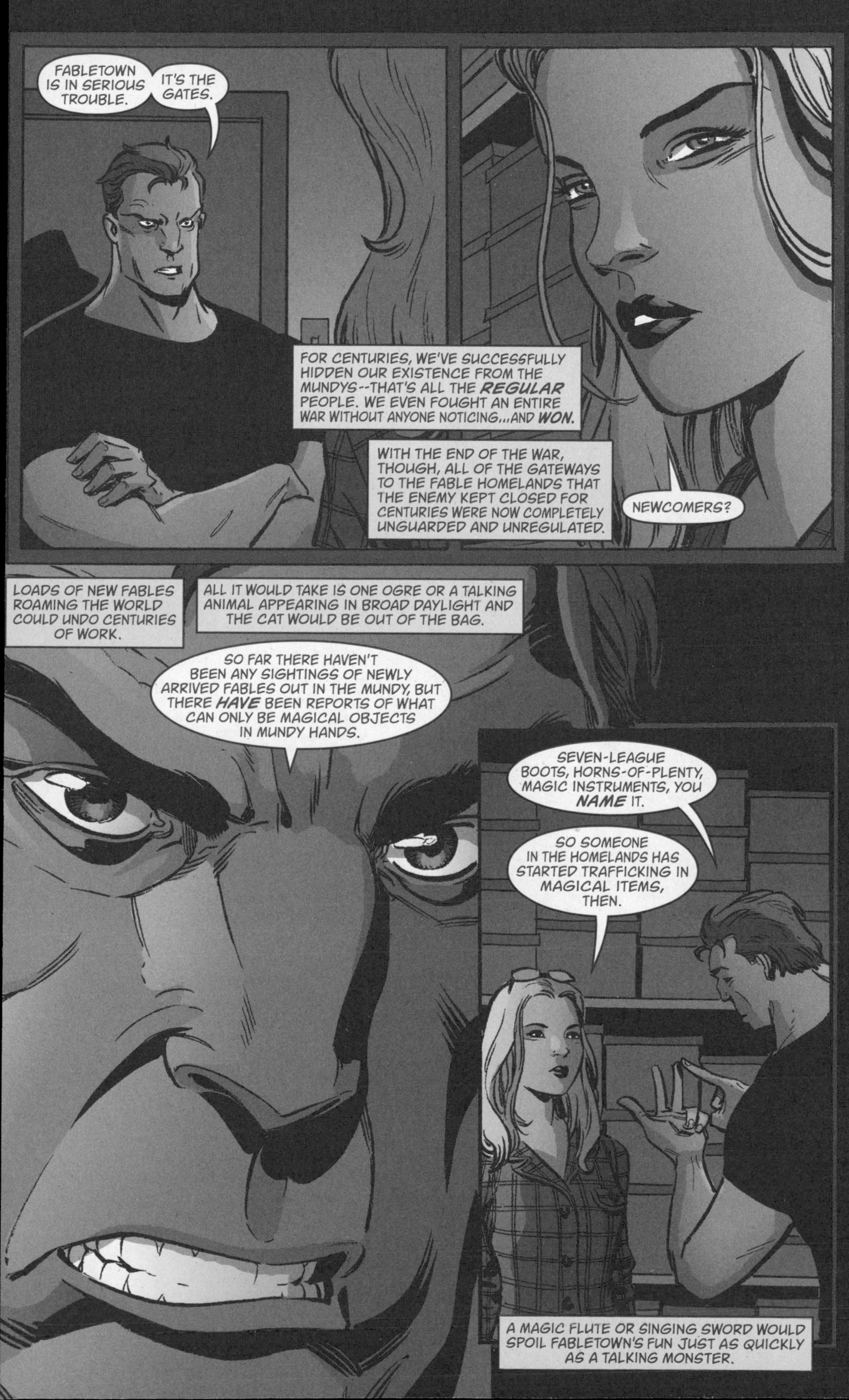
FABLETOWN IS IN SERIOUS TROUBLE.
IT'S THE GATES.
FOR CENTURIES, WE'VE SUCCESSFULLY HIDDEN OUR EXISTENCE FROM THE MUNDYS--THAT'S ALL THE REGULAR PEOPLE. WE EVEN FOUGHT AN ENTIRE WAR WITHOUT ANYONE NOTICING...AND WON.
WITH THE END OF THE WAR, THOUGH, ALL OF THE GATEWAYS TO THE FABLE HOMELANDS THAT THE ENEMY KEPT CLOSED FOR CENTURIES WERE NOW COMPLETELY UNGUARDED AND UNREGULATED.
NEWCOMERS?
LOADS OF NEW FABLES ROAMING THE WORLD COULD UNDO CENTURIES OF WORK.
ALL IT WOULD TAKE IS ONE OGRE OR A TALKING ANIMAL APPEARING IN BROAD DAYLIGHT AND THE CAT WOULD BE OUT OF THE BAG.
SO FAR THERE HAVEN'T BEEN ANY SIGHTINGS OF NEWLY ARRIVED FABLES OUT IN THE MUNDY, BUT THERE HAVE BEEN REPORTS OF WHAT CAN ONLY BE MAGICAL OBJECTS IN MUNDY HANDS.
SEVEN-LEAGUE BOOTS, HORNS-OF-PLENTY, MAGIC INSTRUMENTS, YOU NAME IT.
SO SOMEONE IN THE HOMELANDS HAS STARTED TRAFFICKING IN MAGICAL ITEMS, THEN.
A MAGIC FLUTE OR SINGING SWORD WOULD SPOIL FABLETOWN'S FUN JUST AS QUICKLY AS A TALKING MONSTER.

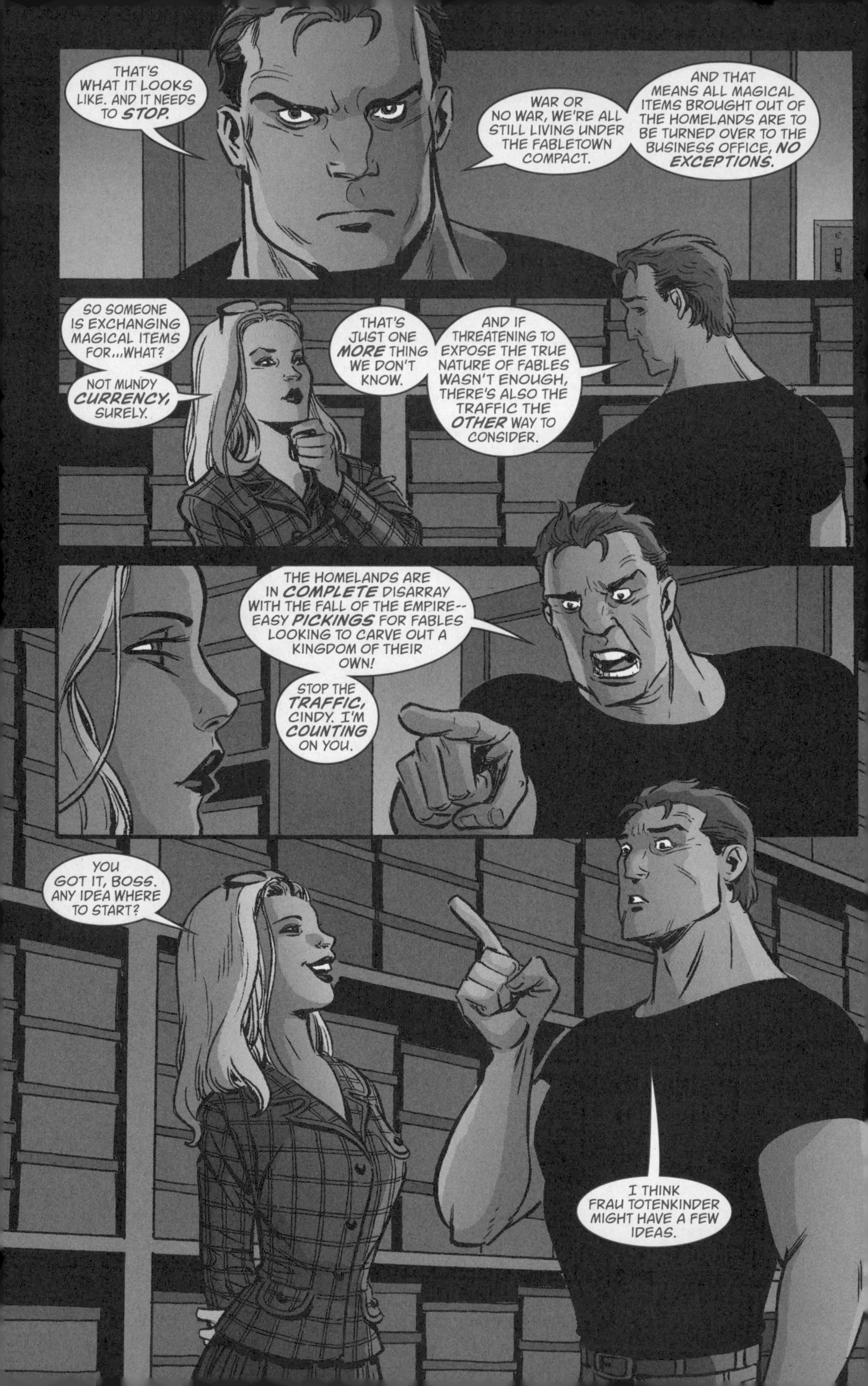
THAT'S WHAT IT LOOKS LIKE. AND IT NEEDS TO STOP.
WAR OR NO WAR, WE'RE ALL STILL LIVING UNDER THE FABLETOWN COMPACT.
AND THAT MEANS ALL MAGICAL ITEMS BROUGHT OUT OF THE HOMELANDS ARE TO BE TURNED OVER TO THE BUSINESS OFFICE, NO EXCEPTIONS.
SO SOMEONE IS EXCHANGING MAGICAL ITEMS FOR...WHAT?
NOT MUNDY CURRENCY, SURELY.
THAT'S JUST ONE MORE THING WE DON'T KNOW.
AND IF THREATENING TO EXPOSE THE TRUE NATURE OF FABLES WASN'T ENOUGH, THERE'S ALSO THE TRAFFIC THE OTHER WAY TO CONSIDER.
THE HOMELANDS ARE IN COMPLETE DISARRAY WITH THE FALL OF THE EMPIRE-- EASY PICKINGS FOR FABLES LOOKING TO CARVE OUT A KINGDOM OF THEIR OWN!
STOP THE TRAFFIC, CINDY. I'M COUNTING ON YOU.
YOU GOT IT, BOSS. ANY IDEA WHERE TO START?
I THINK FRAU TOTENKINDER MIGHT HAVE A FEW IDEAS.

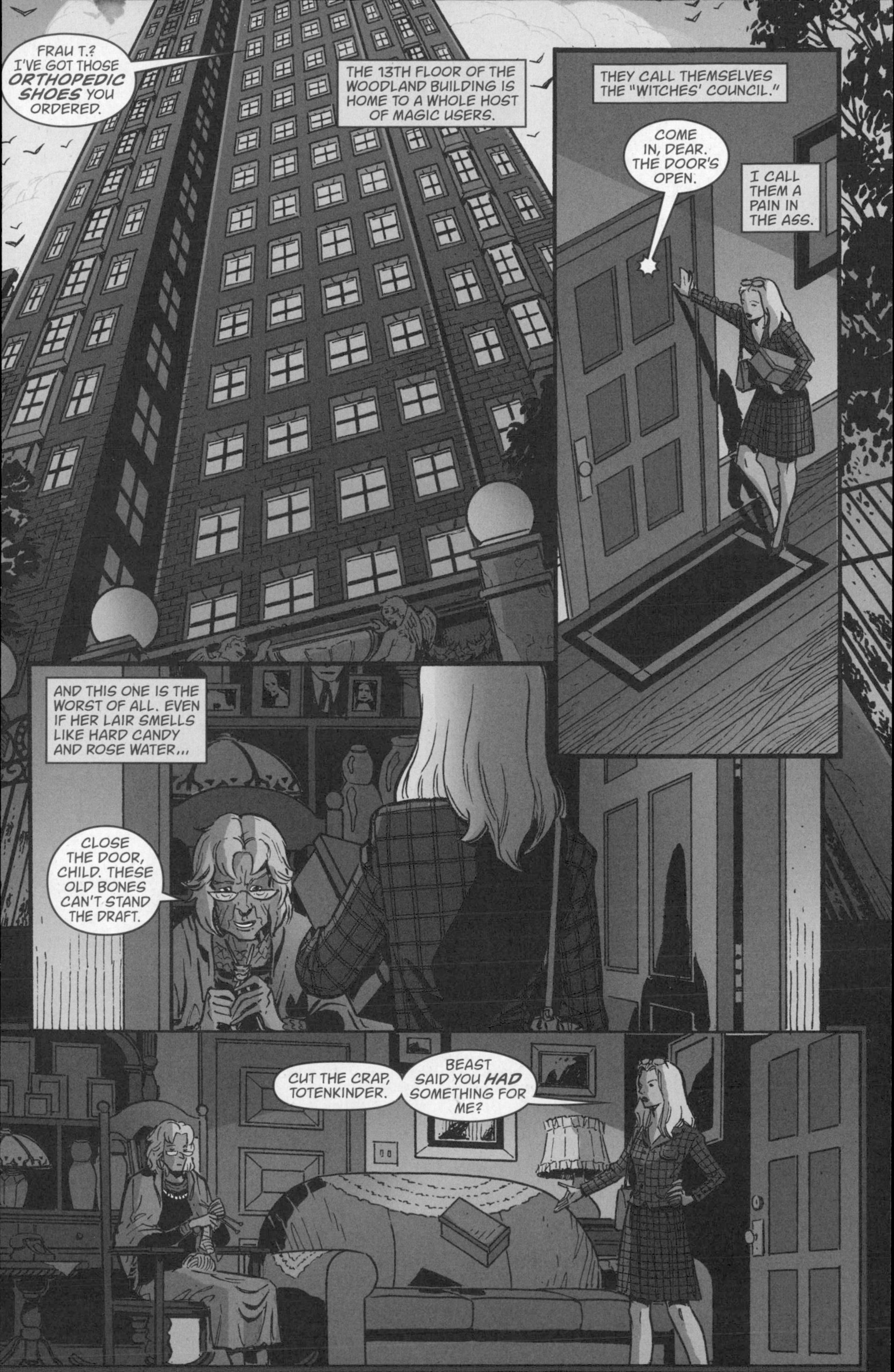
FRAU T.? I'VE GOT THOSE ORTHOPEDIC SHOES YOU ORDERED.
THE 13TH FLOOR OF THE WOODLAND BUILDING IS HOME TO A WHOLE HOST OF MAGIC USERS.
THEY CALL THEMSELVES THE "WITCHES' COUNCIL."
COME IN, DEAR. THE DOOR'S OPEN.
I CALL THEM A PAIN IN THE ASS.
AND THIS ONE IS THE WORST OF ALL. EVEN IF HER LAIR SMELLS LIKE HARD CANDY AND ROSE WATER...
CLOSE THE DOOR, CHILD. THESE OLD BONES CAN'T STAND THE DRAFT.
CUT THE CRAP, TOTENKINDER.
BEAST SAID YOU HAD SOMETHING FOR ME?

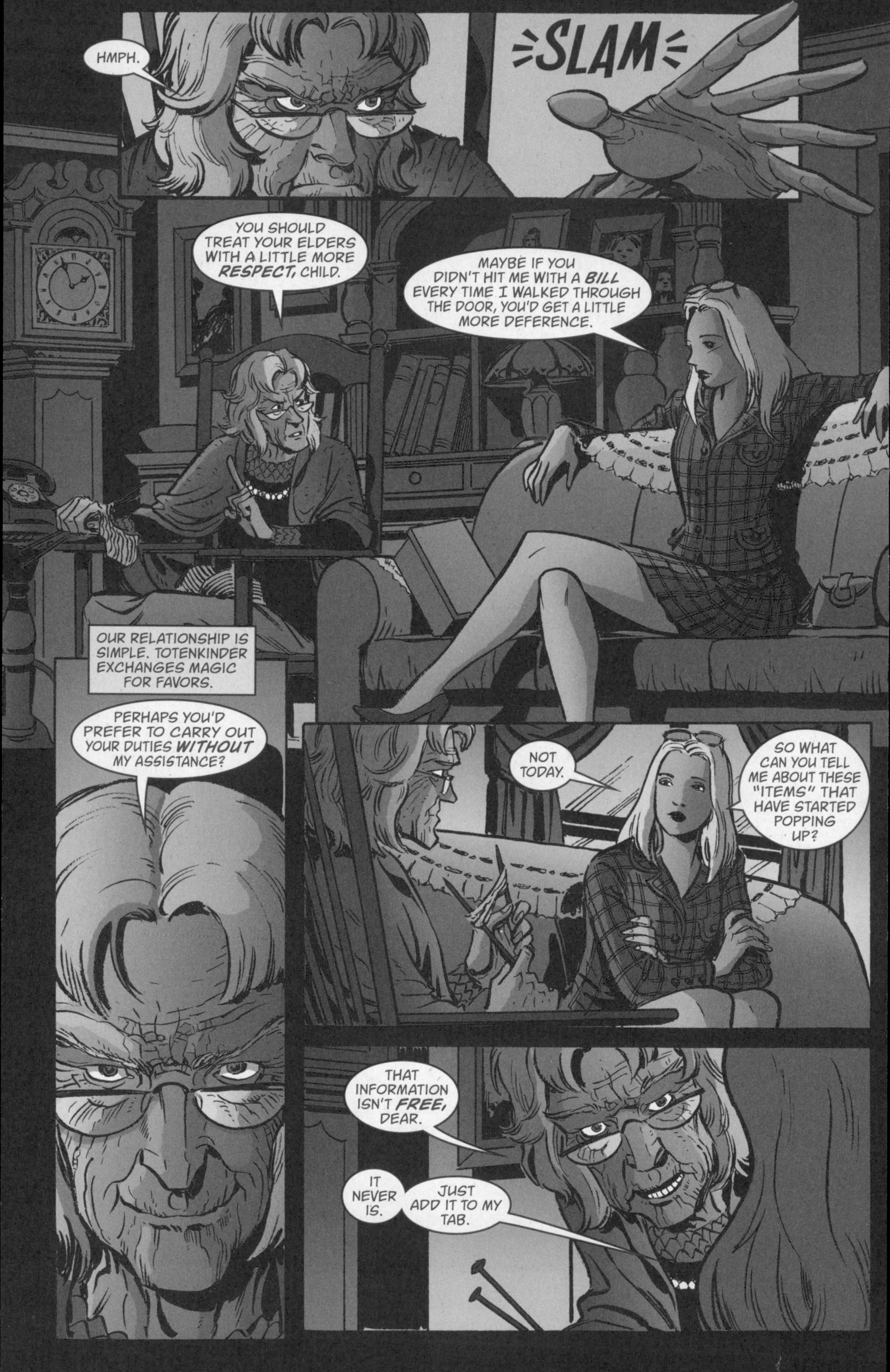
HMPH.
SLAM
YOU SHOULD TREAT YOUR ELDERS WITH A LITTLE MORE RESPECT, CHILD.
MAYBE IF YOU DIDN'T HIT ME WITH A BILL EVERY TIME I WALKED THROUGH THE DOOR, YOU'D GET A LITTLE MORE DEFERENCE.
OUR RELATIONSHIP IS SIMPLE. TOTENKINDER EXCHANGES MAGIC FOR FAVORS.
PERHAPS YOU'D PREFER TO CARRY OUT YOUR DUTIES WITHOUT MY ASSISTANCE?
NOT TODAY.
SO WHAT CAN YOU TELL ME ABOUT THESE "ITEMS" THAT HAVE STARTED POPPING UP?
THAT INFORMATION ISN'T FREE, DEAR.
IT NEVER IS.
JUST ADD IT TO MY TAB.

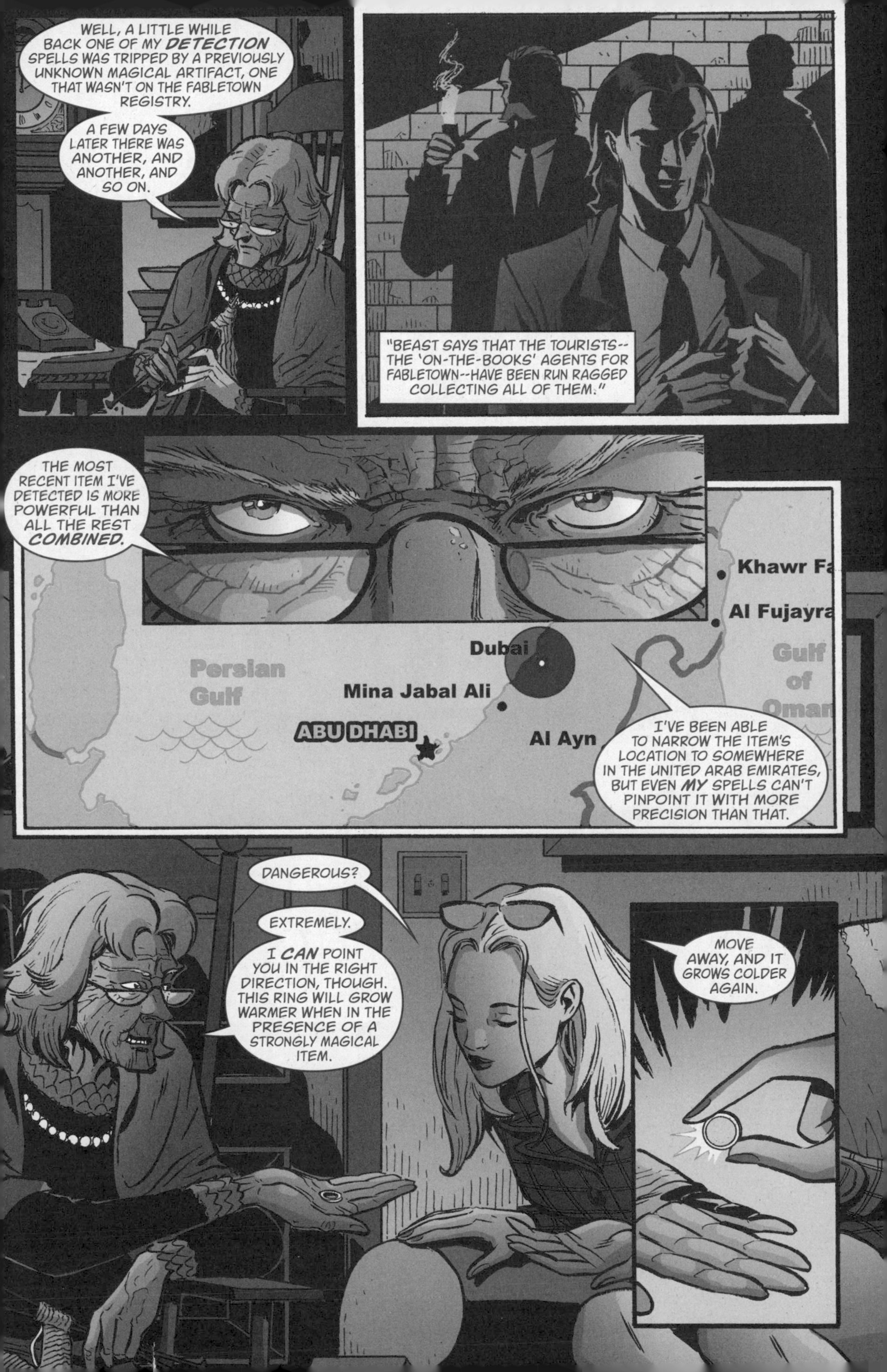
WELL, A LITTLE WHILE BACK ONE OF MY DETECTION SPELLS WAS TRIPPED BY A PREVIOUSLY UNKNOWN MAGICAL ARTIFACT, ONE THAT WASN'T ON THE FABLETOWN REGISTRY.
A FEW DAYS LATER THERE WAS ANOTHER, AND ANOTHER, AND SO ON.
"BEAST SAYS THAT THE TOURISTS--THE 'ON-THE-BOOKS' AGENTS FOR FABLETOWN--HAVE BEEN RUN RAGGED COLLECTING ALL OF THEM."
THE MOST RECENT ITEM I'VE DETECTED IS MORE POWERFUL THAN ALL THE REST COMBINED.
Khawr Fa
Al Fujayra
Dubai
Persian Gulf
Mina Jabal Ali
ABU DHABI
Al Ayn
Gulf of Oman
I'VE BEEN ABLE TO NARROW THE ITEM'S LOCATION TO SOMEWHERE IN THE UNITED ARAB EMIRATES, BUT EVEN MY SPELLS CAN'T PINPOINT IT WITH MORE PRECISION THAN THAT.
DANGEROUS?
EXTREMELY.
I CAN POINT YOU IN THE RIGHT DIRECTION, THOUGH. THIS RING WILL GROW WARMER WHEN IN THE PRESENCE OF A STRONGLY MAGICAL ITEM.
MOVE AWAY, AND IT GROWS COLDER AGAIN.

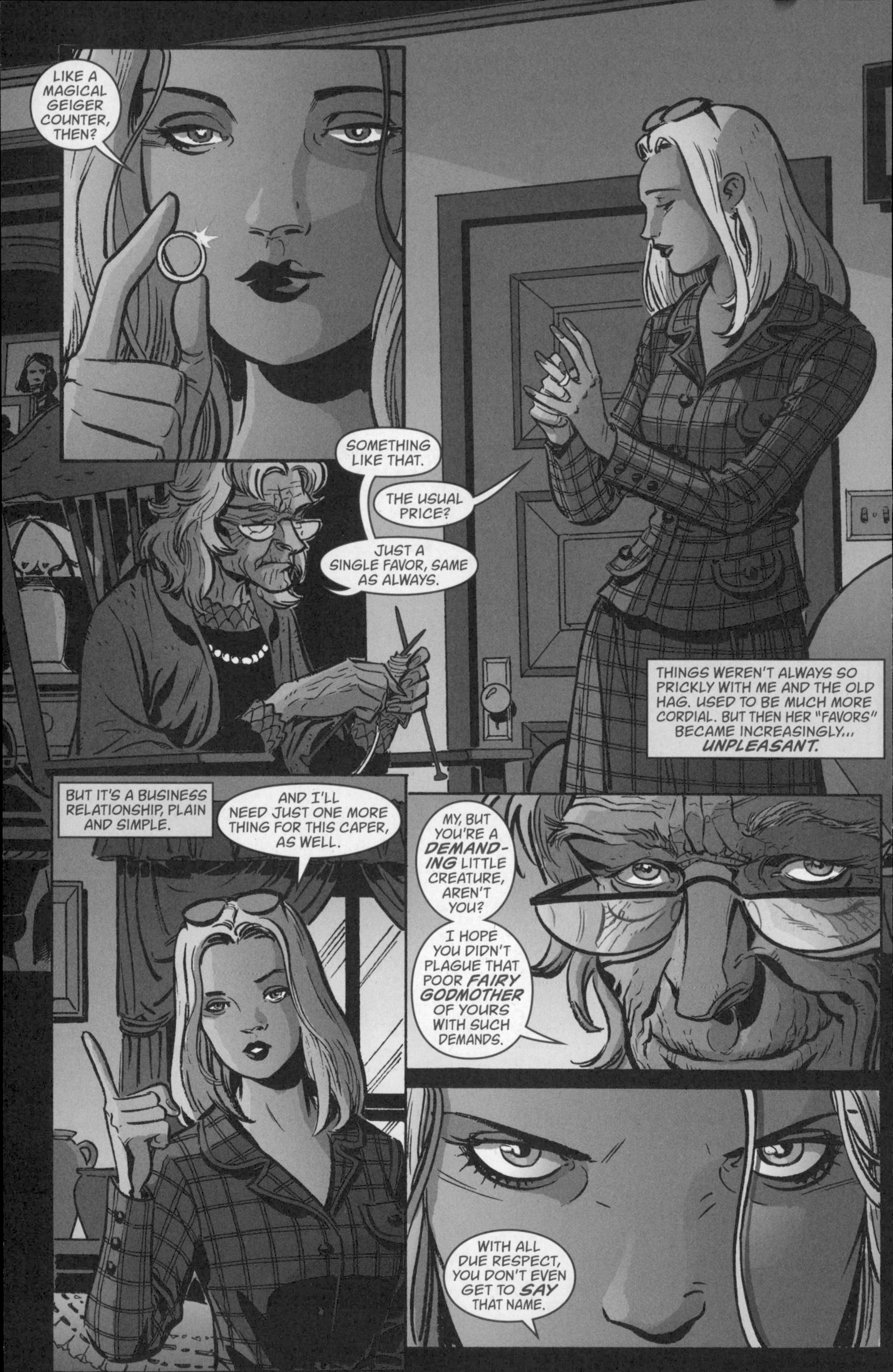
LIKE A MAGICAL GEIGER COUNTER, THEN?
SOMETHING LIKE THAT.
THE USUAL PRICE?
JUST A SINGLE FAVOR, SAME AS ALWAYS.
THINGS WEREN'T ALWAYS SO PRICKLY WITH ME AND THE OLD HAG. USED TO BE MUCH MORE CORDIAL. BUT THEN HER "FAVORS" BECAME INCREASINGLY... UNPLEASANT.
BUT IT'S A BUSINESS RELATIONSHIP, PLAIN AND SIMPLE.
AND I'LL NEED JUST ONE MORE THING FOR THIS CAPER, AS WELL.
MY, BUT YOU'RE A DEMANDING LITTLE CREATURE, AREN'T YOU?
I HOPE YOU DIDN'T PLAGUE THAT POOR FAIRY GODMOTHER OF YOURS WITH SUCH DEMANDS.
WITH ALL DUE RESPECT, YOU DON'T EVEN GET TO SAY THAT NAME.

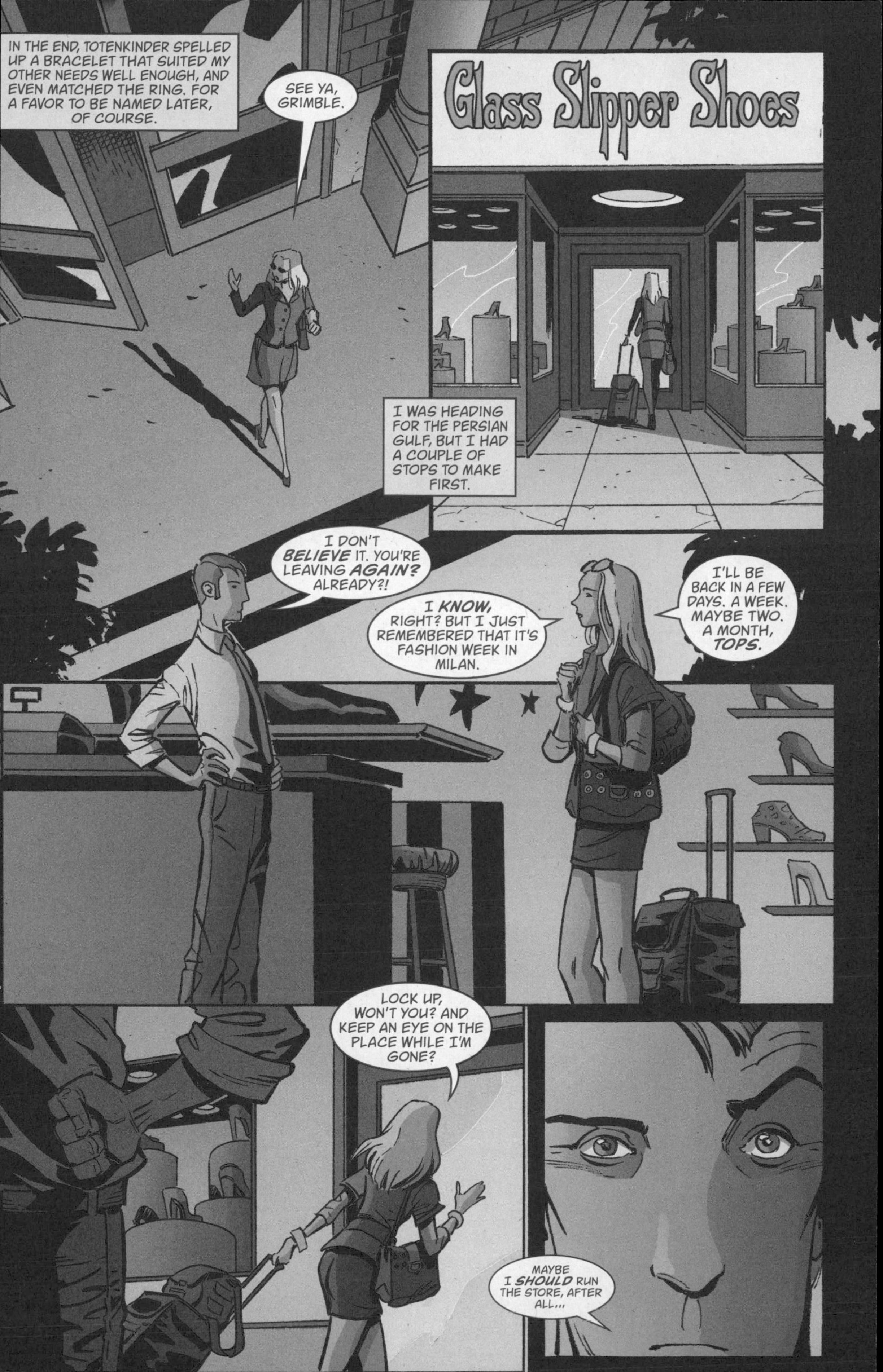
IN THE END, TOTENKINDER SPELLED UP A BRACELET THAT SUITED MY OTHER NEEDS WELL ENOUGH, AND EVEN MATCHED THE RING. FOR A FAVOR TO BE NAMED LATER, OF COURSE.
SEE YA, GRIMBLE.
Glass Slipper Shoes
I WAS HEADING FOR THE PERSIAN GULF, BUT I HAD A COUPLE OF STOPS TO MAKE FIRST.
I DON'T BELIEVE IT. YOU'RE LEAVING AGAIN? ALREADY?!
I KNOW, RIGHT? BUT I JUST REMEMBERED THAT IT'S FASHION WEEK IN MILAN.
I'LL BE BACK IN A FEW DAYS. A WEEK. MAYBE TWO. A MONTH, TOPS.
LOCK UP, WON'T YOU? AND KEEP AN EYE ON THE PLACE WHILE I'M GONE?
MAYBE I SHOULD RUN THE STORE, AFTER ALL...

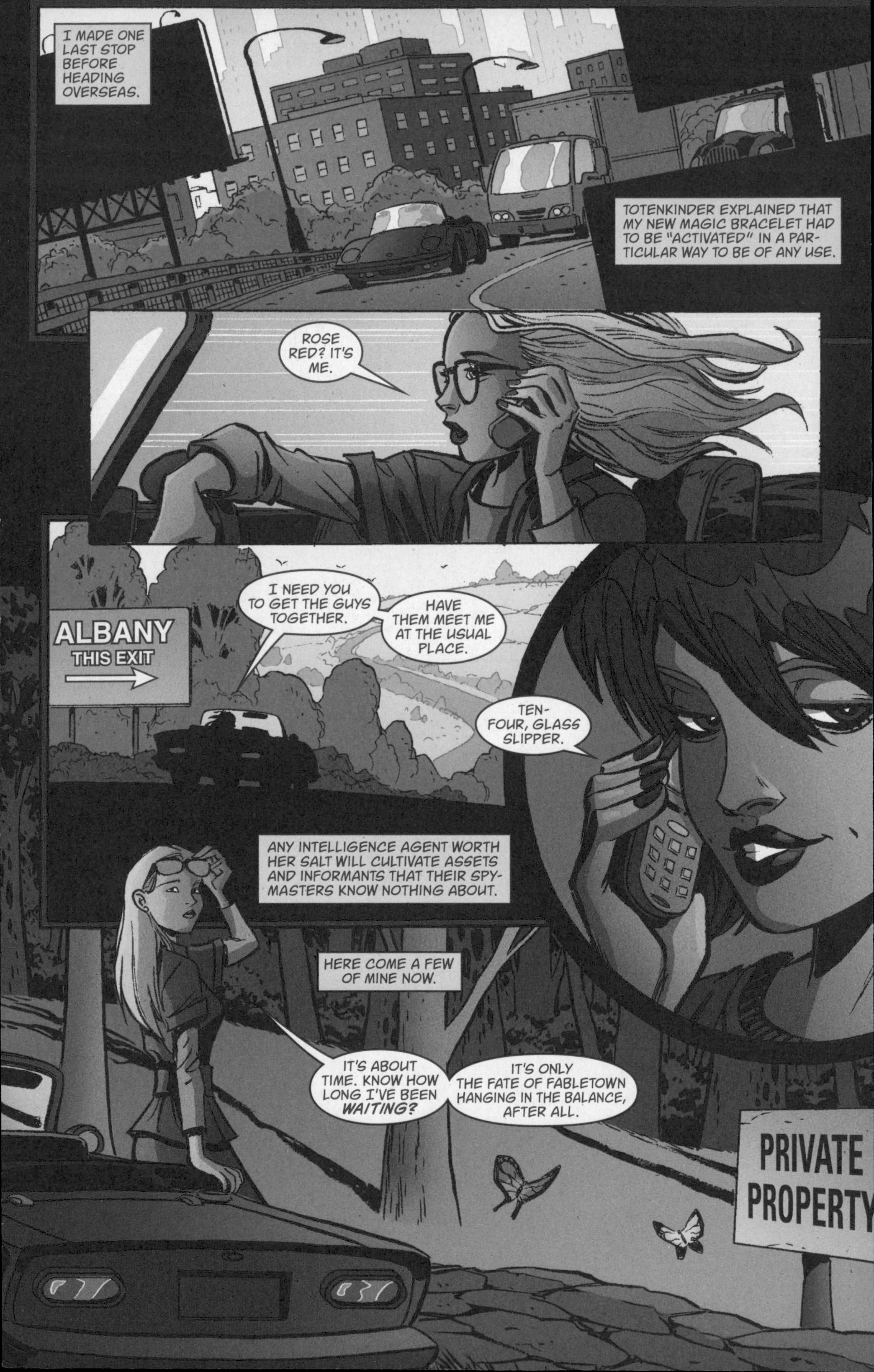
I MADE ONE LAST STOP BEFORE HEADING OVERSEAS.
TOTENKINDER EXPLAINED THAT MY NEW MAGIC BRACELET HAD TO BE "ACTIVATED" IN A PARTICULAR WAY TO BE OF ANY USE.
ROSE RED? IT'S ME.
ALBANY
THIS EXIT
I NEED YOU TO GET THE GUYS TOGETHER.
HAVE THEM MEET ME AT THE USUAL PLACE.
TEN-FOUR, GLASS SLIPPER.
ANY INTELLIGENCE AGENT WORTH HER SALT WILL CULTIVATE ASSETS AND INFORMANTS THAT THEIR SPY-MASTERS KNOW NOTHING ABOUT.
HERE COME A FEW OF MINE NOW.
IT'S ABOUT TIME. KNOW HOW LONG I'VE BEEN *WAITING?*
IT'S ONLY THE FATE OF FABLETOWN HANGING IN THE BALANCE, AFTER ALL.
PRIVATE
PROPERTY

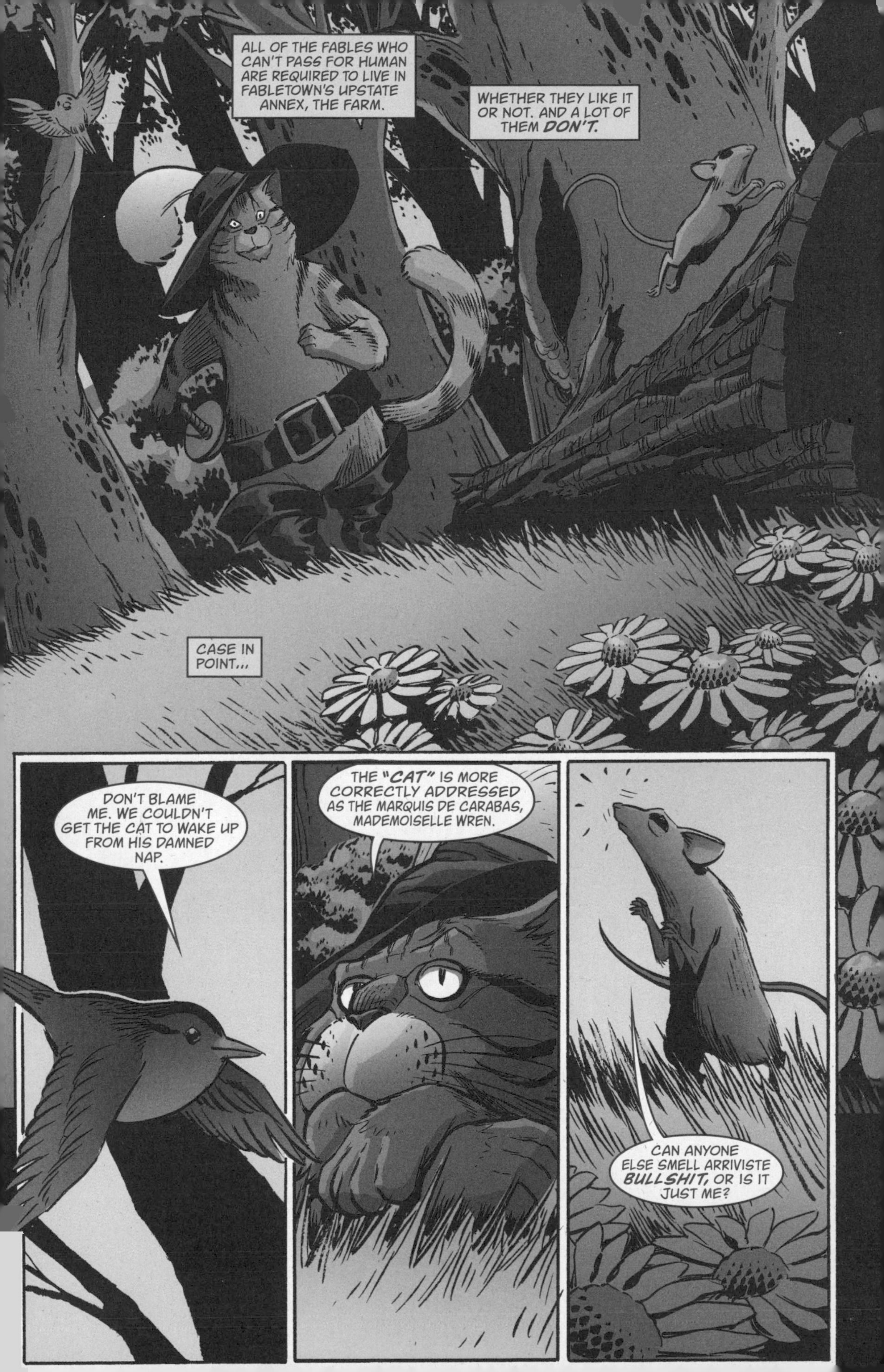
ALL OF THE FABLES WHO CAN'T PASS FOR HUMAN ARE REQUIRED TO LIVE IN FABLETOWN'S UPSTATE ANNEX, THE FARM.
WHETHER THEY LIKE IT OR NOT. AND A LOT OF THEM DON'T.
CASE IN POINT...
DON'T BLAME ME. WE COULDN'T GET THE CAT TO WAKE UP FROM HIS DAMNED NAP.
THE "CAT" IS MORE CORRECTLY ADDRESSED AS THE MARQUIS DE CARABAS, MADEMOISELLE WREN.
CAN ANYONE ELSE SMELL ARRIVISTE BULLSHIT, OR IS IT JUST ME?

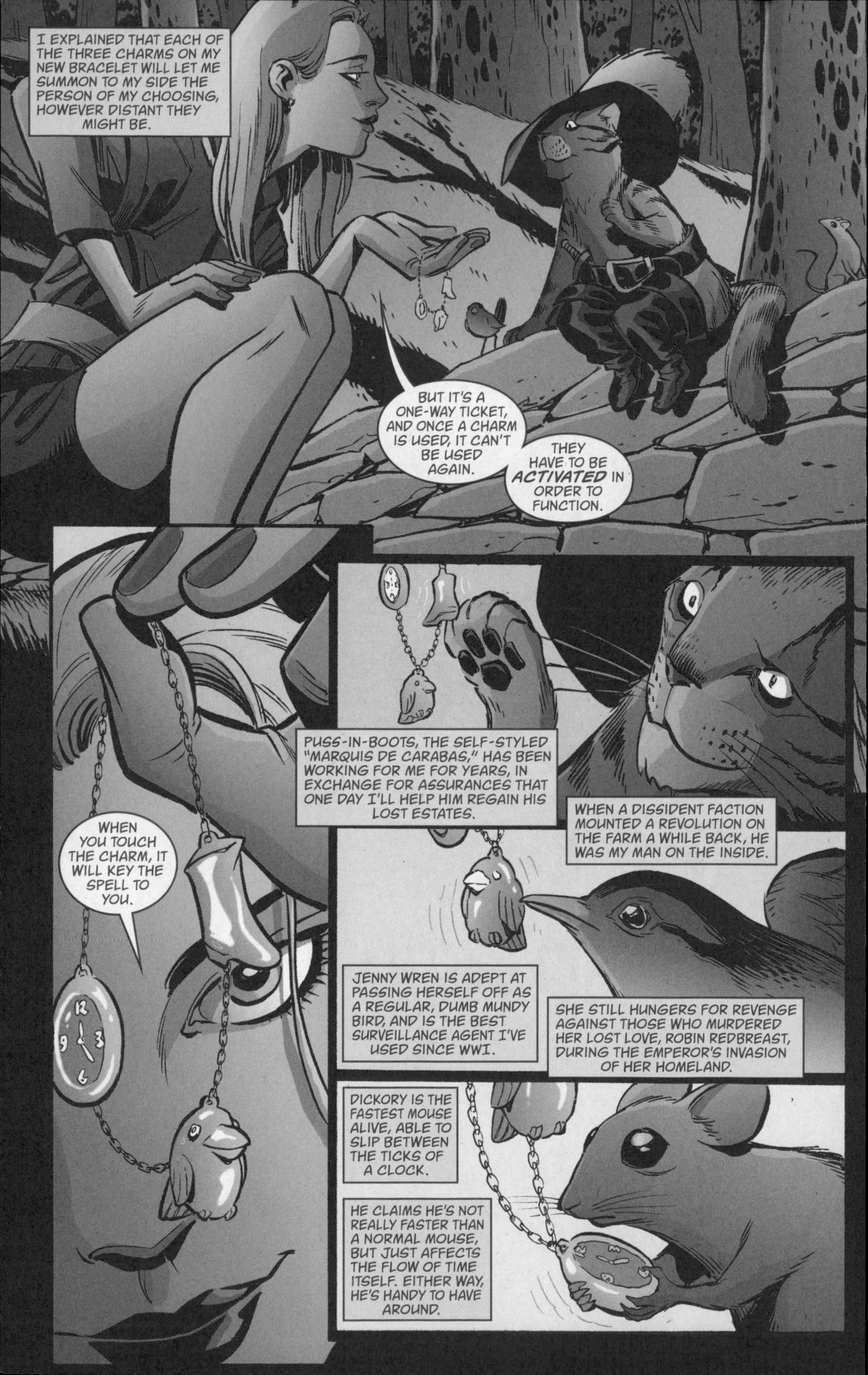
I EXPLAINED THAT EACH OF THE THREE CHARMS ON MY NEW BRACELET WILL LET ME SUMMON TO MY SIDE THE PERSON OF MY CHOOSING, HOWEVER DISTANT THEY MIGHT BE.
BUT IT'S A ONE-WAY TICKET, AND ONCE A CHARM IS USED, IT CAN'T BE USED AGAIN.
THEY HAVE TO BE ACTIVATED IN ORDER TO FUNCTION.
WHEN YOU TOUCH THE CHARM, IT WILL KEY THE SPELL TO YOU.
PUSS-IN-BOOTS, THE SELF-STYLED "MARQUIS DE CARABAS," HAS BEEN WORKING FOR ME FOR YEARS, IN EXCHANGE FOR ASSURANCES THAT ONE DAY I'LL HELP HIM REGAIN HIS LOST ESTATES.
WHEN A DISSIDENT FACTION MOUNTED A REVOLUTION ON THE FARM A WHILE BACK, HE WAS MY MAN ON THE INSIDE.
JENNY WREN IS ADEPT AT PASSING HERSELF OFF AS A REGULAR, DUMB MUNDY BIRD, AND IS THE BEST SURVEILLANCE AGENT I'VE USED SINCE WWI.
SHE STILL HUNGERS FOR REVENGE AGAINST THOSE WHO MURDERED HER LOST LOVE, ROBIN REDBREAST, DURING THE EMPEROR'S INVASION OF HER HOMELAND.
DICKORY IS THE FASTEST MOUSE ALIVE, ABLE TO SLIP BETWEEN THE TICKS OF A CLOCK.
HE CLAIMS HE'S NOT REALLY FASTER THAN A NORMAL MOUSE, BUT JUST AFFECTS THE FLOW OF TIME ITSELF. EITHER WAY, HE'S HANDY TO HAVE AROUND.

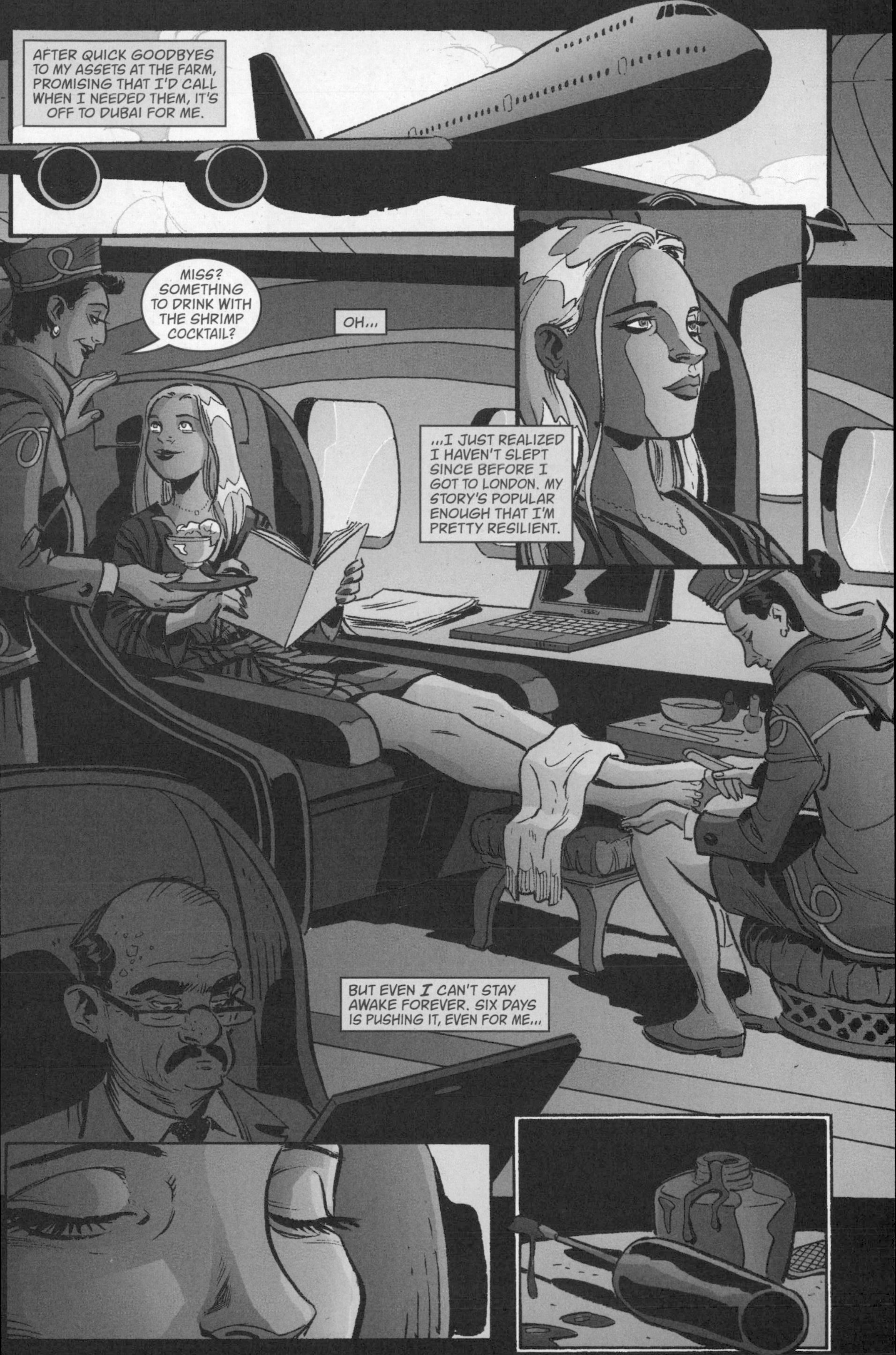
AFTER QUICK GOODBYES TO MY ASSETS AT THE FARM, PROMISING THAT I'D CALL WHEN I NEEDED THEM, IT'S OFF TO DUBAI FOR ME.
MISS? SOMETHING TO DRINK WITH THE SHRIMP COCKTAIL?
OH...
...I JUST REALIZED I HAVEN'T SLEPT SINCE BEFORE I GOT TO LONDON. MY STORY'S POPULAR ENOUGH THAT I'M PRETTY RESILIENT.
BUT EVEN I CAN'T STAY AWAKE FOREVER. SIX DAYS IS PUSHING IT, EVEN FOR ME...

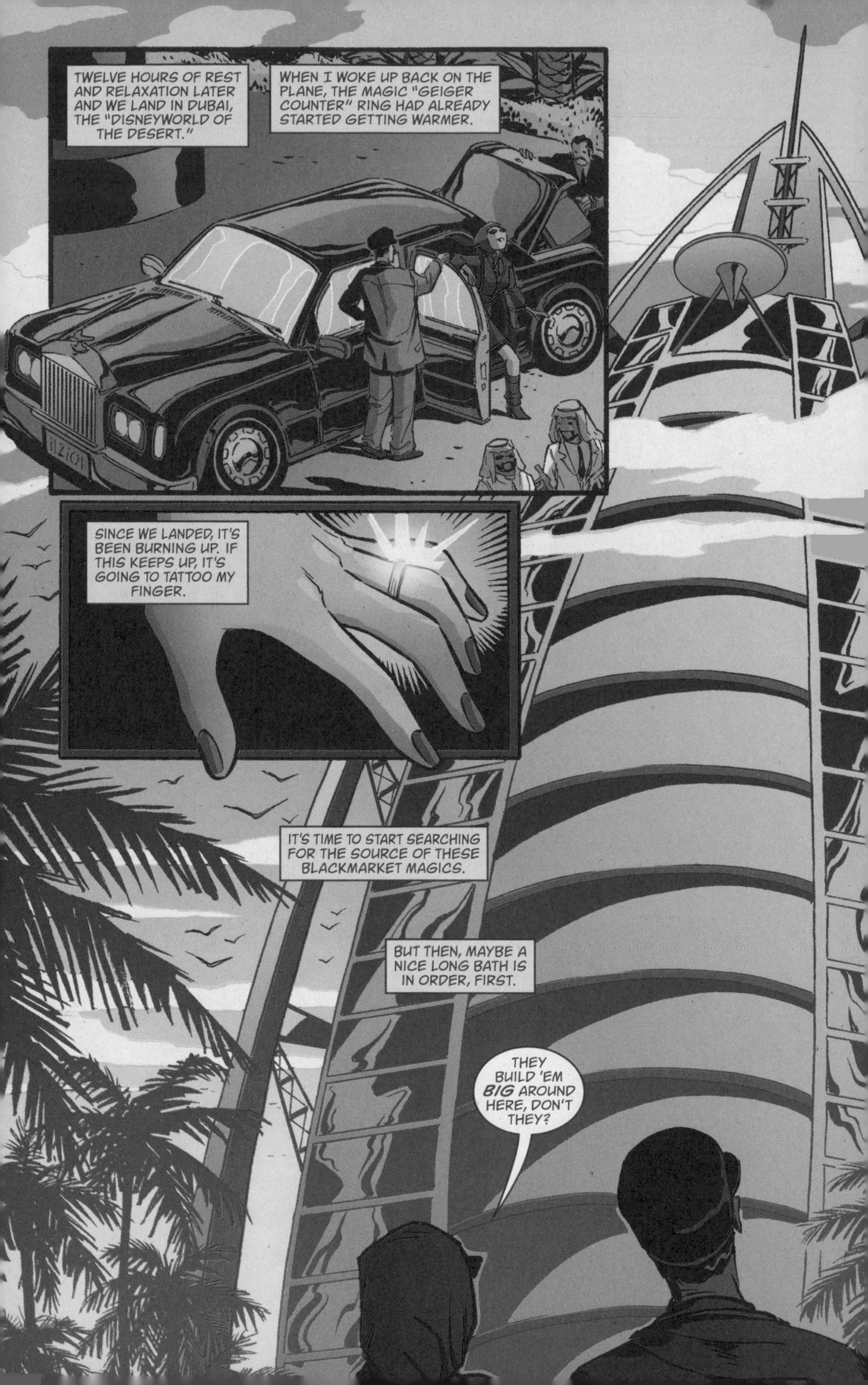
TWELVE HOURS OF REST AND RELAXATION LATER AND WE LAND IN DUBAI, THE "DISNEYWORLD OF THE DESERT."
WHEN I WOKE UP BACK ON THE PLANE, THE MAGIC "GEIGER COUNTER" RING HAD ALREADY STARTED GETTING WARMER.
SINCE WE LANDED, IT'S BEEN BURNING UP. IF THIS KEEPS UP, IT'S GOING TO TATTOO MY FINGER.
IT'S TIME TO START SEARCHING FOR THE SOURCE OF THESE BLACKMARKET MAGICS.
BUT THEN, MAYBE A NICE LONG BATH IS IN ORDER, FIRST.
THEY BUILD 'EM *BIG* AROUND HERE, DON'T THEY?

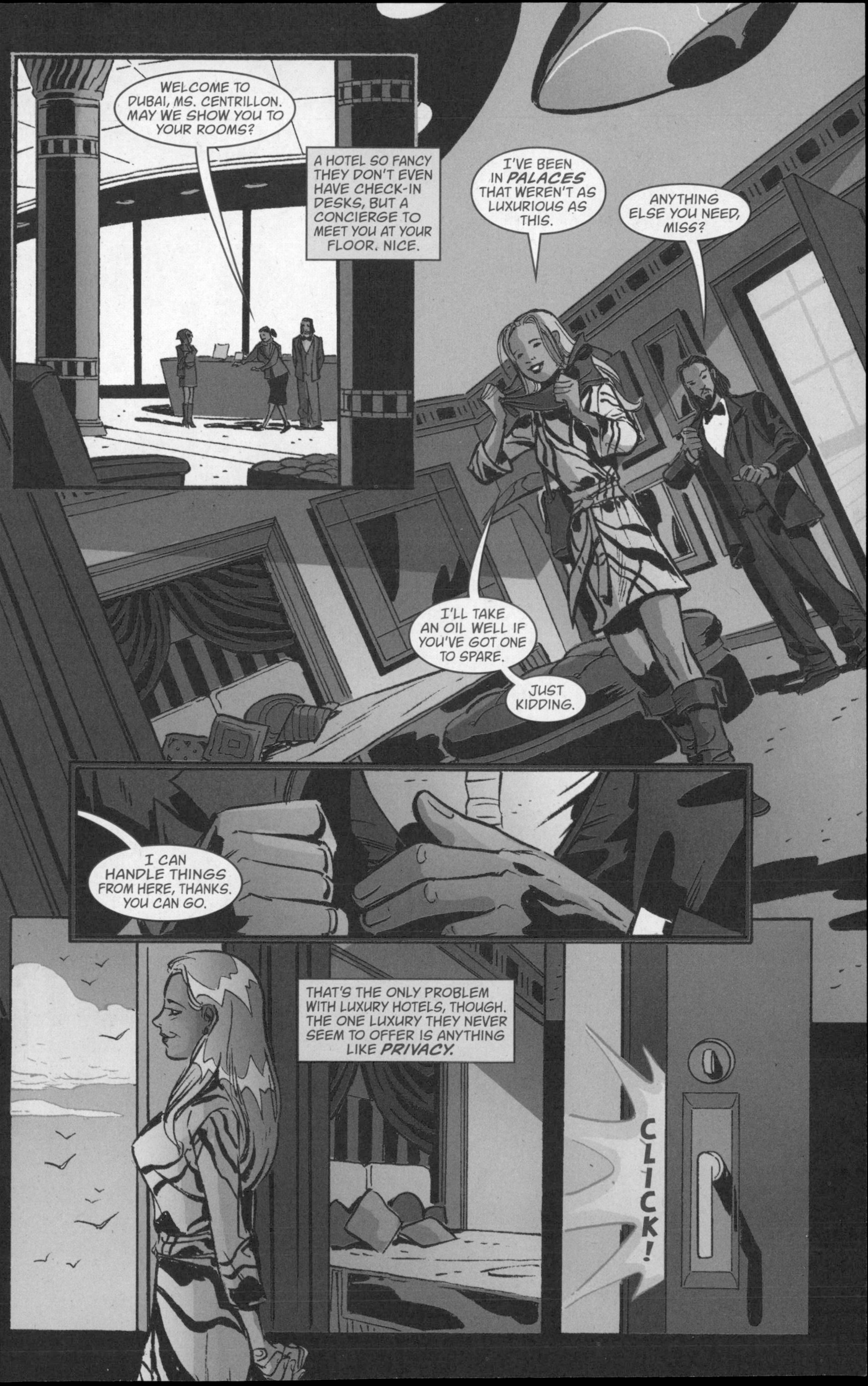

WELCOME TO DUBAI, MS. CENTRILLON. MAY WE SHOW YOU TO YOUR ROOMS?
A HOTEL SO FANCY THEY DON'T EVEN HAVE CHECK-IN DESKS, BUT A CONCIERGE TO MEET YOU AT YOUR FLOOR. NICE.
I'VE BEEN IN PALACES THAT WEREN'T AS LUXURIOUS AS THIS.
ANYTHING ELSE YOU NEED, MISS?
I'LL TAKE AN OIL WELL IF YOU'VE GOT ONE TO SPARE.
JUST KIDDING.
I CAN HANDLE THINGS FROM HERE, THANKS. YOU CAN GO.
THAT'S THE ONLY PROBLEM WITH LUXURY HOTELS, THOUGH. THE ONE LUXURY THEY NEVER SEEM TO OFFER IS ANYTHING LIKE PRIVACY.
CLICK!

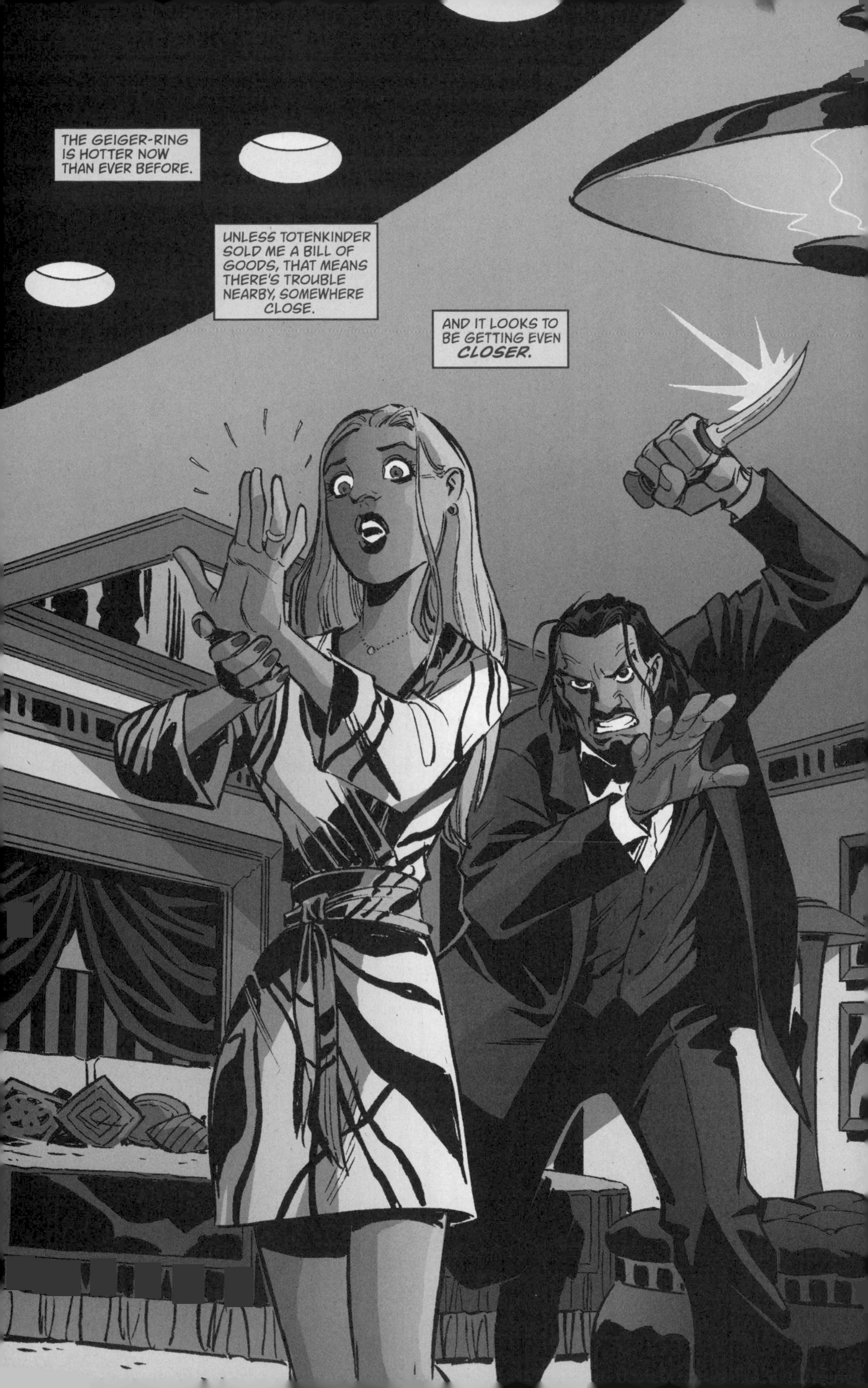
THE GEIGER-RING IS HOTTER NOW THAN EVER BEFORE.
UNLESS TOTENKINDER SOLD ME A BILL OF GOODS, THAT MEANS THERE'S TROUBLE NEARBY, SOMEWHERE CLOSE.
AND IT LOOKS TO BE GETTING EVEN CLOSER.

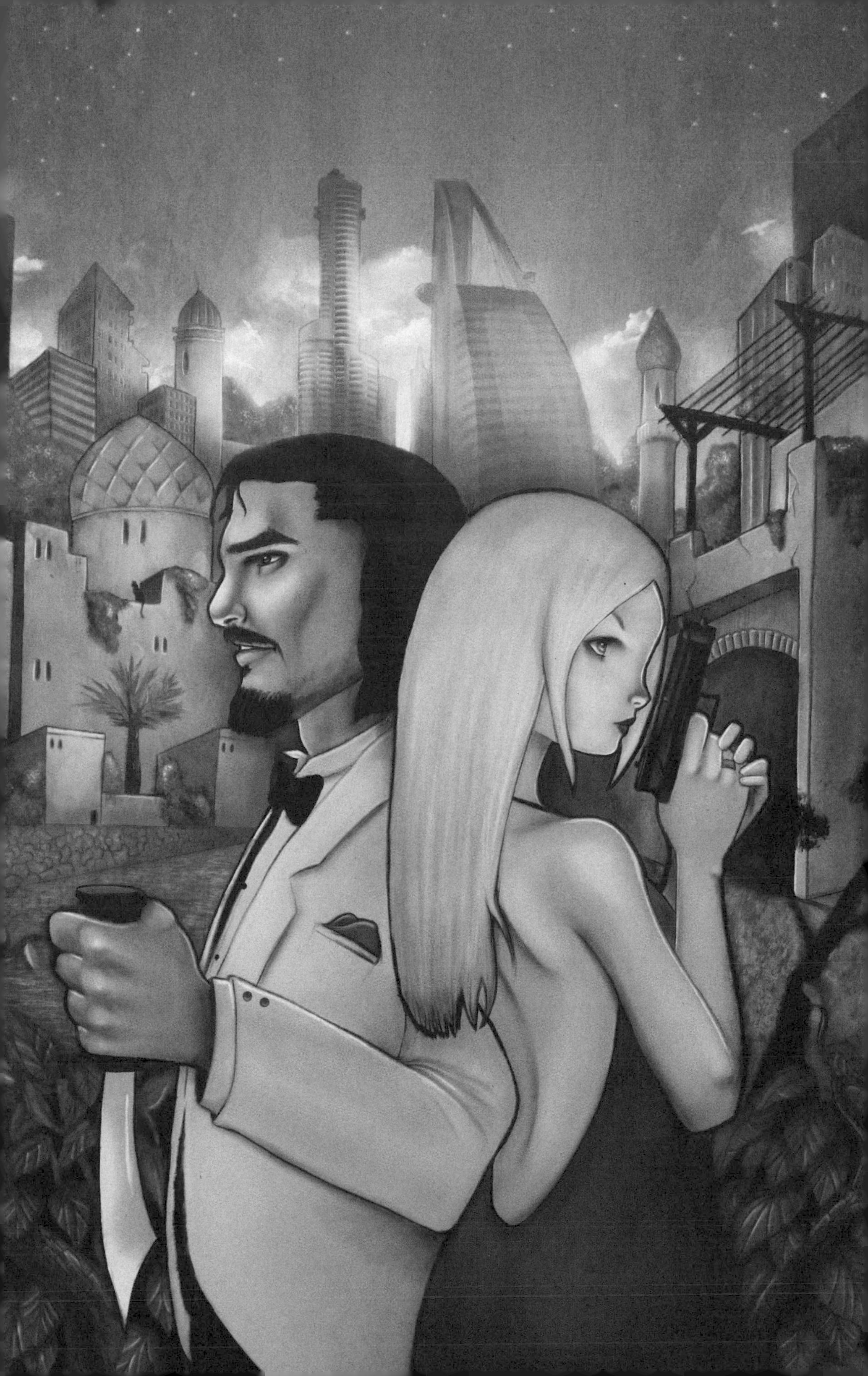

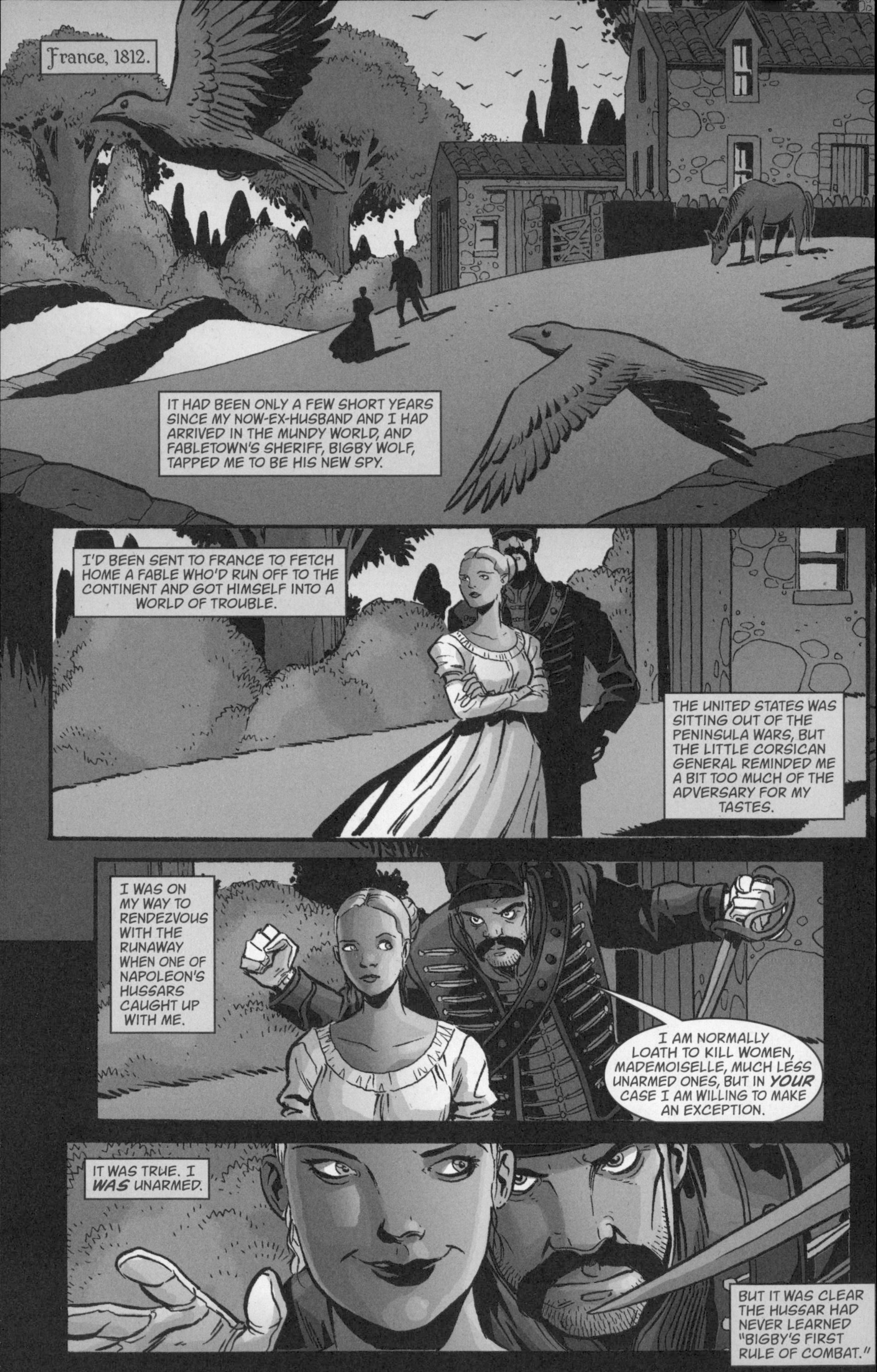
France, 1812.
IT HAD BEEN ONLY A FEW SHORT YEARS SINCE MY NOW-EX-HUSBAND AND I HAD ARRIVED IN THE MUNDY WORLD, AND FABLETOWN'S SHERIFF, BIGBY WOLF, TAPPED ME TO BE HIS NEW SPY.
I'D BEEN SENT TO FRANCE TO FETCH HOME A FABLE WHO'D RUN OFF TO THE CONTINENT AND GOT HIMSELF INTO A WORLD OF TROUBLE.
THE UNITED STATES WAS SITTING OUT OF THE PENINSULA WARS, BUT THE LITTLE CORSICAN GENERAL REMINDED ME A BIT TOO MUCH OF THE ADVERSARY FOR MY TASTES.
I WAS ON MY WAY TO RENDEZVOUS WITH THE RUNAWAY WHEN ONE OF NAPOLEON'S HUSSARS CAUGHT UP WITH ME.
I AM NORMALLY LOATH TO KILL WOMEN, MADEMOISELLE, MUCH LESS UNARMED ONES, BUT IN *YOUR* CASE I AM WILLING TO MAKE AN EXCEPTION.
IT WAS TRUE. I *WAS* UNARMED.
BUT IT WAS CLEAR THE HUSSAR HAD NEVER LEARNED "BIGBY'S FIRST RULE OF COMBAT."

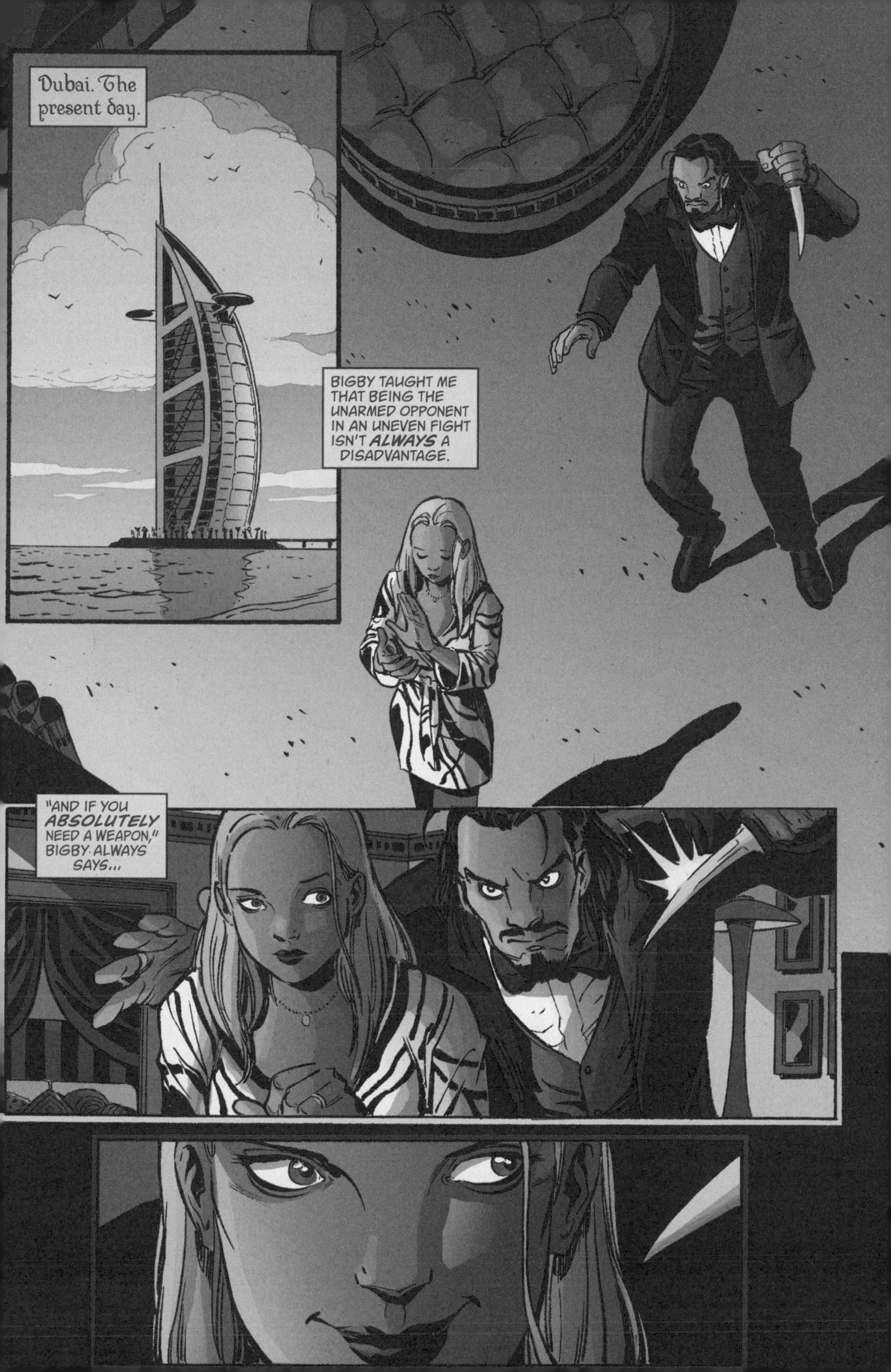
Dubai. The present day.
BIGBY TAUGHT ME THAT BEING THE UNARMED OPPONENT IN AN UNEVEN FIGHT ISN'T ALWAYS A DISADVANTAGE.
"AND IF YOU ABSOLUTELY NEED A WEAPON," BIGBY ALWAYS SAYS...

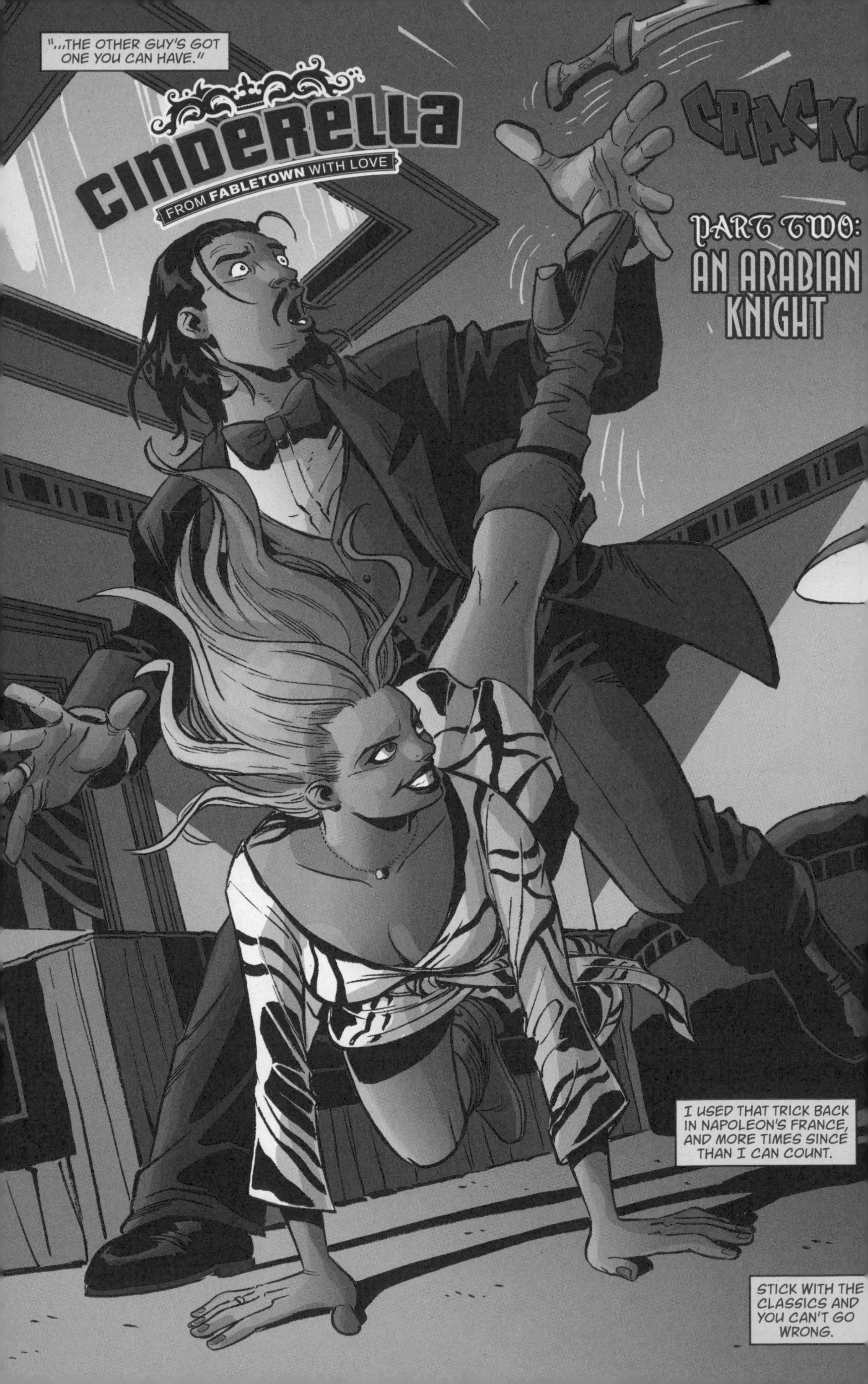

"...THE OTHER GUY'S GOT ONE YOU CAN HAVE."
CINDERELLA
FROM FABLETOWN WITH LOVE
CRACK!
PART TWO: AN ARABIAN KNIGHT
I USED THAT TRICK BACK IN NAPOLEON'S FRANCE, AND MORE TIMES SINCE THAN I CAN COUNT.
STICK WITH THE CLASSICS AND YOU CAN'T GO WRONG.

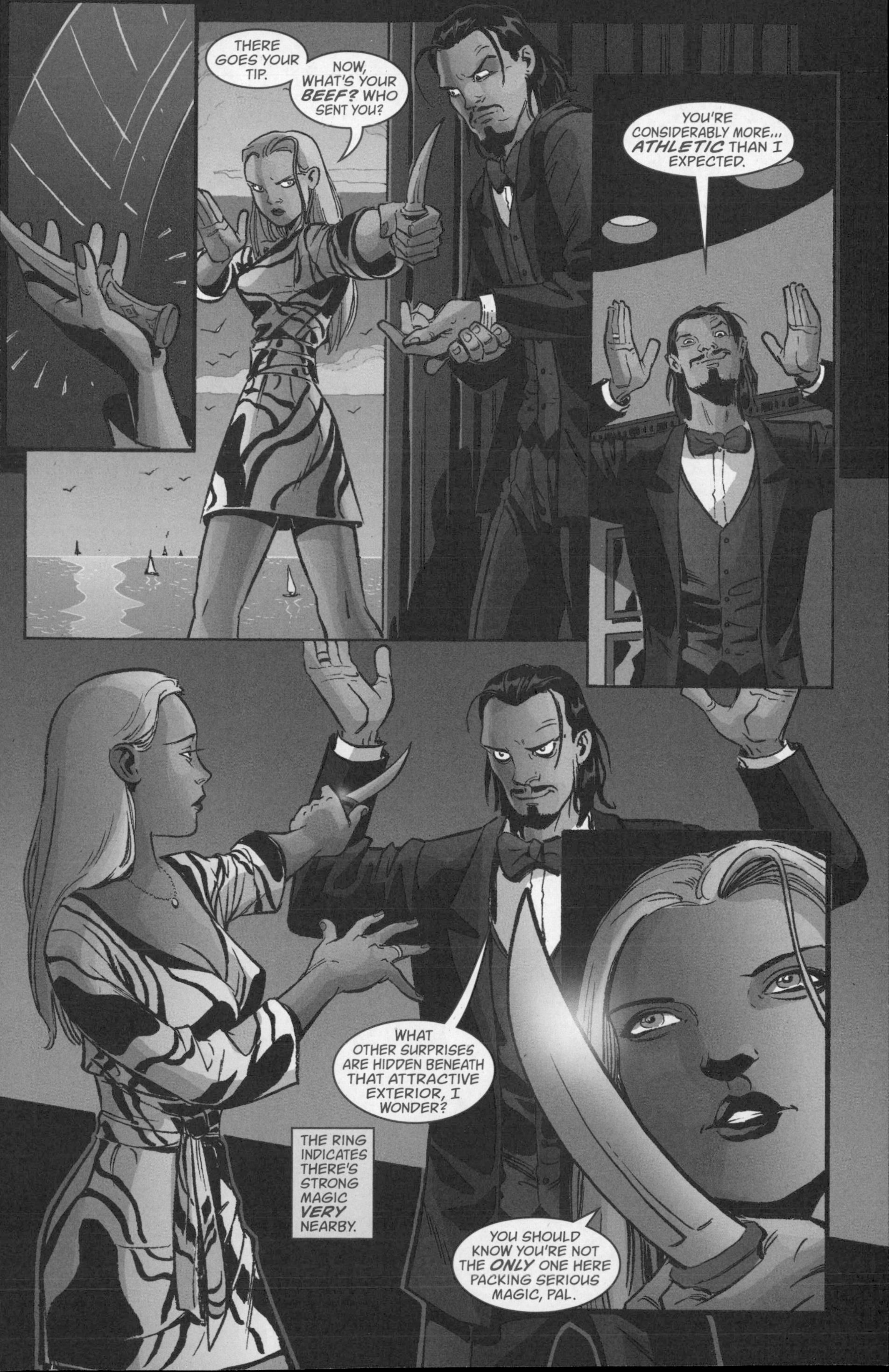
THERE GOES YOUR TIP.
NOW, WHAT'S YOUR BEEF? WHO SENT YOU?
YOU'RE CONSIDERABLY MORE... ATHLETIC THAN I EXPECTED.
WHAT OTHER SURPRISES ARE HIDDEN BENEATH THAT ATTRACTIVE EXTERIOR, I WONDER?
THE RING INDICATES THERE'S STRONG MAGIC VERY NEARBY.
YOU SHOULD KNOW YOU'RE NOT THE ONLY ONE HERE PACKING SERIOUS MAGIC, PAL.

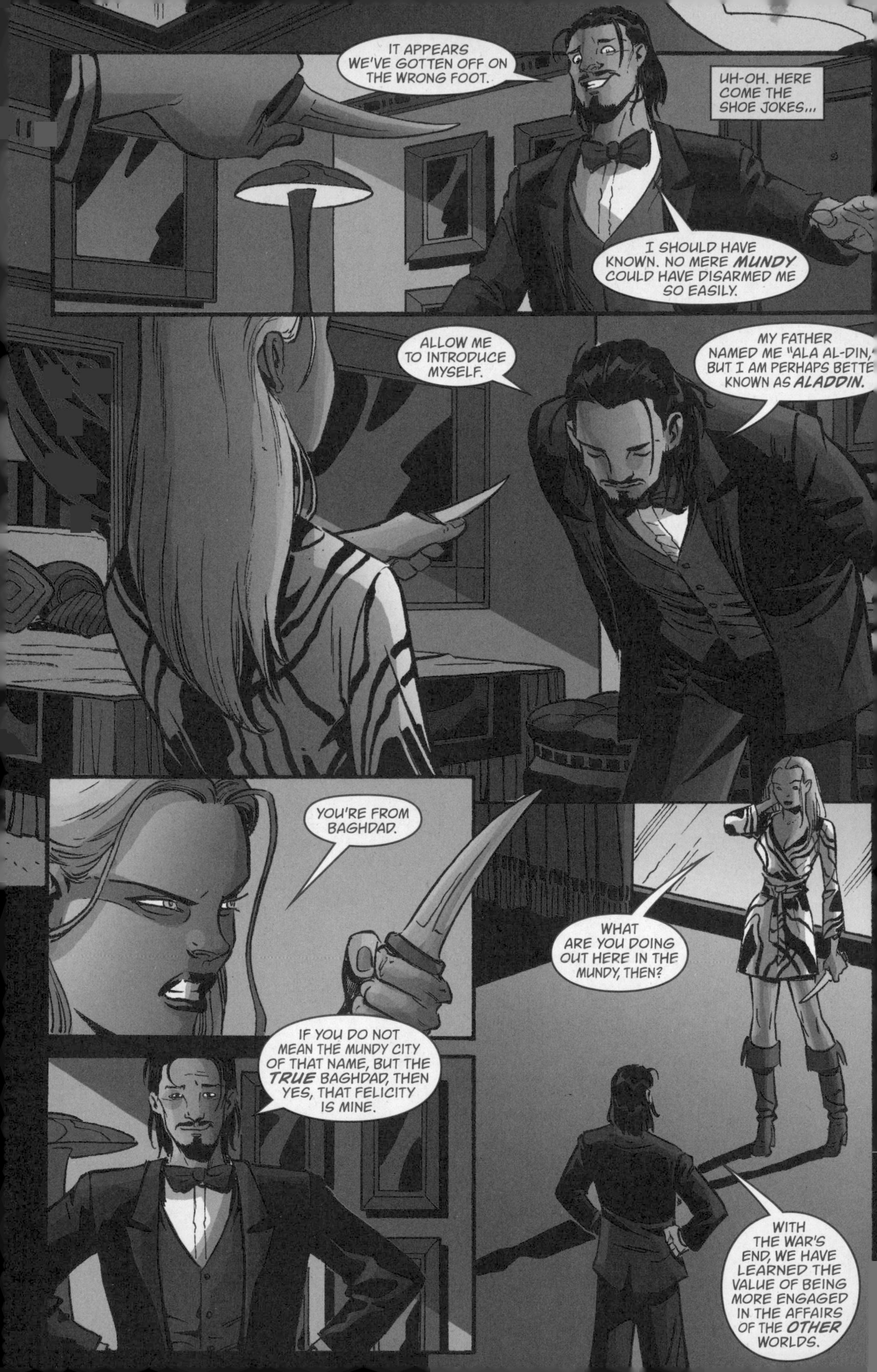
IT APPEARS WE'VE GOTTEN OFF ON THE WRONG FOOT.
UH-OH. HERE COME THE SHOE JOKES...
I SHOULD HAVE KNOWN. NO MERE MUNDY COULD HAVE DISARMED ME SO EASILY.
ALLOW ME TO INTRODUCE MYSELF.
MY FATHER NAMED ME "ALA AL-DIN," BUT I AM PERHAPS BETTE KNOWN AS ALADDIN.
YOU'RE FROM BAGHDAD.
WHAT ARE YOU DOING OUT HERE IN THE MUNDY, THEN?
IF YOU DO NOT MEAN THE MUNDY CITY OF THAT NAME, BUT THE TRUE BAGHDAD, THEN YES, THAT FELICITY IS MINE.
WITH THE WAR'S END, WE HAVE LEARNED THE VALUE OF BEING MORE ENGAGED IN THE AFFAIRS OF THE OTHER WORLDS.

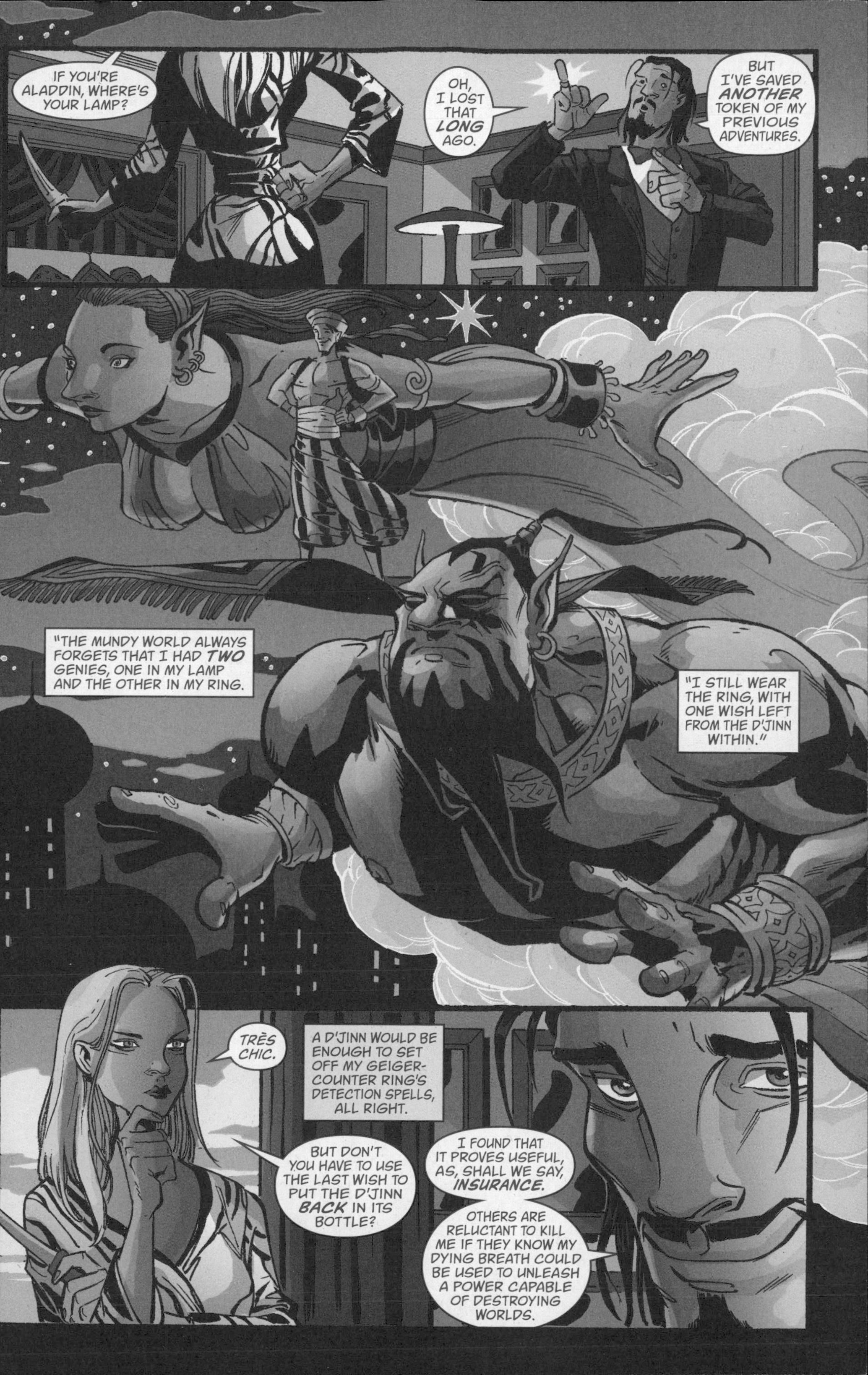
IF YOU'RE ALADDIN, WHERE'S YOUR LAMP?
OH, I LOST THAT LONG AGO.
BUT I'VE SAVED ANOTHER TOKEN OF MY PREVIOUS ADVENTURES.
"THE MUNDY WORLD ALWAYS FORGETS THAT I HAD TWO GENIES, ONE IN MY LAMP AND THE OTHER IN MY RING.
"I STILL WEAR THE RING, WITH ONE WISH LEFT FROM THE D'JINN WITHIN."
TRÈS CHIC.
A D'JINN WOULD BE ENOUGH TO SET OFF MY GEIGER-COUNTER RING'S DETECTION SPELLS, ALL RIGHT.
BUT DON'T YOU HAVE TO USE THE LAST WISH TO PUT THE D'JINN BACK IN ITS BOTTLE?
I FOUND THAT IT PROVES USEFUL, AS, SHALL WE SAY, INSURANCE.
OTHERS ARE RELUCTANT TO KILL ME IF THEY KNOW MY DYING BREATH COULD BE USED TO UNLEASH A POWER CAPABLE OF DESTROYING WORLDS.

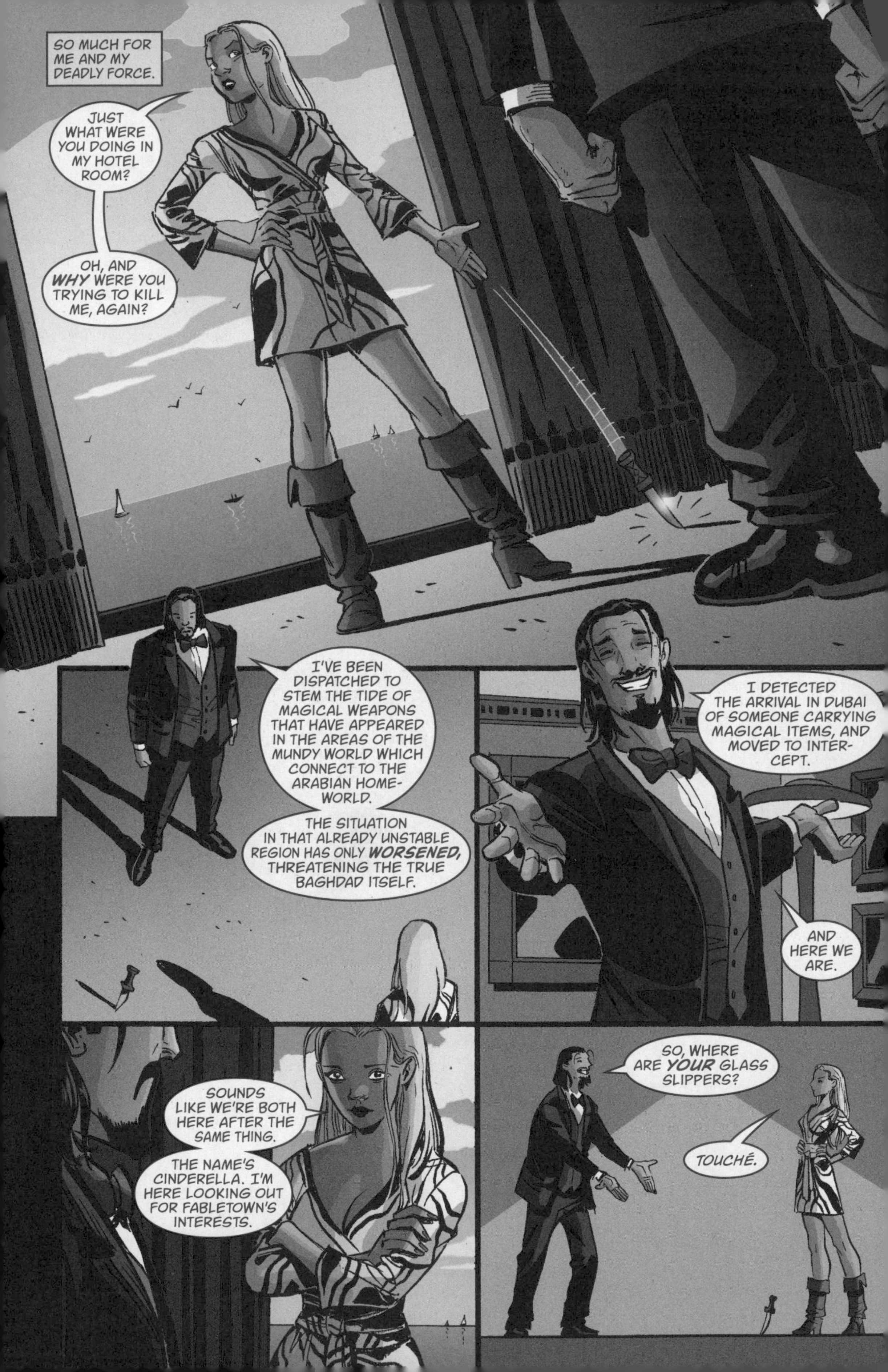
SO MUCH FOR ME AND MY DEADLY FORCE.
JUST WHAT WERE YOU DOING IN MY HOTEL ROOM?
OH, AND WHY WERE YOU TRYING TO KILL ME, AGAIN?
I'VE BEEN DISPATCHED TO STEM THE TIDE OF MAGICAL WEAPONS THAT HAVE APPEARED IN THE AREAS OF THE MUNDY WORLD WHICH CONNECT TO THE ARABIAN HOME-WORLD.
THE SITUATION IN THAT ALREADY UNSTABLE REGION HAS ONLY WORSENED, THREATENING THE TRUE BAGHDAD ITSELF.
I DETECTED THE ARRIVAL IN DUBAI OF SOMEONE CARRYING MAGICAL ITEMS, AND MOVED TO INTER-CEPT.
AND HERE WE ARE.
SOUNDS LIKE WE'RE BOTH HERE AFTER THE SAME THING.
THE NAME'S CINDERELLA. I'M HERE LOOKING OUT FOR FABLETOWN'S INTERESTS.
SO, WHERE ARE YOUR GLASS SLIPPERS?
TOUCHÉ.

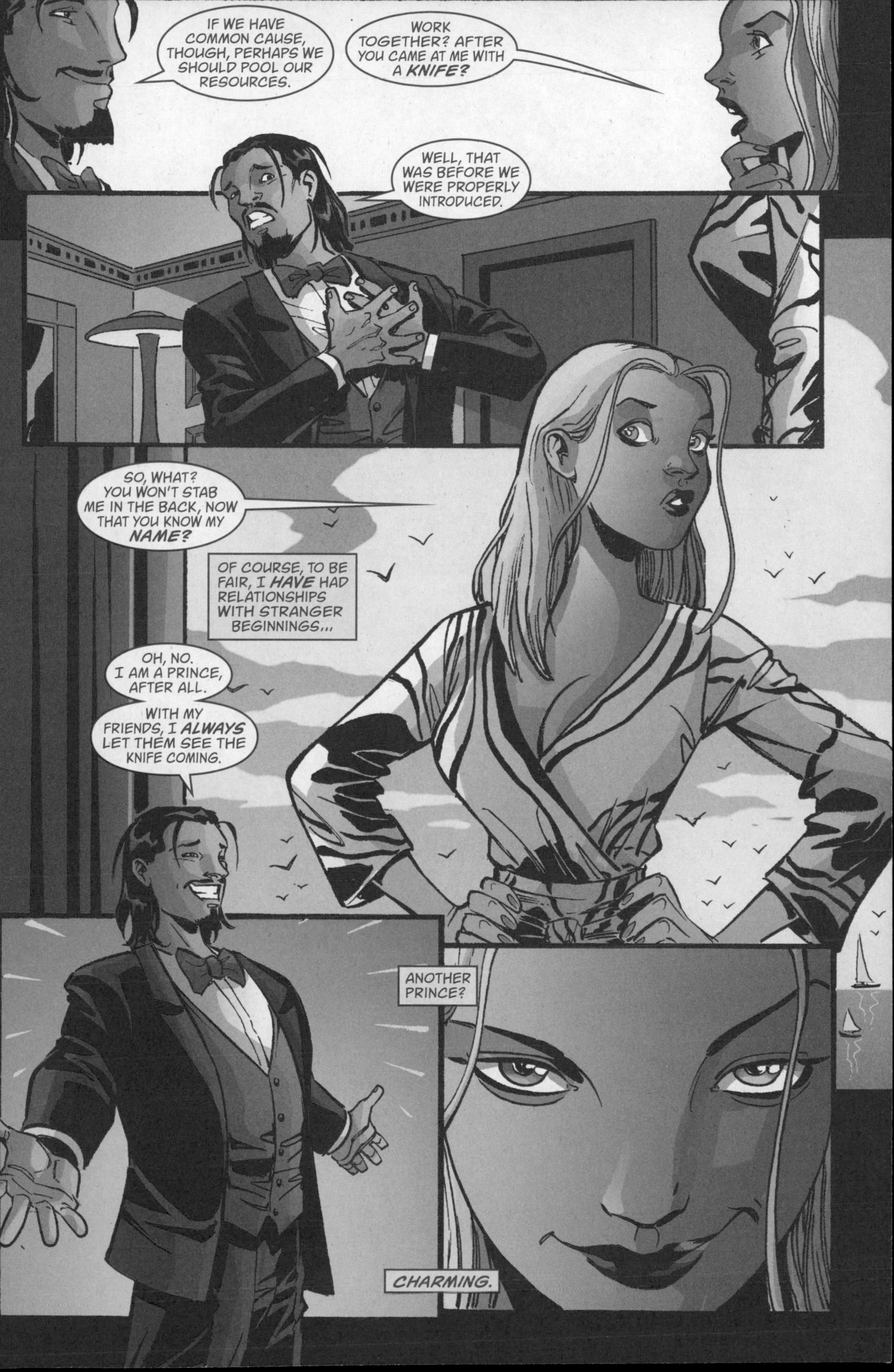
IF WE HAVE COMMON CAUSE, THOUGH, PERHAPS WE SHOULD POOL OUR RESOURCES.
WORK TOGETHER? AFTER YOU CAME AT ME WITH A KNIFE?
WELL, THAT WAS BEFORE WE WERE PROPERLY INTRODUCED.
SO, WHAT? YOU WON'T STAB ME IN THE BACK, NOW THAT YOU KNOW MY NAME?
OF COURSE, TO BE FAIR, I HAVE HAD RELATIONSHIPS WITH STRANGER BEGINNINGS...
OH, NO. I AM A PRINCE, AFTER ALL.
WITH MY FRIENDS, I ALWAYS LET THEM SEE THE KNIFE COMING.
ANOTHER PRINCE?
CHARMING.

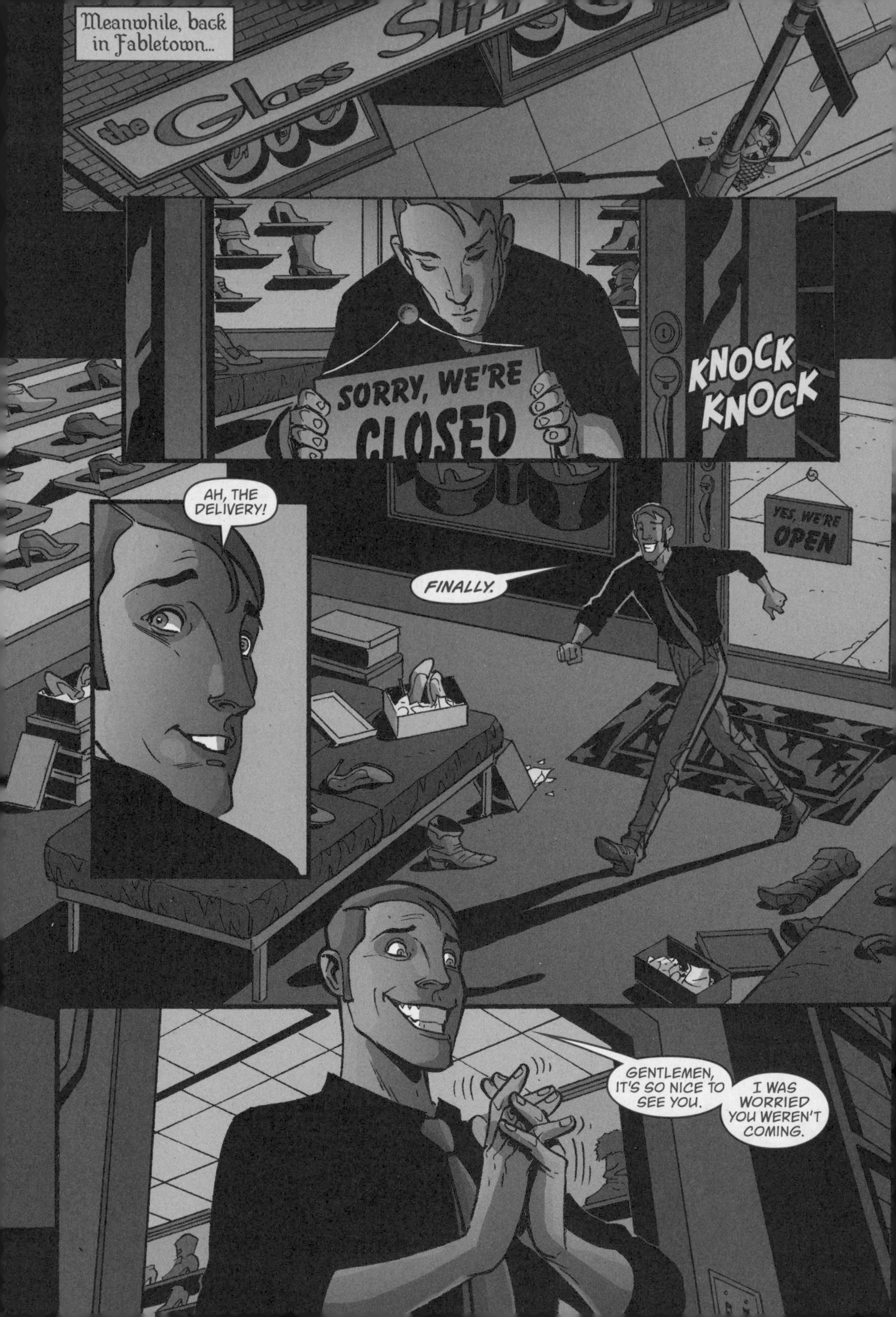

Meanwhile, back in Fabletown...
the Glass Slipper
SORRY, WE'RE CLOSED
KNOCK KNOCK
AH, THE DELIVERY!
FINALLY.
YES, WE'RE OPEN
GENTLEMEN, IT'S SO NICE TO SEE YOU.
I WAS WORRIED YOU WEREN'T COMING.

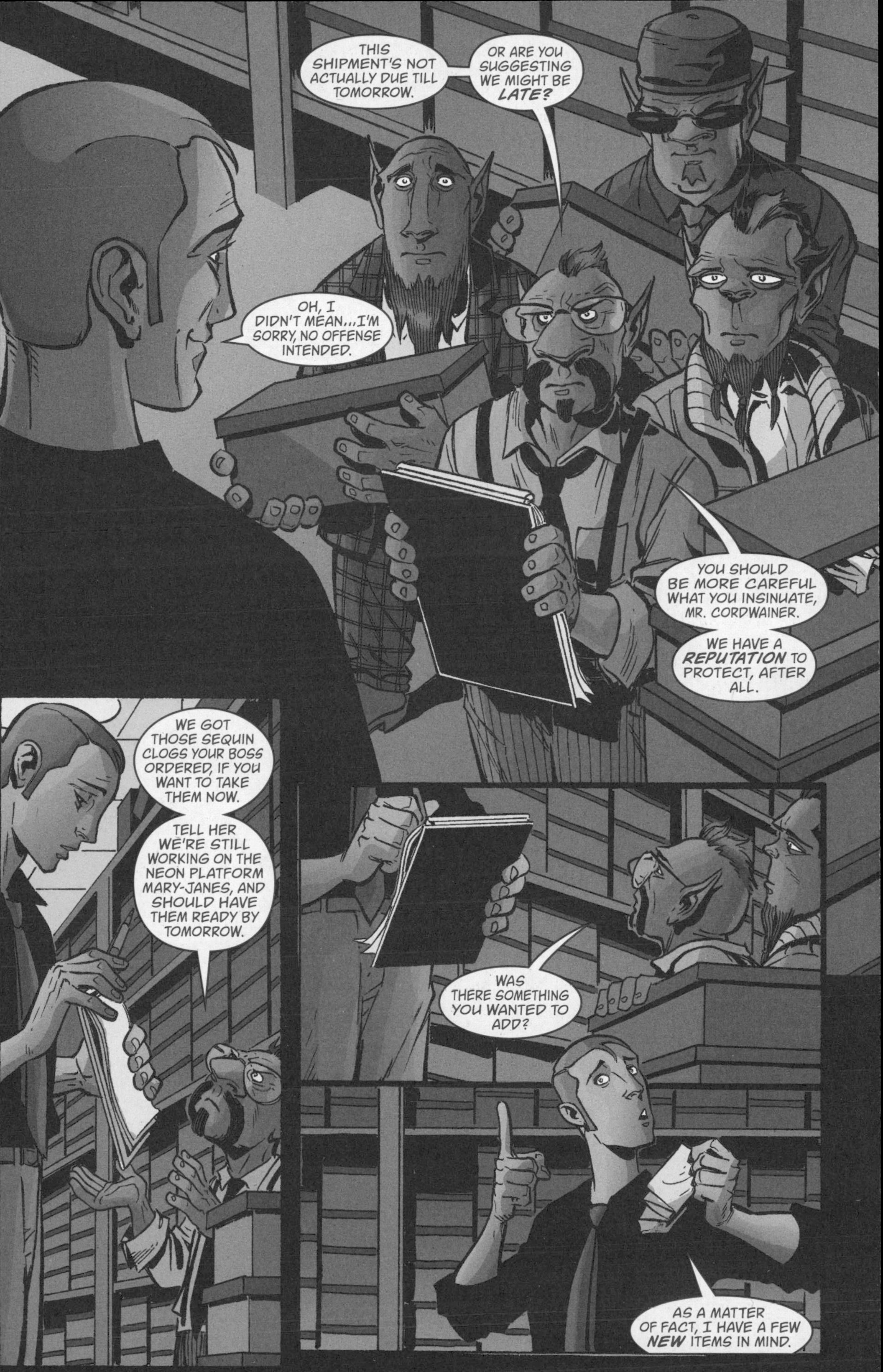
THIS SHIPMENT'S NOT ACTUALLY DUE TILL TOMORROW.
OR ARE YOU SUGGESTING WE MIGHT BE *LATE?*
OH, I DIDN'T MEAN...I'M SORRY, NO OFFENSE INTENDED.
YOU SHOULD BE MORE CAREFUL WHAT YOU INSINUATE, MR. CORDWAINER.
WE HAVE A *REPUTATION* TO PROTECT, AFTER ALL.
WE GOT THOSE SEQUIN CLOGS YOUR BOSS ORDERED, IF YOU WANT TO TAKE THEM NOW.
TELL HER WE'RE STILL WORKING ON THE NEON PLATFORM MARY-JANES, AND SHOULD HAVE THEM READY BY TOMORROW.
WAS THERE SOMETHING YOU WANTED TO ADD?
AS A MATTER OF FACT, I HAVE A FEW *NEW* ITEMS IN MIND.

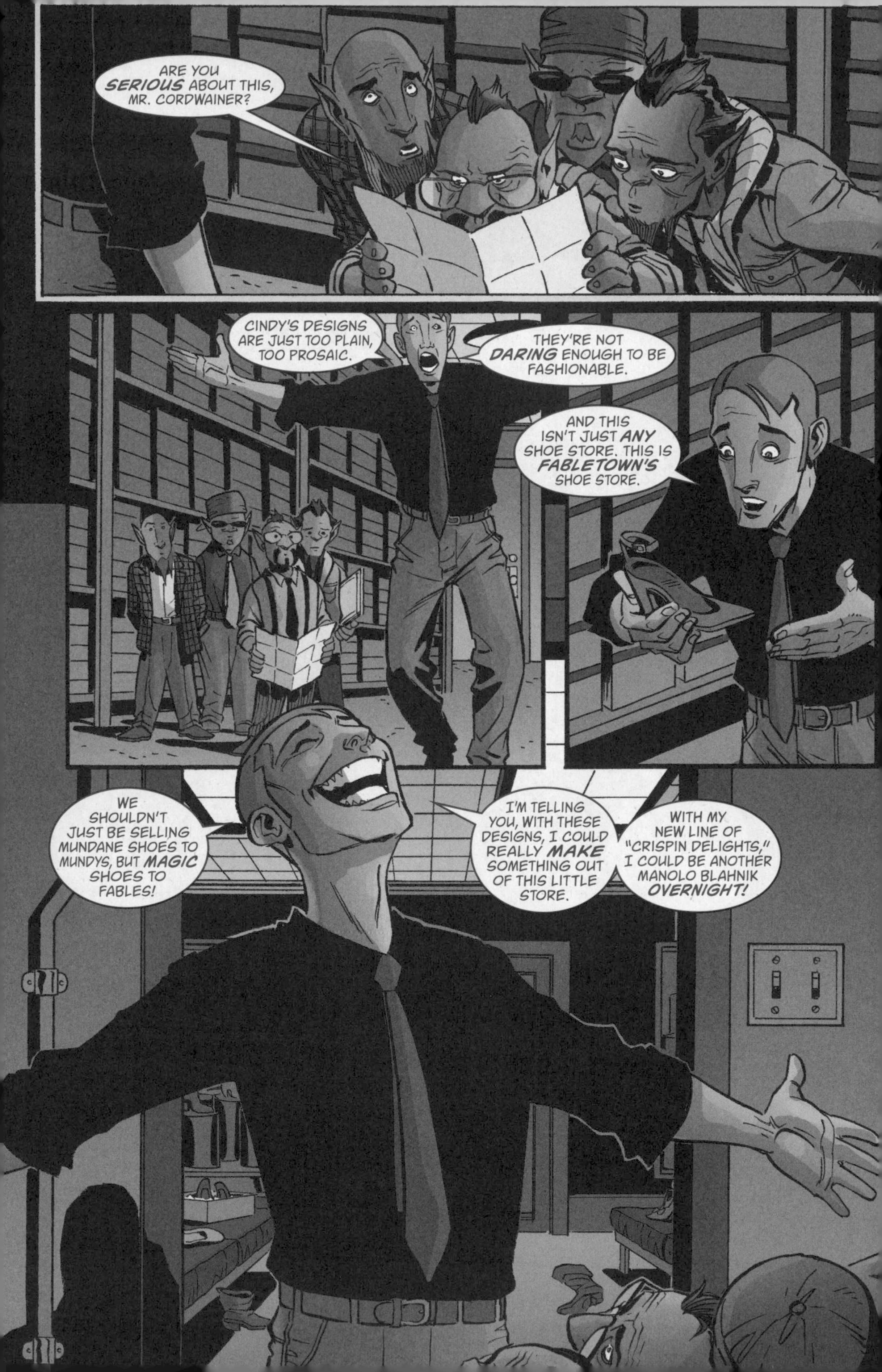
ARE YOU SERIOUS ABOUT THIS, MR. CORDWAINER?
CINDY'S DESIGNS ARE JUST TOO PLAIN, TOO PROSAIC.
THEY'RE NOT DARING ENOUGH TO BE FASHIONABLE.
AND THIS ISN'T JUST ANY SHOE STORE. THIS IS FABLETOWN'S SHOE STORE.
WE SHOULDN'T JUST BE SELLING MUNDANE SHOES TO MUNDYS, BUT MAGIC SHOES TO FABLES!
I'M TELLING YOU, WITH THESE DESIGNS, I COULD REALLY MAKE SOMETHING OUT OF THIS LITTLE STORE.
WITH MY NEW LINE OF "CRISPIN DELIGHTS," I COULD BE ANOTHER MANOLO BLAHNIK OVERNIGHT!

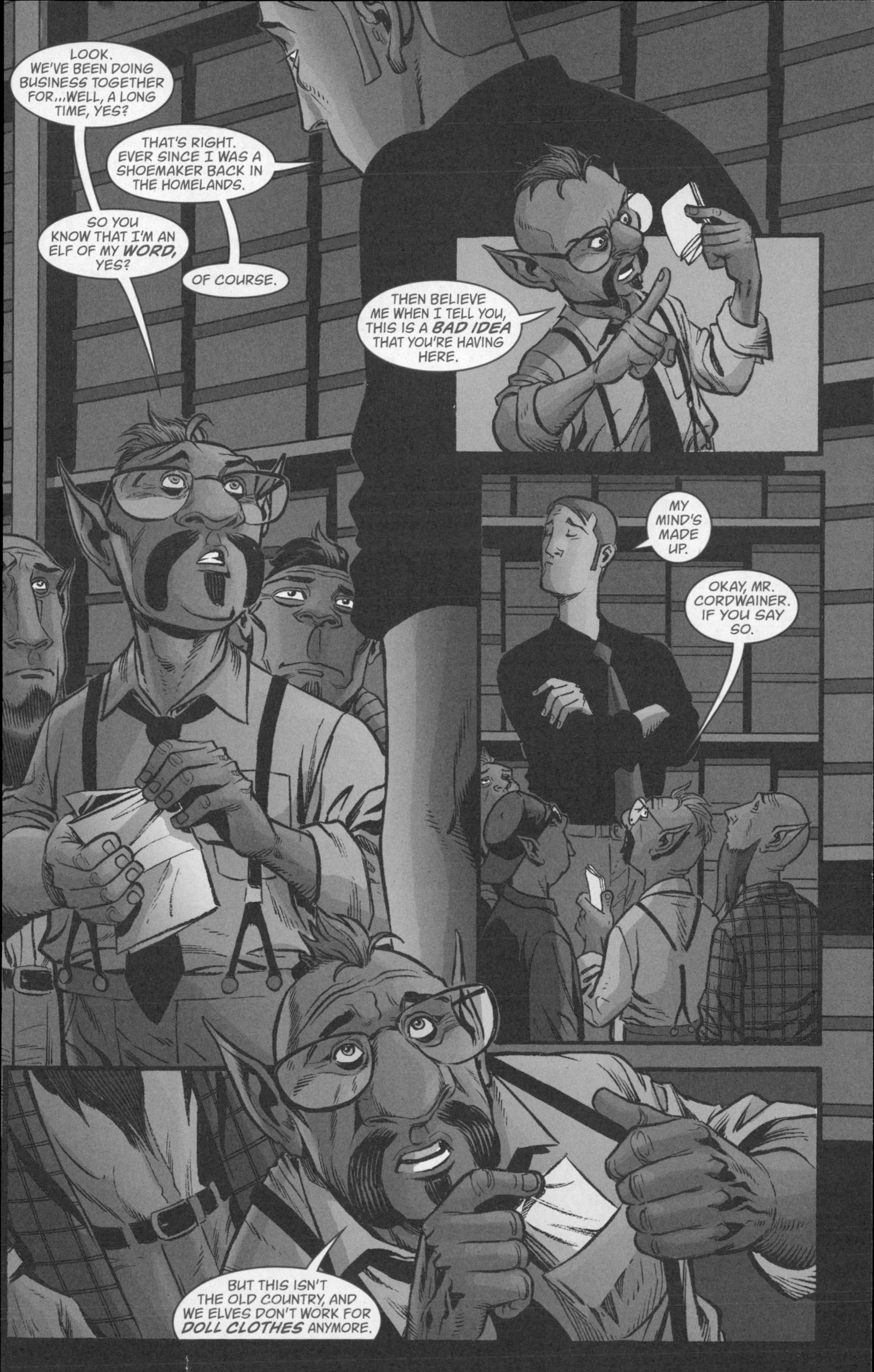

LOOK. WE'VE BEEN DOING BUSINESS TOGETHER FOR...WELL, A LONG TIME, YES?
THAT'S RIGHT. EVER SINCE I WAS A SHOEMAKER BACK IN THE HOMELANDS.
SO YOU KNOW THAT I'M AN ELF OF MY WORD, YES?
OF COURSE.
THEN BELIEVE ME WHEN I TELL YOU, THIS IS A BAD IDEA THAT YOU'RE HAVING HERE.
MY MIND'S MADE UP.
OKAY, MR. CORDWAINER. IF YOU SAY SO.
BUT THIS ISN'T THE OLD COUNTRY, AND WE ELVES DON'T WORK FOR DOLL CLOTHES ANYMORE.

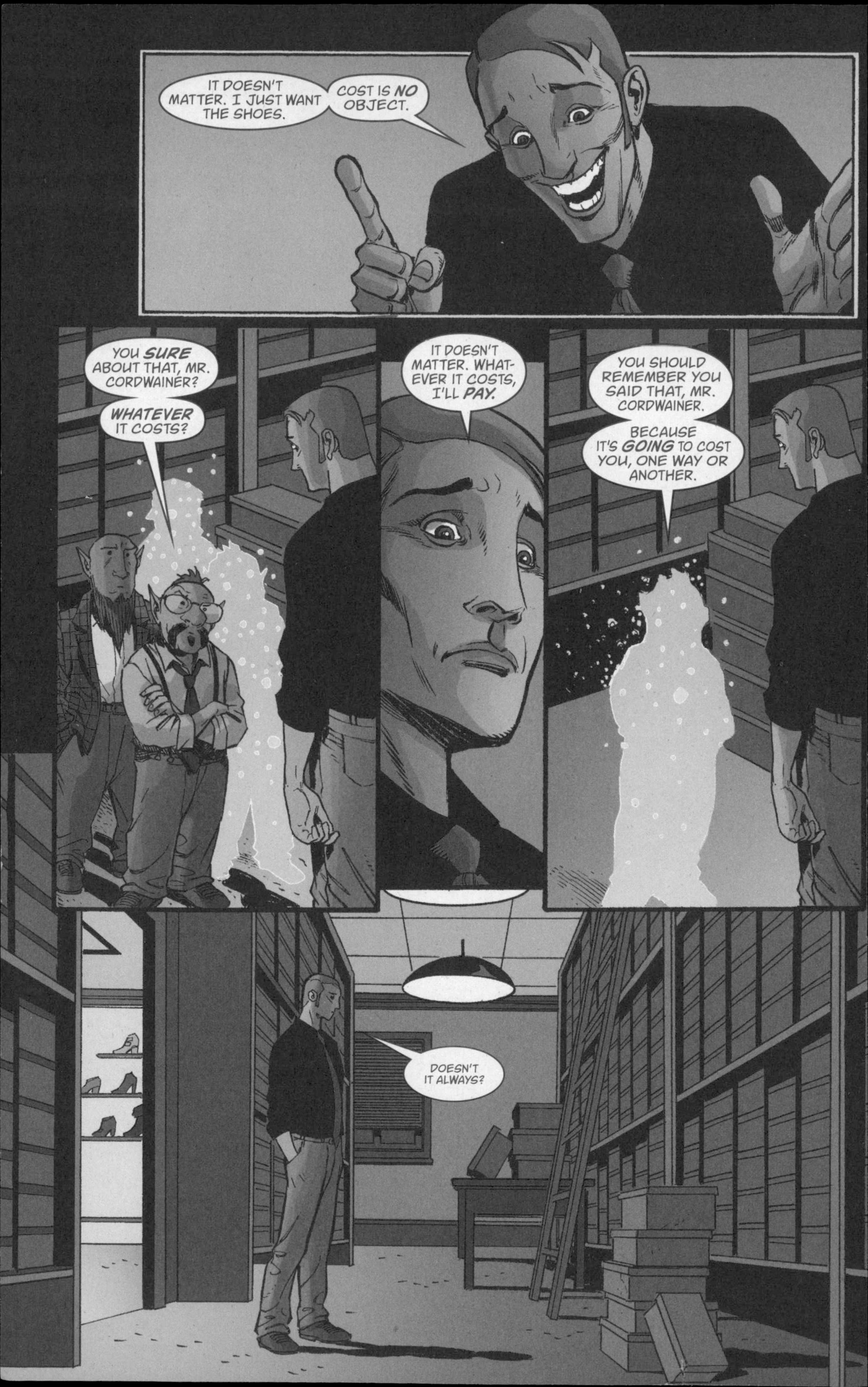
IT DOESN'T MATTER. I JUST WANT THE SHOES.
COST IS NO OBJECT.
YOU SURE ABOUT THAT, MR. CORDWAINER?
WHATEVER IT COSTS?
IT DOESN'T MATTER. WHATEVER IT COSTS, I'LL PAY.
YOU SHOULD REMEMBER YOU SAID THAT, MR. CORDWAINER.
BECAUSE IT'S GOING TO COST YOU, ONE WAY OR ANOTHER.
DOESN'T IT ALWAYS?

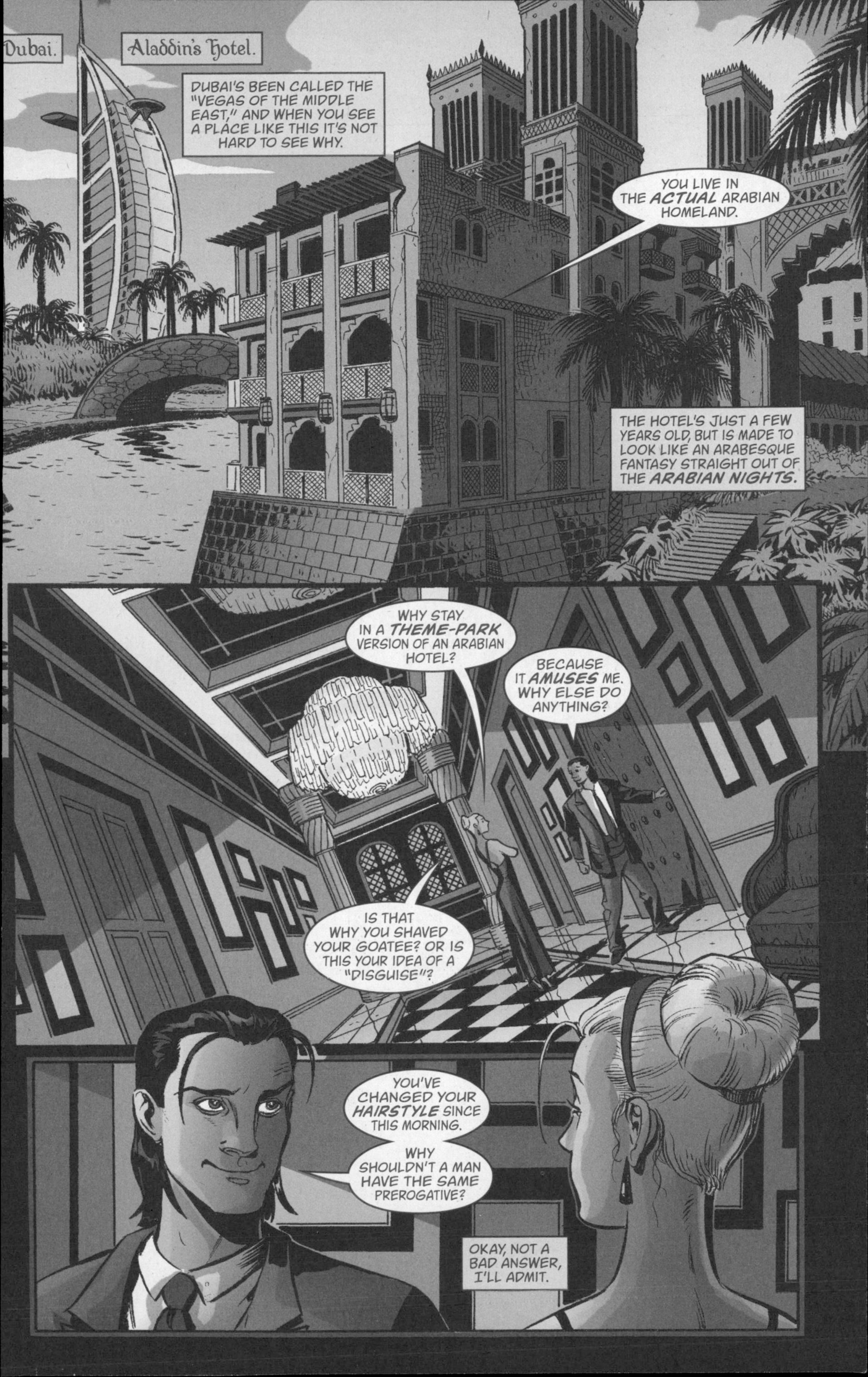
Dubai.
Aladdin's Hotel.
DUBAI'S BEEN CALLED THE "VEGAS OF THE MIDDLE EAST," AND WHEN YOU SEE A PLACE LIKE THIS IT'S NOT HARD TO SEE WHY.
YOU LIVE IN THE ACTUAL ARABIAN HOMELAND.
THE HOTEL'S JUST A FEW YEARS OLD, BUT IS MADE TO LOOK LIKE AN ARABESQUE FANTASY STRAIGHT OUT OF THE ARABIAN NIGHTS.
WHY STAY IN A THEME-PARK VERSION OF AN ARABIAN HOTEL?
BECAUSE IT AMUSES ME. WHY ELSE DO ANYTHING?
IS THAT WHY YOU SHAVED YOUR GOATEE? OR IS THIS YOUR IDEA OF A "DISGUISE"?
YOU'VE CHANGED YOUR HAIRSTYLE SINCE THIS MORNING.
WHY SHOULDN'T A MAN HAVE THE SAME PREROGATIVE?
OKAY, NOT A BAD ANSWER, I'LL ADMIT.

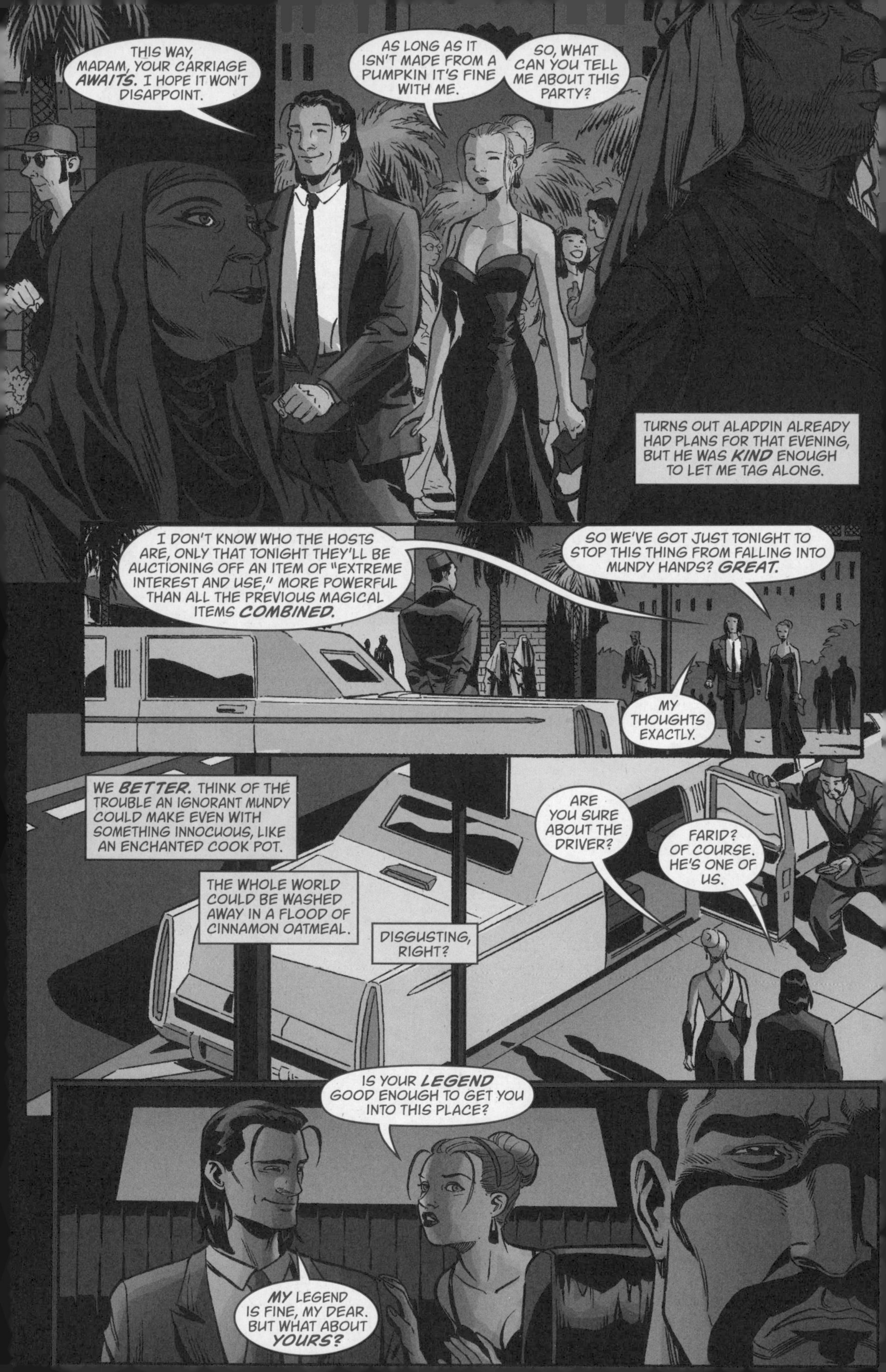
THIS WAY, MADAM, YOUR CARRIAGE AWAITS. I HOPE IT WON'T DISAPPOINT.
AS LONG AS IT ISN'T MADE FROM A PUMPKIN IT'S FINE WITH ME.
SO, WHAT CAN YOU TELL ME ABOUT THIS PARTY?
TURNS OUT ALADDIN ALREADY HAD PLANS FOR THAT EVENING, BUT HE WAS KIND ENOUGH TO LET ME TAG ALONG.
I DON'T KNOW WHO THE HOSTS ARE, ONLY THAT TONIGHT THEY'LL BE AUCTIONING OFF AN ITEM OF "EXTREME INTEREST AND USE," MORE POWERFUL THAN ALL THE PREVIOUS MAGICAL ITEMS COMBINED.
SO WE'VE GOT JUST TONIGHT TO STOP THIS THING FROM FALLING INTO MUNDY HANDS? GREAT.
MY THOUGHTS EXACTLY.
WE BETTER. THINK OF THE TROUBLE AN IGNORANT MUNDY COULD MAKE EVEN WITH SOMETHING INNOCUOUS, LIKE AN ENCHANTED COOK POT.
THE WHOLE WORLD COULD BE WASHED AWAY IN A FLOOD OF CINNAMON OATMEAL.
DISGUSTING, RIGHT?
ARE YOU SURE ABOUT THE DRIVER?
FARID? OF COURSE. HE'S ONE OF US.
IS YOUR LEGEND GOOD ENOUGH TO GET YOU INTO THIS PLACE?
MY LEGEND IS FINE, MY DEAR. BUT WHAT ABOUT YOURS?

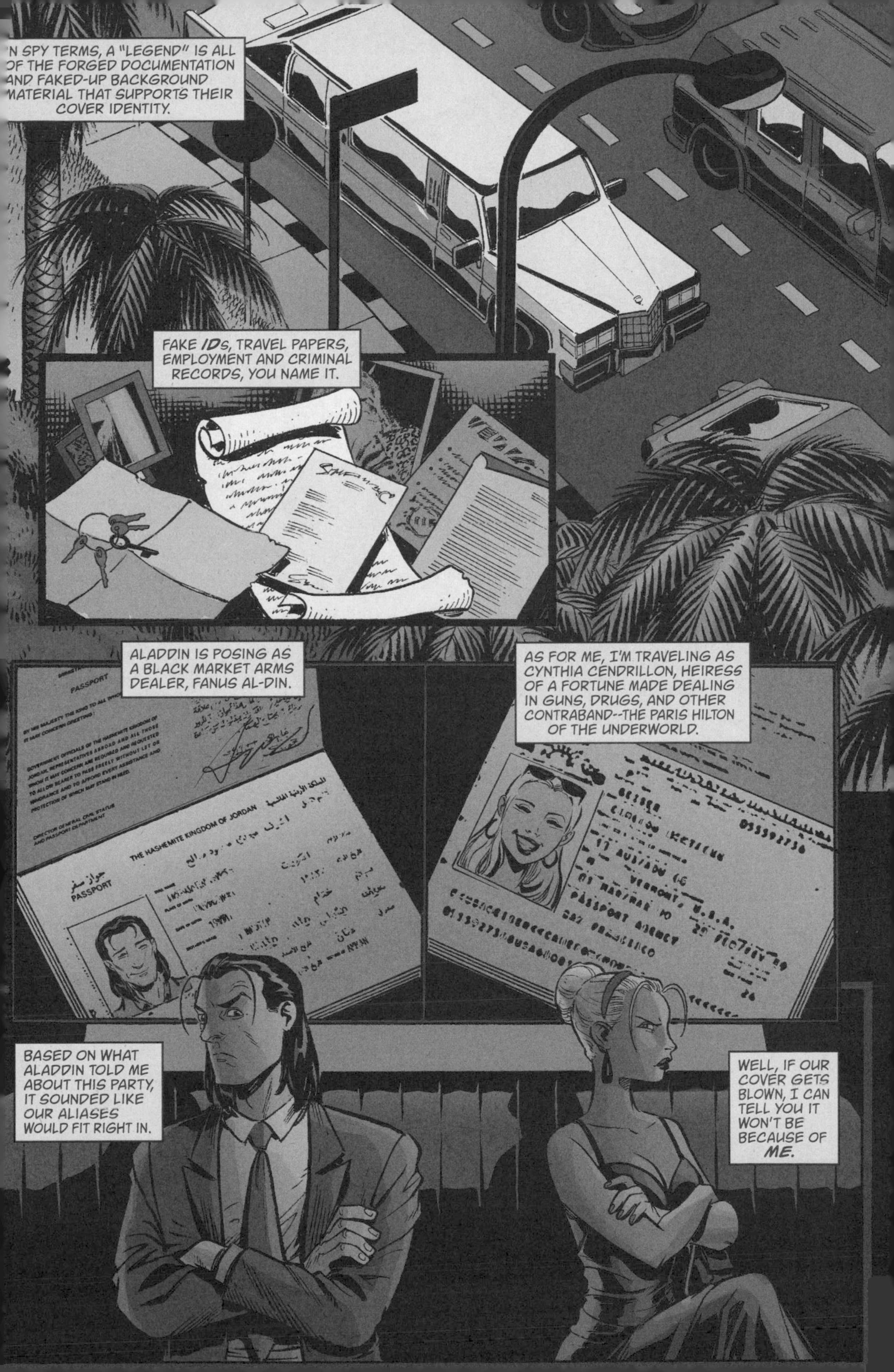
IN SPY TERMS, A "LEGEND" IS ALL OF THE FORGED DOCUMENTATION AND FAKED-UP BACKGROUND MATERIAL THAT SUPPORTS THEIR COVER IDENTITY.
FAKE IDs, TRAVEL PAPERS, EMPLOYMENT AND CRIMINAL RECORDS, YOU NAME IT.
ALADDIN IS POSING AS A BLACK MARKET ARMS DEALER, FANUS AL-DIN.
AS FOR ME, I'M TRAVELING AS CYNTHIA CENDRILLON, HEIRESS OF A FORTUNE MADE DEALING IN GUNS, DRUGS, AND OTHER CONTRABAND--THE PARIS HILTON OF THE UNDERWORLD.
PASSPORT
THE HASHEMITE KINGDOM OF JORDAN
PASSPORT
BASED ON WHAT ALADDIN TOLD ME ABOUT THIS PARTY, IT SOUNDED LIKE OUR ALIASES WOULD FIT RIGHT IN.
WELL, IF OUR COVER GETS BLOWN, I CAN TELL YOU IT WON'T BE BECAUSE OF ME.

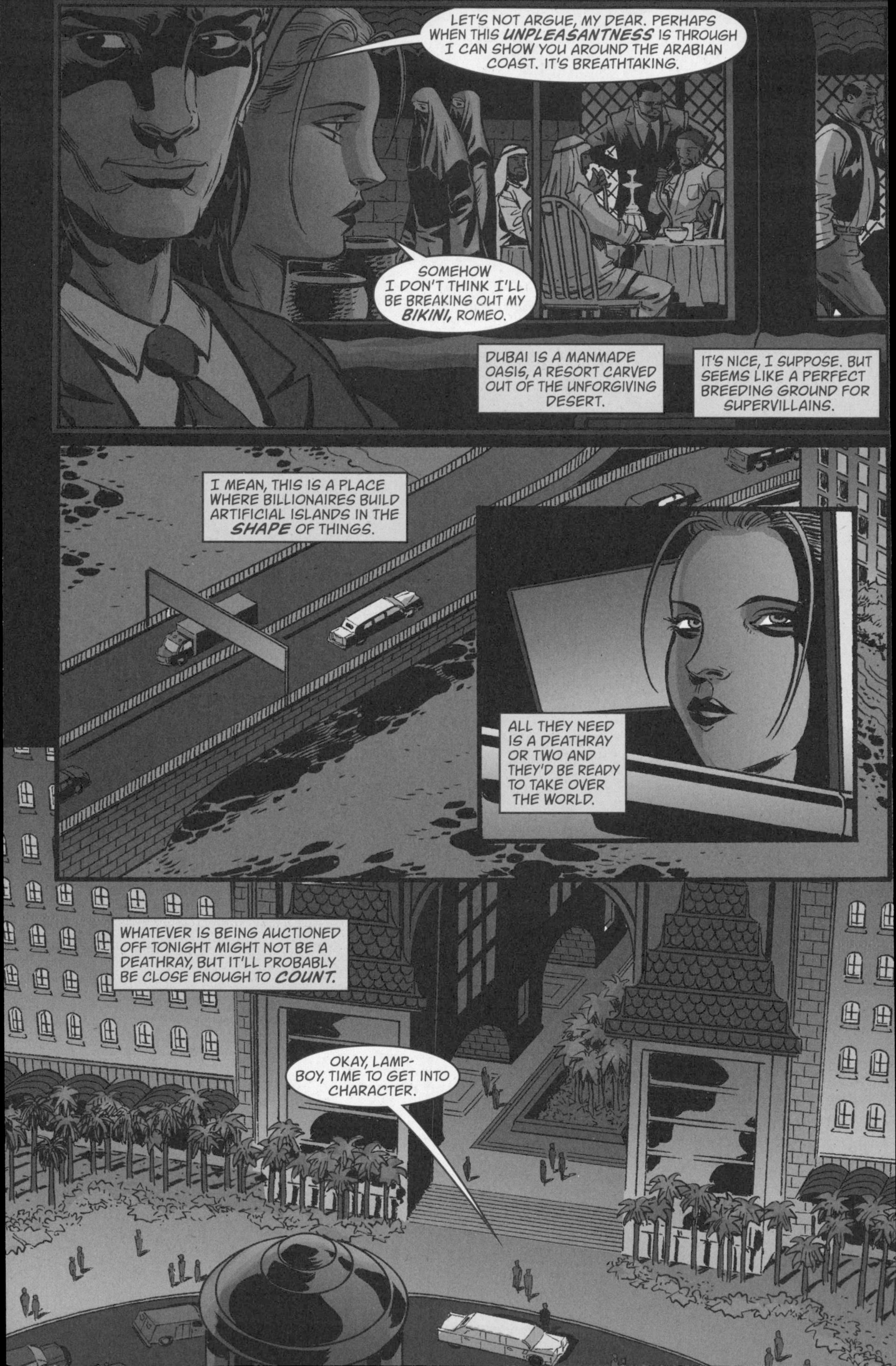
LET'S NOT ARGUE, MY DEAR. PERHAPS WHEN THIS UNPLEASANTNESS IS THROUGH I CAN SHOW YOU AROUND THE ARABIAN COAST. IT'S BREATHTAKING.
SOMEHOW I DON'T THINK I'LL BE BREAKING OUT MY BIKINI, ROMEO.
DUBAI IS A MANMADE OASIS, A RESORT CARVED OUT OF THE UNFORGIVING DESERT.
IT'S NICE, I SUPPOSE. BUT SEEMS LIKE A PERFECT BREEDING GROUND FOR SUPERVILLAINS.
I MEAN, THIS IS A PLACE WHERE BILLIONAIRES BUILD ARTIFICIAL ISLANDS IN THE SHAPE OF THINGS.
ALL THEY NEED IS A DEATHRAY OR TWO AND THEY'D BE READY TO TAKE OVER THE WORLD.
WHATEVER IS BEING AUCTIONED OFF TONIGHT MIGHT NOT BE A DEATHRAY, BUT IT'LL PROBABLY BE CLOSE ENOUGH TO COUNT.
OKAY, LAMP-BOY, TIME TO GET INTO CHARACTER.

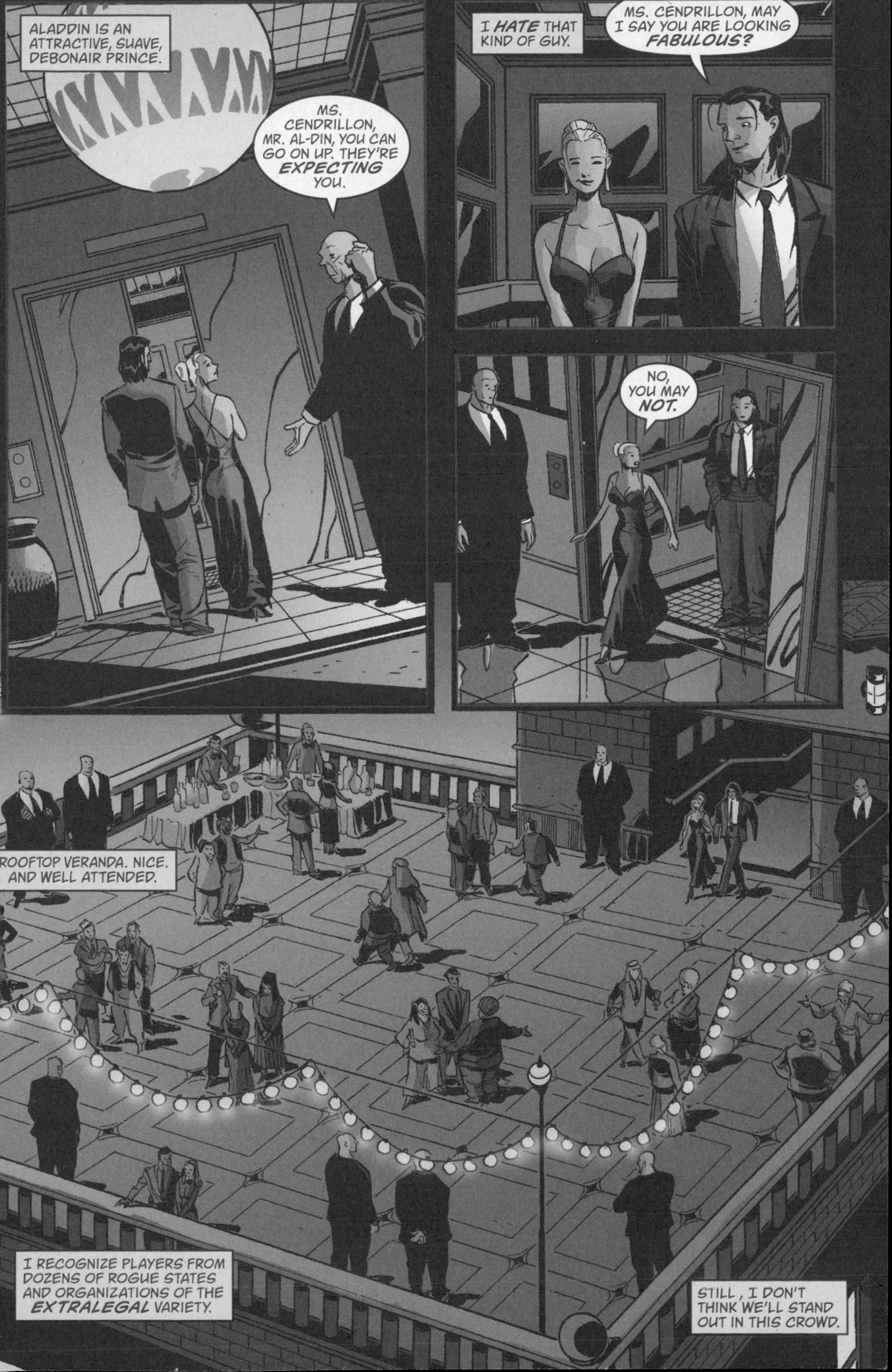

ALADDIN IS AN ATTRACTIVE, SUAVE, DEBONAIR PRINCE.
MS. CENDRILLON, MR. AL-DIN, YOU CAN GO ON UP. THEY'RE EXPECTING YOU.
I HATE THAT KIND OF GUY.
MS. CENDRILLON, MAY I SAY YOU ARE LOOKING FABULOUS?
NO, YOU MAY NOT.
ROOFTOP VERANDA. NICE. AND WELL ATTENDED.
I RECOGNIZE PLAYERS FROM DOZENS OF ROGUE STATES AND ORGANIZATIONS OF THE EXTRALEGAL VARIETY.
STILL, I DON'T THINK WE'LL STAND OUT IN THIS CROWD.

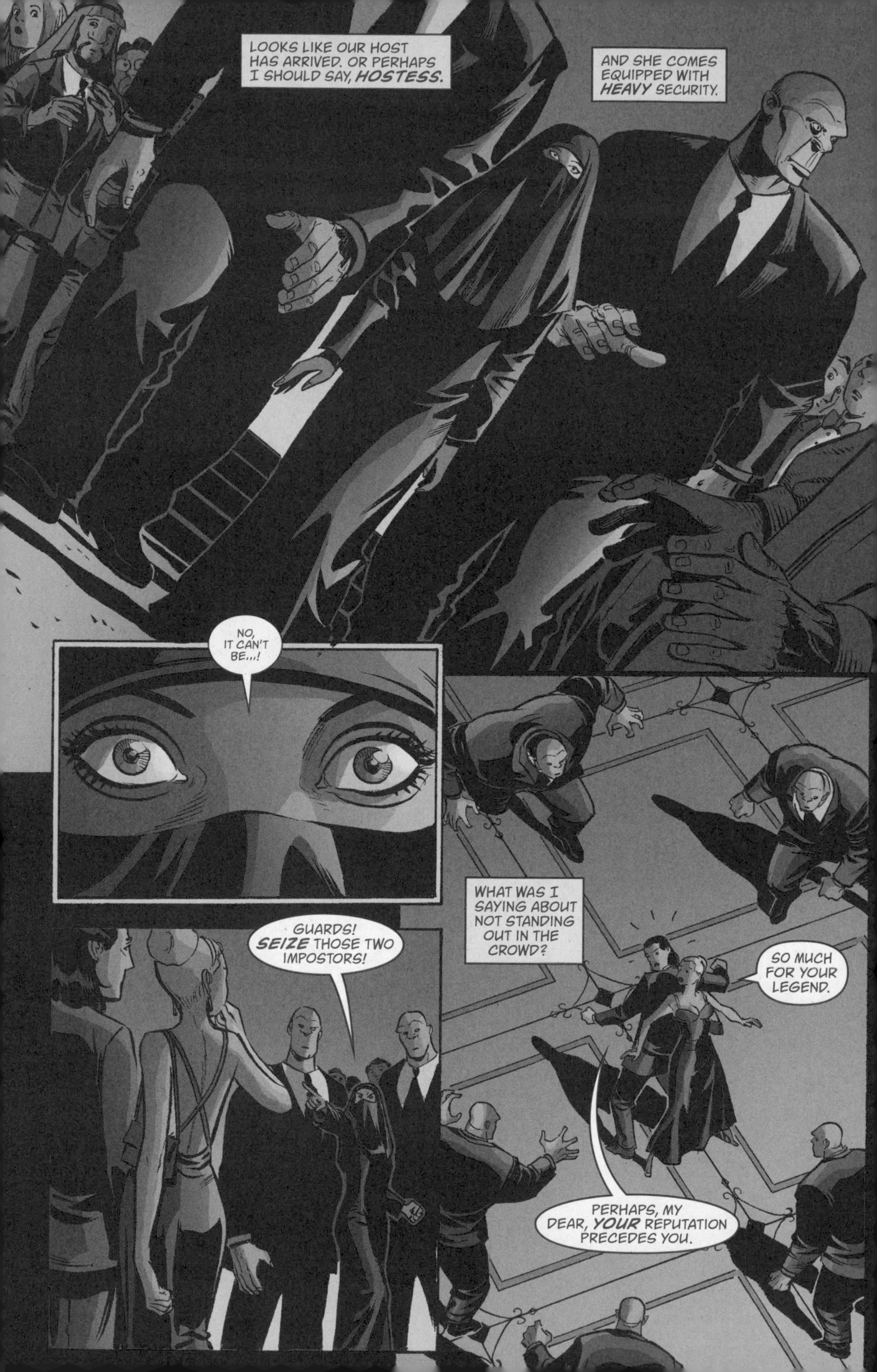
LOOKS LIKE OUR HOST HAS ARRIVED. OR PERHAPS I SHOULD SAY, *HOSTESS.*
AND SHE COMES EQUIPPED WITH *HEAVY* SECURITY.
NO, IT CAN'T BE...!
GUARDS! *SEIZE* THOSE TWO IMPOSTORS!
WHAT WAS I SAYING ABOUT NOT STANDING OUT IN THE CROWD?
SO MUCH FOR YOUR LEGEND.
PERHAPS, MY DEAR, *YOUR* REPUTATION PRECEDES YOU.

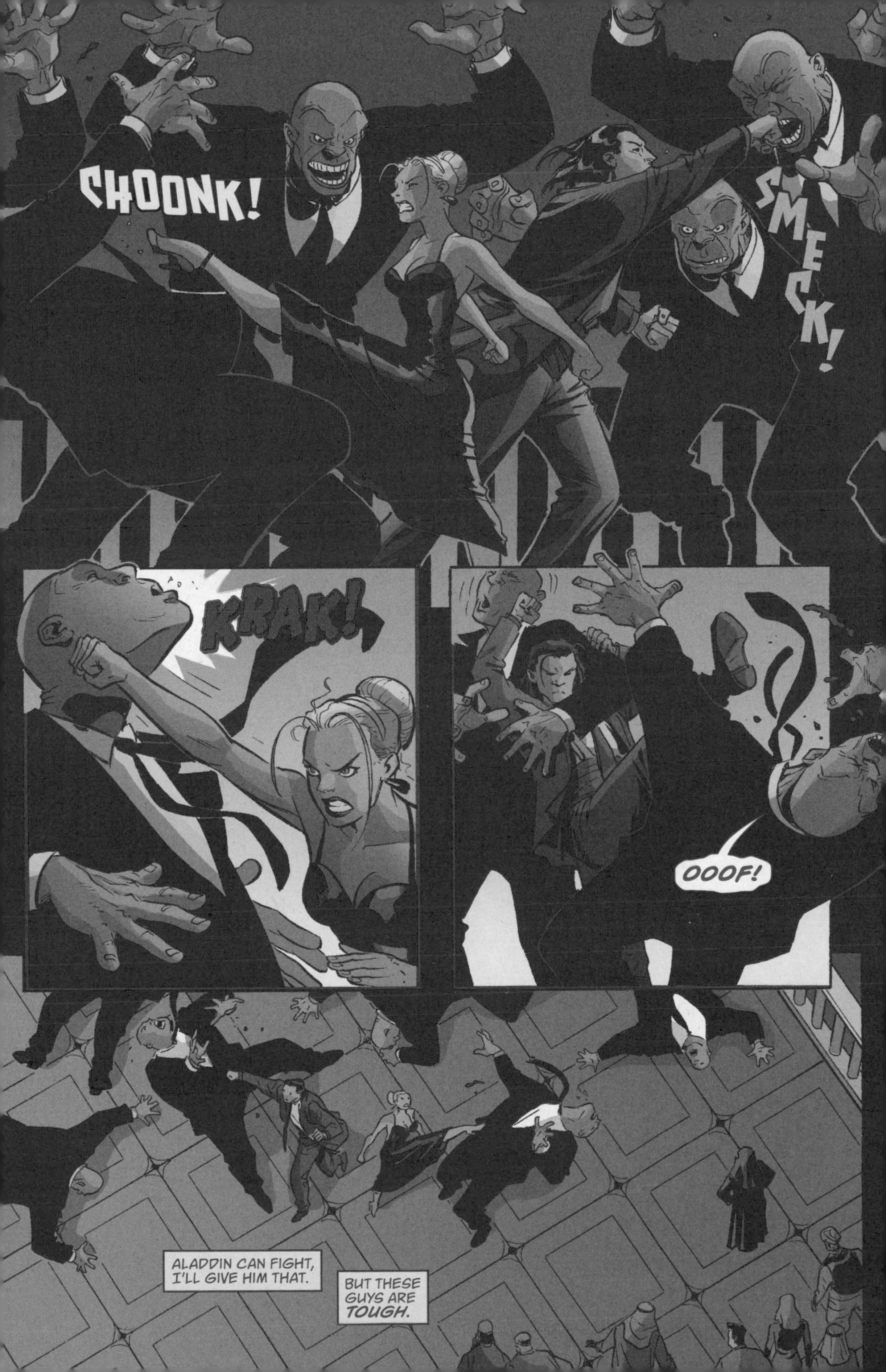
CHOONK!
SMECK!
KRAK!
OOOF!
ALADDIN CAN FIGHT, I'LL GIVE HIM THAT.
BUT THESE GUYS ARE TOUGH.

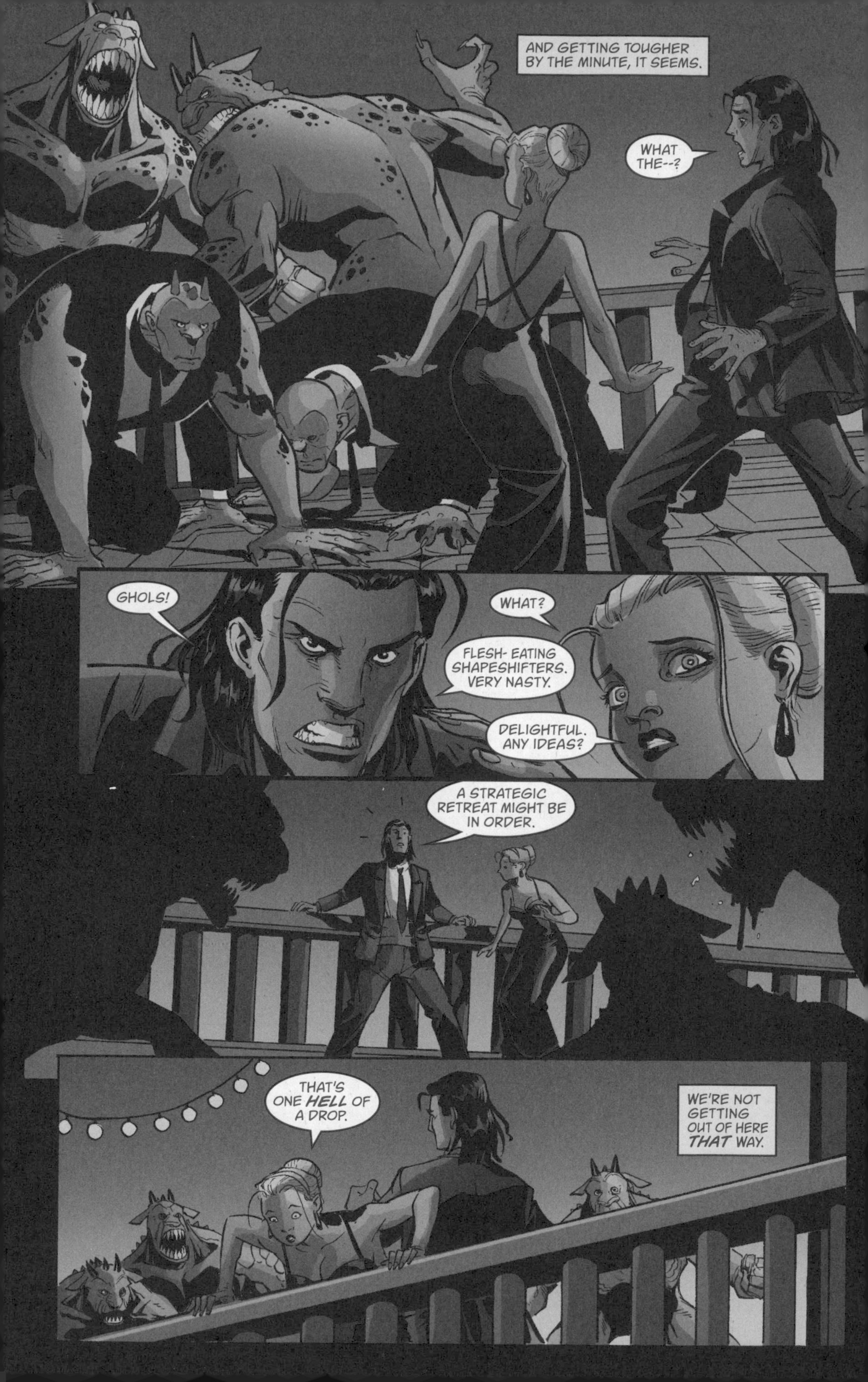
AND GETTING TOUGHER BY THE MINUTE, IT SEEMS.
WHAT THE--?
GHOLS!
WHAT?
FLESH- EATING SHAPESHIFTERS. VERY NASTY.
DELIGHTFUL. ANY IDEAS?
A STRATEGIC RETREAT MIGHT BE IN ORDER.
THAT'S ONE HELL OF A DROP.
WE'RE NOT GETTING OUT OF HERE THAT WAY.

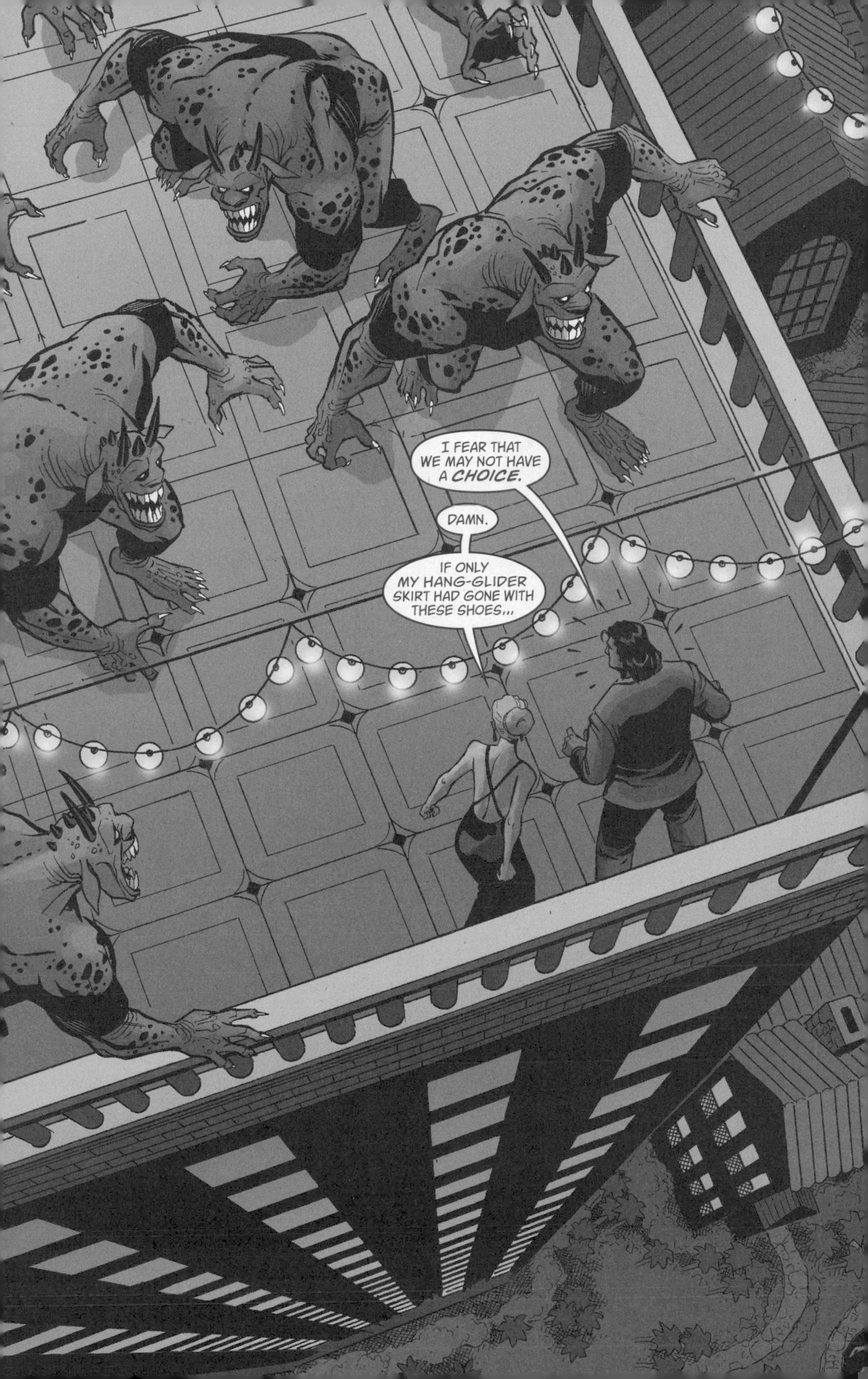
I FEAR THAT WE MAY NOT HAVE A CHOICE.
DAMN.
IF ONLY MY HANG-GLIDER SKIRT HAD GONE WITH THESE SHOES...

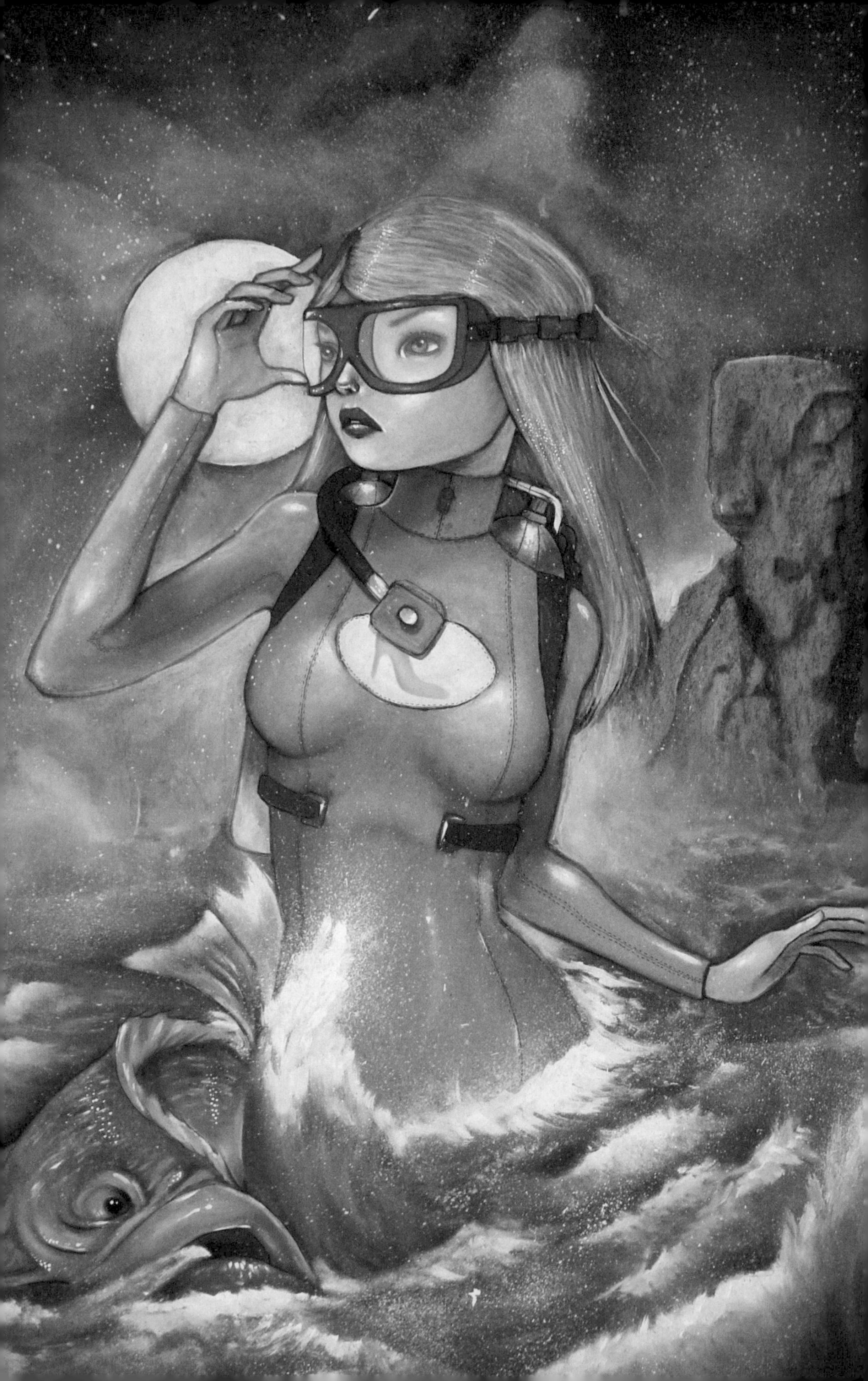

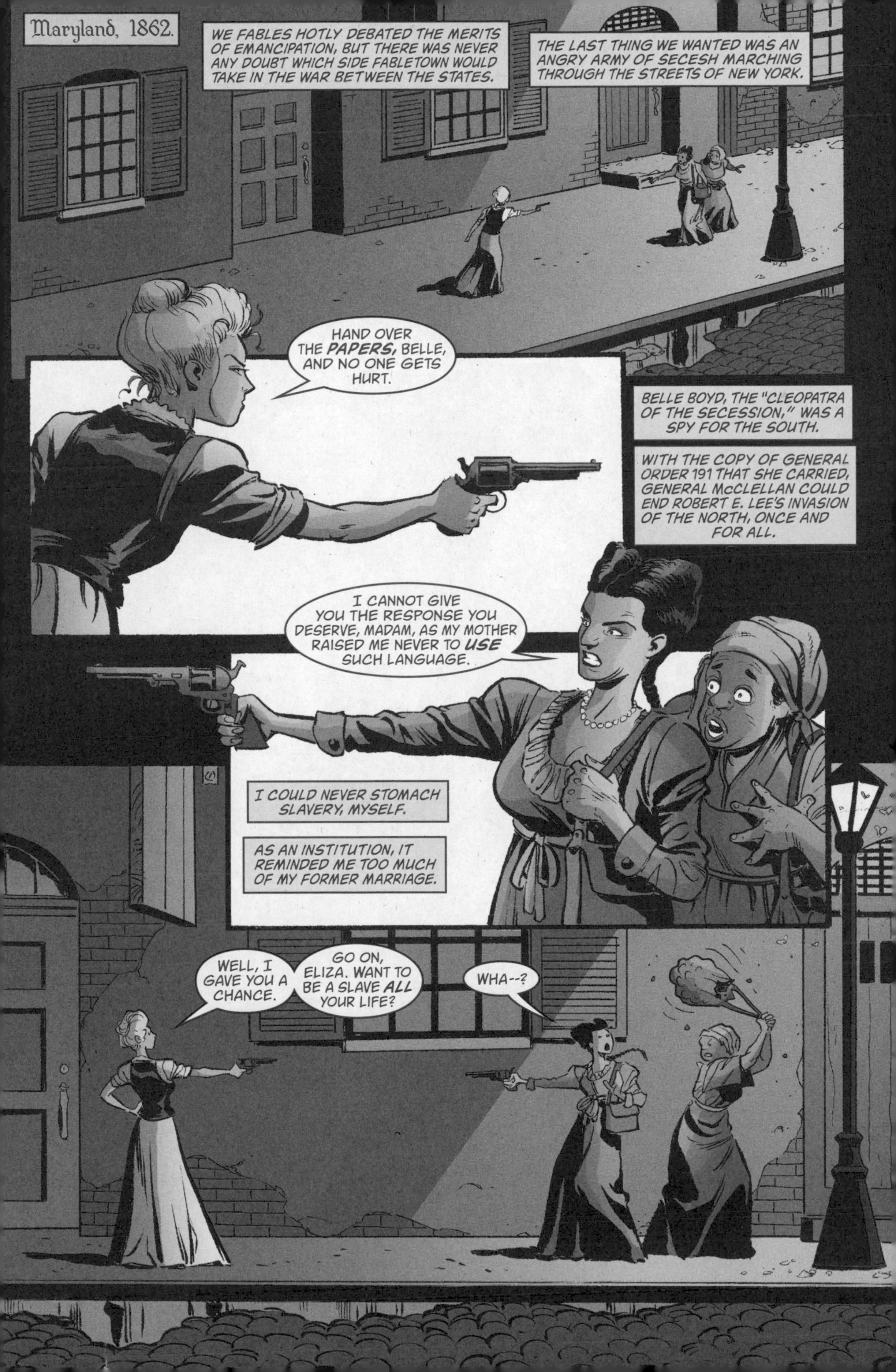

Maryland, 1862.
WE FABLES HOTLY DEBATED THE MERITS OF EMANCIPATION, BUT THERE WAS NEVER ANY DOUBT WHICH SIDE FABLETOWN WOULD TAKE IN THE WAR BETWEEN THE STATES.
THE LAST THING WE WANTED WAS AN ANGRY ARMY OF SECESH MARCHING THROUGH THE STREETS OF NEW YORK.
HAND OVER THE PAPERS, BELLE, AND NO ONE GETS HURT.
BELLE BOYD, THE "CLEOPATRA OF THE SECESSION," WAS A SPY FOR THE SOUTH.
WITH THE COPY OF GENERAL ORDER 191 THAT SHE CARRIED, GENERAL McCLELLAN COULD END ROBERT E. LEE'S INVASION OF THE NORTH, ONCE AND FOR ALL.
I CANNOT GIVE YOU THE RESPONSE YOU DESERVE, MADAM, AS MY MOTHER RAISED ME NEVER TO USE SUCH LANGUAGE.
I COULD NEVER STOMACH SLAVERY, MYSELF.
AS AN INSTITUTION, IT REMINDED ME TOO MUCH OF MY FORMER MARRIAGE.
WELL, I GAVE YOU A CHANCE.
GO ON, ELIZA. WANT TO BE A SLAVE ALL YOUR LIFE?
WHA--?

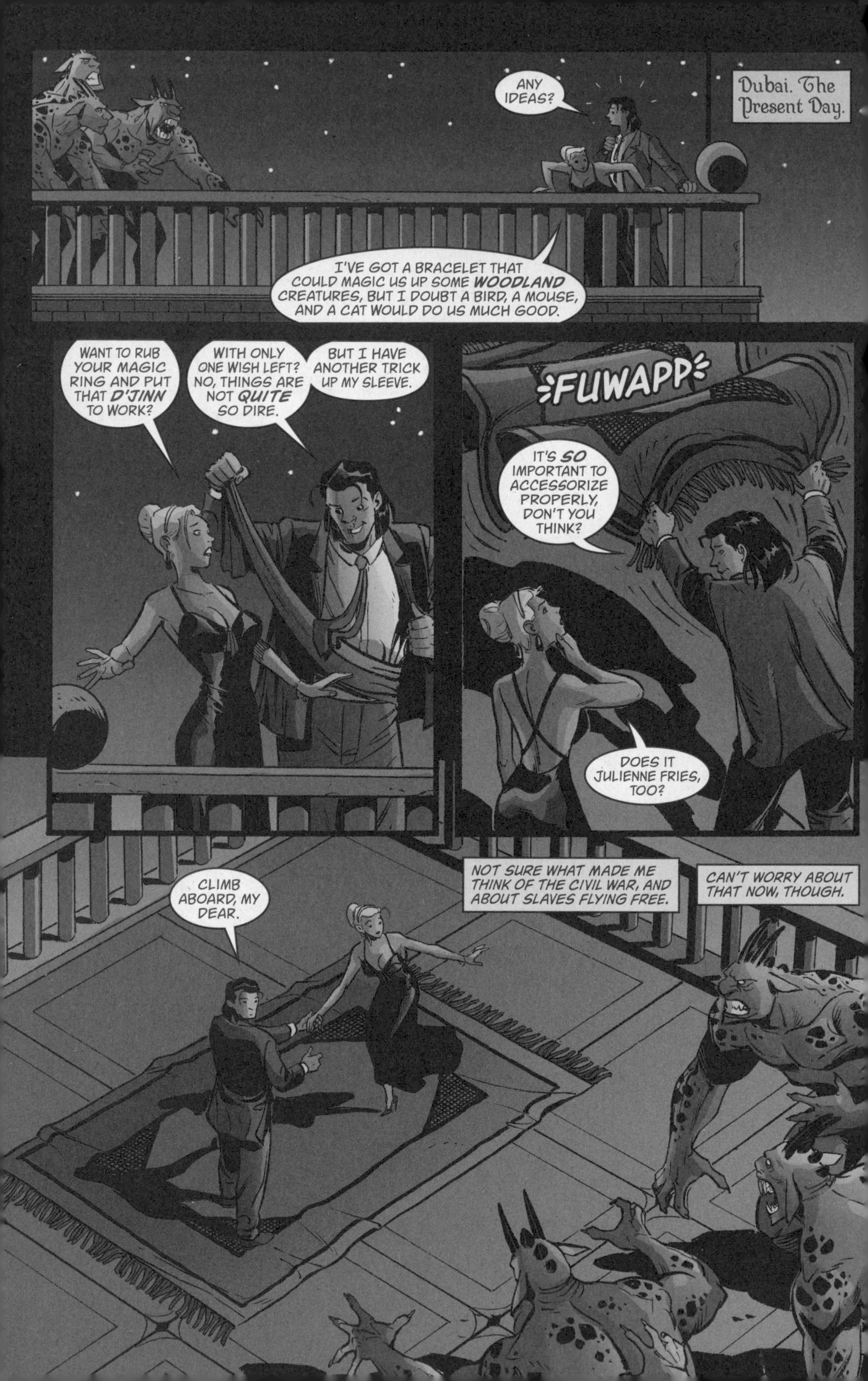
Dubai. The Present Day.
ANY IDEAS?
I'VE GOT A BRACELET THAT COULD MAGIC US UP SOME WOODLAND CREATURES, BUT I DOUBT A BIRD, A MOUSE, AND A CAT WOULD DO US MUCH GOOD.
WANT TO RUB YOUR MAGIC RING AND PUT THAT D'JINN TO WORK?
WITH ONLY ONE WISH LEFT? NO, THINGS ARE NOT QUITE SO DIRE.
BUT I HAVE ANOTHER TRICK UP MY SLEEVE.
FUWAPP
IT'S SO IMPORTANT TO ACCESSORIZE PROPERLY, DON'T YOU THINK?
DOES IT JULIENNE FRIES, TOO?
CLIMB ABOARD, MY DEAR.
NOT SURE WHAT MADE ME THINK OF THE CIVIL WAR, AND ABOUT SLAVES FLYING FREE.
CAN'T WORRY ABOUT THAT NOW, THOUGH.

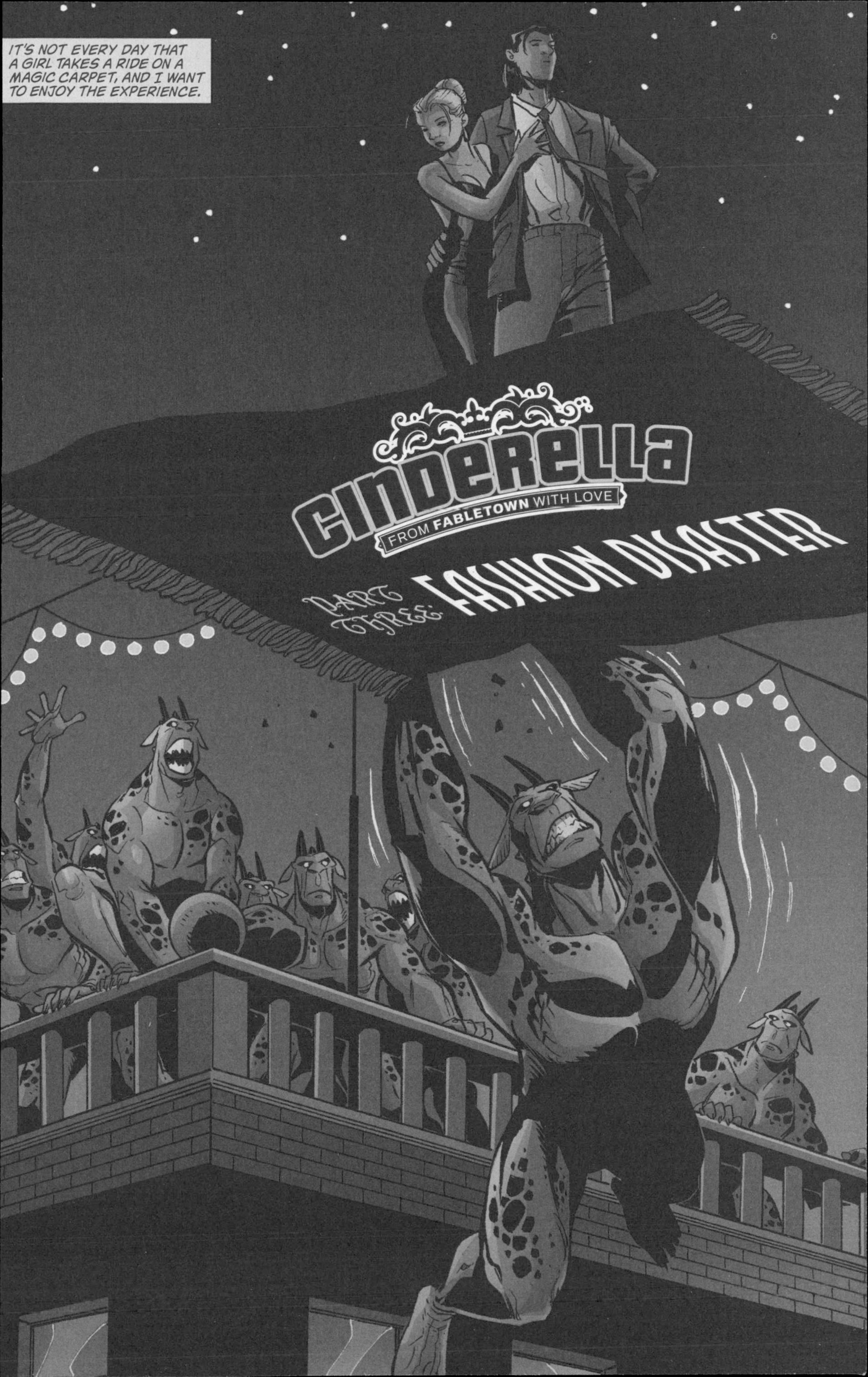
IT'S NOT EVERY DAY THAT A GIRL TAKES A RIDE ON A MAGIC CARPET, AND I WANT TO ENJOY THE EXPERIENCE.
CINDERELLA
FROM FABLETOWN WITH LOVE
PART THREE: FASHION DISASTER

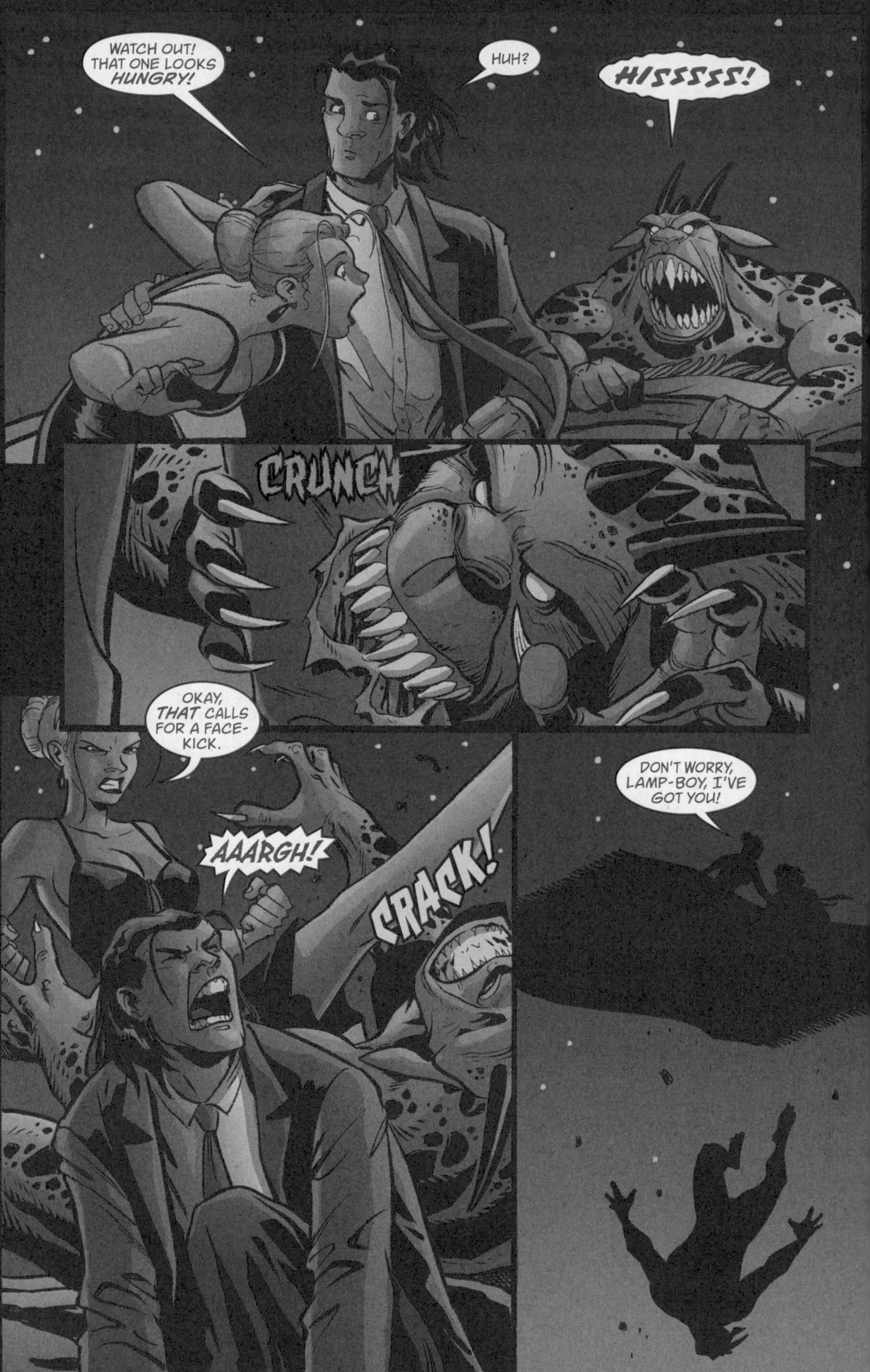
WATCH OUT! THAT ONE LOOKS HUNGRY!
HUH?
HISSSSS!
CRUNCH
OKAY, THAT CALLS FOR A FACE-KICK.
AAARGH!
CRACK!
DON'T WORRY, LAMP-BOY, I'VE GOT YOU!

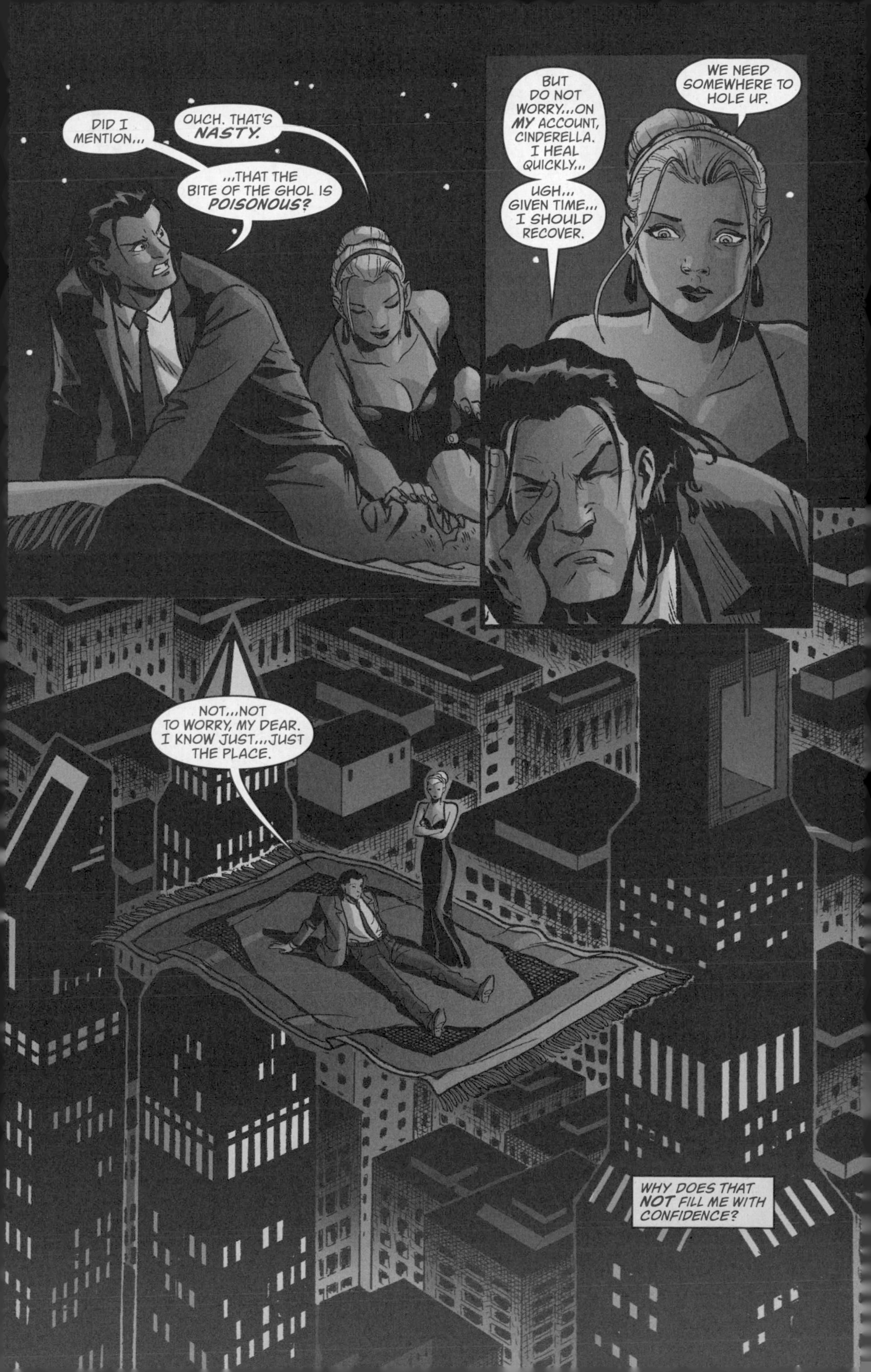
DID I MENTION...
OUCH. THAT'S NASTY.
...THAT THE BITE OF THE GHOL IS POISONOUS?
BUT DO NOT WORRY...ON MY ACCOUNT, CINDERELLA. I HEAL QUICKLY...
UGH... GIVEN TIME... I SHOULD RECOVER.
WE NEED SOMEWHERE TO HOLE UP.
NOT...NOT TO WORRY, MY DEAR. I KNOW JUST...JUST THE PLACE.
WHY DOES THAT NOT FILL ME WITH CONFIDENCE?

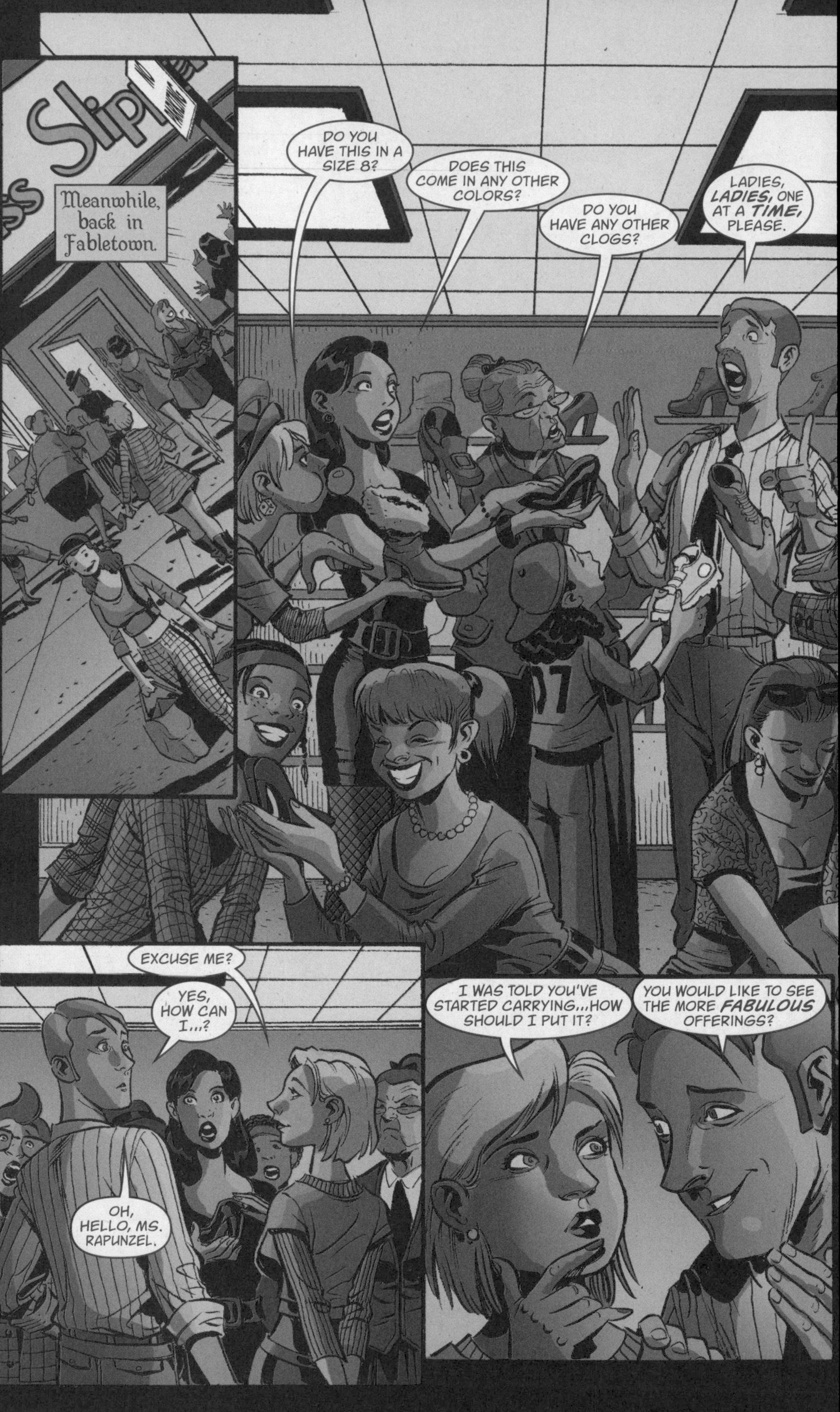

Slip
Meanwhile, back in Fabletown.
DO YOU HAVE THIS IN A SIZE 8?
DOES THIS COME IN ANY OTHER COLORS?
DO YOU HAVE ANY OTHER CLOGS?
LADIES, LADIES, ONE AT A TIME, PLEASE.
07
EXCUSE ME?
YES, HOW CAN I...?
OH, HELLO, MS. RAPUNZEL.
I WAS TOLD YOU'VE STARTED CARRYING...HOW SHOULD I PUT IT?
YOU WOULD LIKE TO SEE THE MORE FABULOUS OFFERINGS?

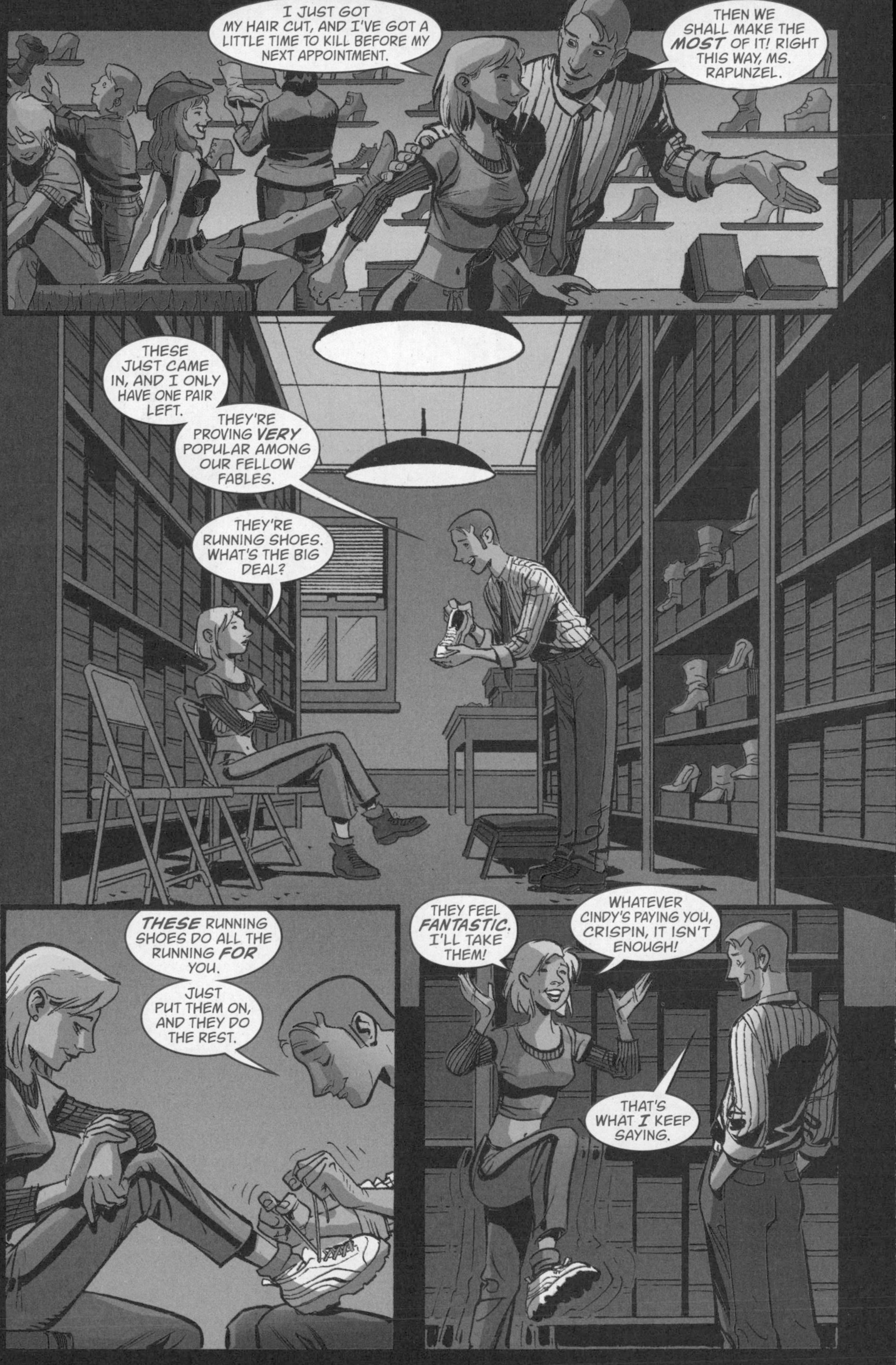
I JUST GOT MY HAIR CUT, AND I'VE GOT A LITTLE TIME TO KILL BEFORE MY NEXT APPOINTMENT.
THEN WE SHALL MAKE THE MOST OF IT! RIGHT THIS WAY, MS. RAPUNZEL.
THESE JUST CAME IN, AND I ONLY HAVE ONE PAIR LEFT.
THEY'RE PROVING VERY POPULAR AMONG OUR FELLOW FABLES.
THEY'RE RUNNING SHOES. WHAT'S THE BIG DEAL?
THESE RUNNING SHOES DO ALL THE RUNNING FOR YOU.
JUST PUT THEM ON, AND THEY DO THE REST.
THEY FEEL FANTASTIC. I'LL TAKE THEM!
WHATEVER CINDY'S PAYING YOU, CRISPIN, IT ISN'T ENOUGH!
THAT'S WHAT I KEEP SAYING.

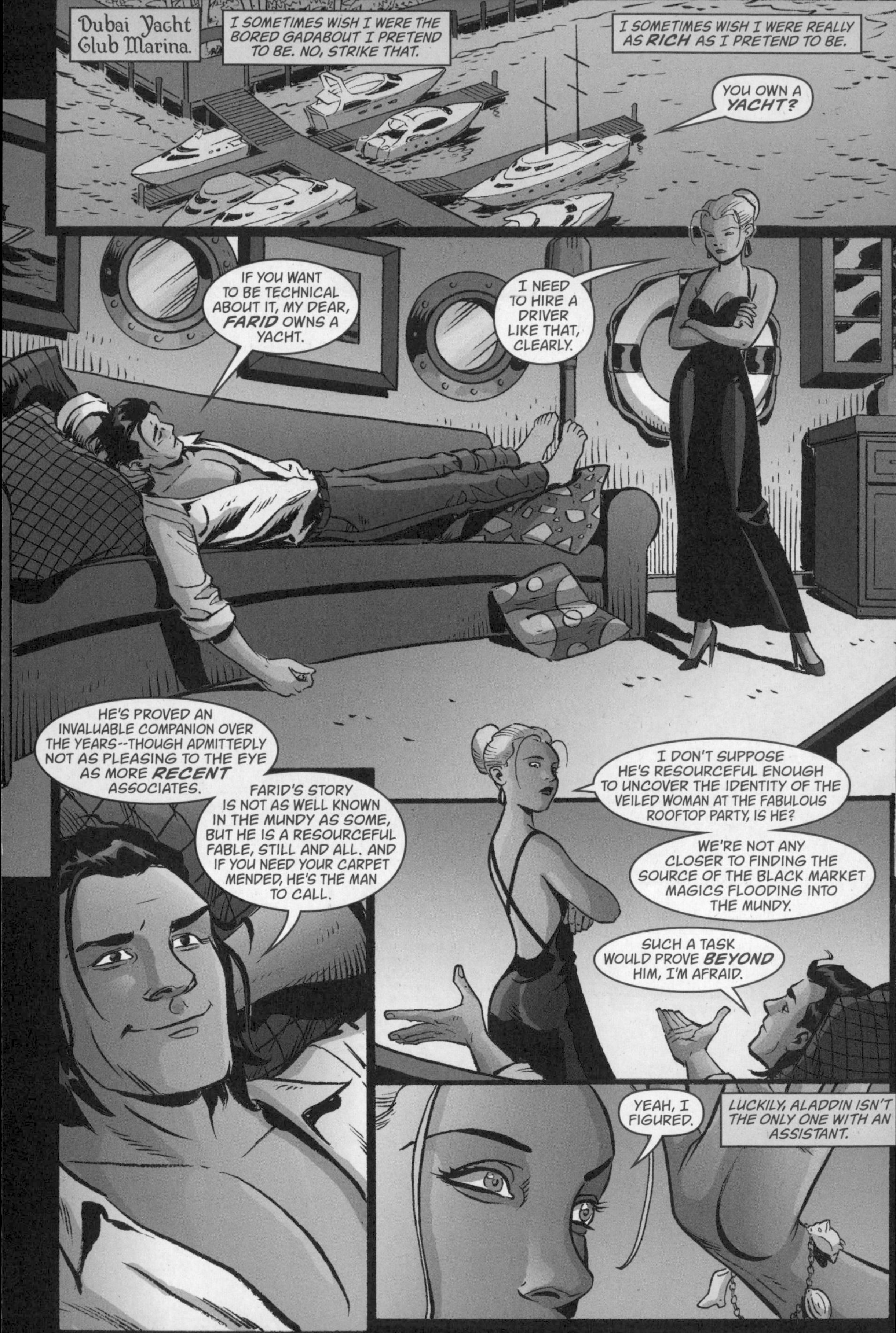
Dubai Yacht Club Marina.
I SOMETIMES WISH I WERE THE BORED GADABOUT I PRETEND TO BE. NO, STRIKE THAT.
I SOMETIMES WISH I WERE REALLY AS RICH AS I PRETEND TO BE.
YOU OWN A YACHT?
IF YOU WANT TO BE TECHNICAL ABOUT IT, MY DEAR, FARID OWNS A YACHT.
I NEED TO HIRE A DRIVER LIKE THAT, CLEARLY.
HE'S PROVED AN INVALUABLE COMPANION OVER THE YEARS--THOUGH ADMITTEDLY NOT AS PLEASING TO THE EYE AS MORE RECENT ASSOCIATES.
FARID'S STORY IS NOT AS WELL KNOWN IN THE MUNDY AS SOME, BUT HE IS A RESOURCEFUL FABLE, STILL AND ALL. AND IF YOU NEED YOUR CARPET MENDED, HE'S THE MAN TO CALL.
I DON'T SUPPOSE HE'S RESOURCEFUL ENOUGH TO UNCOVER THE IDENTITY OF THE VEILED WOMAN AT THE FABULOUS ROOFTOP PARTY, IS HE?
WE'RE NOT ANY CLOSER TO FINDING THE SOURCE OF THE BLACK MARKET MAGICS FLOODING INTO THE MUNDY.
SUCH A TASK WOULD PROVE BEYOND HIM, I'M AFRAID.
YEAH, I FIGURED.
LUCKILY, ALADDIN ISN'T THE ONLY ONE WITH AN ASSISTANT.

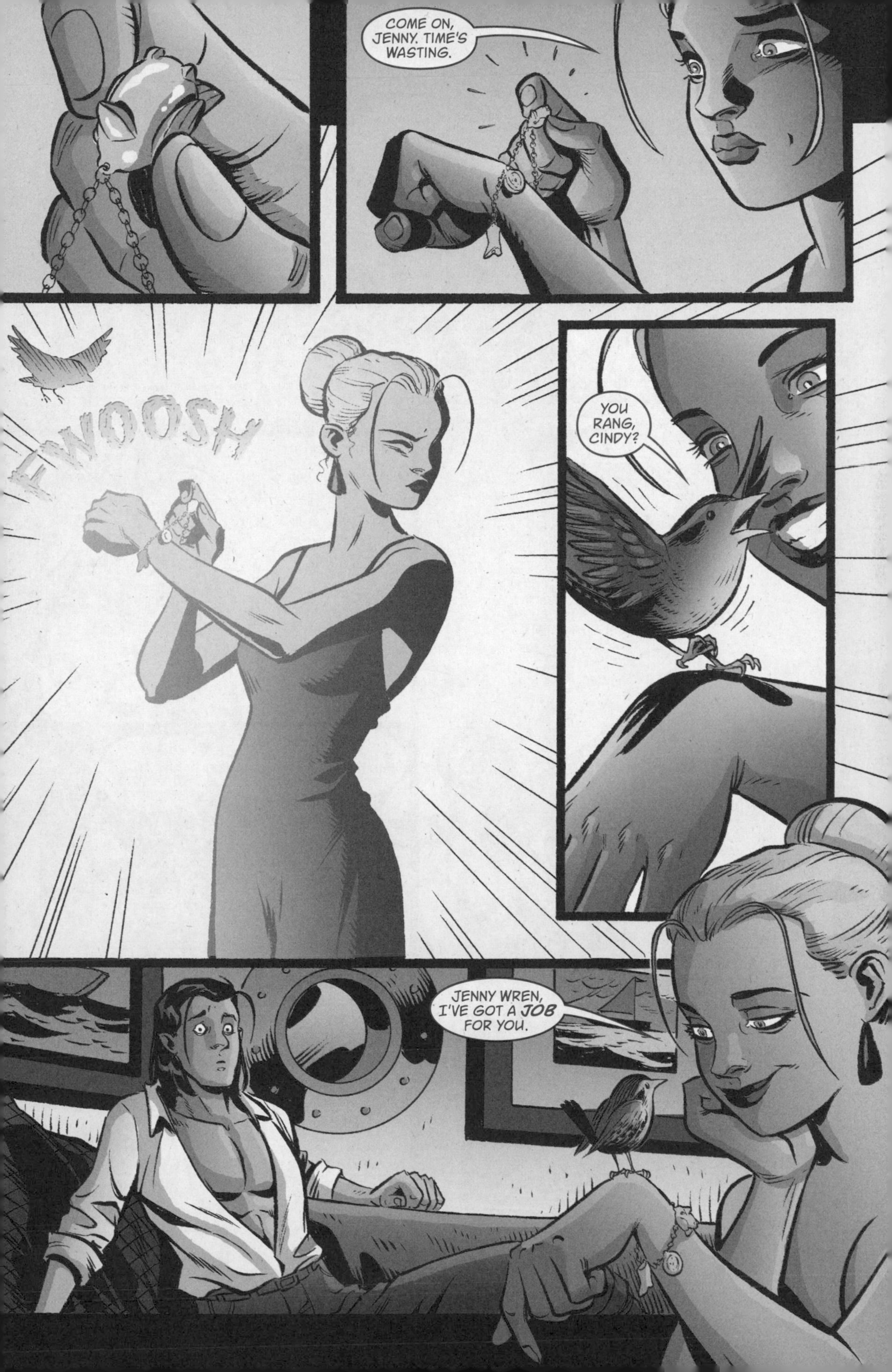
COME ON, JENNY. TIME'S WASTING.
FWOOSH
YOU RANG, CINDY?
JENNY WREN, I'VE GOT A JOB FOR YOU.

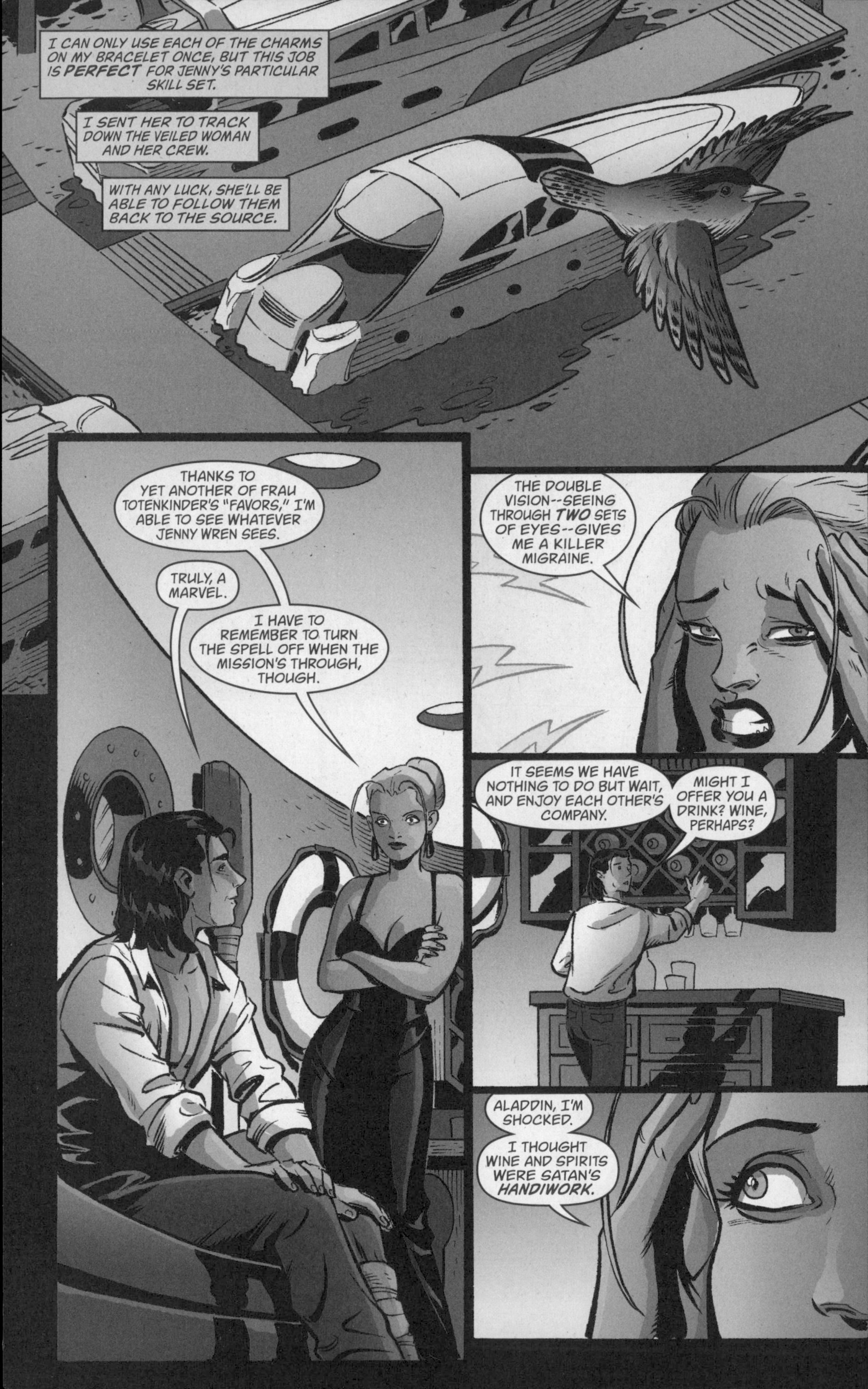
I CAN ONLY USE EACH OF THE CHARMS ON MY BRACELET ONCE, BUT THIS JOB IS PERFECT FOR JENNY'S PARTICULAR SKILL SET.
I SENT HER TO TRACK DOWN THE VEILED WOMAN AND HER CREW.
WITH ANY LUCK, SHE'LL BE ABLE TO FOLLOW THEM BACK TO THE SOURCE.
THANKS TO YET ANOTHER OF FRAU TOTENKINDER'S "FAVORS," I'M ABLE TO SEE WHATEVER JENNY WREN SEES.
TRULY, A MARVEL.
I HAVE TO REMEMBER TO TURN THE SPELL OFF WHEN THE MISSION'S THROUGH, THOUGH.
THE DOUBLE VISION--SEEING THROUGH TWO SETS OF EYES--GIVES ME A KILLER MIGRAINE.
IT SEEMS WE HAVE NOTHING TO DO BUT WAIT, AND ENJOY EACH OTHER'S COMPANY.
MIGHT I OFFER YOU A DRINK? WINE, PERHAPS?
ALADDIN, I'M SHOCKED.
I THOUGHT WINE AND SPIRITS WERE SATAN'S HANDIWORK.

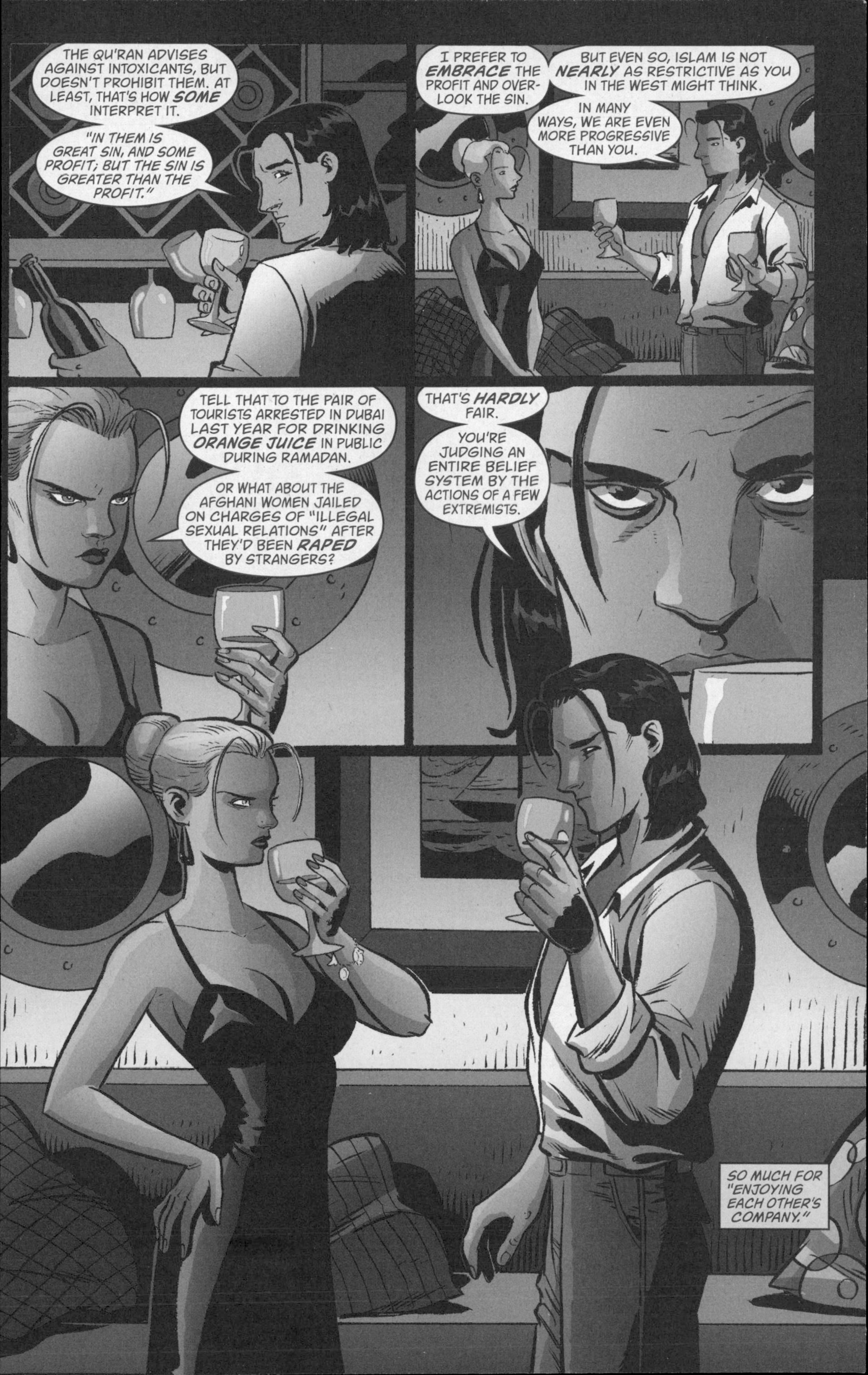
THE QU'RAN ADVISES AGAINST INTOXICANTS, BUT DOESN'T PROHIBIT THEM. AT LEAST, THAT'S HOW *SOME* INTERPRET IT.
"IN THEM IS GREAT SIN, AND SOME PROFIT; BUT THE SIN IS GREATER THAN THE PROFIT."
I PREFER TO *EMBRACE* THE PROFIT AND OVERLOOK THE SIN.
BUT EVEN SO, ISLAM IS NOT *NEARLY* AS RESTRICTIVE AS YOU IN THE WEST MIGHT THINK.
IN MANY WAYS, WE ARE EVEN MORE PROGRESSIVE THAN YOU.
TELL THAT TO THE PAIR OF TOURISTS ARRESTED IN DUBAI LAST YEAR FOR DRINKING *ORANGE JUICE* IN PUBLIC DURING RAMADAN.
OR WHAT ABOUT THE AFGHANI WOMEN JAILED ON CHARGES OF "ILLEGAL SEXUAL RELATIONS" AFTER THEY'D BEEN *RAPED* BY STRANGERS?
THAT'S *HARDLY* FAIR.
YOU'RE JUDGING AN ENTIRE BELIEF SYSTEM BY THE ACTIONS OF A FEW EXTREMISTS.
SO MUCH FOR "ENJOYING EACH OTHER'S COMPANY."

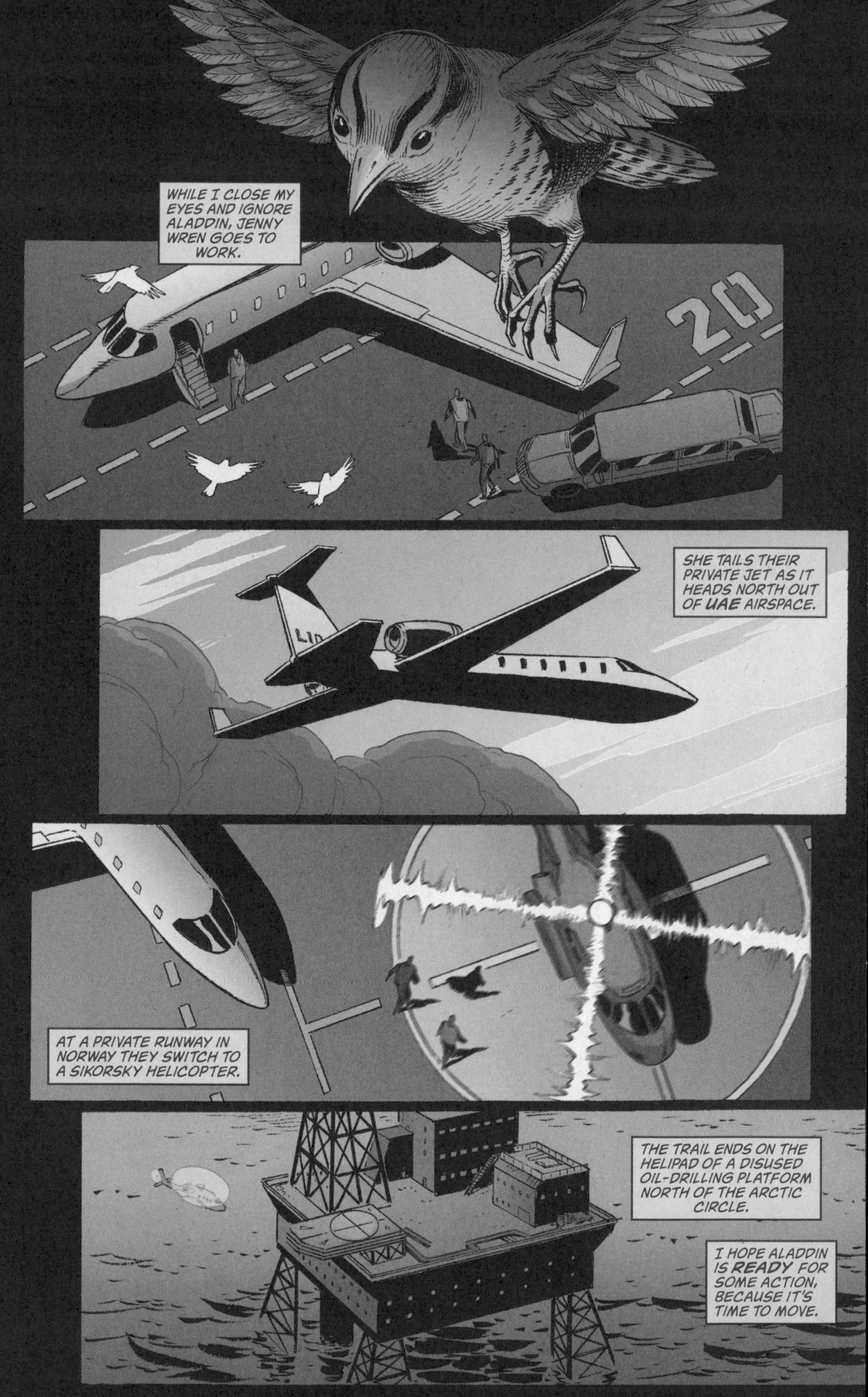
WHILE I CLOSE MY EYES AND IGNORE ALADDIN, JENNY WREN GOES TO WORK.
20
SHE TAILS THEIR PRIVATE JET AS IT HEADS NORTH OUT OF UAE AIRSPACE.
AT A PRIVATE RUNWAY IN NORWAY THEY SWITCH TO A SIKORSKY HELICOPTER.
THE TRAIL ENDS ON THE HELIPAD OF A DISUSED OIL-DRILLING PLATFORM NORTH OF THE ARCTIC CIRCLE.
I HOPE ALADDIN IS READY FOR SOME ACTION, BECAUSE IT'S TIME TO MOVE.

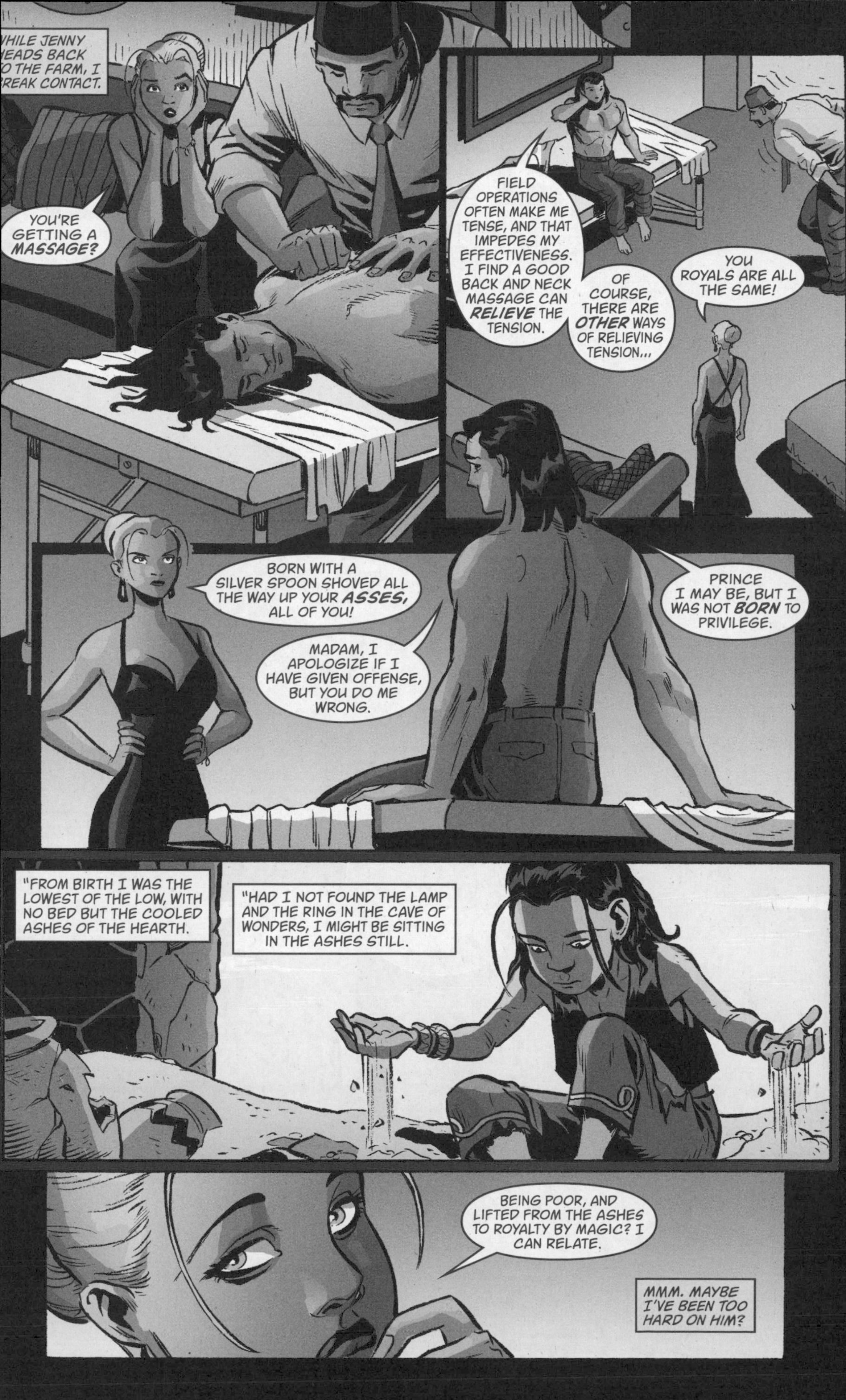
WHILE JENNY HEADS BACK TO THE FARM, I BREAK CONTACT.
YOU'RE GETTING A MASSAGE?
FIELD OPERATIONS OFTEN MAKE ME TENSE, AND THAT IMPEDES MY EFFECTIVENESS. I FIND A GOOD BACK AND NECK MASSAGE CAN RELIEVE THE TENSION.
OF COURSE, THERE ARE OTHER WAYS OF RELIEVING TENSION...
YOU ROYALS ARE ALL THE SAME!
BORN WITH A SILVER SPOON SHOVED ALL THE WAY UP YOUR ASSES, ALL OF YOU!
MADAM, I APOLOGIZE IF I HAVE GIVEN OFFENSE, BUT YOU DO ME WRONG.
PRINCE I MAY BE, BUT I WAS NOT BORN TO PRIVILEGE.
"FROM BIRTH I WAS THE LOWEST OF THE LOW, WITH NO BED BUT THE COOLED ASHES OF THE HEARTH.
"HAD I NOT FOUND THE LAMP AND THE RING IN THE CAVE OF WONDERS, I MIGHT BE SITTING IN THE ASHES STILL.
BEING POOR, AND LIFTED FROM THE ASHES TO ROYALTY BY MAGIC? I CAN RELATE.
MMM. MAYBE I'VE BEEN TOO HARD ON HIM?

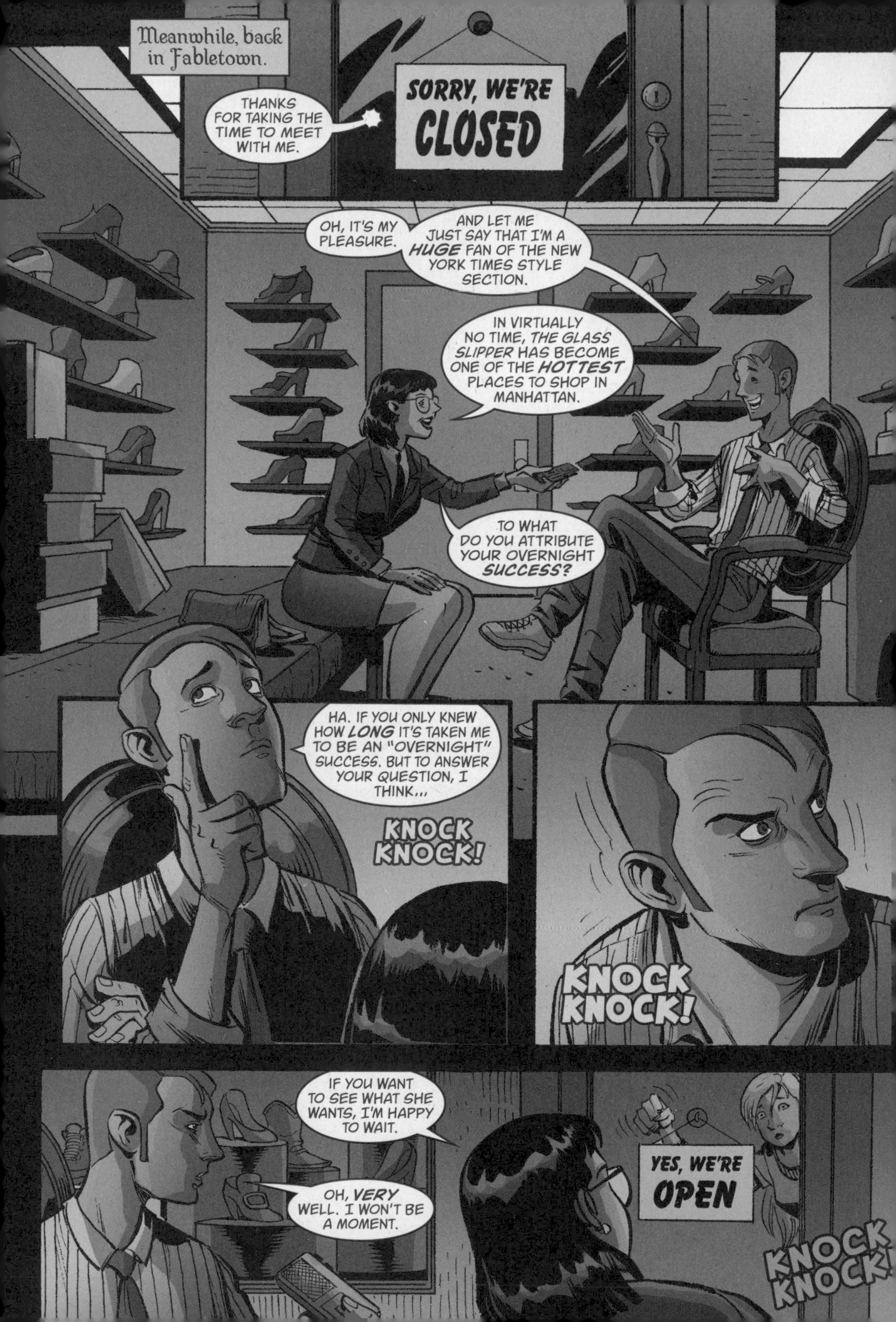
Meanwhile, back in Fabletown.
SORRY, WE'RE CLOSED
THANKS FOR TAKING THE TIME TO MEET WITH ME.
OH, IT'S MY PLEASURE.
AND LET ME JUST SAY THAT I'M A HUGE FAN OF THE NEW YORK TIMES STYLE SECTION.
IN VIRTUALLY NO TIME, THE GLASS SLIPPER HAS BECOME ONE OF THE HOTTEST PLACES TO SHOP IN MANHATTAN.
TO WHAT DO YOU ATTRIBUTE YOUR OVERNIGHT SUCCESS?
HA. IF YOU ONLY KNEW HOW LONG IT'S TAKEN ME TO BE AN "OVERNIGHT" SUCCESS. BUT TO ANSWER YOUR QUESTION, I THINK...
KNOCK KNOCK!
KNOCK KNOCK!
IF YOU WANT TO SEE WHAT SHE WANTS, I'M HAPPY TO WAIT.
OH, VERY WELL. I WON'T BE A MOMENT.
YES, WE'RE OPEN
KNOCK KNOCK!

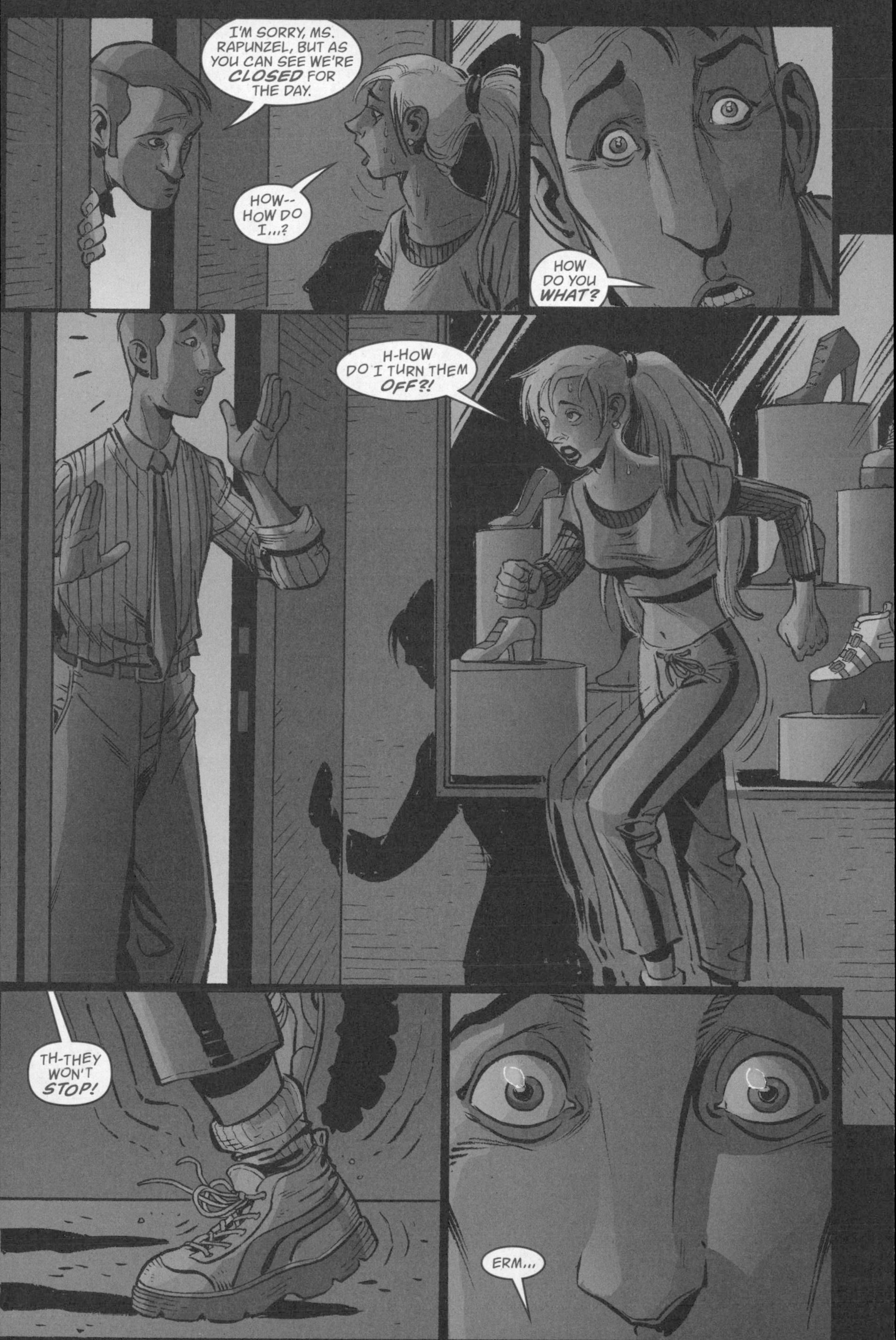
I'M SORRY, MS. RAPUNZEL, BUT AS YOU CAN SEE WE'RE CLOSED FOR THE DAY.
HOW-- HOW DO I...?
HOW DO YOU WHAT?
H-HOW DO I TURN THEM OFF?!
TH-THEY WON'T STOP!
ERM...

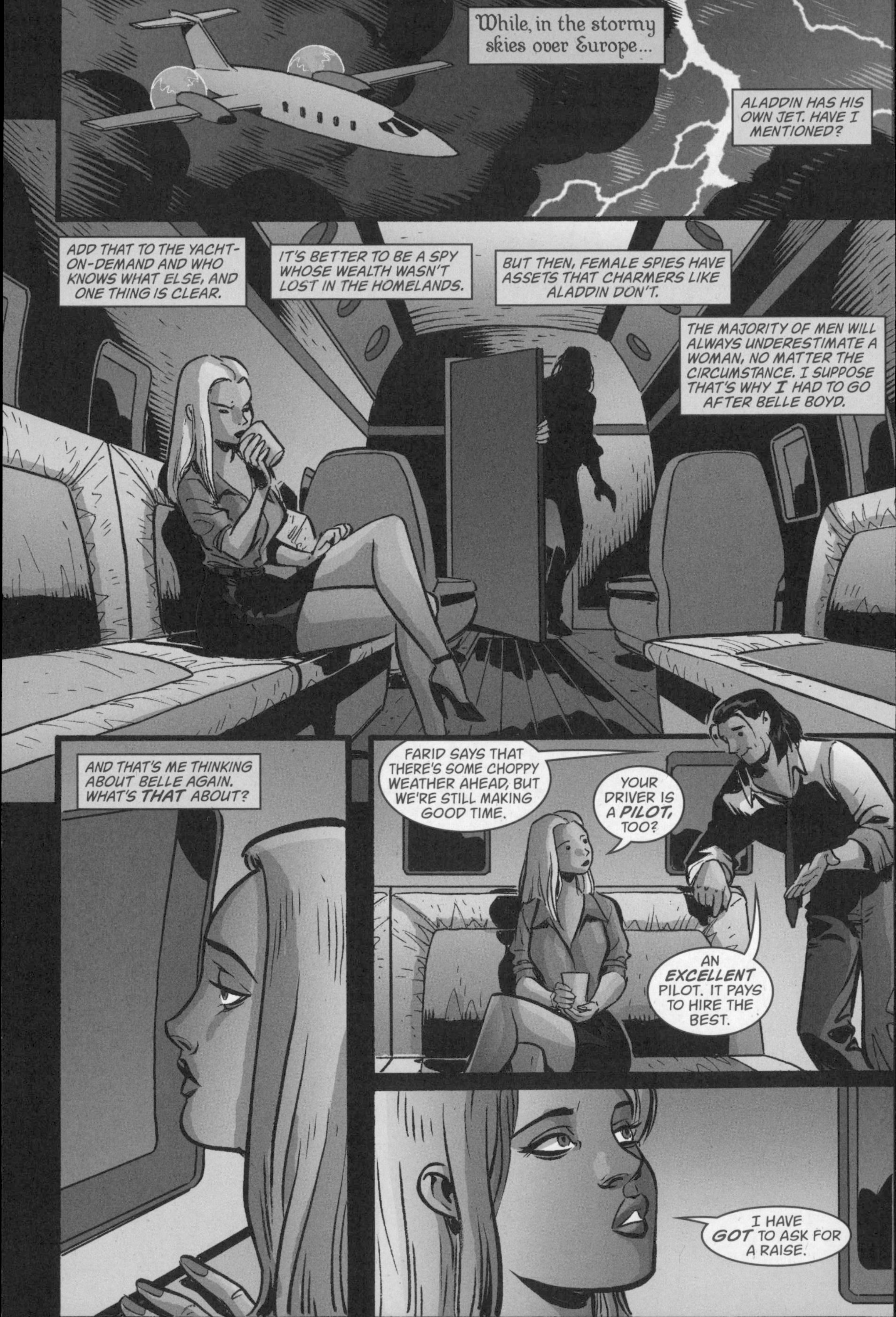
While, in the stormy skies over Europe...
ALADDIN HAS HIS OWN JET. HAVE I MENTIONED?
ADD THAT TO THE YACHT-ON-DEMAND AND WHO KNOWS WHAT ELSE, AND ONE THING IS CLEAR.
IT'S BETTER TO BE A SPY WHOSE WEALTH WASN'T LOST IN THE HOMELANDS.
BUT THEN, FEMALE SPIES HAVE ASSETS THAT CHARMERS LIKE ALADDIN DON'T.
THE MAJORITY OF MEN WILL ALWAYS UNDERESTIMATE A WOMAN, NO MATTER THE CIRCUMSTANCE. I SUPPOSE THAT'S WHY I HAD TO GO AFTER BELLE BOYD.
AND THAT'S ME THINKING ABOUT BELLE AGAIN. WHAT'S THAT ABOUT?
FARID SAYS THAT THERE'S SOME CHOPPY WEATHER AHEAD, BUT WE'RE STILL MAKING GOOD TIME.
YOUR DRIVER IS A PILOT, TOO?
AN EXCELLENT PILOT. IT PAYS TO HIRE THE BEST.
I HAVE GOT TO ASK FOR A RAISE.

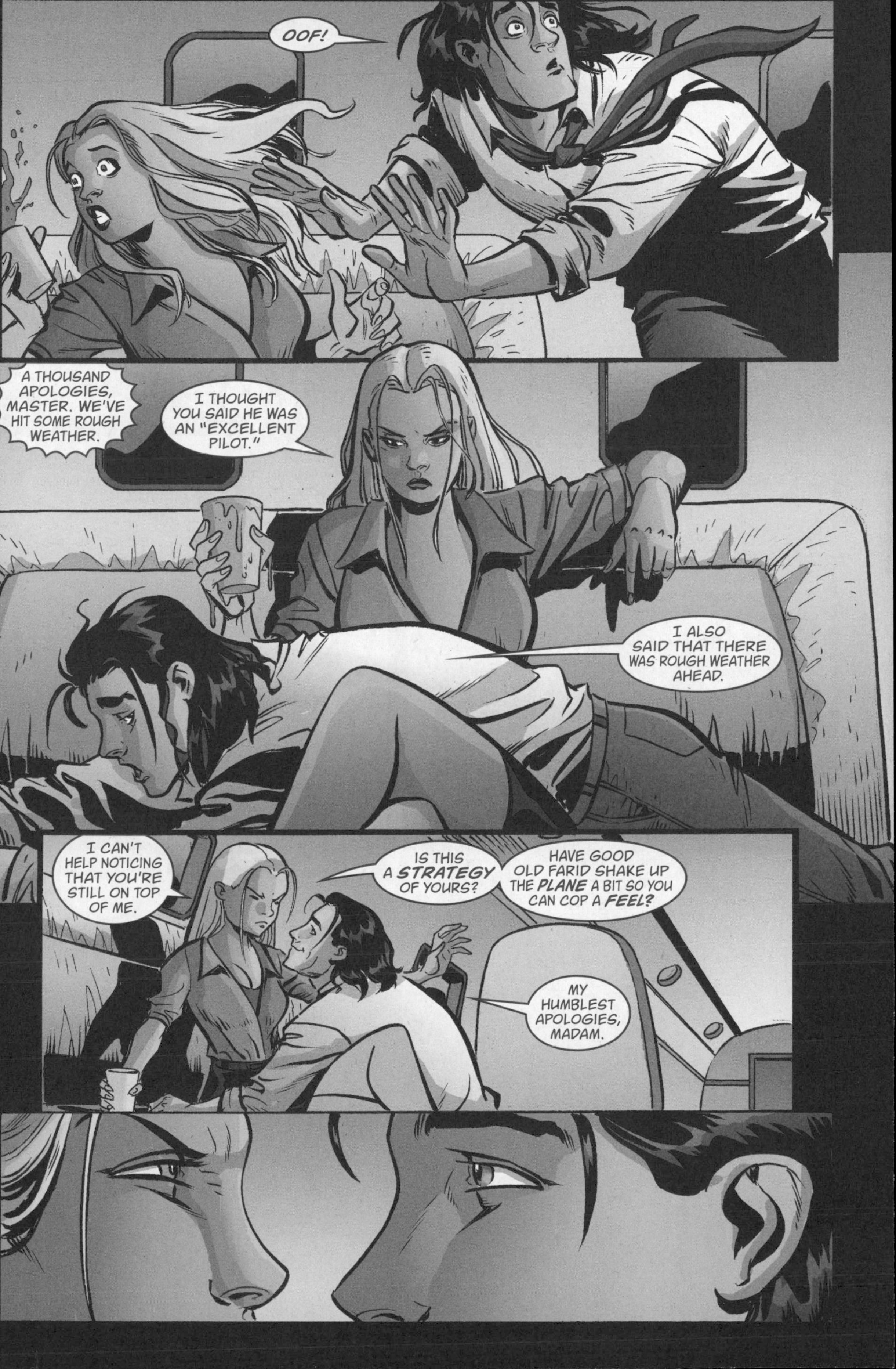
OOF!
A THOUSAND APOLOGIES, MASTER. WE'VE HIT SOME ROUGH WEATHER.
I THOUGHT YOU SAID HE WAS AN "EXCELLENT PILOT."
I ALSO SAID THAT THERE WAS ROUGH WEATHER AHEAD.
I CAN'T HELP NOTICING THAT YOU'RE STILL ON TOP OF ME.
IS THIS A STRATEGY OF YOURS?
HAVE GOOD OLD FARID SHAKE UP THE PLANE A BIT SO YOU CAN COP A FEEL?
MY HUMBLEST APOLOGIES, MADAM.

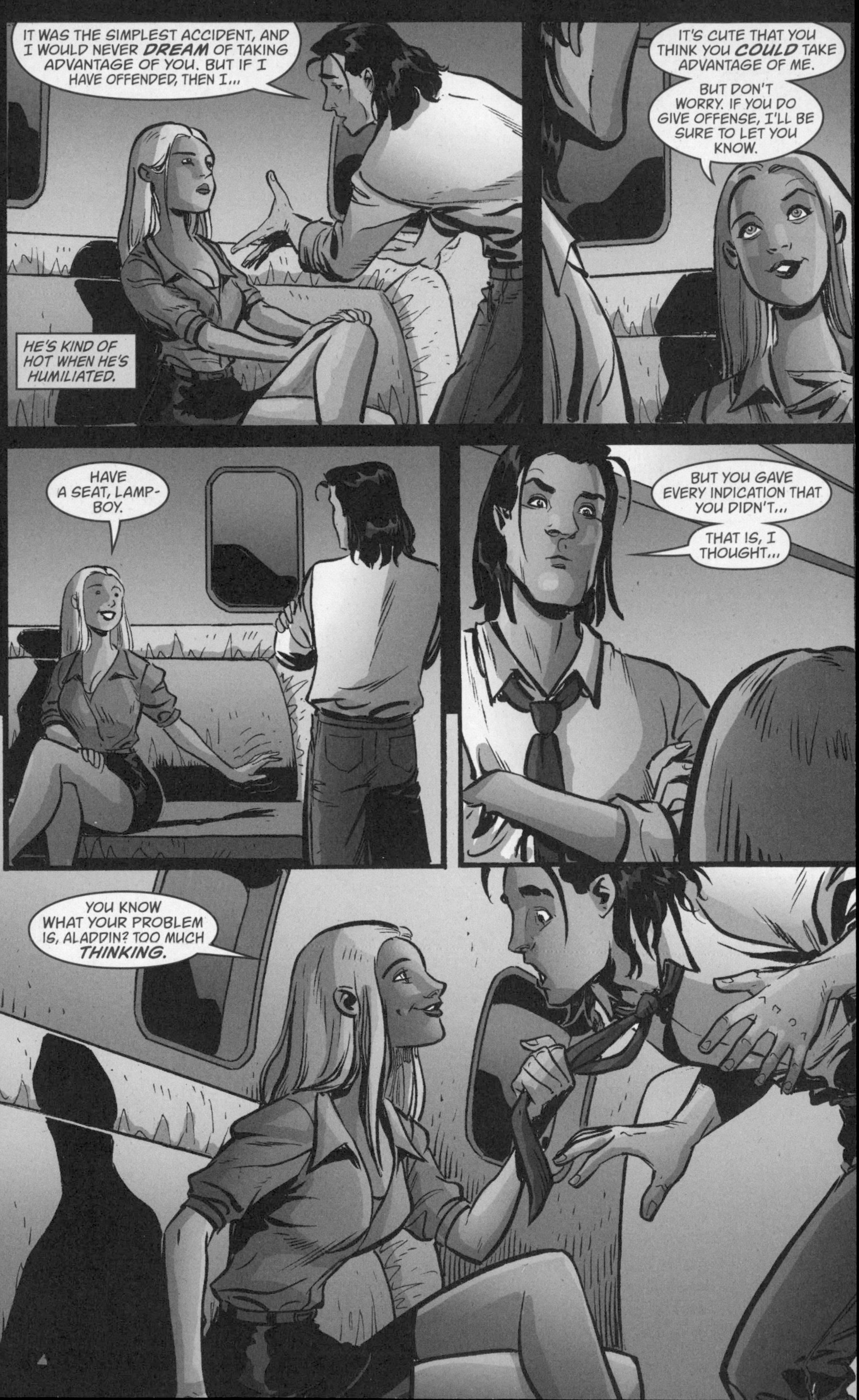

IT WAS THE SIMPLEST ACCIDENT, AND I WOULD NEVER DREAM OF TAKING ADVANTAGE OF YOU. BUT IF I HAVE OFFENDED, THEN I...
HE'S KIND OF HOT WHEN HE'S HUMILIATED.
IT'S CUTE THAT YOU THINK YOU COULD TAKE ADVANTAGE OF ME.
BUT DON'T WORRY. IF YOU DO GIVE OFFENSE, I'LL BE SURE TO LET YOU KNOW.
HAVE A SEAT, LAMP-BOY.
BUT YOU GAVE EVERY INDICATION THAT YOU DIDN'T...
THAT IS, I THOUGHT...
YOU KNOW WHAT YOUR PROBLEM IS, ALADDIN? TOO MUCH THINKING.

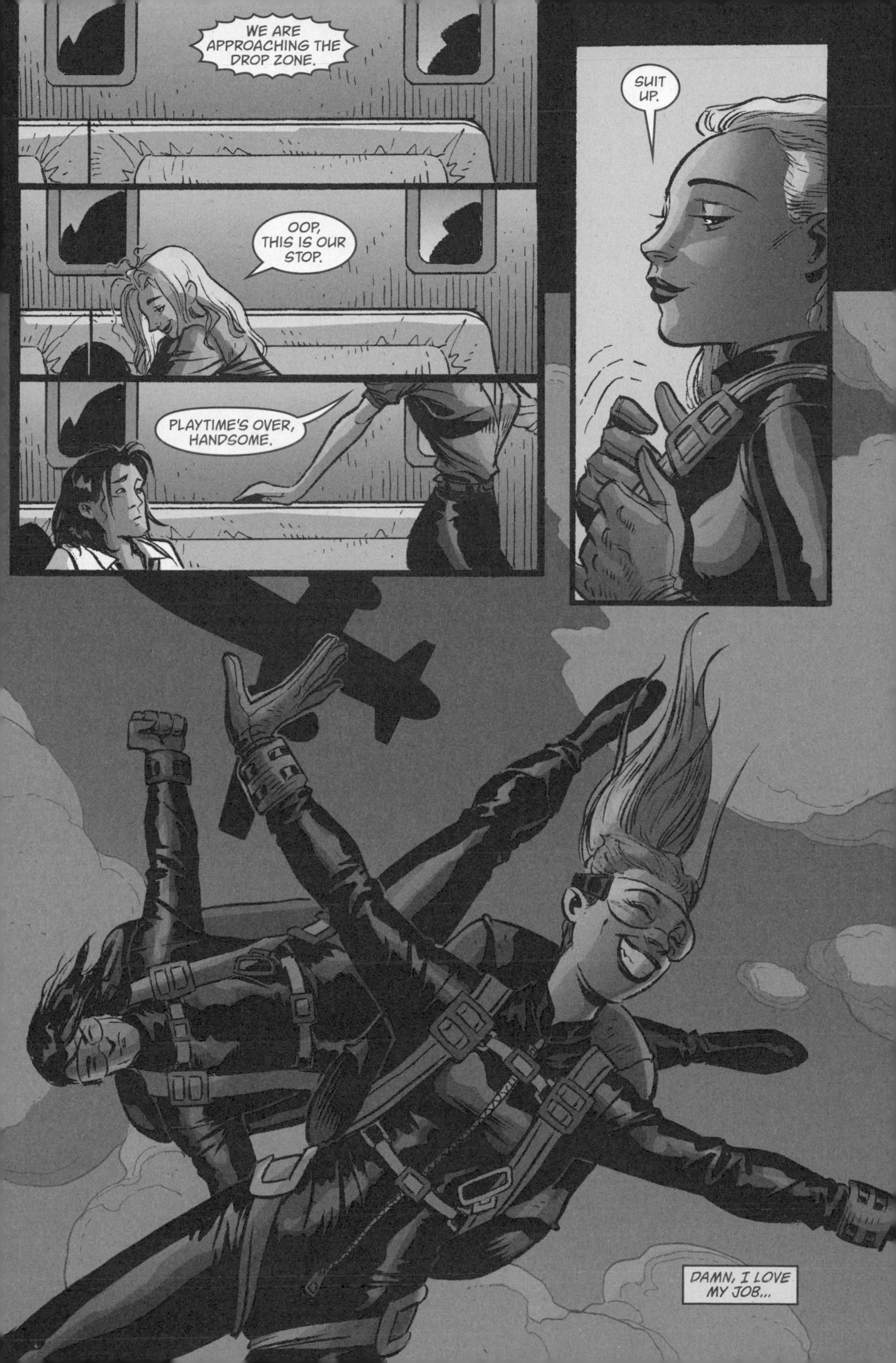
WE ARE APPROACHING THE DROP ZONE.
SUIT UP.
OOP, THIS IS OUR STOP.
PLAYTIME'S OVER, HANDSOME.
DAMN, I LOVE MY JOB...

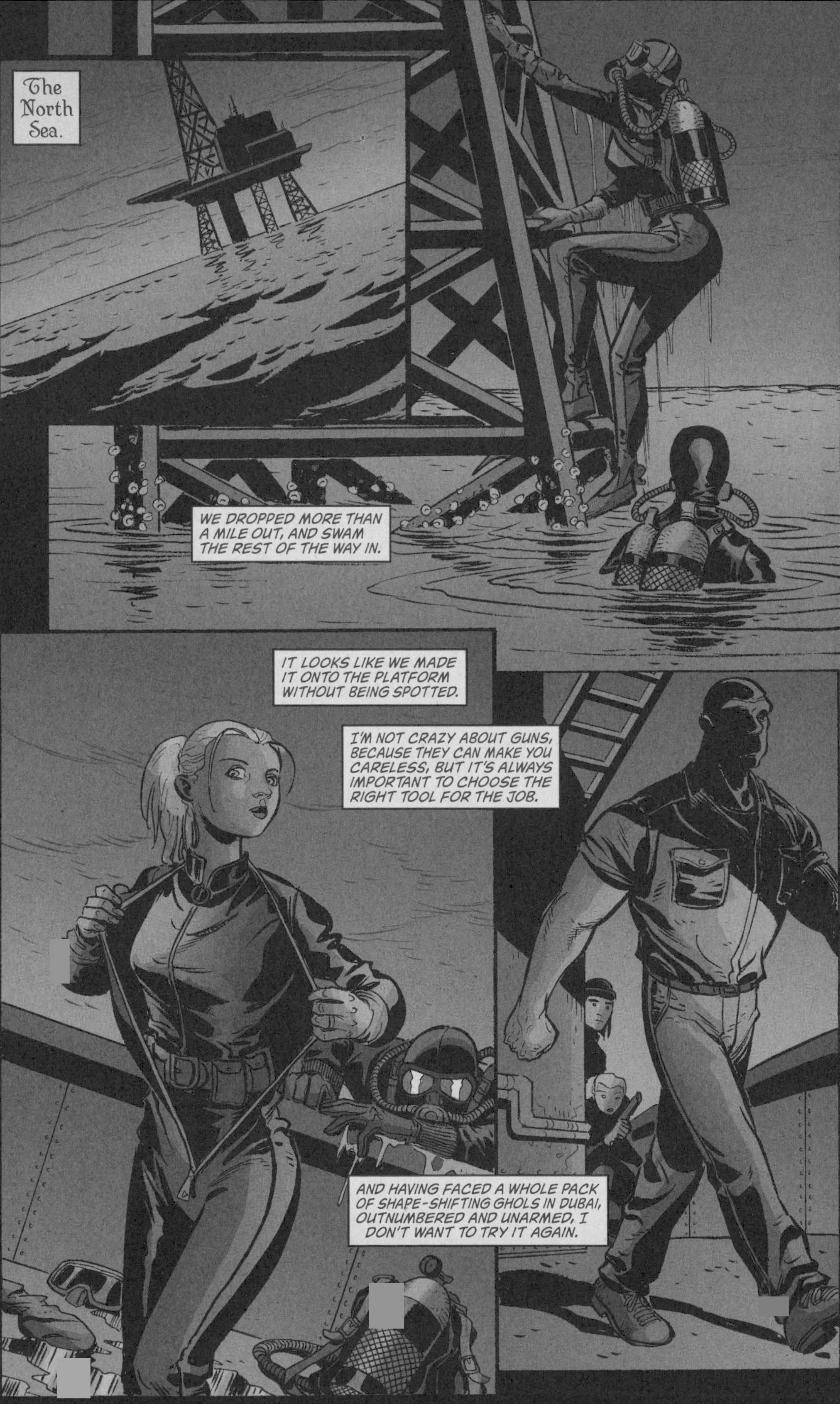
The North Sea.
WE DROPPED MORE THAN A MILE OUT, AND SWAM THE REST OF THE WAY IN.
IT LOOKS LIKE WE MADE IT ONTO THE PLATFORM WITHOUT BEING SPOTTED.
I'M NOT CRAZY ABOUT GUNS, BECAUSE THEY CAN MAKE YOU CARELESS, BUT IT'S ALWAYS IMPORTANT TO CHOOSE THE RIGHT TOOL FOR THE JOB.
AND HAVING FACED A WHOLE PACK OF SHAPE-SHIFTING GHOLS IN DUBAI, OUTNUMBERED AND UNARMED, I DON'T WANT TO TRY IT AGAIN.

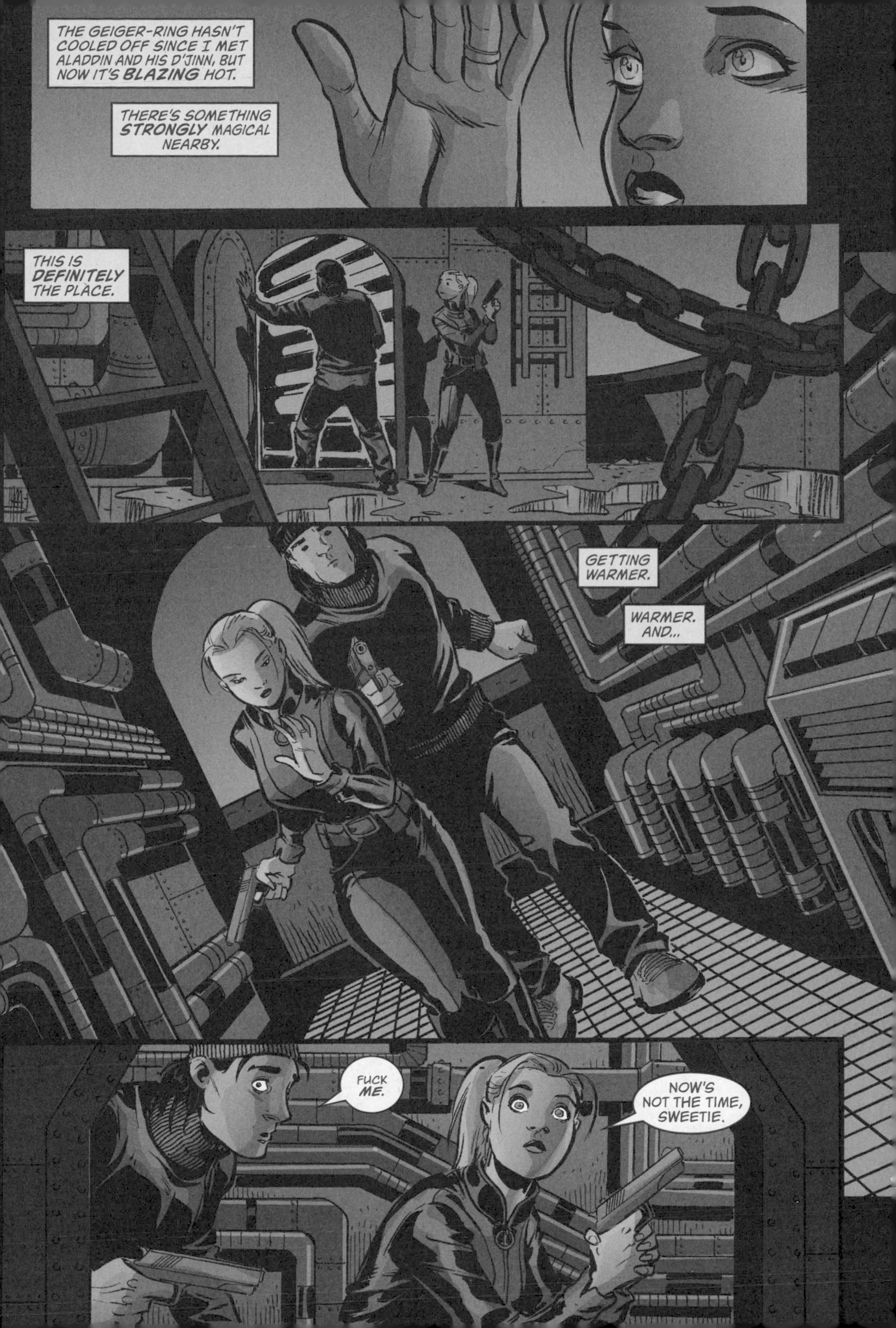
THE GEIGER-RING HASN'T COOLED OFF SINCE I MET ALADDIN AND HIS D'JINN, BUT NOW IT'S **BLAZING** HOT.
THERE'S SOMETHING **STRONGLY** MAGICAL NEARBY.
THIS IS **DEFINITELY** THE PLACE.
GETTING WARMER.
WARMER. AND...
FUCK **ME**.
NOW'S NOT THE TIME, SWEETIE.

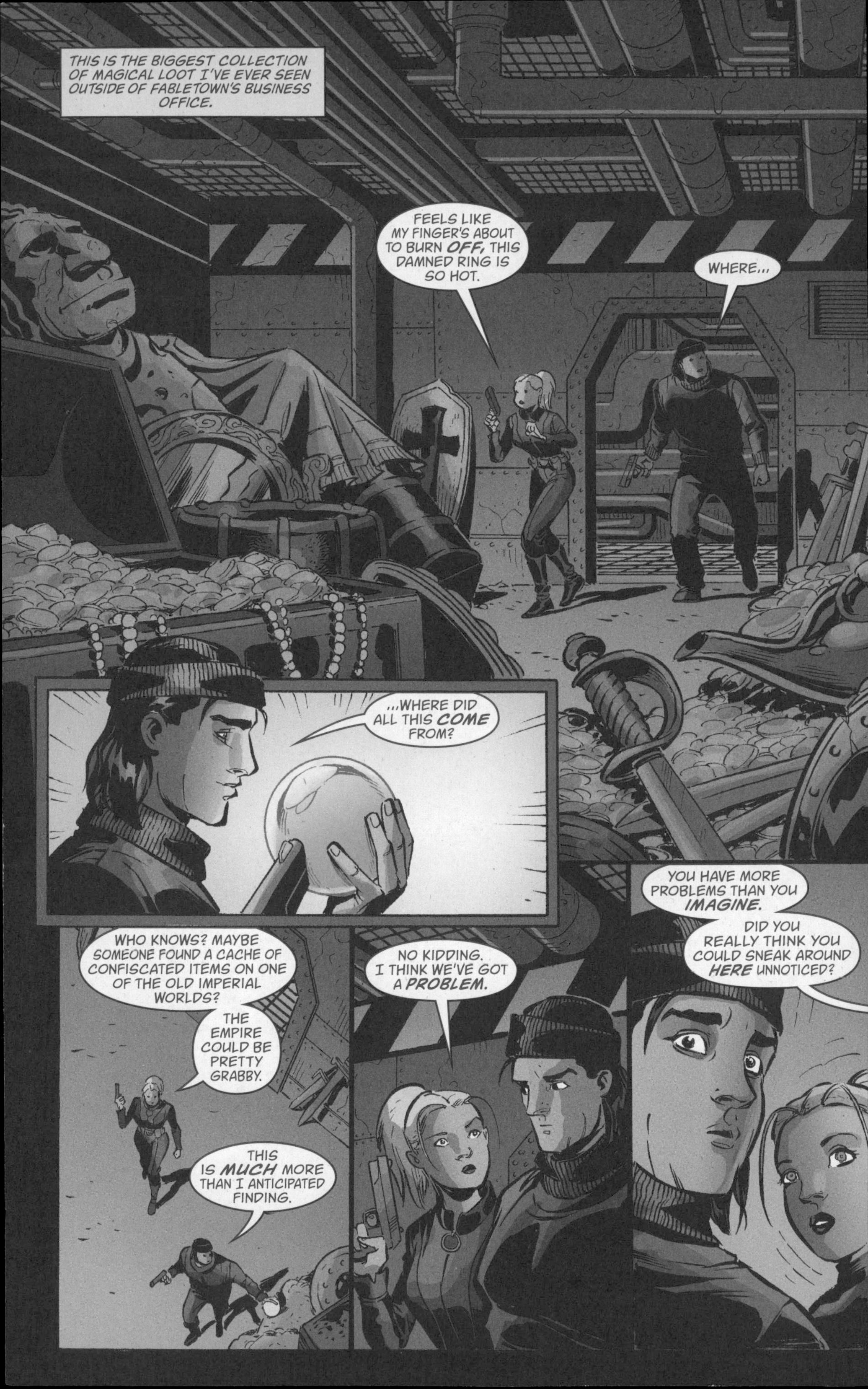
THIS IS THE BIGGEST COLLECTION OF MAGICAL LOOT I'VE EVER SEEN OUTSIDE OF FABLETOWN'S BUSINESS OFFICE.
FEELS LIKE MY FINGER'S ABOUT TO BURN OFF, THIS DAMNED RING IS SO HOT.
WHERE...
...WHERE DID ALL THIS COME FROM?
WHO KNOWS? MAYBE SOMEONE FOUND A CACHE OF CONFISCATED ITEMS ON ONE OF THE OLD IMPERIAL WORLDS?
THE EMPIRE COULD BE PRETTY GRABBY.
THIS IS MUCH MORE THAN I ANTICIPATED FINDING.
NO KIDDING. I THINK WE'VE GOT A PROBLEM.
YOU HAVE MORE PROBLEMS THAN YOU IMAGINE.
DID YOU REALLY THINK YOU COULD SNEAK AROUND HERE UNNOTICED?

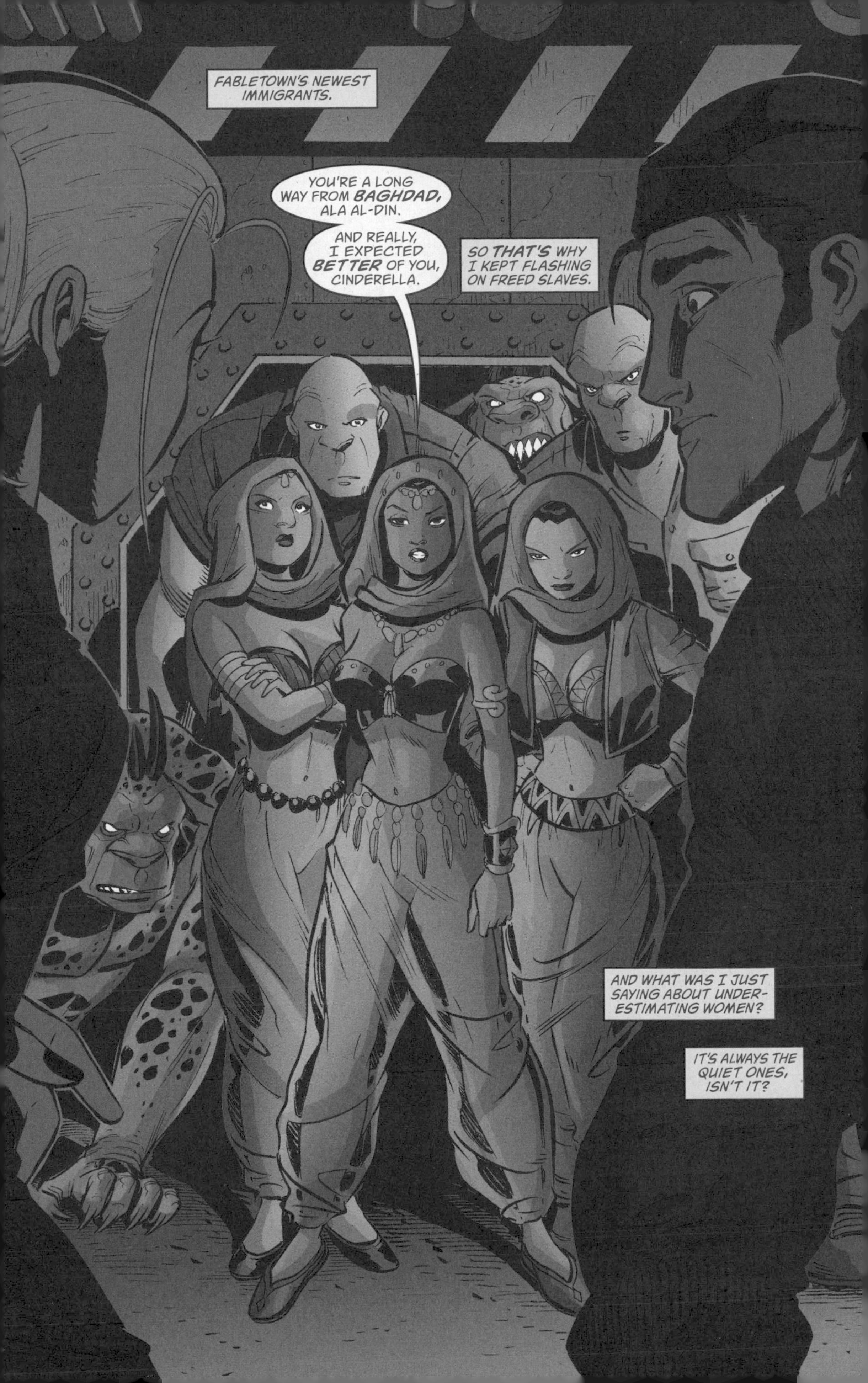
FABLETOWN'S NEWEST IMMIGRANTS.
YOU'RE A LONG WAY FROM BAGHDAD, ALA AL-DIN.
AND REALLY, I EXPECTED BETTER OF YOU, CINDERELLA.
SO THAT'S WHY I KEPT FLASHING ON FREED SLAVES.
AND WHAT WAS I JUST SAYING ABOUT UNDER-ESTIMATING WOMEN?
IT'S ALWAYS THE QUIET ONES, ISN'T IT?

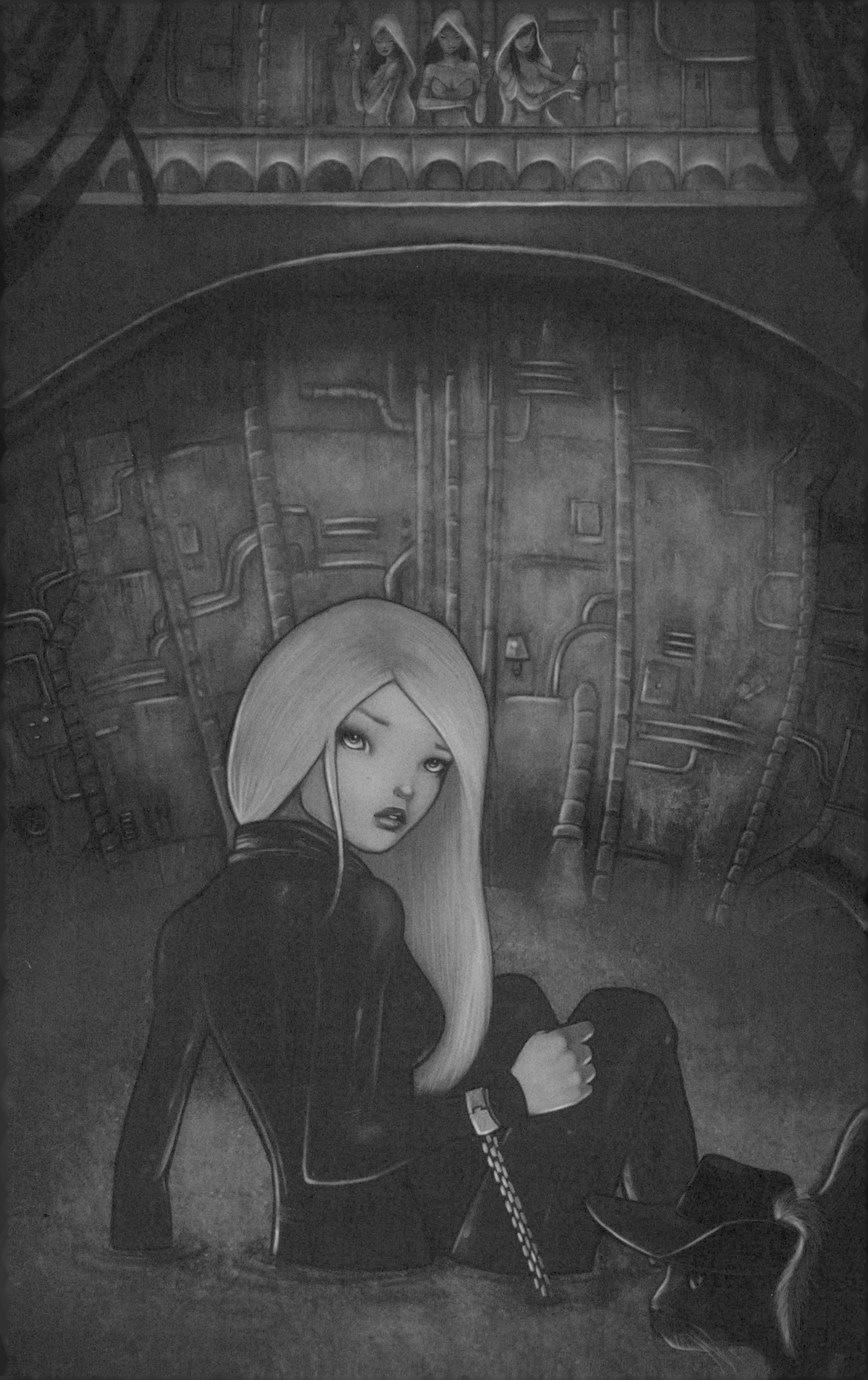

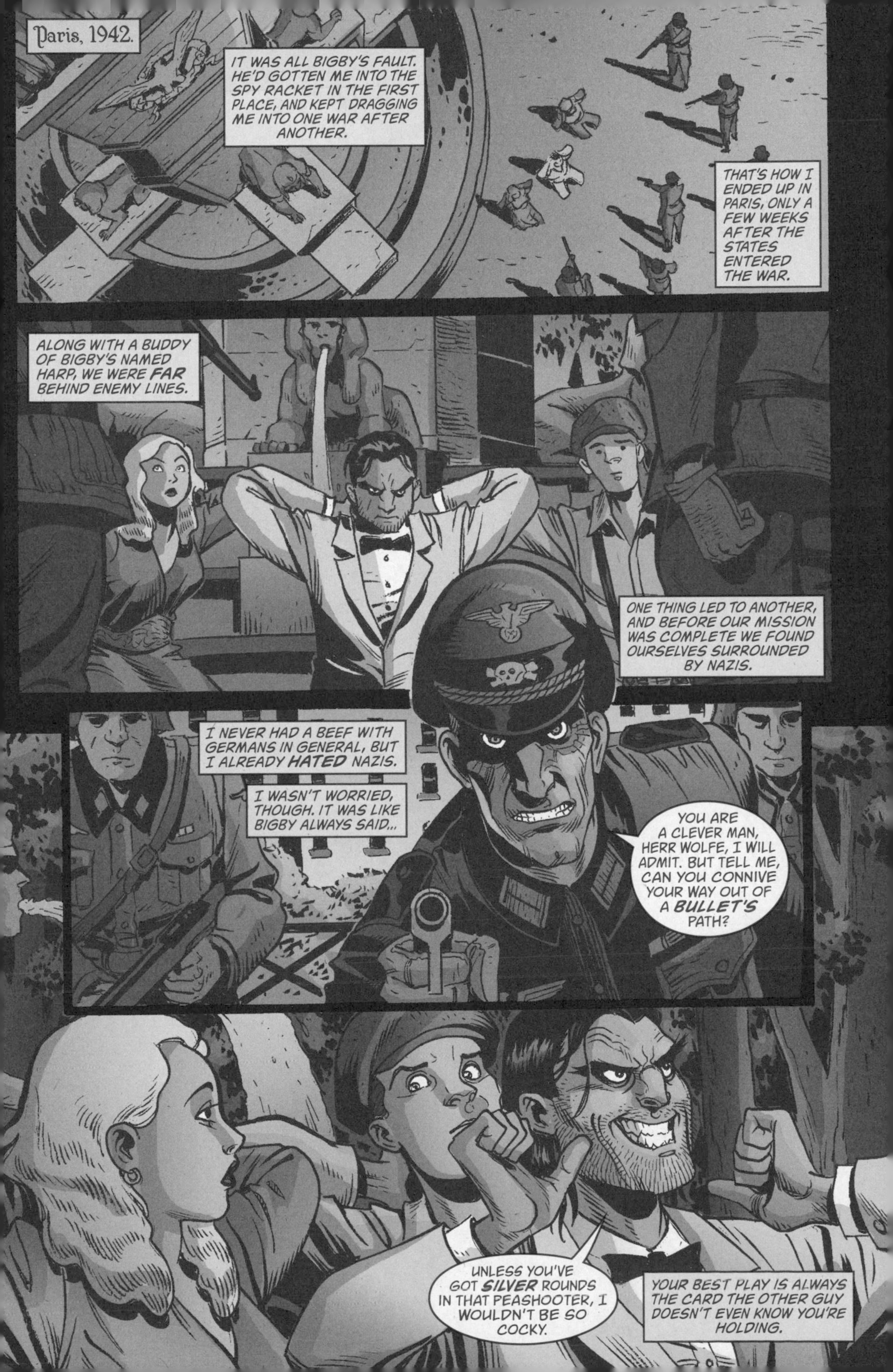
Paris, 1942.
IT WAS ALL BIGBY'S FAULT. HE'D GOTTEN ME INTO THE SPY RACKET IN THE FIRST PLACE, AND KEPT DRAGGING ME INTO ONE WAR AFTER ANOTHER.
THAT'S HOW I ENDED UP IN PARIS, ONLY A FEW WEEKS AFTER THE STATES ENTERED THE WAR.
ALONG WITH A BUDDY OF BIGBY'S NAMED HARP, WE WERE FAR BEHIND ENEMY LINES.
ONE THING LED TO ANOTHER, AND BEFORE OUR MISSION WAS COMPLETE WE FOUND OURSELVES SURROUNDED BY NAZIS.
I NEVER HAD A BEEF WITH GERMANS IN GENERAL, BUT I ALREADY HATED NAZIS.
I WASN'T WORRIED, THOUGH. IT WAS LIKE BIGBY ALWAYS SAID...
YOU ARE A CLEVER MAN, HERR WOLFE, I WILL ADMIT. BUT TELL ME, CAN YOU CONNIVE YOUR WAY OUT OF A BULLET'S PATH?
UNLESS YOU'VE GOT SILVER ROUNDS IN THAT PEASHOOTER, I WOULDN'T BE SO COCKY.
YOUR BEST PLAY IS ALWAYS THE CARD THE OTHER GUY DOESN'T EVEN KNOW YOU'RE HOLDING.

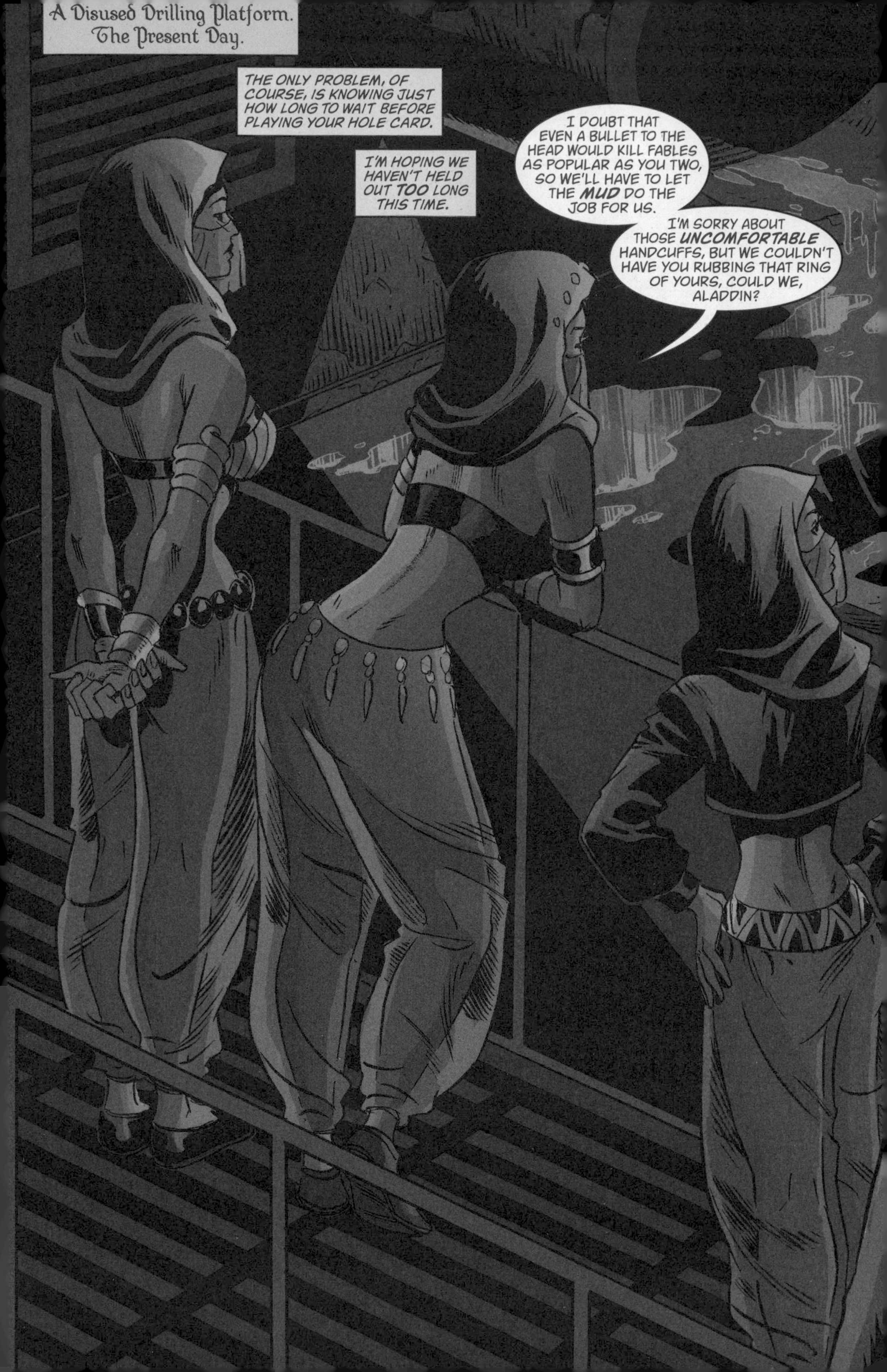
A Disused Drilling Platform. The Present Day.
THE ONLY PROBLEM, OF COURSE, IS KNOWING JUST HOW LONG TO WAIT BEFORE PLAYING YOUR HOLE CARD.
I'M HOPING WE HAVEN'T HELD OUT TOO LONG THIS TIME.
I DOUBT THAT EVEN A BULLET TO THE HEAD WOULD KILL FABLES AS POPULAR AS YOU TWO, SO WE'LL HAVE TO LET THE MUD DO THE JOB FOR US.
I'M SORRY ABOUT THOSE UNCOMFORTABLE HANDCUFFS, BUT WE COULDN'T HAVE YOU RUBBING THAT RING OF YOURS, COULD WE, ALADDIN?

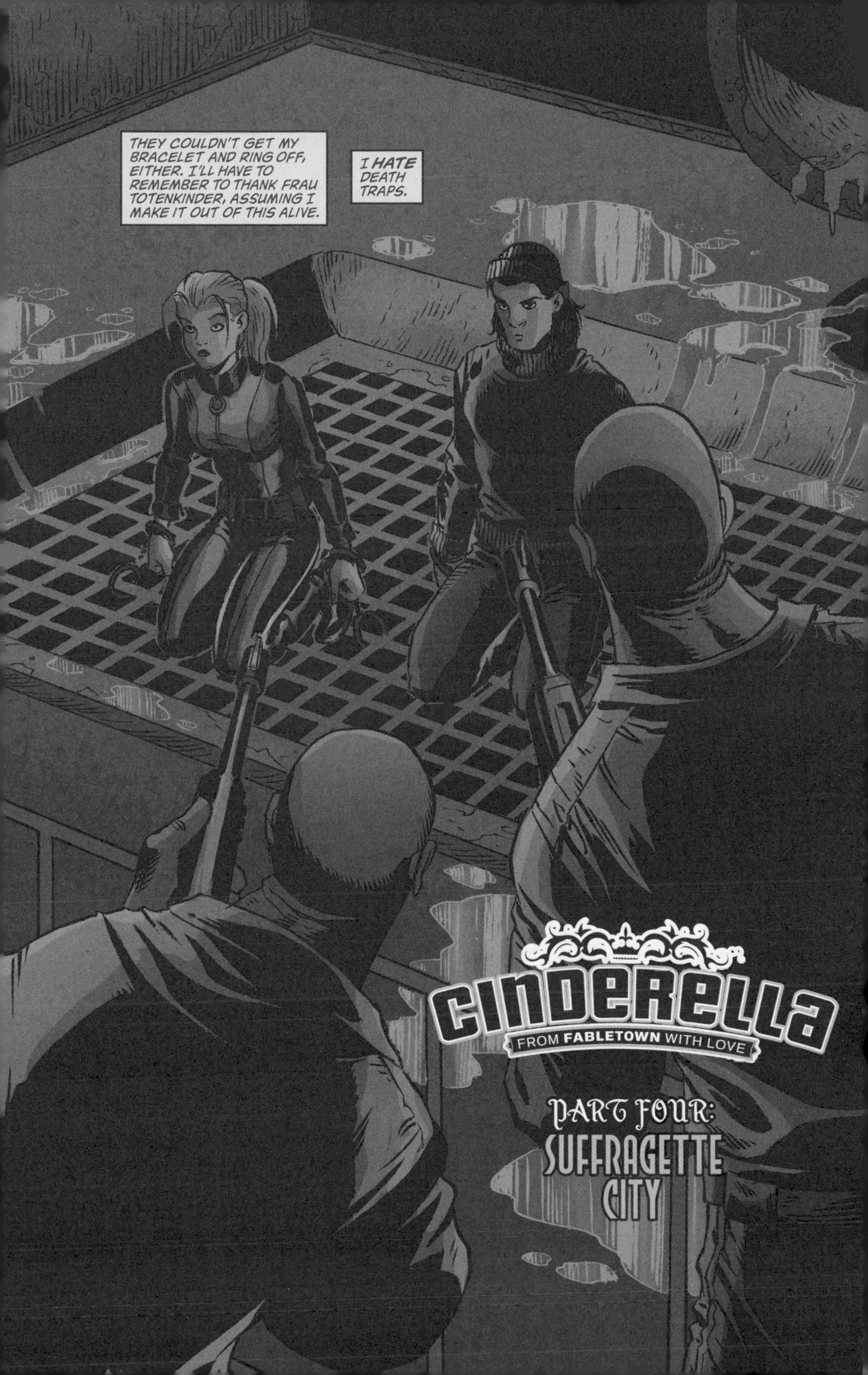
THEY COULDN'T GET MY BRACELET AND RING OFF, EITHER. I'LL HAVE TO REMEMBER TO THANK FRAU TOTENKINDER, ASSUMING I MAKE IT OUT OF THIS ALIVE.
I HATE DEATH TRAPS.
CINDERELLA
FROM FABLETOWN WITH LOVE
PART FOUR:
SUFFRAGETTE CITY

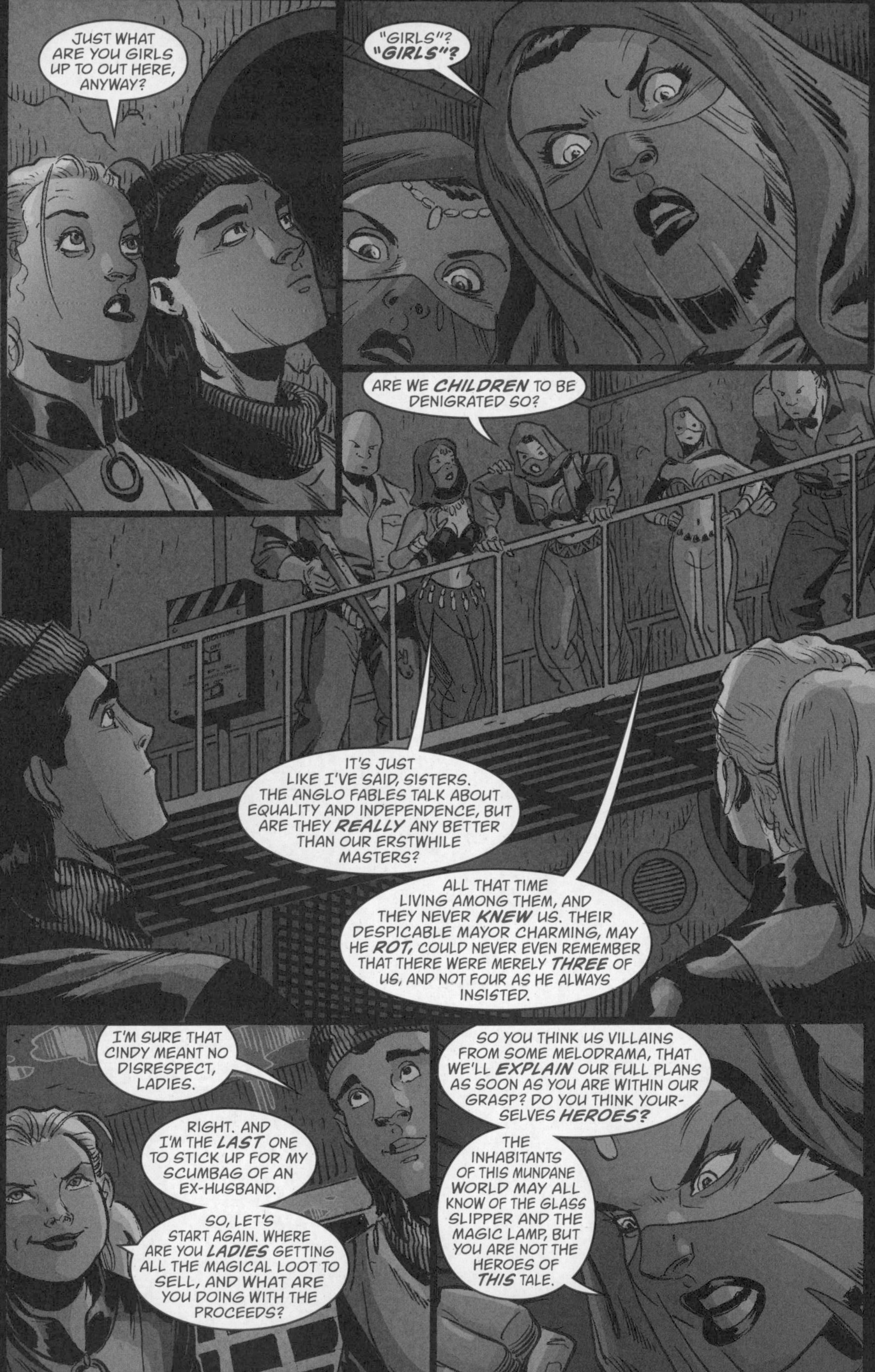

JUST WHAT ARE YOU GIRLS UP TO OUT HERE, ANYWAY?
"GIRLS"? **"GIRLS"?**
ARE WE **CHILDREN** TO BE DENIGRATED SO?
IT'S JUST LIKE I'VE SAID, SISTERS. THE ANGLO FABLES TALK ABOUT EQUALITY AND INDEPENDENCE, BUT ARE THEY **REALLY** ANY BETTER THAN OUR ERSTWHILE MASTERS?
ALL THAT TIME LIVING AMONG THEM, AND THEY NEVER **KNEW** US. THEIR DESPICABLE MAYOR CHARMING, MAY HE **ROT,** COULD NEVER EVEN REMEMBER THAT THERE WERE MERELY **THREE** OF US, AND NOT FOUR AS HE ALWAYS INSISTED.
I'M SURE THAT CINDY MEANT NO DISRESPECT, LADIES.
RIGHT. AND I'M THE **LAST** ONE TO STICK UP FOR MY SCUMBAG OF AN EX-HUSBAND.
SO, LET'S START AGAIN. WHERE ARE YOU **LADIES** GETTING ALL THE MAGICAL LOOT TO SELL, AND WHAT ARE YOU DOING WITH THE PROCEEDS?
SO YOU THINK US VILLAINS FROM SOME MELODRAMA, THAT WE'LL **EXPLAIN** OUR FULL PLANS AS SOON AS YOU ARE WITHIN OUR GRASP? DO YOU THINK YOURSELVES **HEROES?**
THE INHABITANTS OF THIS MUNDANE WORLD MAY ALL KNOW OF THE GLASS SLIPPER AND THE MAGIC LAMP, BUT YOU ARE NOT THE HEROES OF **THIS** TALE.

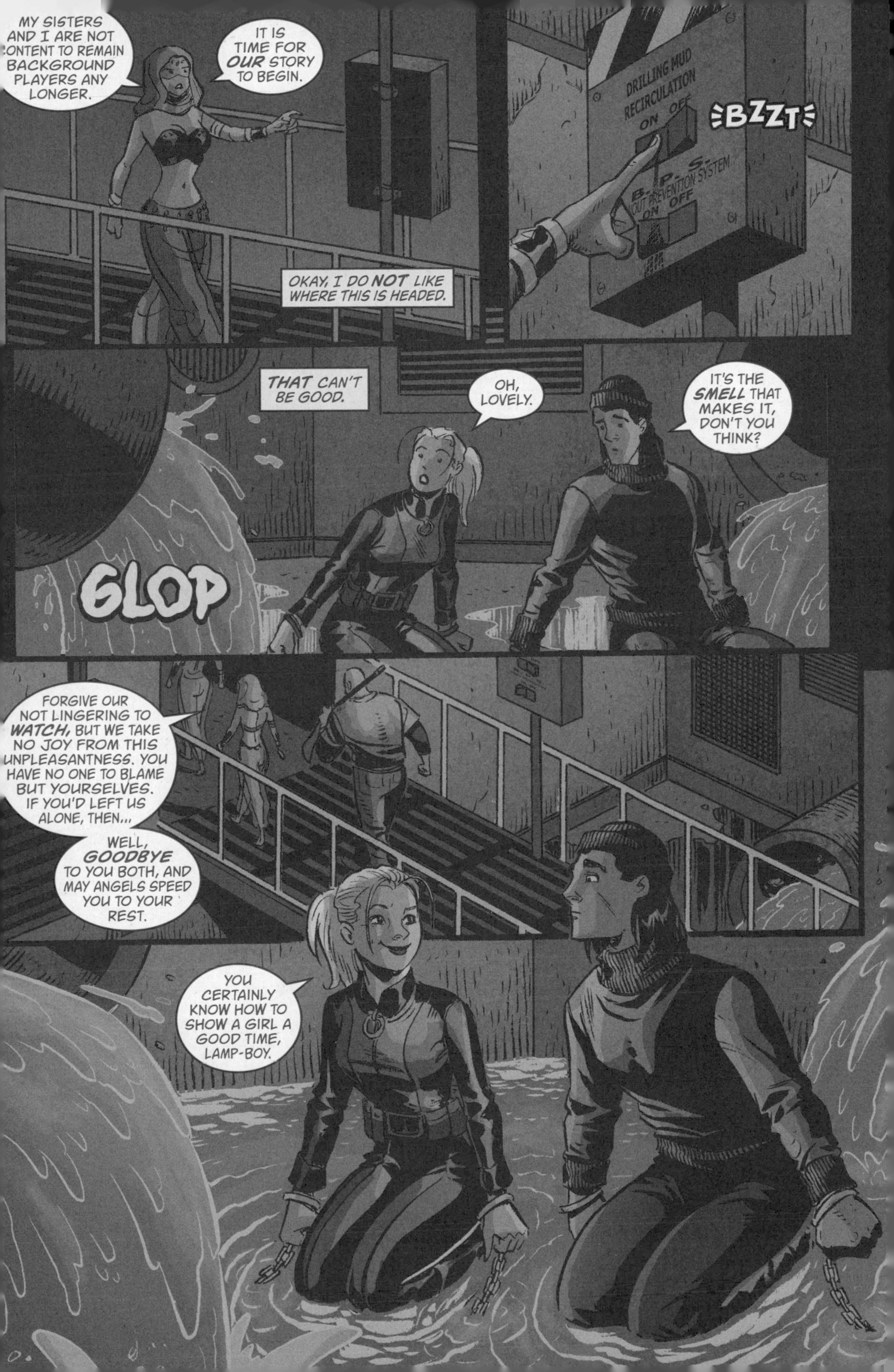
MY SISTERS AND I ARE NOT CONTENT TO REMAIN BACKGROUND PLAYERS ANY LONGER.
IT IS TIME FOR OUR STORY TO BEGIN.
OKAY, I DO NOT LIKE WHERE THIS IS HEADED.
DRILLING MUD RECIRCULATION ON OFF
B.P.S. BLOWOUT PREVENTION SYSTEM ON OFF
BZZT
THAT CAN'T BE GOOD.
OH, LOVELY.
IT'S THE SMELL THAT MAKES IT, DON'T YOU THINK?
GLOP
FORGIVE OUR NOT LINGERING TO WATCH, BUT WE TAKE NO JOY FROM THIS UNPLEASANTNESS. YOU HAVE NO ONE TO BLAME BUT YOURSELVES. IF YOU'D LEFT US ALONE, THEN...
WELL, GOODBYE TO YOU BOTH, AND MAY ANGELS SPEED YOU TO YOUR REST.
YOU CERTAINLY KNOW HOW TO SHOW A GIRL A GOOD TIME, LAMP-BOY.

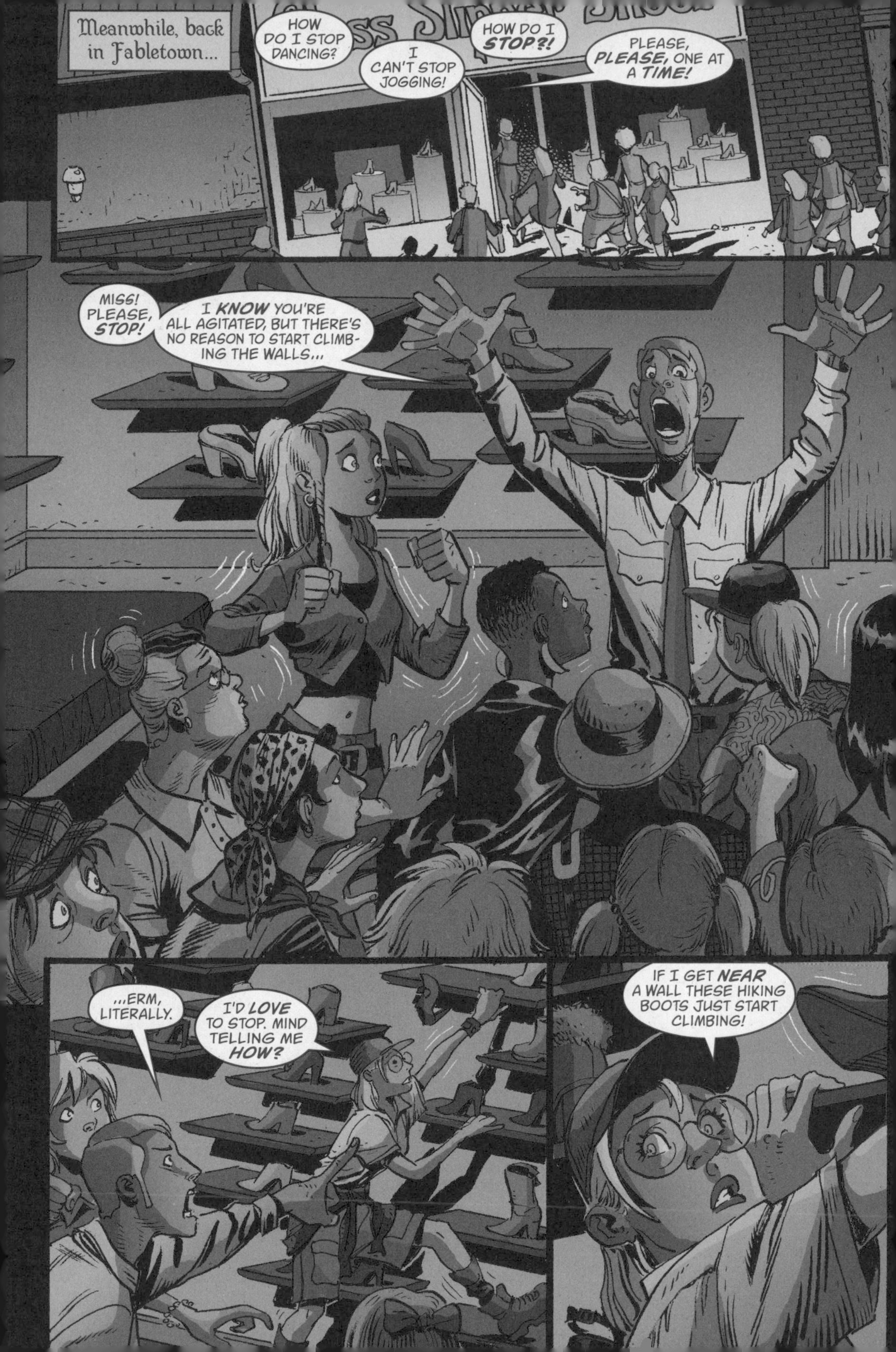
Meanwhile, back in Fabletown...
HOW DO I STOP DANCING?
I CAN'T STOP JOGGING!
HOW DO I STOP?!
PLEASE, PLEASE, ONE AT A TIME!
MISS! PLEASE, STOP!
I KNOW YOU'RE ALL AGITATED, BUT THERE'S NO REASON TO START CLIMBING THE WALLS...
...ERM, LITERALLY.
I'D LOVE TO STOP. MIND TELLING ME HOW?
IF I GET NEAR A WALL THESE HIKING BOOTS JUST START CLIMBING!

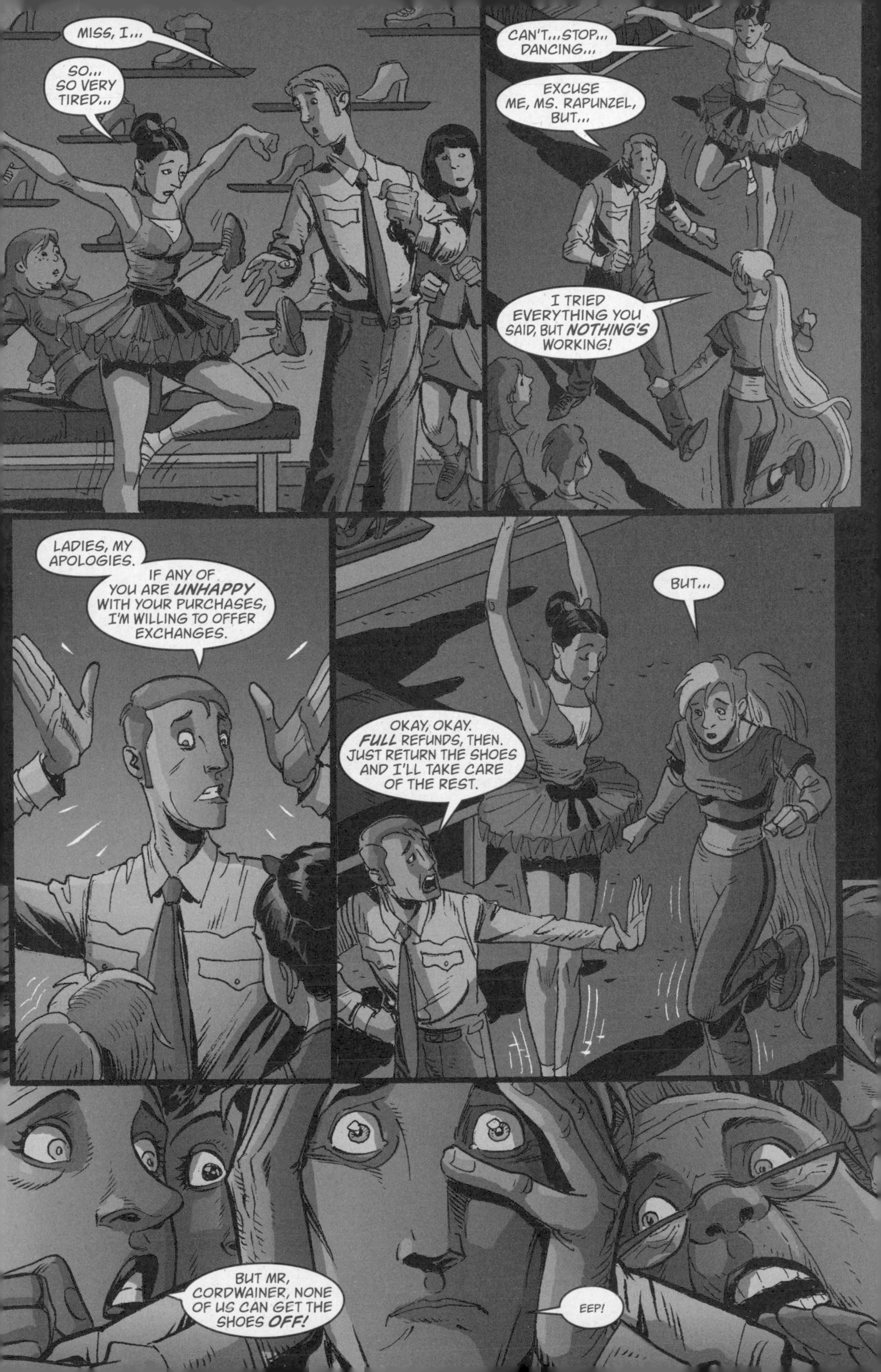

MISS, I...
SO... SO VERY TIRED...
CAN'T...STOP... DANCING...
EXCUSE ME, MS. RAPUNZEL, BUT...
I TRIED EVERYTHING YOU SAID, BUT **NOTHING'S** WORKING!
LADIES, MY APOLOGIES.
IF ANY OF YOU ARE **UNHAPPY** WITH YOUR PURCHASES, I'M WILLING TO OFFER EXCHANGES.
BUT...
OKAY, OKAY. **FULL** REFUNDS, THEN. JUST RETURN THE SHOES AND I'LL TAKE CARE OF THE REST.
BUT MR, CORDWAINER, NONE OF US CAN GET THE SHOES **OFF!**
EEP!

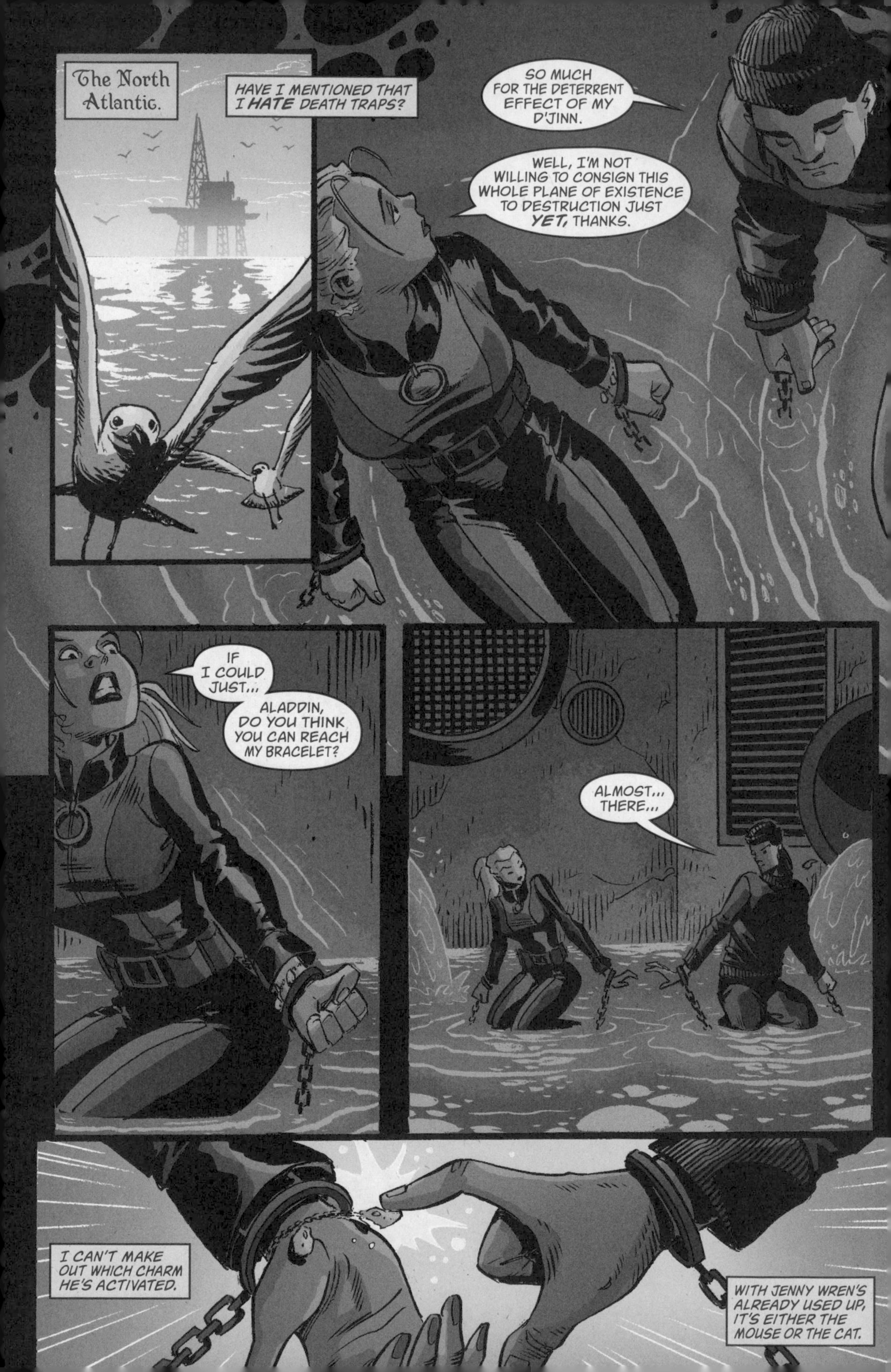
The North Atlantic.
HAVE I MENTIONED THAT I HATE DEATH TRAPS?
SO MUCH FOR THE DETERRENT EFFECT OF MY D'JINN.
WELL, I'M NOT WILLING TO CONSIGN THIS WHOLE PLANE OF EXISTENCE TO DESTRUCTION JUST YET, THANKS.
IF I COULD JUST...
ALADDIN, DO YOU THINK YOU CAN REACH MY BRACELET?
ALMOST... THERE...
I CAN'T MAKE OUT WHICH CHARM HE'S ACTIVATED.
WITH JENNY WREN'S ALREADY USED UP, IT'S EITHER THE MOUSE OR THE CAT.

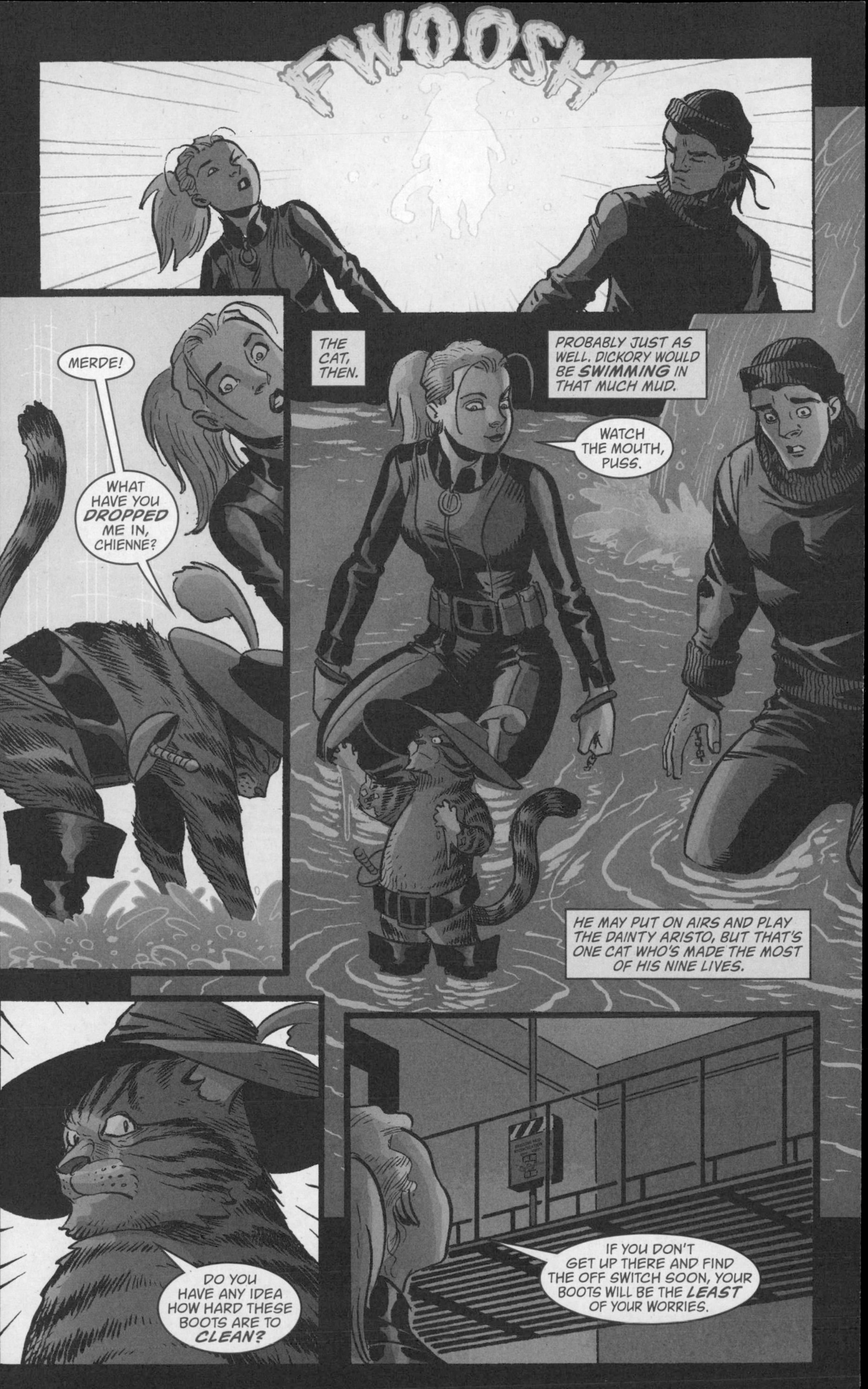
FWOOSH
MERDE!
WHAT HAVE YOU DROPPED ME IN, CHIENNE?
THE CAT, THEN.
PROBABLY JUST AS WELL. DICKORY WOULD BE SWIMMING IN THAT MUCH MUD.
WATCH THE MOUTH, PUSS.
HE MAY PUT ON AIRS AND PLAY THE DAINTY ARISTO, BUT THAT'S ONE CAT WHO'S MADE THE MOST OF HIS NINE LIVES.
DO YOU HAVE ANY IDEA HOW HARD THESE BOOTS ARE TO CLEAN?
IF YOU DON'T GET UP THERE AND FIND THE OFF SWITCH SOON, YOUR BOOTS WILL BE THE LEAST OF YOUR WORRIES.

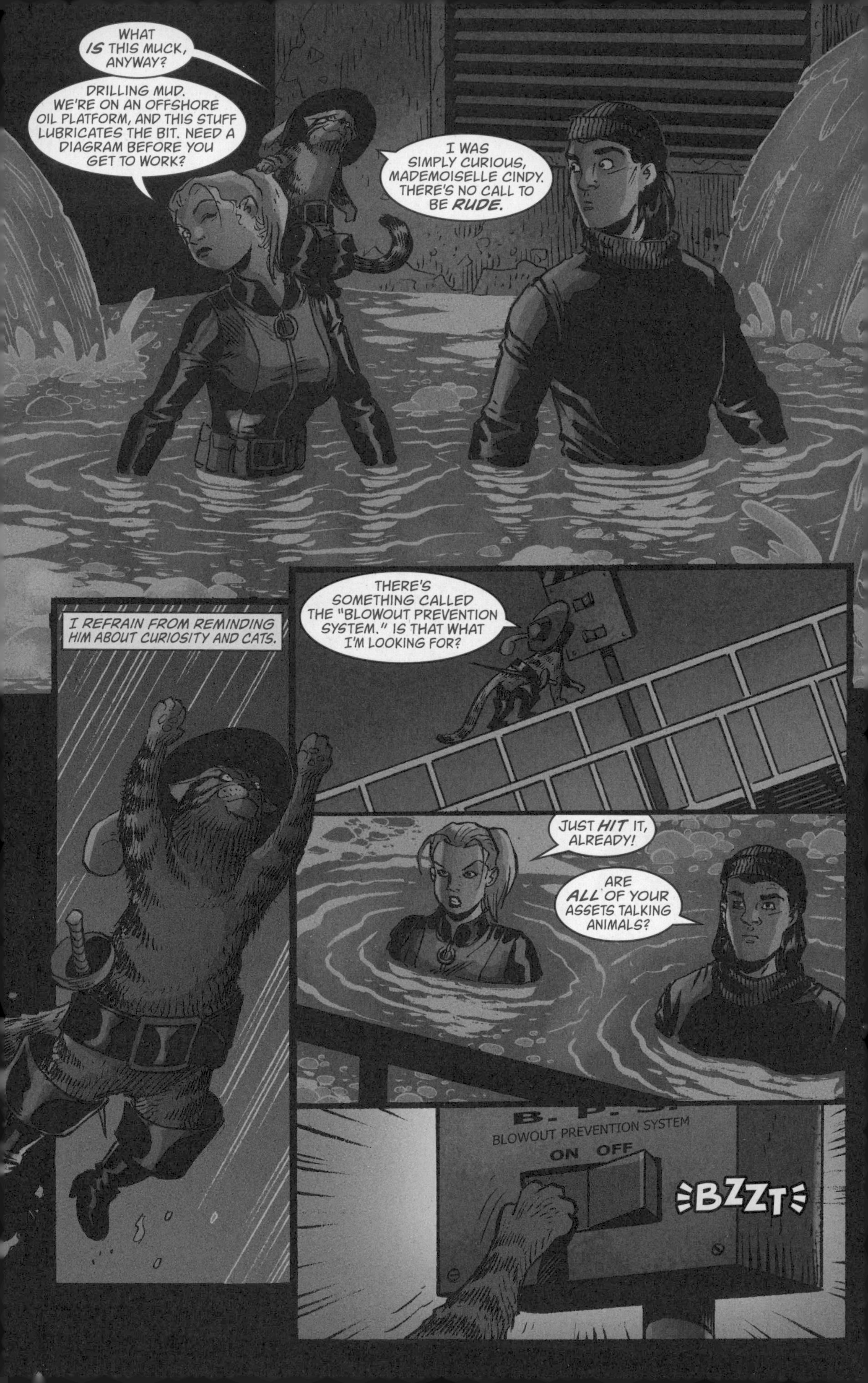
WHAT IS THIS MUCK, ANYWAY?
DRILLING MUD. WE'RE ON AN OFFSHORE OIL PLATFORM, AND THIS STUFF LUBRICATES THE BIT. NEED A DIAGRAM BEFORE YOU GET TO WORK?
I WAS SIMPLY CURIOUS, MADEMOISELLE CINDY. THERE'S NO CALL TO BE RUDE.
I REFRAIN FROM REMINDING HIM ABOUT CURIOSITY AND CATS.
THERE'S SOMETHING CALLED THE "BLOWOUT PREVENTION SYSTEM." IS THAT WHAT I'M LOOKING FOR?
JUST HIT IT, ALREADY!
ARE ALL OF YOUR ASSETS TALKING ANIMALS?
BLOWOUT PREVENTION SYSTEM
ON OFF
BZZT

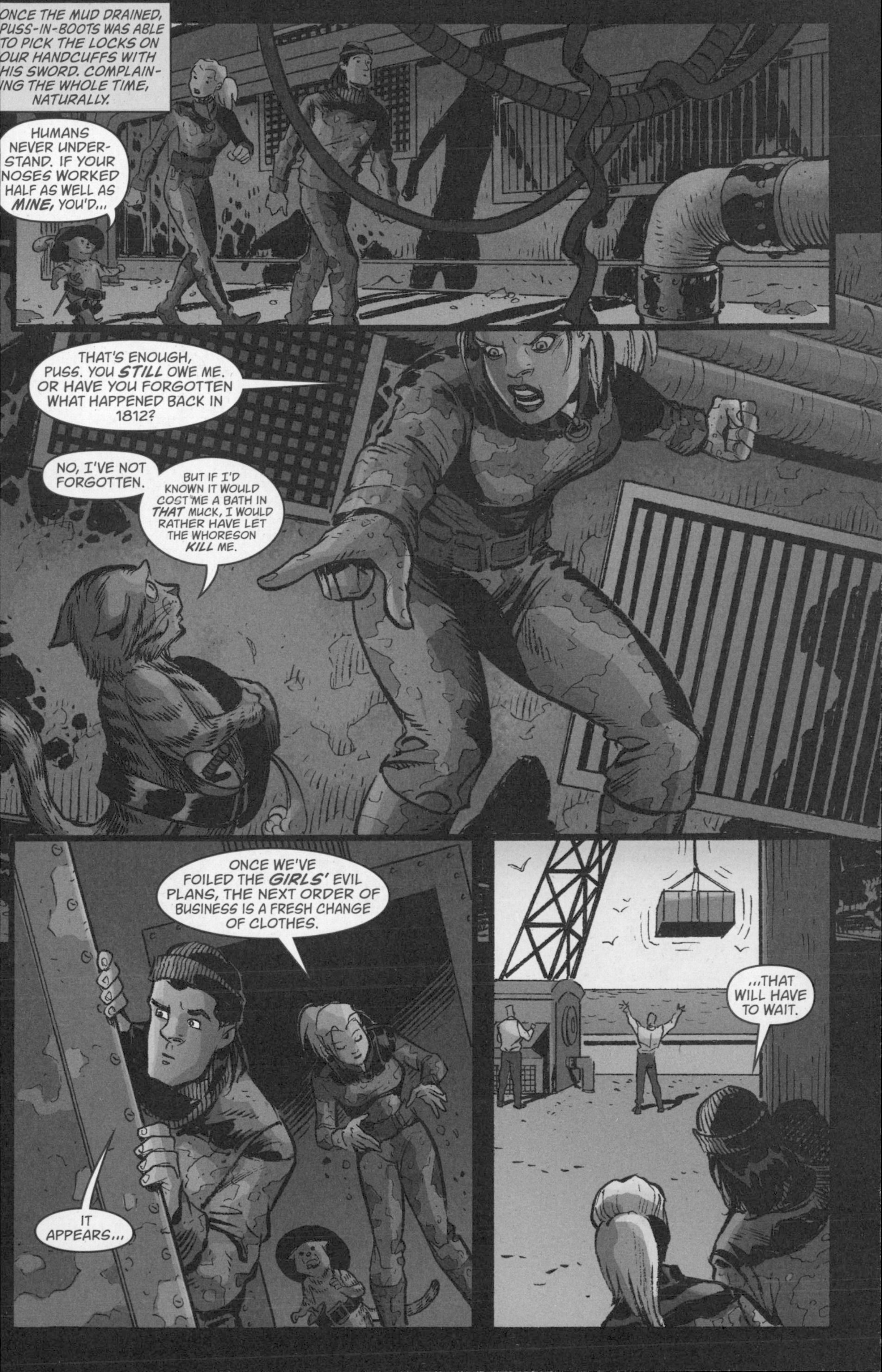

ONCE THE MUD DRAINED, PUSS-IN-BOOTS WAS ABLE TO PICK THE LOCKS ON OUR HANDCUFFS WITH HIS SWORD. COMPLAINING THE WHOLE TIME, NATURALLY.
HUMANS NEVER UNDERSTAND. IF YOUR NOSES WORKED HALF AS WELL AS MINE, YOU'D...
THAT'S ENOUGH, PUSS. YOU STILL OWE ME. OR HAVE YOU FORGOTTEN WHAT HAPPENED BACK IN 1812?
NO, I'VE NOT FORGOTTEN.
BUT IF I'D KNOWN IT WOULD COST ME A BATH IN THAT MUCK, I WOULD RATHER HAVE LET THE WHORESON KILL ME.
ONCE WE'VE FOILED THE GIRLS' EVIL PLANS, THE NEXT ORDER OF BUSINESS IS A FRESH CHANGE OF CLOTHES.
IT APPEARS...
...THAT WILL HAVE TO WAIT.

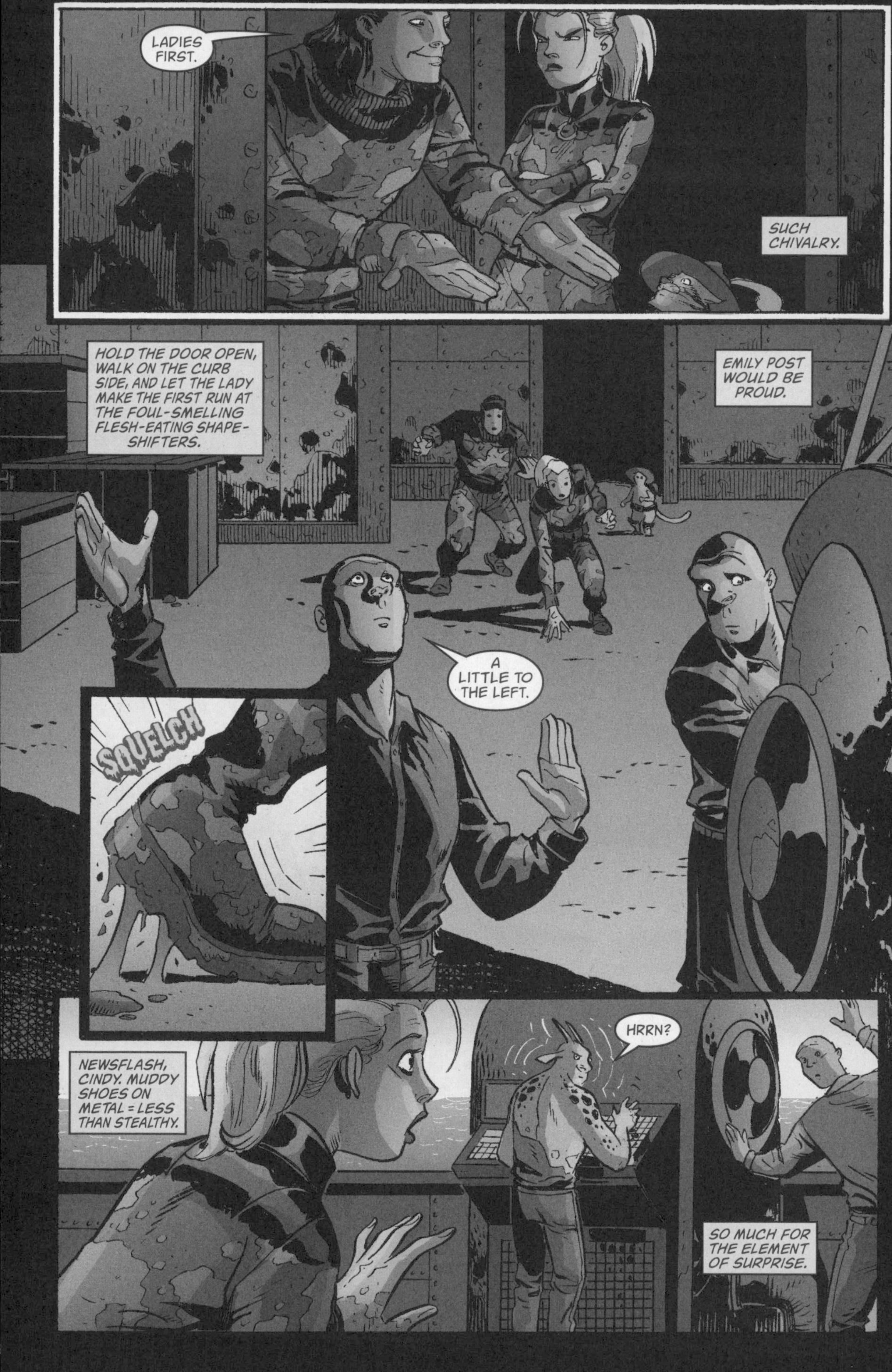
LADIES FIRST.
SUCH CHIVALRY.
HOLD THE DOOR OPEN, WALK ON THE CURB SIDE, AND LET THE LADY MAKE THE FIRST RUN AT THE FOUL-SMELLING FLESH-EATING SHAPE-SHIFTERS.
EMILY POST WOULD BE PROUD.
A LITTLE TO THE LEFT.
SQUELCH
NEWSFLASH, CINDY. MUDDY SHOES ON METAL = LESS THAN STEALTHY.
HRRN?
SO MUCH FOR THE ELEMENT OF SURPRISE.

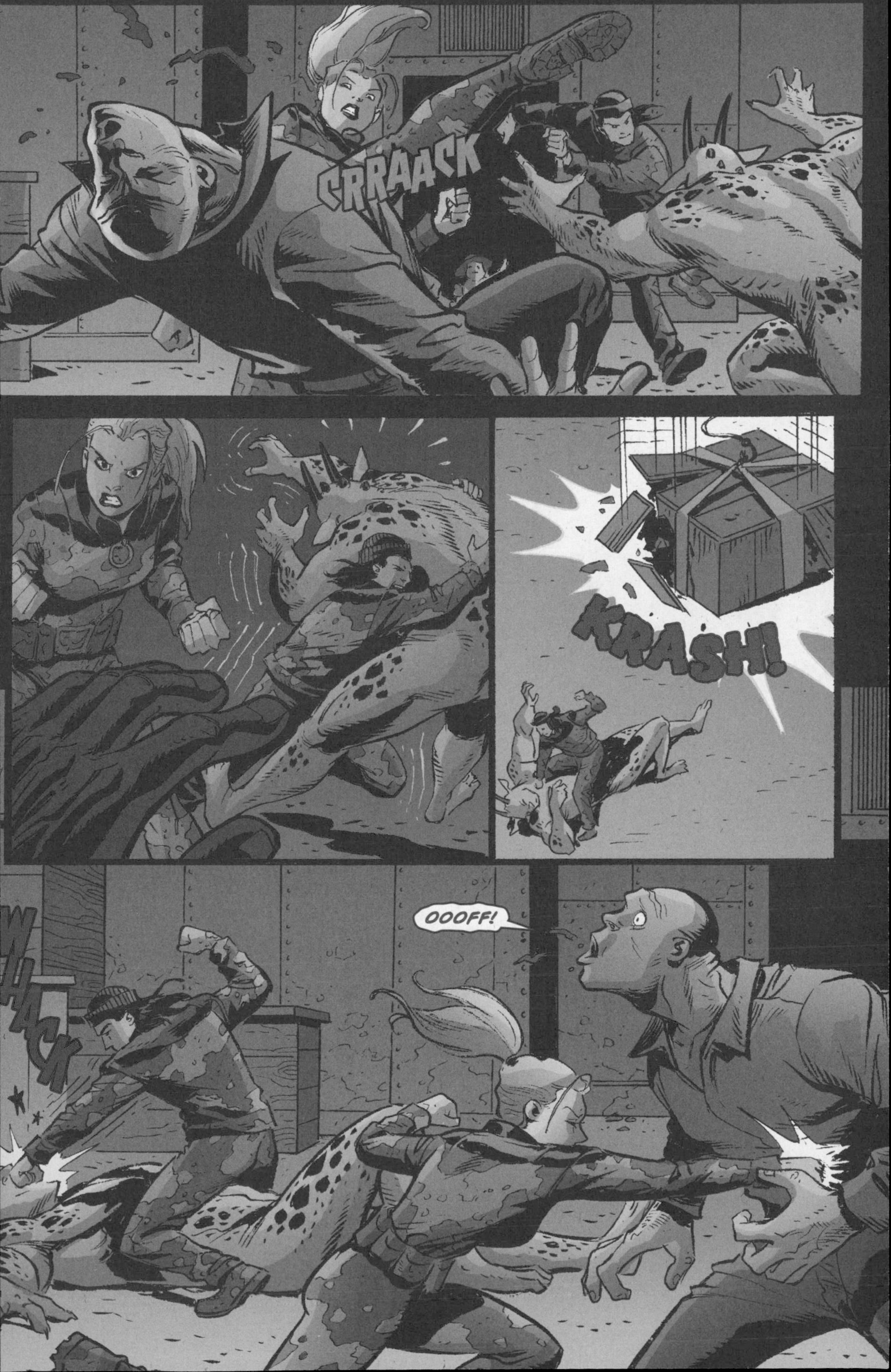
CRRAACK
KRASH!
OOOFF!
WHACK

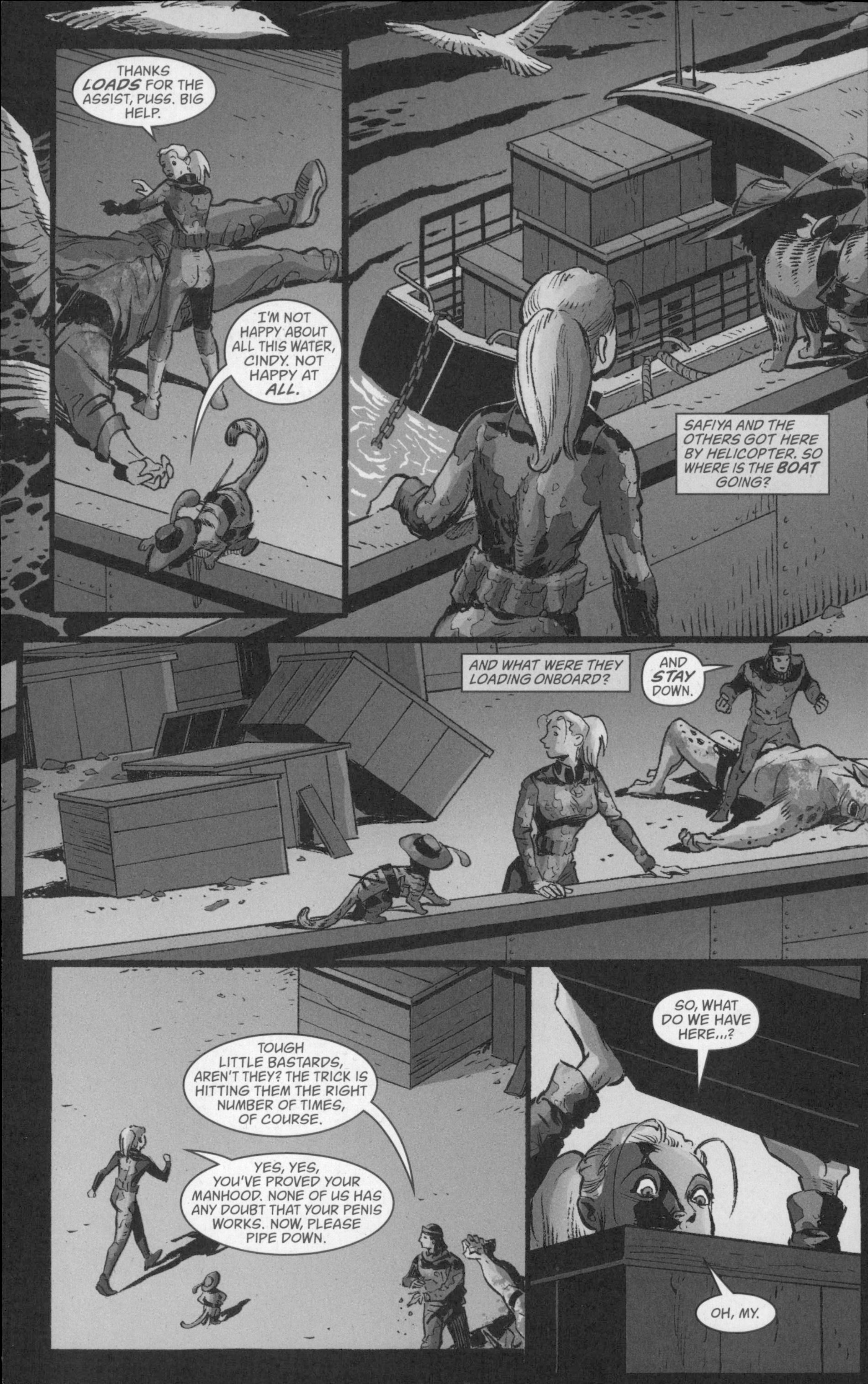
THANKS LOADS FOR THE ASSIST, PUSS. BIG HELP.
I'M NOT HAPPY ABOUT ALL THIS WATER, CINDY. NOT HAPPY AT ALL.
SAFIYA AND THE OTHERS GOT HERE BY HELICOPTER. SO WHERE IS THE BOAT GOING?
AND WHAT WERE THEY LOADING ONBOARD?
AND STAY DOWN.
TOUGH LITTLE BASTARDS, AREN'T THEY? THE TRICK IS HITTING THEM THE RIGHT NUMBER OF TIMES, OF COURSE.
YES, YES, YOU'VE PROVED YOUR MANHOOD. NONE OF US HAS ANY DOUBT THAT YOUR PENIS WORKS. NOW, PLEASE PIPE DOWN.
SO, WHAT DO WE HAVE HERE...?
OH, MY.

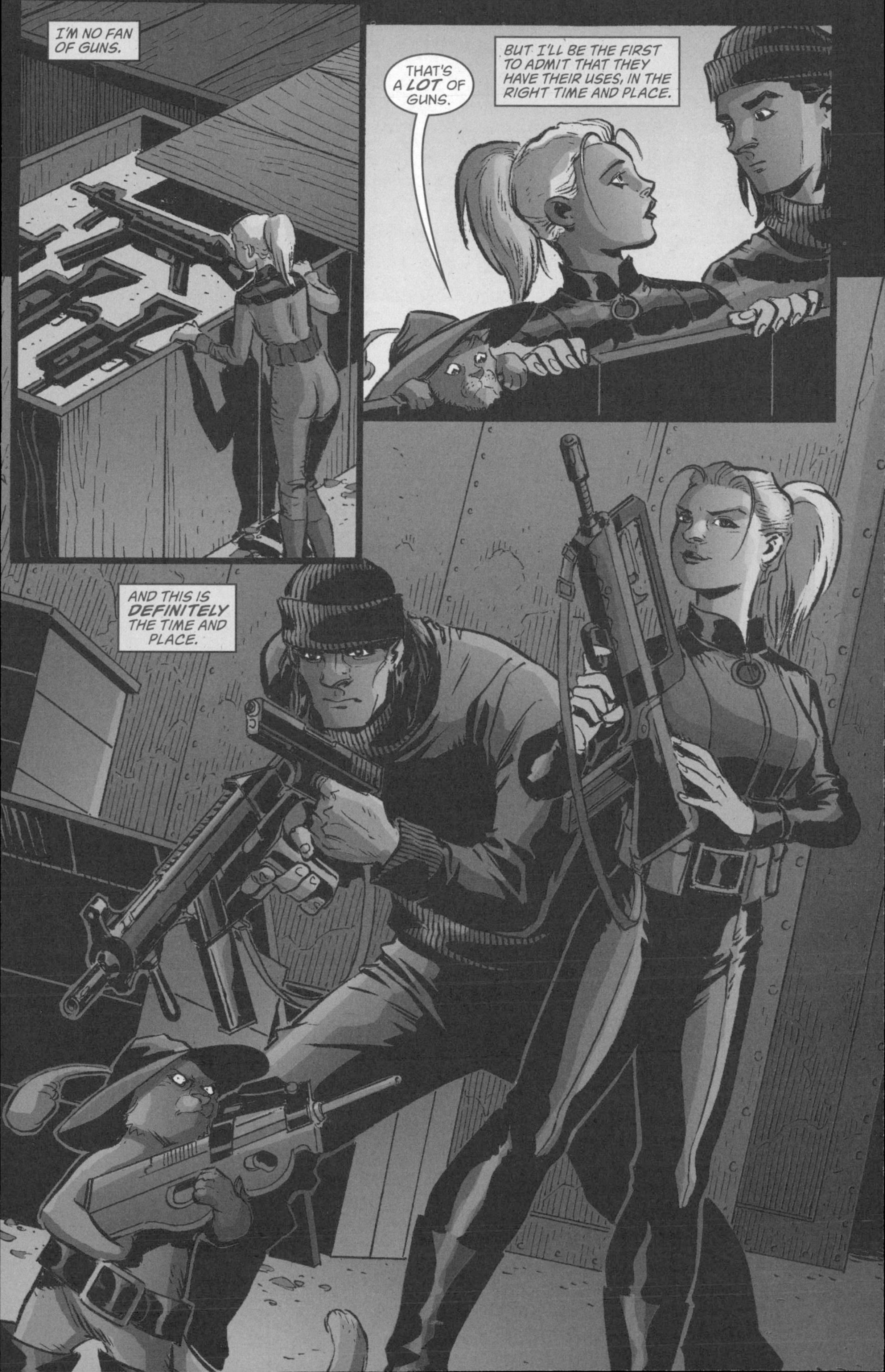
I'M NO FAN OF GUNS.
THAT'S A **LOT** OF GUNS.
BUT I'LL BE THE FIRST TO ADMIT THAT THEY HAVE THEIR USES, IN THE RIGHT TIME AND PLACE.
AND THIS IS **DEFINITELY** THE TIME AND PLACE.

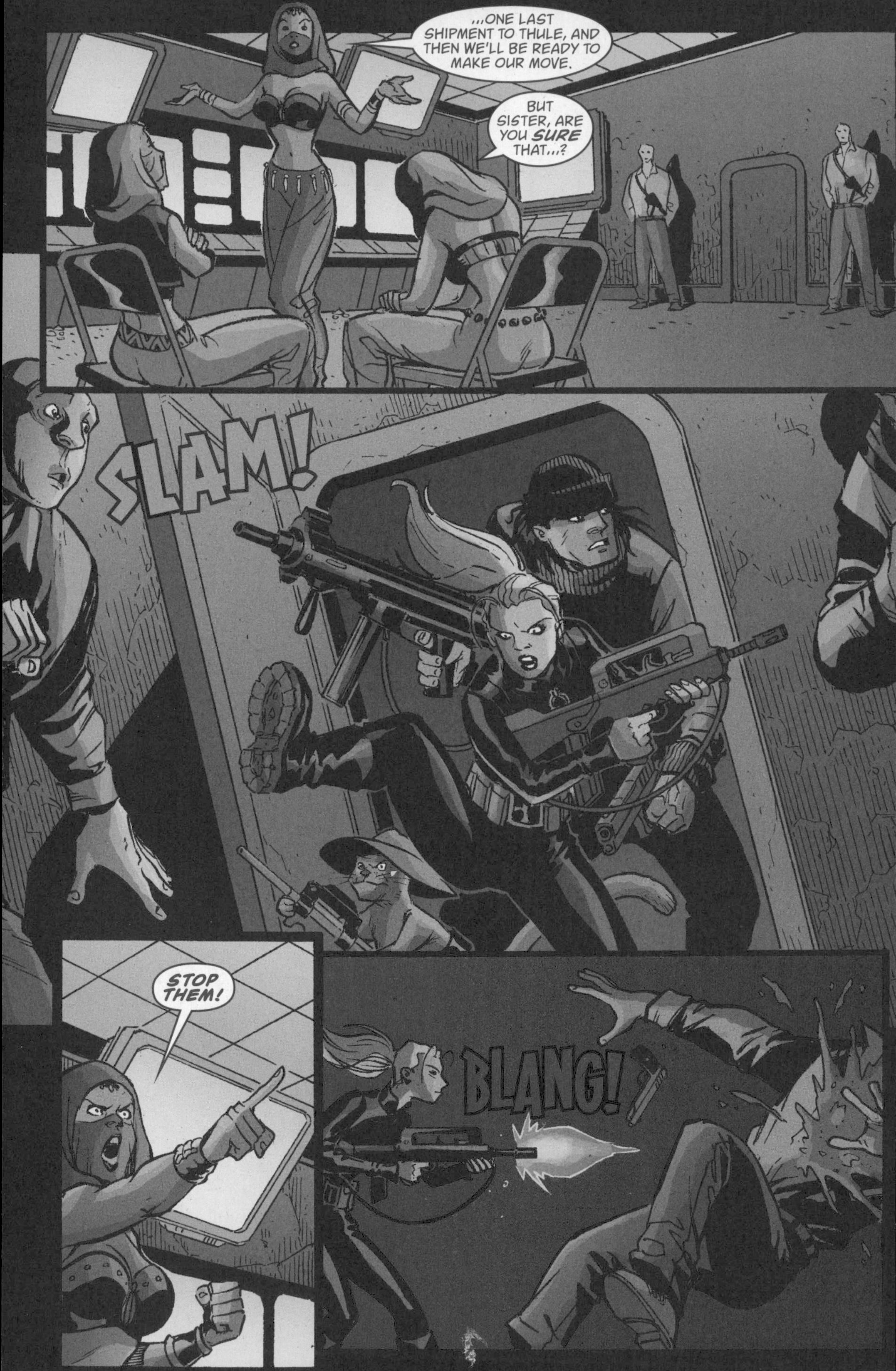
...ONE LAST SHIPMENT TO THULE, AND THEN WE'LL BE READY TO MAKE OUR MOVE.
BUT SISTER, ARE YOU SURE THAT...?
SLAM!
STOP THEM!
BLANG!

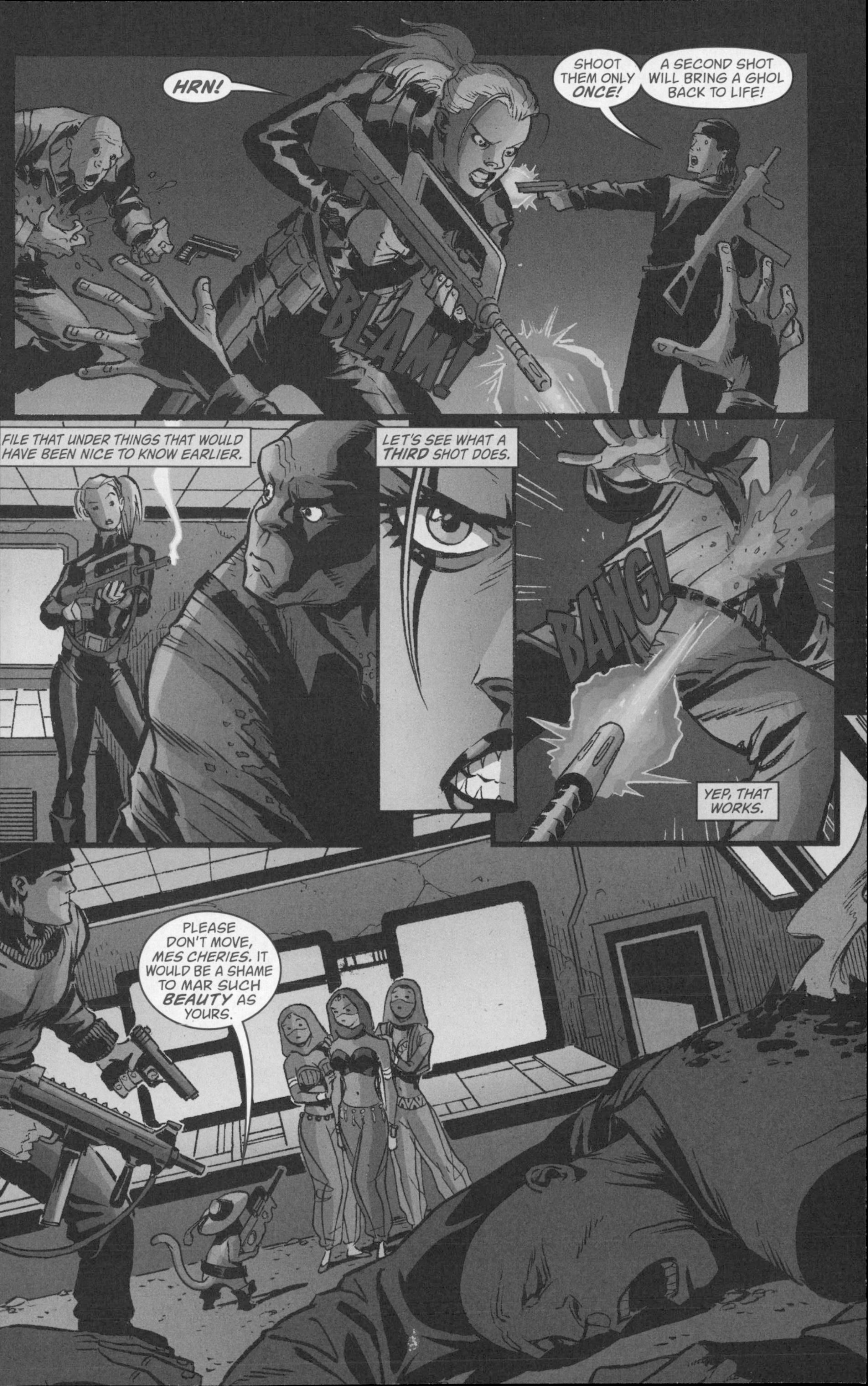
HRN!
SHOOT THEM ONLY ONCE!
A SECOND SHOT WILL BRING A GHOL BACK TO LIFE!
BLAM!
FILE THAT UNDER THINGS THAT WOULD HAVE BEEN NICE TO KNOW EARLIER.
LET'S SEE WHAT A THIRD SHOT DOES.
BANG!
YEP, THAT WORKS.
PLEASE DON'T MOVE, MES CHERIES. IT WOULD BE A SHAME TO MAR SUCH BEAUTY AS YOURS.

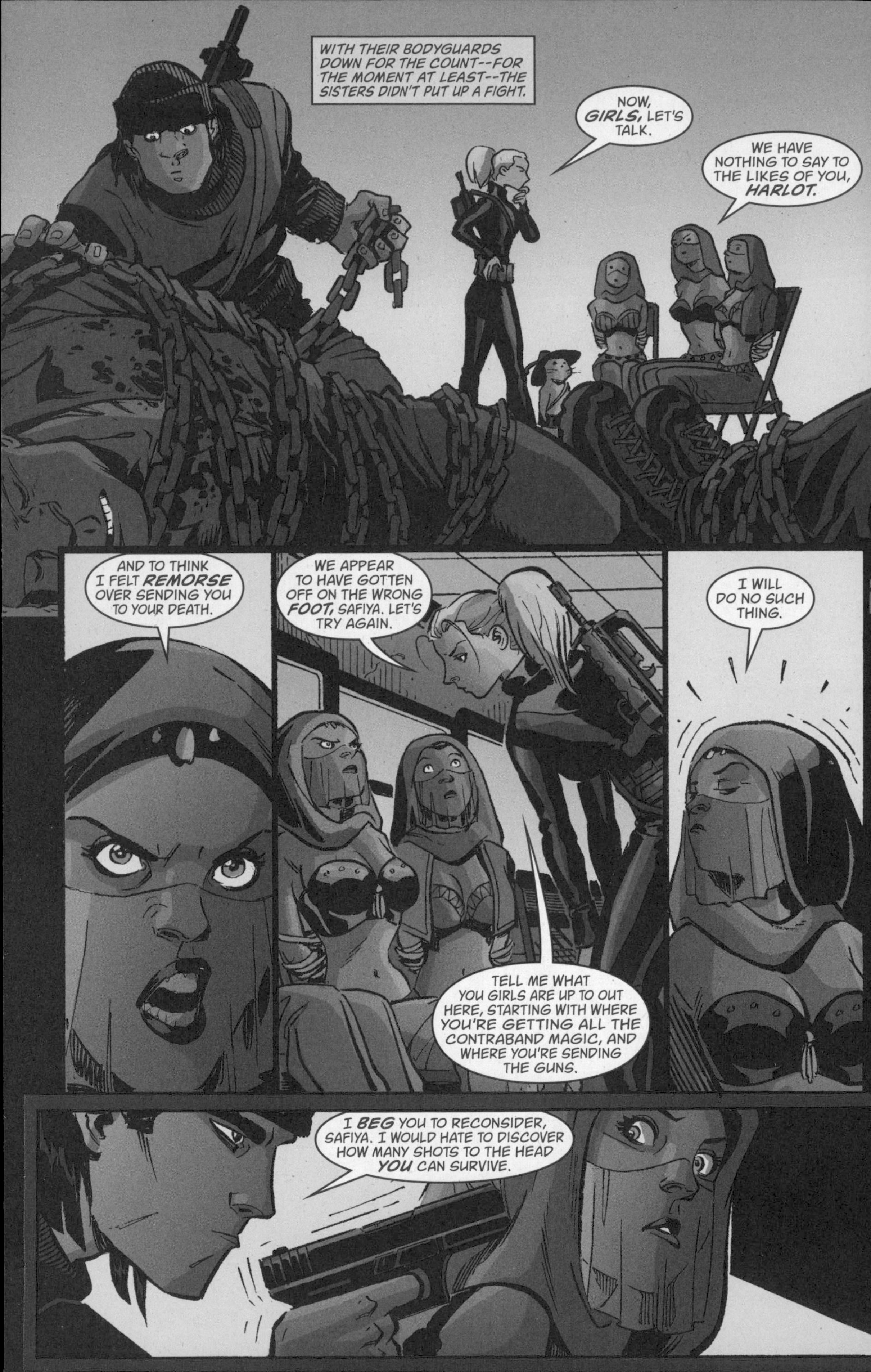
WITH THEIR BODYGUARDS DOWN FOR THE COUNT--FOR THE MOMENT AT LEAST--THE SISTERS DIDN'T PUT UP A FIGHT.
NOW, GIRLS, LET'S TALK.
WE HAVE NOTHING TO SAY TO THE LIKES OF YOU, HARLOT.
AND TO THINK I FELT REMORSE OVER SENDING YOU TO YOUR DEATH.
WE APPEAR TO HAVE GOTTEN OFF ON THE WRONG FOOT, SAFIYA. LET'S TRY AGAIN.
TELL ME WHAT YOU GIRLS ARE UP TO OUT HERE, STARTING WITH WHERE YOU'RE GETTING ALL THE CONTRABAND MAGIC, AND WHERE YOU'RE SENDING THE GUNS.
I WILL DO NO SUCH THING.
I BEG YOU TO RECONSIDER, SAFIYA. I WOULD HATE TO DISCOVER HOW MANY SHOTS TO THE HEAD YOU CAN SURVIVE.

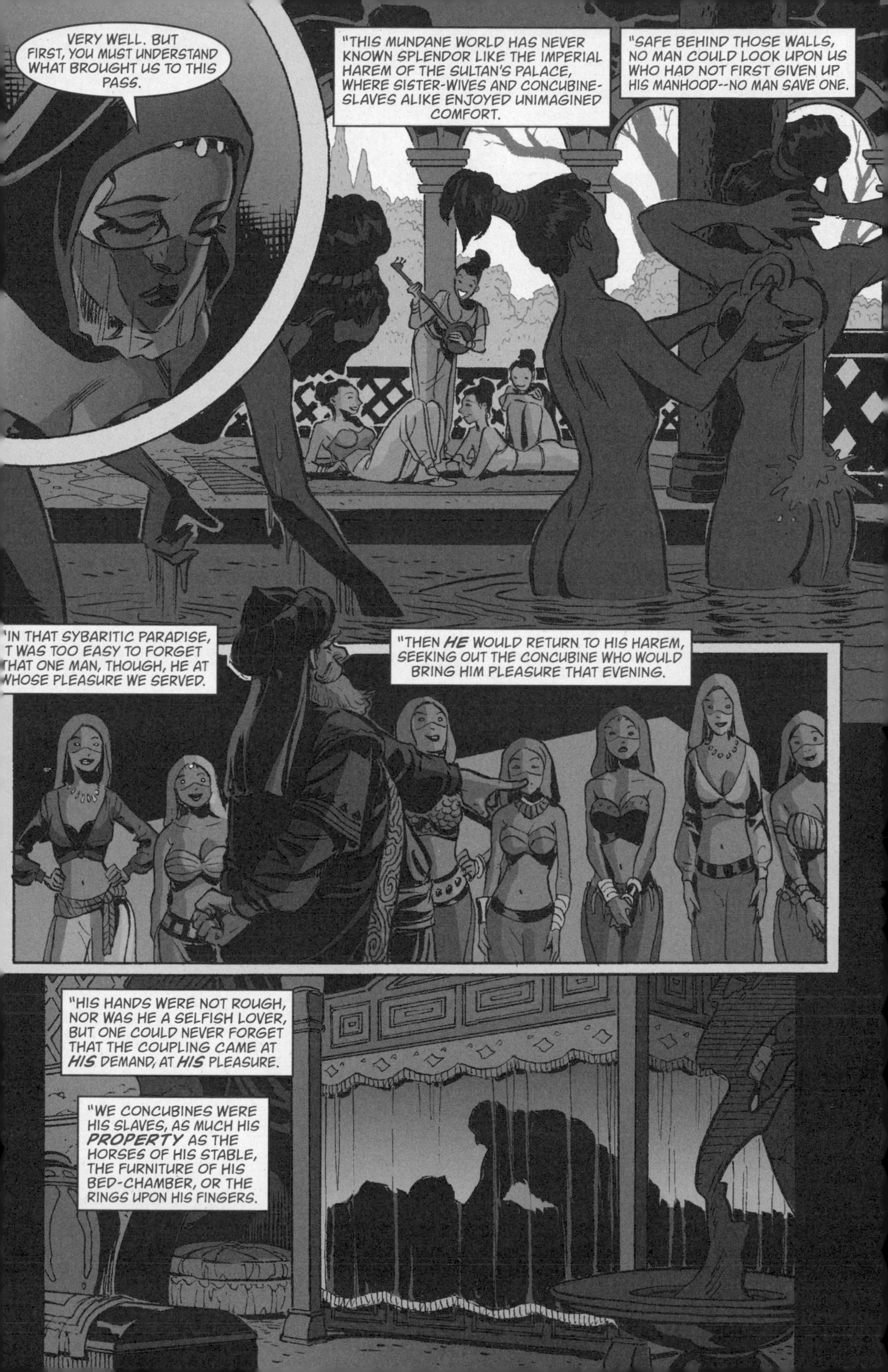
VERY WELL. BUT FIRST, YOU MUST UNDERSTAND WHAT BROUGHT US TO THIS PASS.
"THIS MUNDANE WORLD HAS NEVER KNOWN SPLENDOR LIKE THE IMPERIAL HAREM OF THE SULTAN'S PALACE, WHERE SISTER-WIVES AND CONCUBINE-SLAVES ALIKE ENJOYED UNIMAGINED COMFORT.
"SAFE BEHIND THOSE WALLS, NO MAN COULD LOOK UPON US WHO HAD NOT FIRST GIVEN UP HIS MANHOOD--NO MAN SAVE ONE.
"IN THAT SYBARITIC PARADISE, IT WAS TOO EASY TO FORGET THAT ONE MAN, THOUGH, HE AT WHOSE PLEASURE WE SERVED.
"THEN HE WOULD RETURN TO HIS HAREM, SEEKING OUT THE CONCUBINE WHO WOULD BRING HIM PLEASURE THAT EVENING.
"HIS HANDS WERE NOT ROUGH, NOR WAS HE A SELFISH LOVER, BUT ONE COULD NEVER FORGET THAT THE COUPLING CAME AT HIS DEMAND, AT HIS PLEASURE.
"WE CONCUBINES WERE HIS SLAVES, AS MUCH HIS PROPERTY AS THE HORSES OF HIS STABLE, THE FURNITURE OF HIS BED-CHAMBER, OR THE RINGS UPON HIS FINGERS.

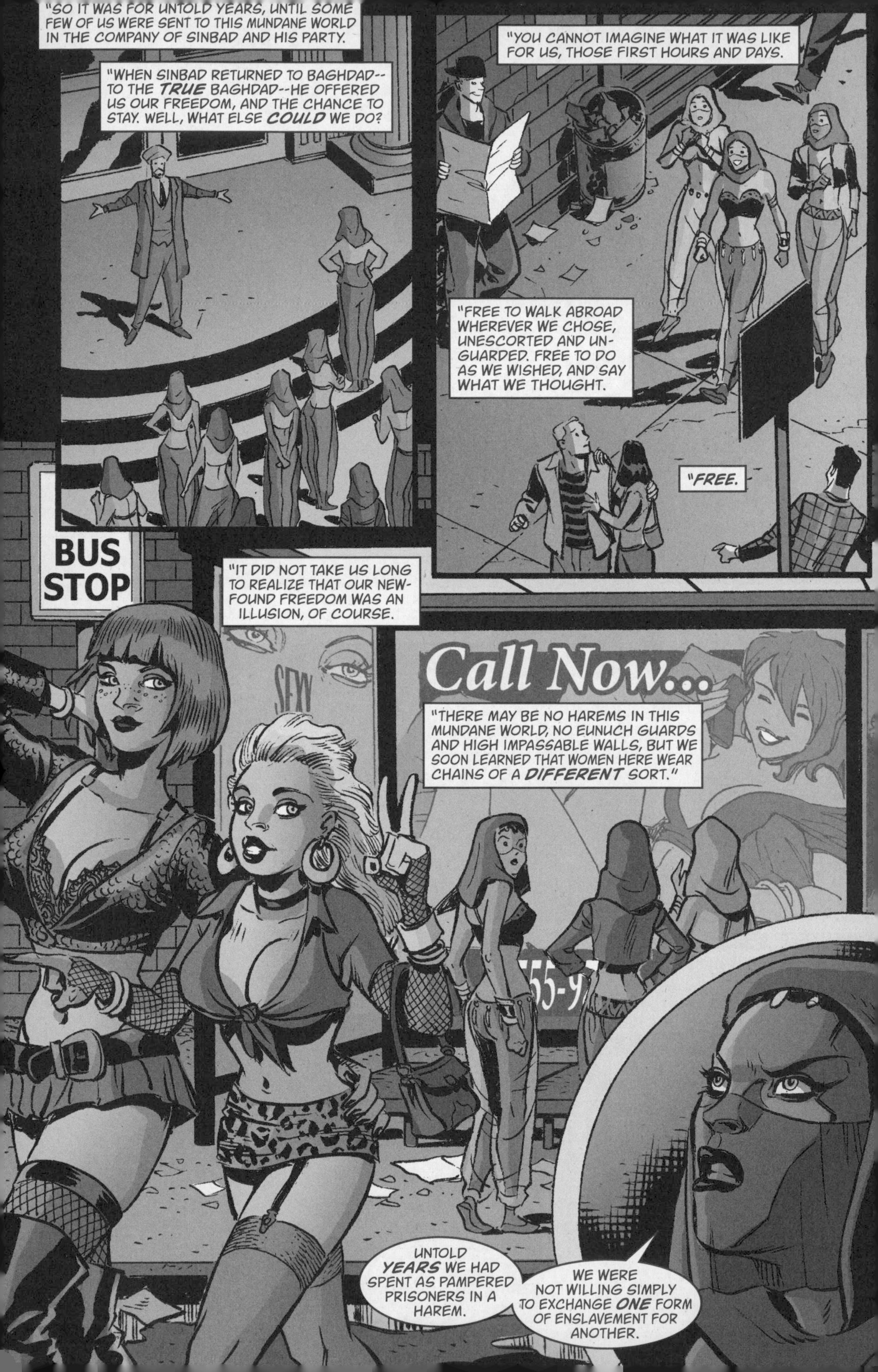
"SO IT WAS FOR UNTOLD YEARS, UNTIL SOME FEW OF US WERE SENT TO THIS MUNDANE WORLD IN THE COMPANY OF SINBAD AND HIS PARTY.
"WHEN SINBAD RETURNED TO BAGHDAD--TO THE TRUE BAGHDAD--HE OFFERED US OUR FREEDOM, AND THE CHANCE TO STAY. WELL, WHAT ELSE COULD WE DO?
"YOU CANNOT IMAGINE WHAT IT WAS LIKE FOR US, THOSE FIRST HOURS AND DAYS.
"FREE TO WALK ABROAD WHEREVER WE CHOSE, UNESCORTED AND UNGUARDED. FREE TO DO AS WE WISHED, AND SAY WHAT WE THOUGHT.
"FREE.
BUS STOP
"IT DID NOT TAKE US LONG TO REALIZE THAT OUR NEWFOUND FREEDOM WAS AN ILLUSION, OF COURSE.
SEXY
Call Now...
"THERE MAY BE NO HAREMS IN THIS MUNDANE WORLD, NO EUNUCH GUARDS AND HIGH IMPASSABLE WALLS, BUT WE SOON LEARNED THAT WOMEN HERE WEAR CHAINS OF A DIFFERENT SORT."
UNTOLD YEARS WE HAD SPENT AS PAMPERED PRISONERS IN A HAREM.
WE WERE NOT WILLING SIMPLY TO EXCHANGE ONE FORM OF ENSLAVEMENT FOR ANOTHER.

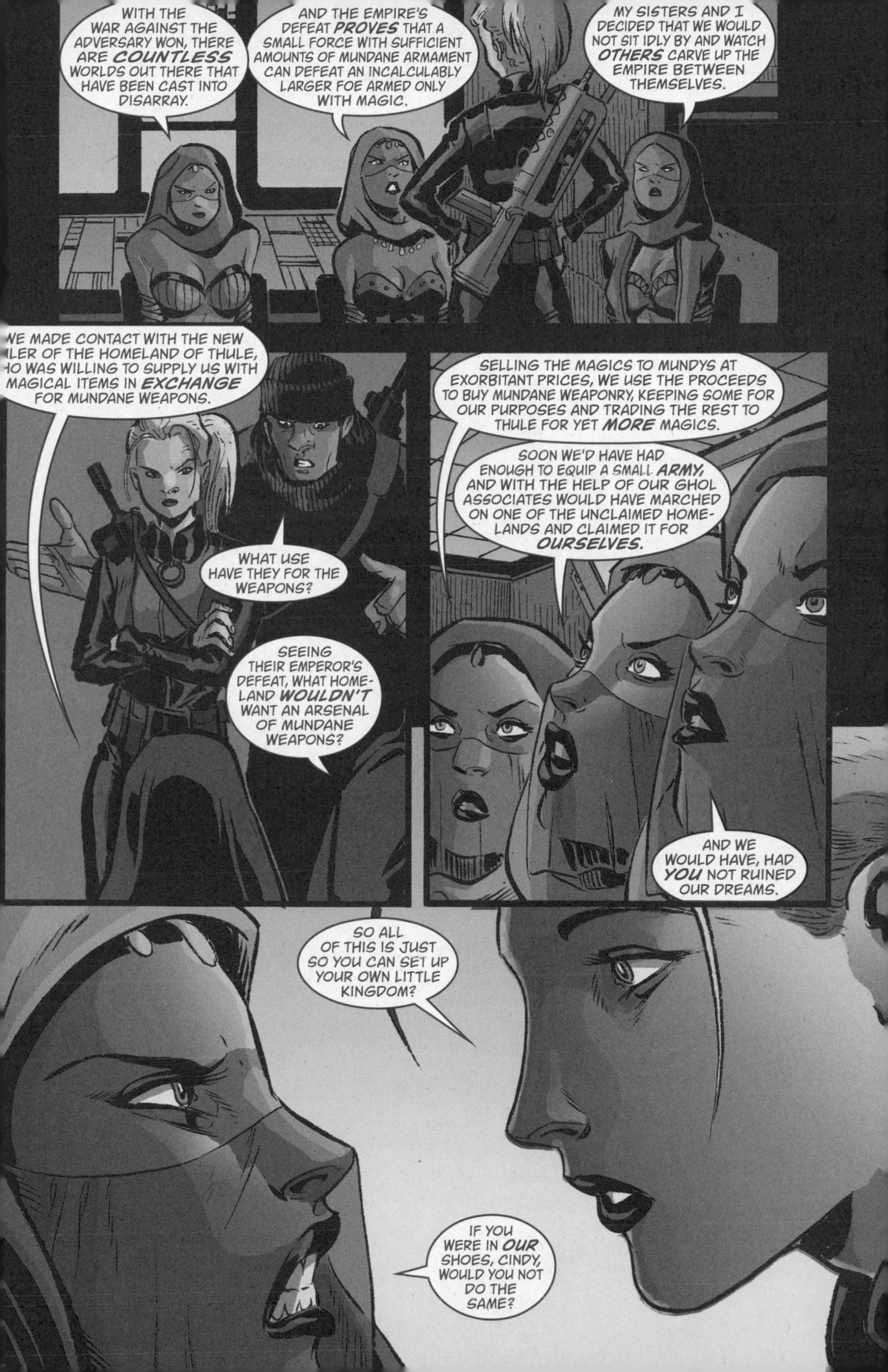

WITH THE WAR AGAINST THE ADVERSARY WON, THERE ARE COUNTLESS WORLDS OUT THERE THAT HAVE BEEN CAST INTO DISARRAY.
AND THE EMPIRE'S DEFEAT PROVES THAT A SMALL FORCE WITH SUFFICIENT AMOUNTS OF MUNDANE ARMAMENT CAN DEFEAT AN INCALCULABLY LARGER FOE ARMED ONLY WITH MAGIC.
MY SISTERS AND I DECIDED THAT WE WOULD NOT SIT IDLY BY AND WATCH OTHERS CARVE UP THE EMPIRE BETWEEN THEMSELVES.
WE MADE CONTACT WITH THE NEW ILER OF THE HOMELAND OF THULE, HO WAS WILLING TO SUPPLY US WITH MAGICAL ITEMS IN EXCHANGE FOR MUNDANE WEAPONS.
WHAT USE HAVE THEY FOR THE WEAPONS?
SEEING THEIR EMPEROR'S DEFEAT, WHAT HOMELAND WOULDN'T WANT AN ARSENAL OF MUNDANE WEAPONS?
SELLING THE MAGICS TO MUNDYS AT EXORBITANT PRICES, WE USE THE PROCEEDS TO BUY MUNDANE WEAPONRY, KEEPING SOME FOR OUR PURPOSES AND TRADING THE REST TO THULE FOR YET MORE MAGICS.
SOON WE'D HAVE HAD ENOUGH TO EQUIP A SMALL ARMY, AND WITH THE HELP OF OUR GHOL ASSOCIATES WOULD HAVE MARCHED ON ONE OF THE UNCLAIMED HOMELANDS AND CLAIMED IT FOR OURSELVES.
AND WE WOULD HAVE, HAD YOU NOT RUINED OUR DREAMS.
SO ALL OF THIS IS JUST SO YOU CAN SET UP YOUR OWN LITTLE KINGDOM?
IF YOU WERE IN OUR SHOES, CINDY, WOULD YOU NOT DO THE SAME?

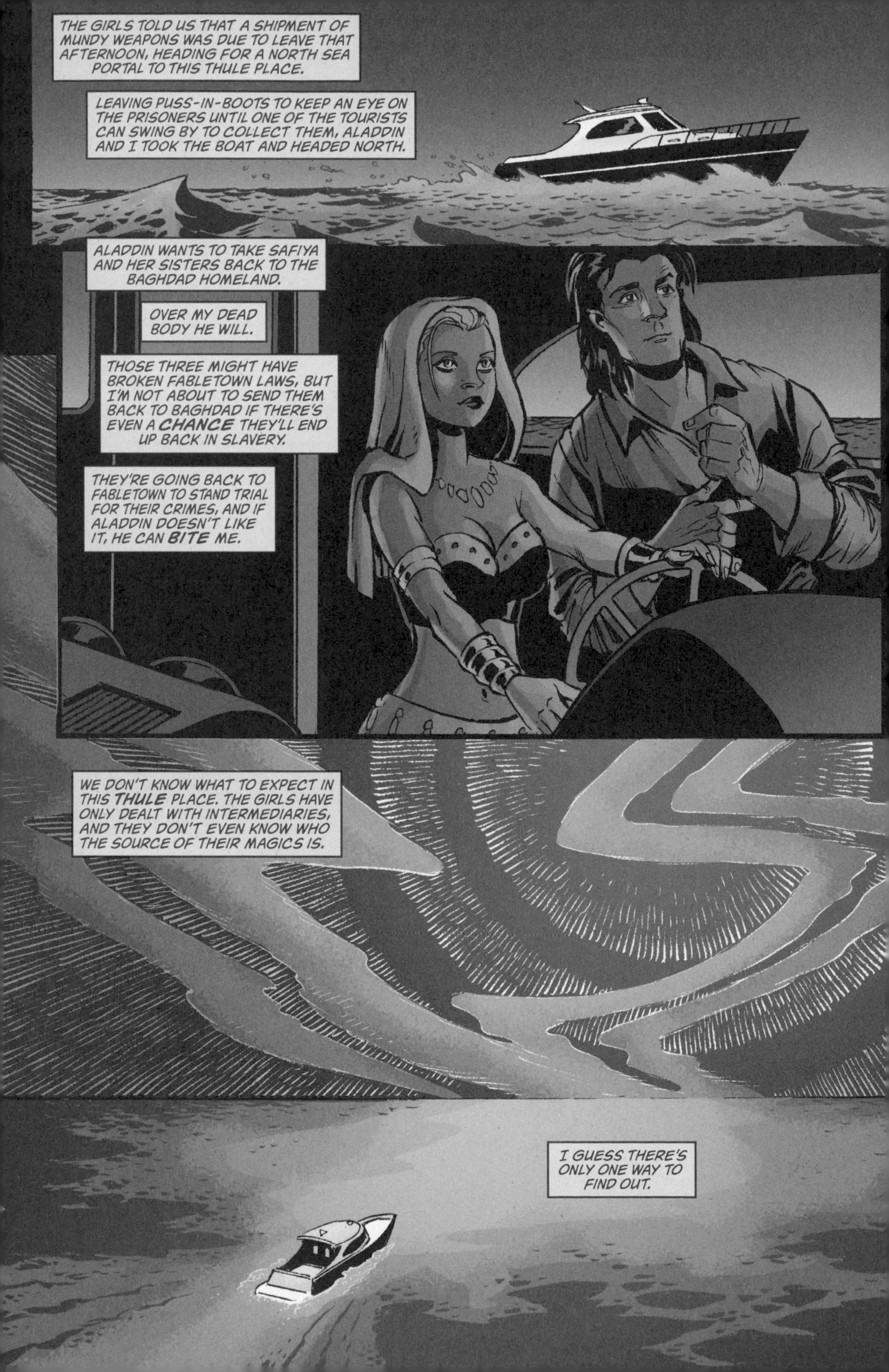
THE GIRLS TOLD US THAT A SHIPMENT OF MUNDY WEAPONS WAS DUE TO LEAVE THAT AFTERNOON, HEADING FOR A NORTH SEA PORTAL TO THIS THULE PLACE.
LEAVING PUSS-IN-BOOTS TO KEEP AN EYE ON THE PRISONERS UNTIL ONE OF THE TOURISTS CAN SWING BY TO COLLECT THEM, ALADDIN AND I TOOK THE BOAT AND HEADED NORTH.
ALADDIN WANTS TO TAKE SAFIYA AND HER SISTERS BACK TO THE BAGHDAD HOMELAND.
OVER MY DEAD BODY HE WILL.
THOSE THREE MIGHT HAVE BROKEN FABLETOWN LAWS, BUT I'M NOT ABOUT TO SEND THEM BACK TO BAGHDAD IF THERE'S EVEN A CHANCE THEY'LL END UP BACK IN SLAVERY.
THEY'RE GOING BACK TO FABLETOWN TO STAND TRIAL FOR THEIR CRIMES, AND IF ALADDIN DOESN'T LIKE IT, HE CAN BITE ME.
WE DON'T KNOW WHAT TO EXPECT IN THIS THULE PLACE. THE GIRLS HAVE ONLY DEALT WITH INTERMEDIARIES, AND THEY DON'T EVEN KNOW WHO THE SOURCE OF THEIR MAGICS IS.
I GUESS THERE'S ONLY ONE WAY TO FIND OUT.

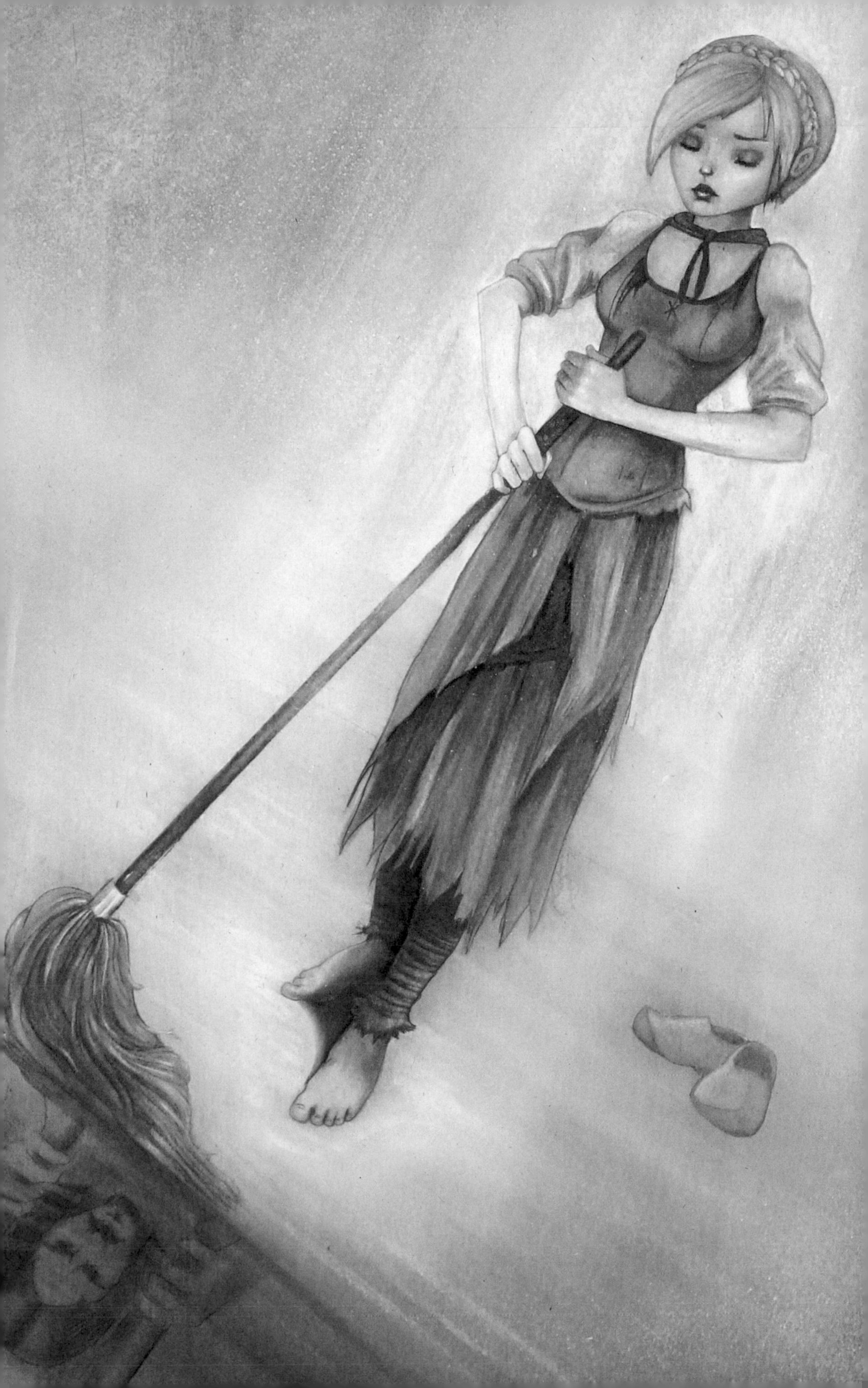

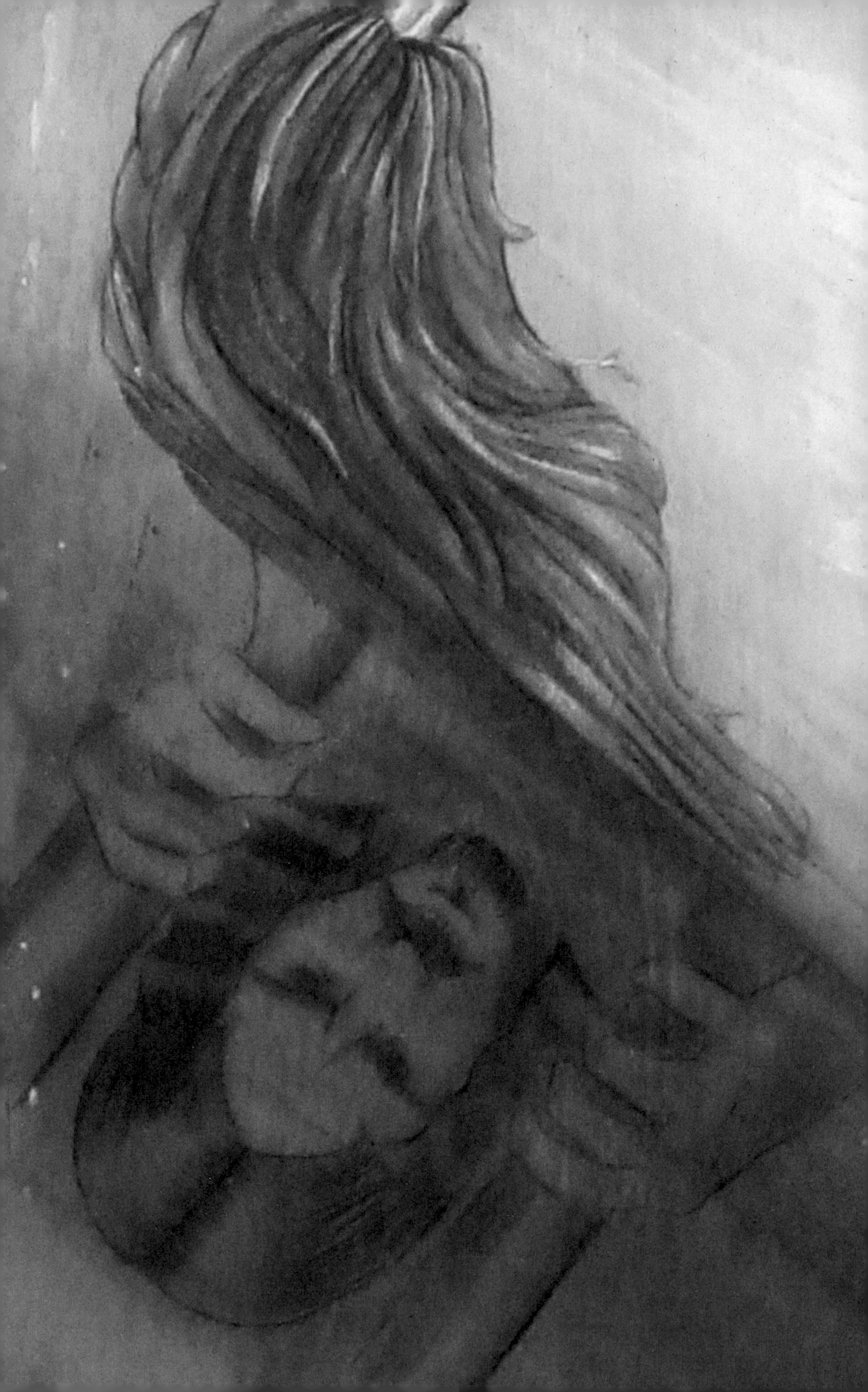

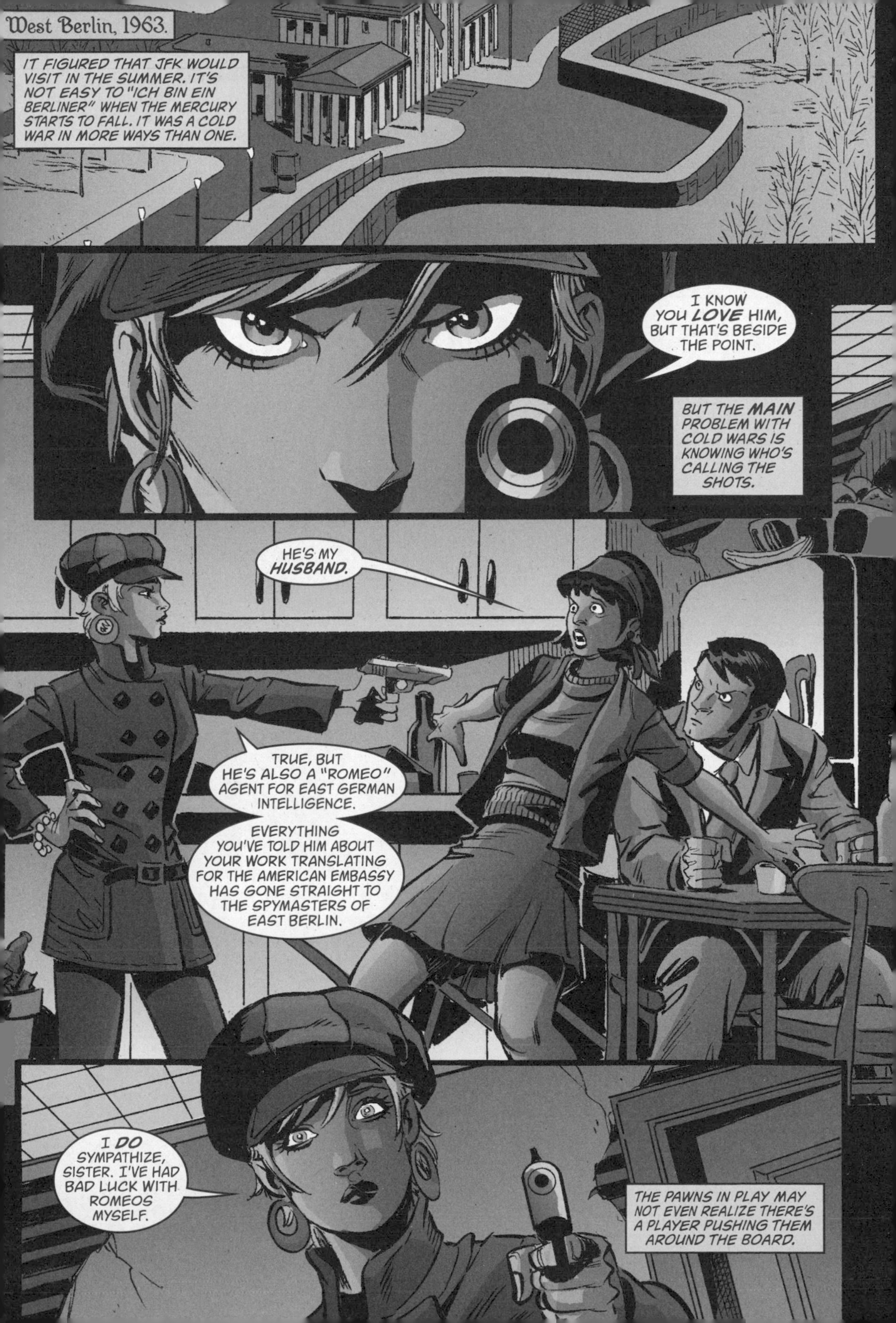
West Berlin, 1963.
IT FIGURED THAT JFK WOULD VISIT IN THE SUMMER. IT'S NOT EASY TO "ICH BIN EIN BERLINER" WHEN THE MERCURY STARTS TO FALL. IT WAS A COLD WAR IN MORE WAYS THAN ONE.
I KNOW YOU LOVE HIM, BUT THAT'S BESIDE THE POINT.
BUT THE MAIN PROBLEM WITH COLD WARS IS KNOWING WHO'S CALLING THE SHOTS.
HE'S MY HUSBAND.
TRUE, BUT HE'S ALSO A "ROMEO" AGENT FOR EAST GERMAN INTELLIGENCE.
EVERYTHING YOU'VE TOLD HIM ABOUT YOUR WORK TRANSLATING FOR THE AMERICAN EMBASSY HAS GONE STRAIGHT TO THE SPYMASTERS OF EAST BERLIN.
I DO SYMPATHIZE, SISTER. I'VE HAD BAD LUCK WITH ROMEOS MYSELF.
THE PAWNS IN PLAY MAY NOT EVEN REALIZE THERE'S A PLAYER PUSHING THEM AROUND THE BOARD.

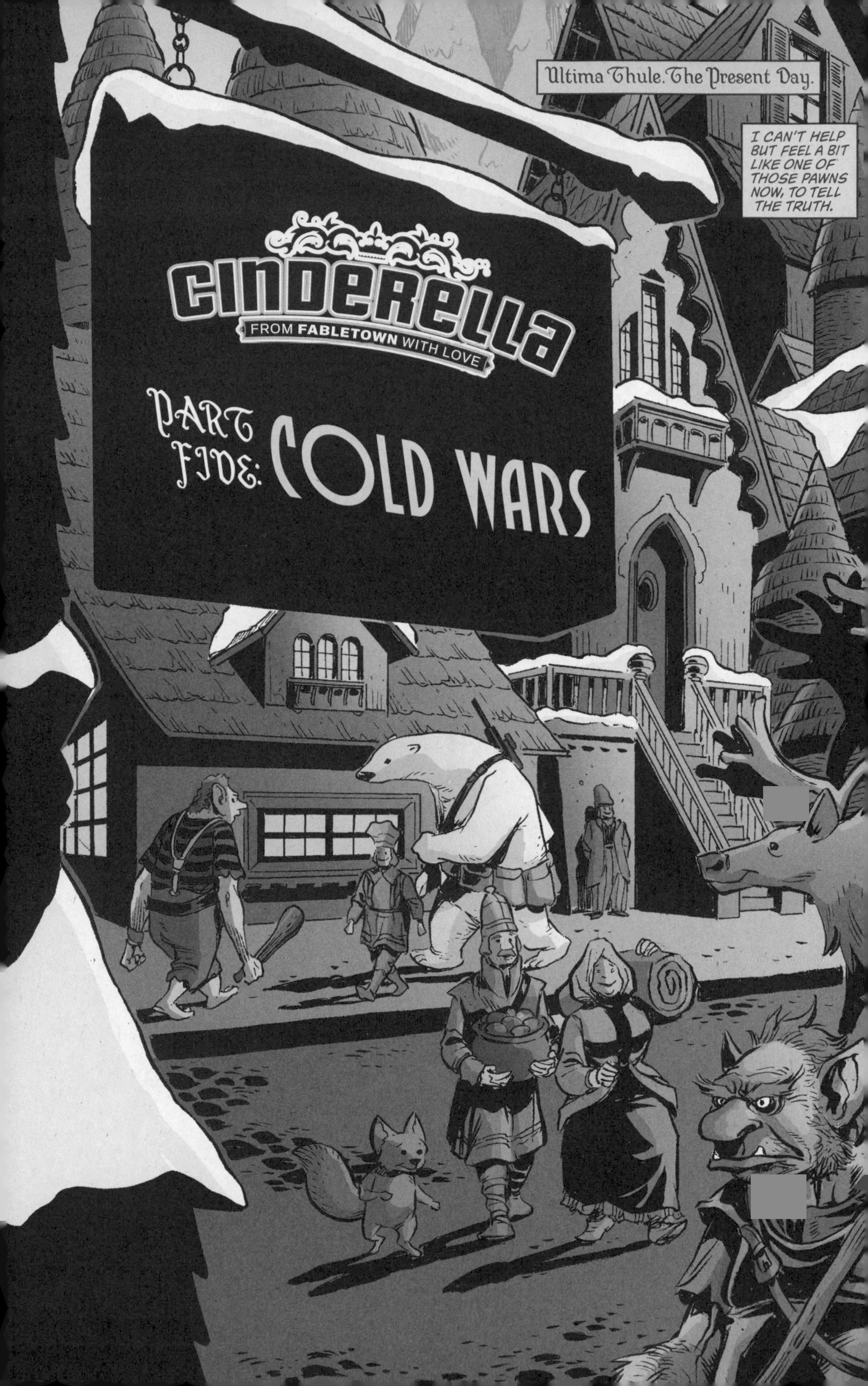
Ultima Thule. The Present Day.
I CAN'T HELP BUT FEEL A BIT LIKE ONE OF THOSE PAWNS NOW, TO TELL THE TRUTH.
CINDERELLA
FROM FABLETOWN WITH LOVE
PART FIVE: COLD WARS

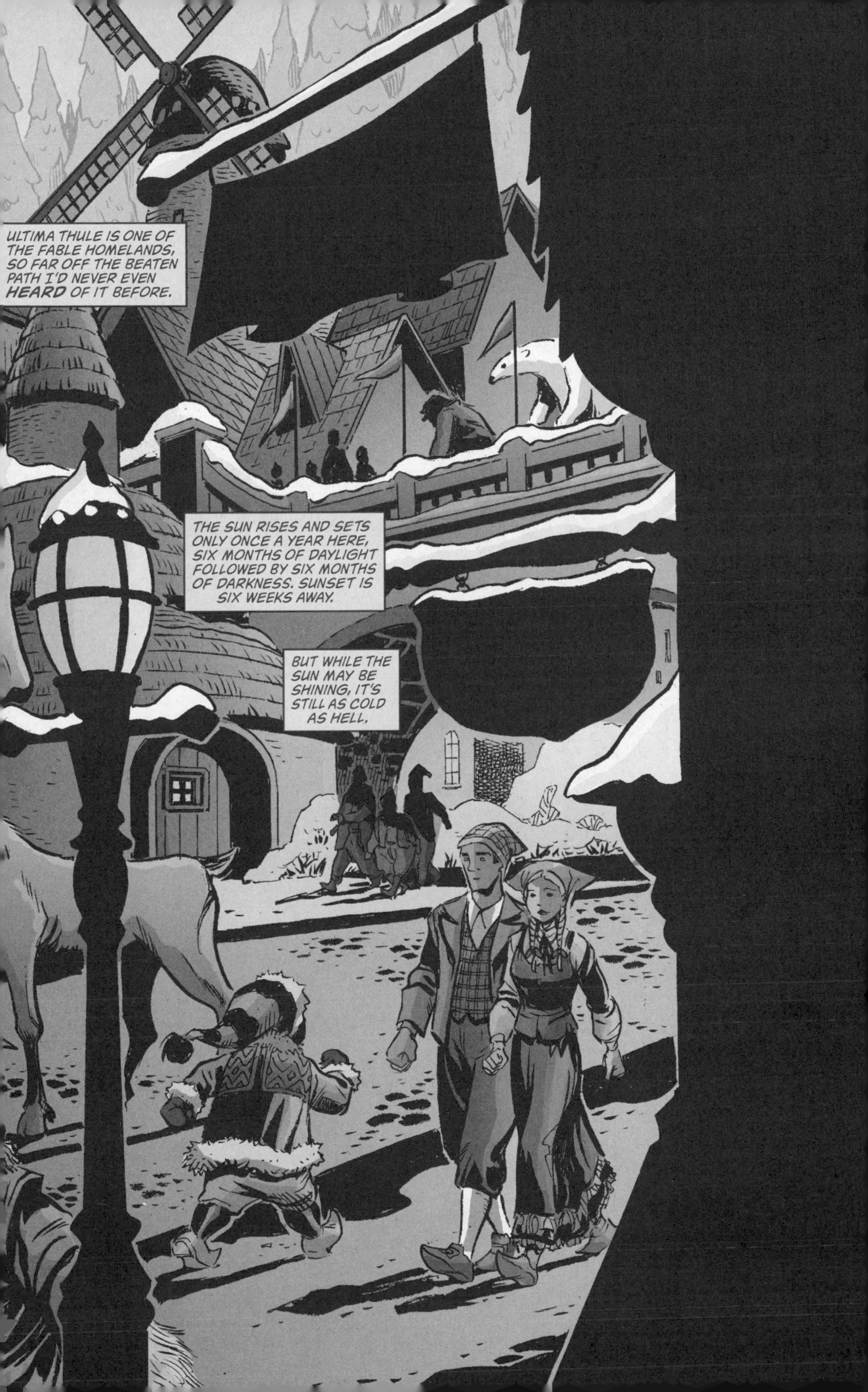
ULTIMA THULE IS ONE OF THE FABLE HOMELANDS, SO FAR OFF THE BEATEN PATH I'D NEVER EVEN **HEARD** OF IT BEFORE.
THE SUN RISES AND SETS ONLY ONCE A YEAR HERE, SIX MONTHS OF DAYLIGHT FOLLOWED BY SIX MONTHS OF DARKNESS. SUNSET IS SIX WEEKS AWAY.
BUT WHILE THE SUN MAY BE SHINING, IT'S STILL AS COLD AS HELL.

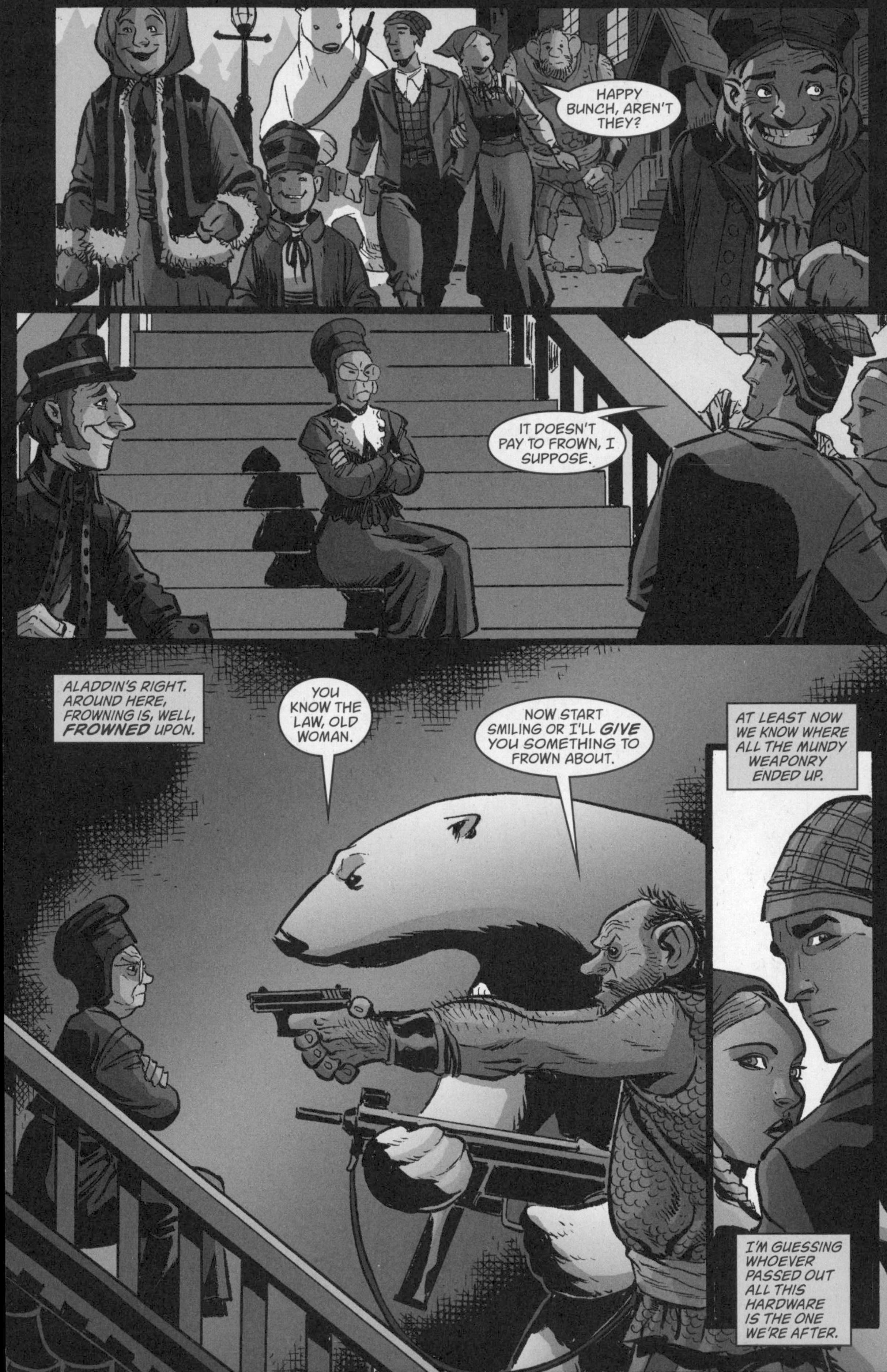
HAPPY BUNCH, AREN'T THEY?
IT DOESN'T PAY TO FROWN, I SUPPOSE.
ALADDIN'S RIGHT. AROUND HERE, FROWNING IS, WELL, ***FROWNED*** UPON.
YOU KNOW THE LAW, OLD WOMAN.
NOW START SMILING OR I'LL ***GIVE*** YOU SOMETHING TO FROWN ABOUT.
AT LEAST NOW WE KNOW WHERE ALL THE MUNDY WEAPONRY ENDED UP.
I'M GUESSING WHOEVER PASSED OUT ALL THIS HARDWARE IS THE ONE WE'RE AFTER.

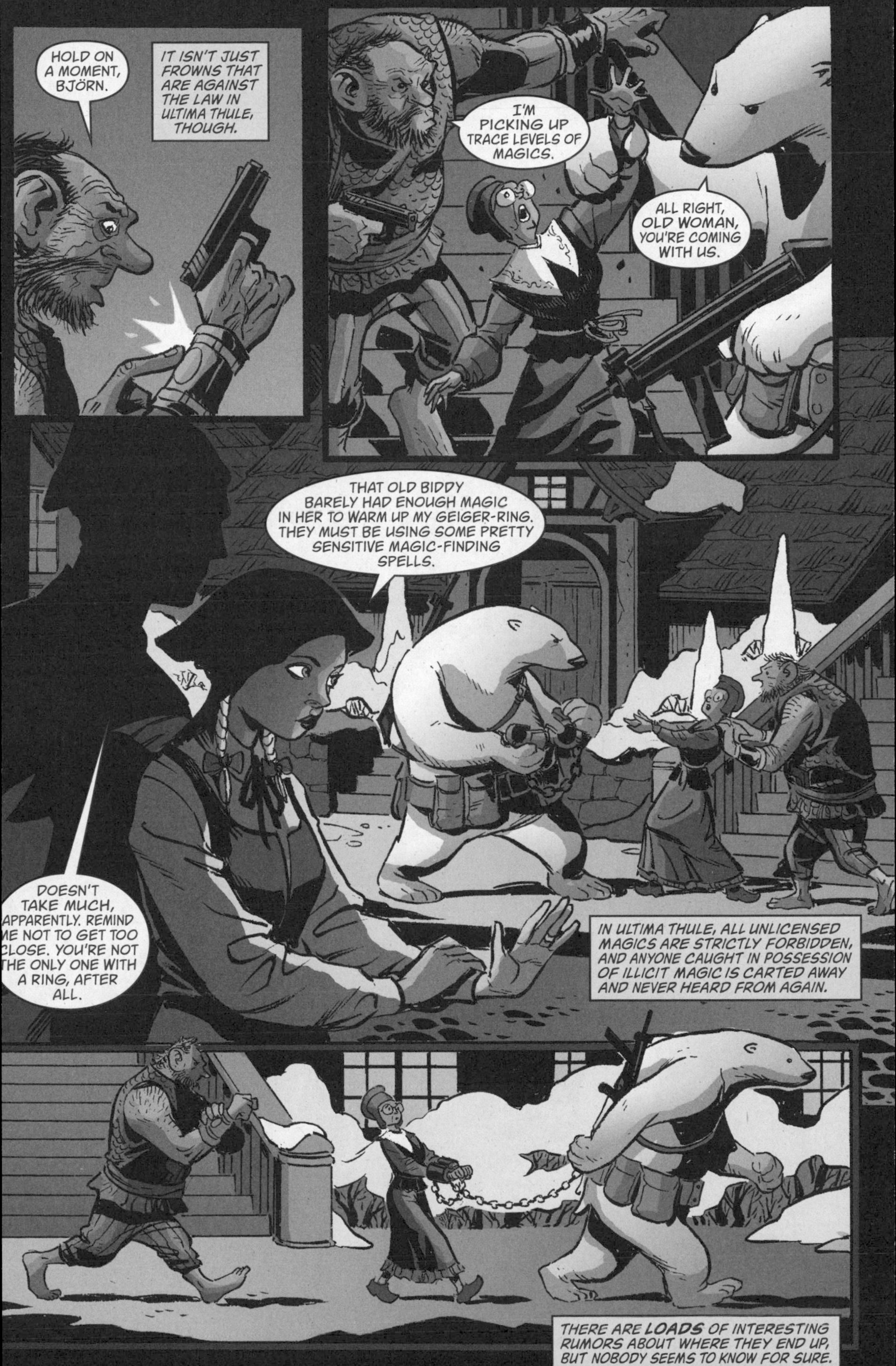

HOLD ON A MOMENT, BJÖRN.
IT ISN'T JUST FROWNS THAT ARE AGAINST THE LAW IN ULTIMA THULE, THOUGH.
I'M PICKING UP TRACE LEVELS OF MAGICS.
ALL RIGHT, OLD WOMAN, YOU'RE COMING WITH US.
THAT OLD BIDDY BARELY HAD ENOUGH MAGIC IN HER TO WARM UP MY GEIGER-RING. THEY MUST BE USING SOME PRETTY SENSITIVE MAGIC-FINDING SPELLS.
DOESN'T TAKE MUCH, APPARENTLY. REMIND ME NOT TO GET TOO CLOSE. YOU'RE NOT THE ONLY ONE WITH A RING, AFTER ALL.
IN ULTIMA THULE, ALL UNLICENSED MAGICS ARE STRICTLY FORBIDDEN, AND ANYONE CAUGHT IN POSSESSION OF ILLICIT MAGIC IS CARTED AWAY AND NEVER HEARD FROM AGAIN.
THERE ARE LOADS OF INTERESTING RUMORS ABOUT WHERE THEY END UP, BUT NOBODY SEEMS TO KNOW FOR SURE.

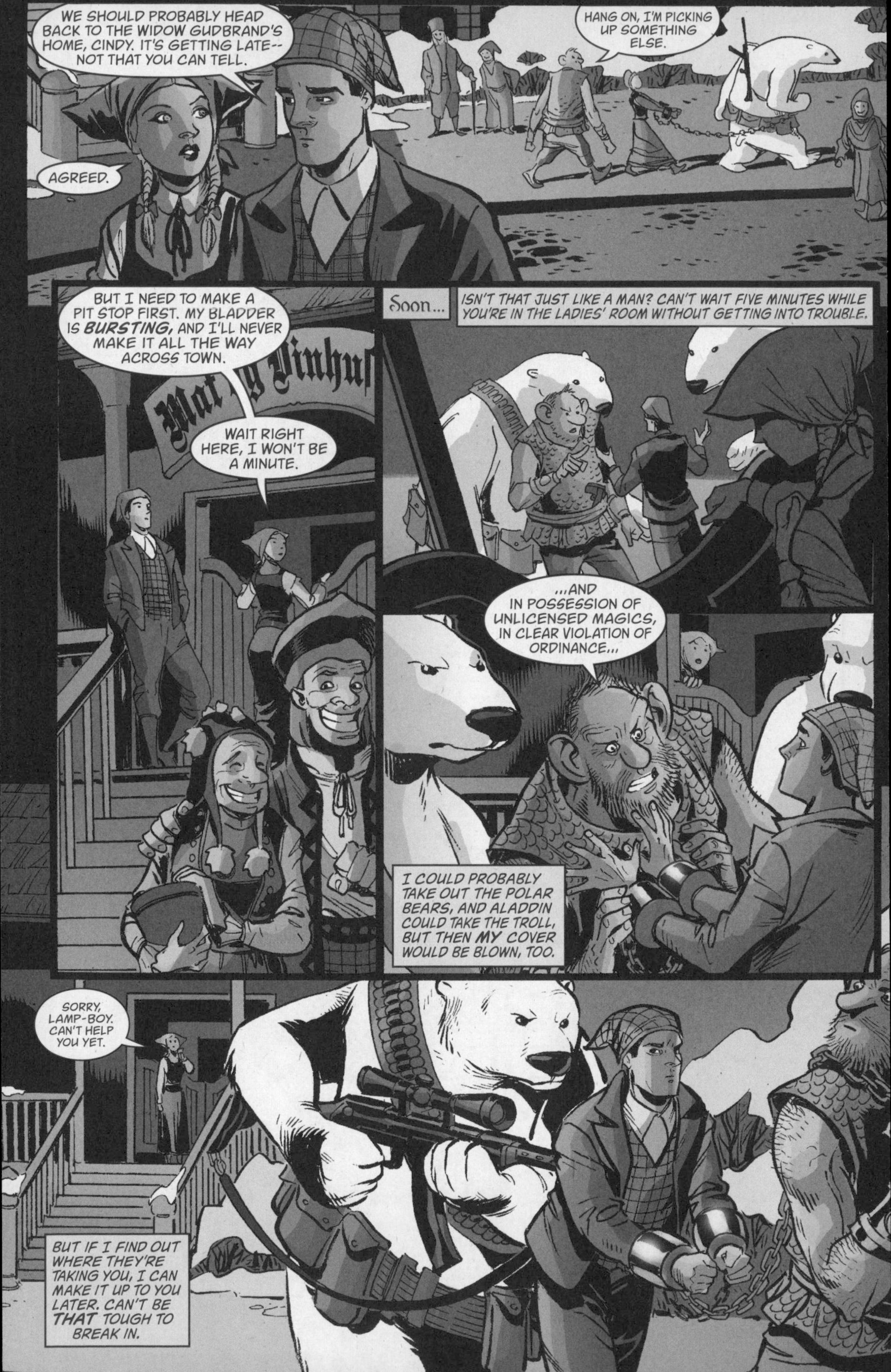
WE SHOULD PROBABLY HEAD BACK TO THE WIDOW GUDBRAND'S HOME, CINDY. IT'S GETTING LATE-- NOT THAT YOU CAN TELL.
AGREED.
HANG ON, I'M PICKING UP SOMETHING ELSE.
BUT I NEED TO MAKE A PIT STOP FIRST. MY BLADDER IS BURSTING, AND I'LL NEVER MAKE IT ALL THE WAY ACROSS TOWN.
WAIT RIGHT HERE, I WON'T BE A MINUTE.
Soon...
ISN'T THAT JUST LIKE A MAN? CAN'T WAIT FIVE MINUTES WHILE YOU'RE IN THE LADIES' ROOM WITHOUT GETTING INTO TROUBLE.
...AND IN POSSESSION OF UNLICENSED MAGICS, IN CLEAR VIOLATION OF ORDINANCE...
I COULD PROBABLY TAKE OUT THE POLAR BEARS, AND ALADDIN COULD TAKE THE TROLL, BUT THEN MY COVER WOULD BE BLOWN, TOO.
SORRY, LAMP-BOY. CAN'T HELP YOU YET.
BUT IF I FIND OUT WHERE THEY'RE TAKING YOU, I CAN MAKE IT UP TO YOU LATER. CAN'T BE THAT TOUGH TO BREAK IN.

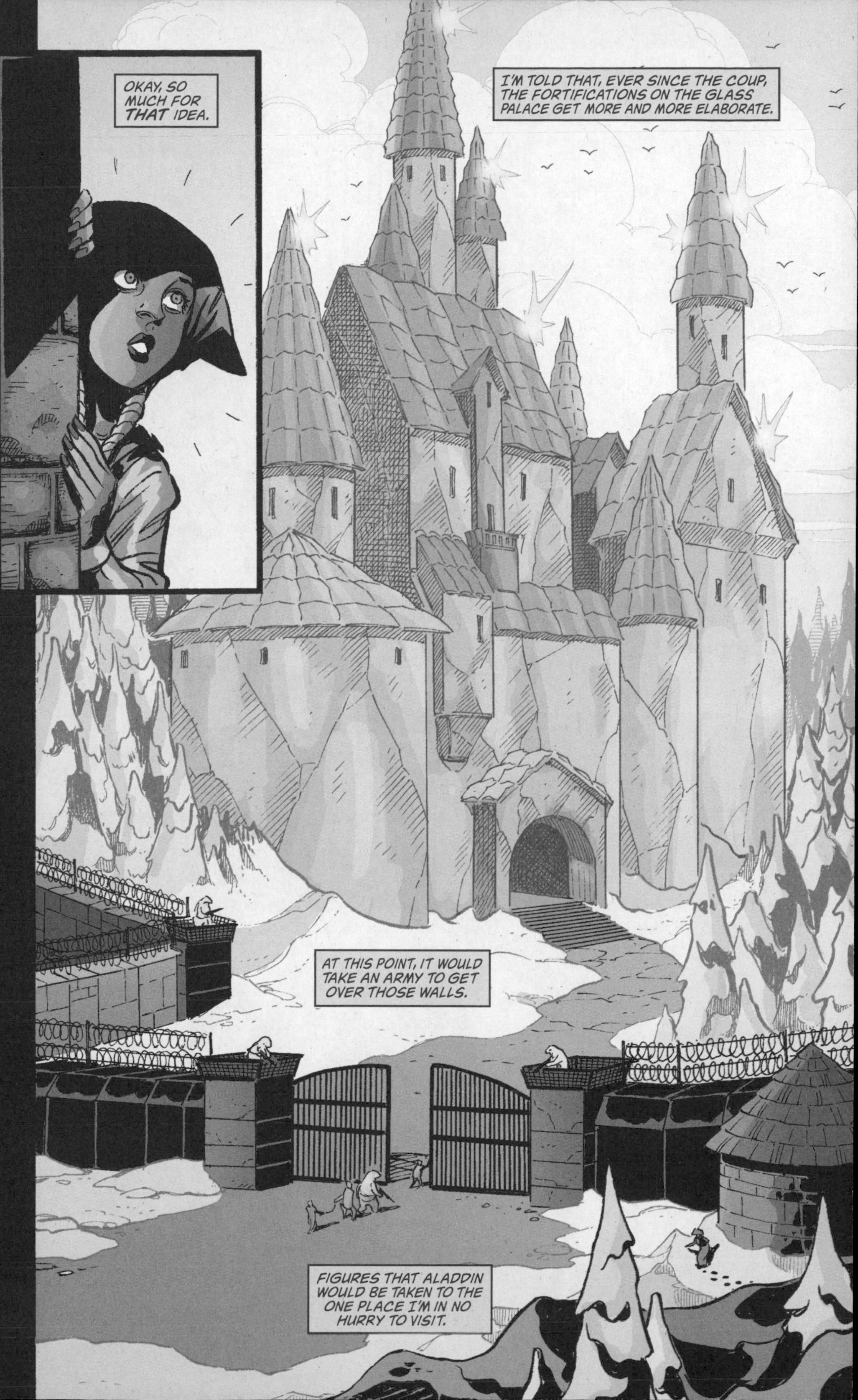
OKAY, SO MUCH FOR THAT IDEA.
I'M TOLD THAT, EVER SINCE THE COUP, THE FORTIFICATIONS ON THE GLASS PALACE GET MORE AND MORE ELABORATE.
AT THIS POINT, IT WOULD TAKE AN ARMY TO GET OVER THOSE WALLS.
FIGURES THAT ALADDIN WOULD BE TAKEN TO THE ONE PLACE I'M IN NO HURRY TO VISIT.

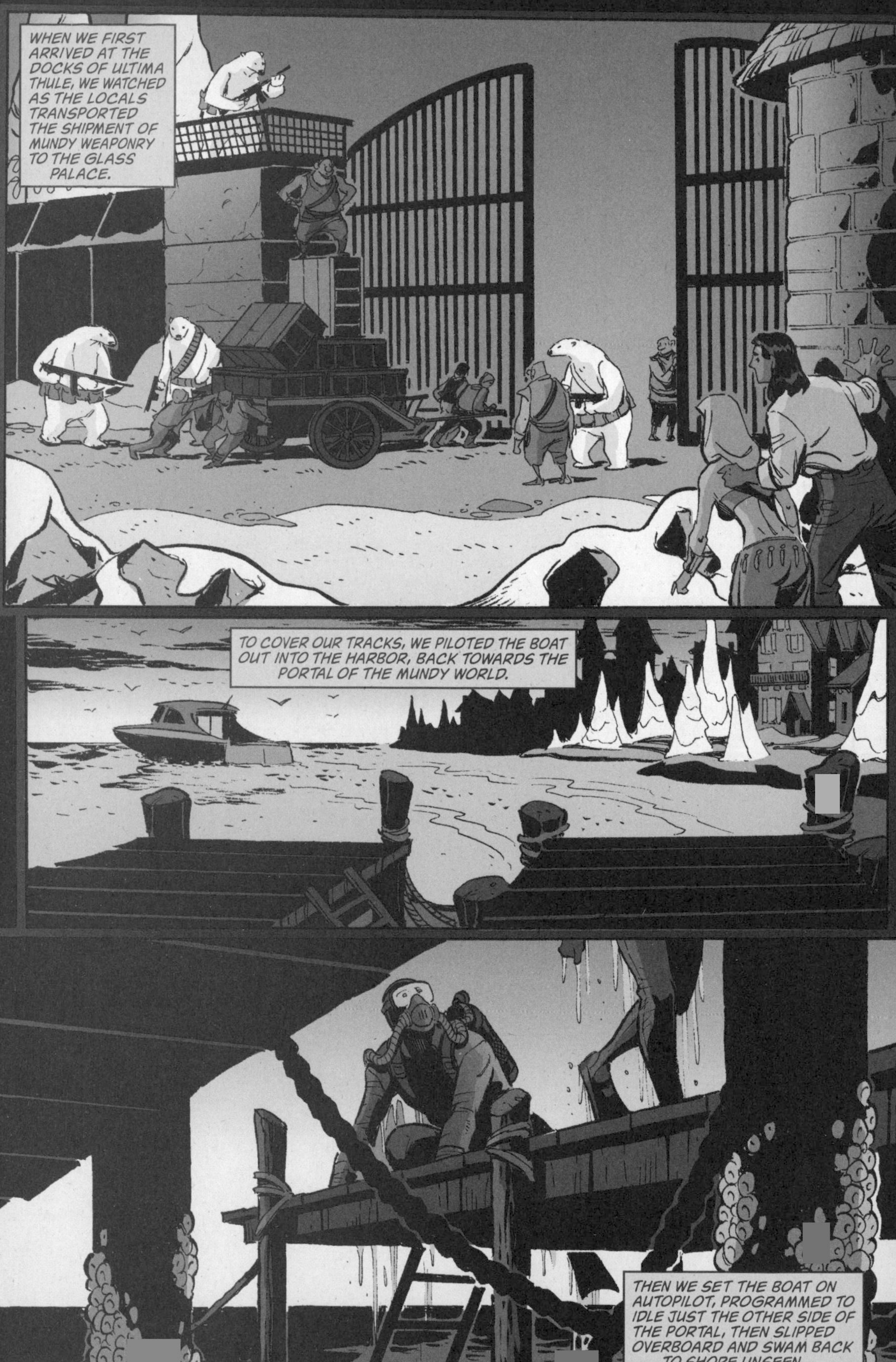
WHEN WE FIRST ARRIVED AT THE DOCKS OF ULTIMA THULE, WE WATCHED AS THE LOCALS TRANSPORTED THE SHIPMENT OF MUNDY WEAPONRY TO THE GLASS PALACE.
TO COVER OUR TRACKS, WE PILOTED THE BOAT OUT INTO THE HARBOR, BACK TOWARDS THE PORTAL OF THE MUNDY WORLD.
THEN WE SET THE BOAT ON AUTOPILOT, PROGRAMMED TO IDLE JUST THE OTHER SIDE OF THE PORTAL, THEN SLIPPED OVERBOARD AND SWAM BACK TO SHORE UNSEEN.

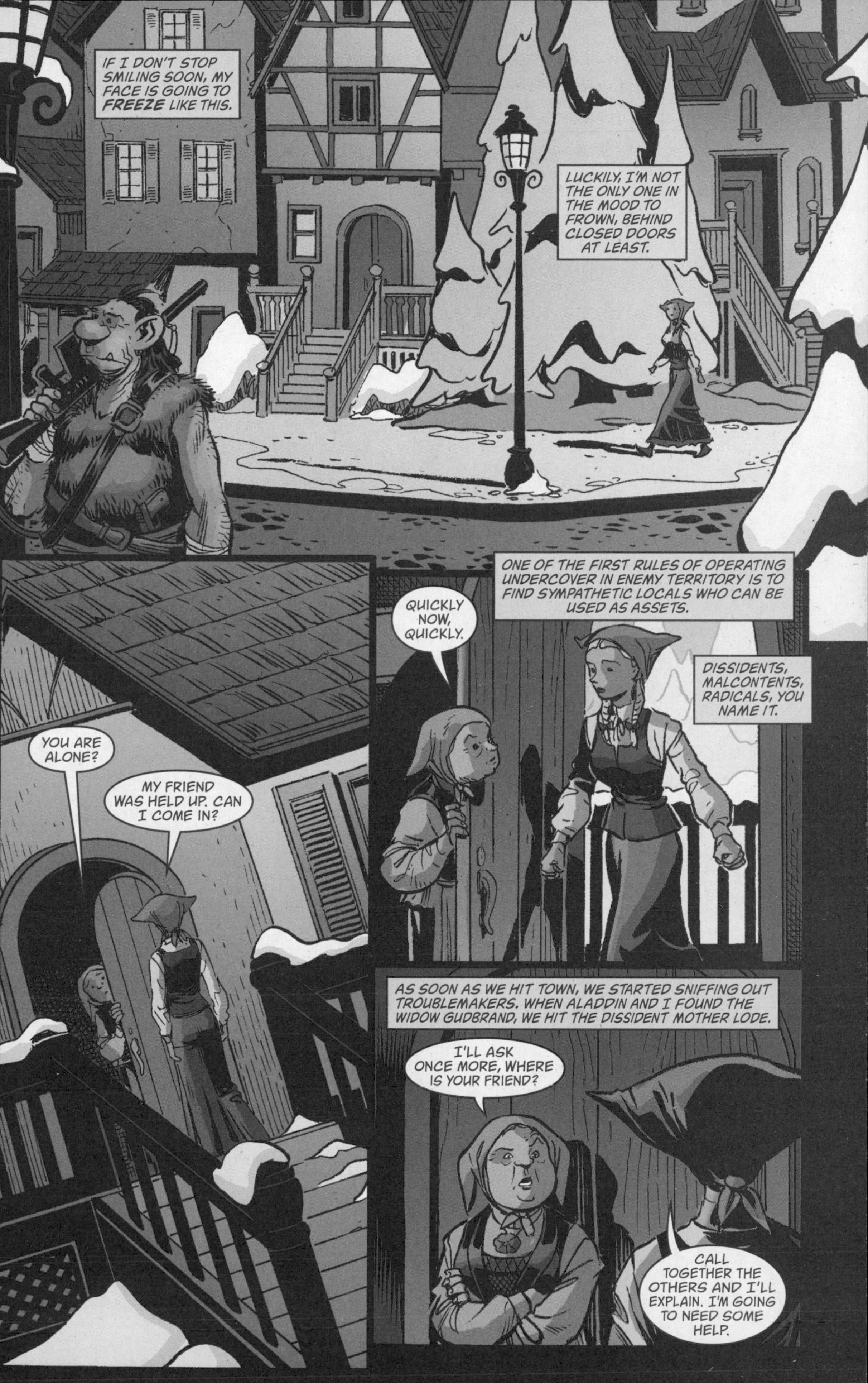
IF I DON'T STOP SMILING SOON, MY FACE IS GOING TO **FREEZE** LIKE THIS.
LUCKILY, I'M NOT THE ONLY ONE IN THE MOOD TO FROWN, BEHIND CLOSED DOORS AT LEAST.
YOU ARE ALONE?
MY FRIEND WAS HELD UP. CAN I COME IN?
ONE OF THE FIRST RULES OF OPERATING UNDERCOVER IN ENEMY TERRITORY IS TO FIND SYMPATHETIC LOCALS WHO CAN BE USED AS ASSETS.
QUICKLY NOW, QUICKLY.
DISSIDENTS, MALCONTENTS, RADICALS, YOU NAME IT.
AS SOON AS WE HIT TOWN, WE STARTED SNIFFING OUT TROUBLEMAKERS. WHEN ALADDIN AND I FOUND THE WIDOW GUDBRAND, WE HIT THE DISSIDENT MOTHER LODE.
I'LL ASK ONCE MORE, WHERE IS YOUR FRIEND?
CALL TOGETHER THE OTHERS AND I'LL EXPLAIN. I'M GOING TO NEED SOME HELP.

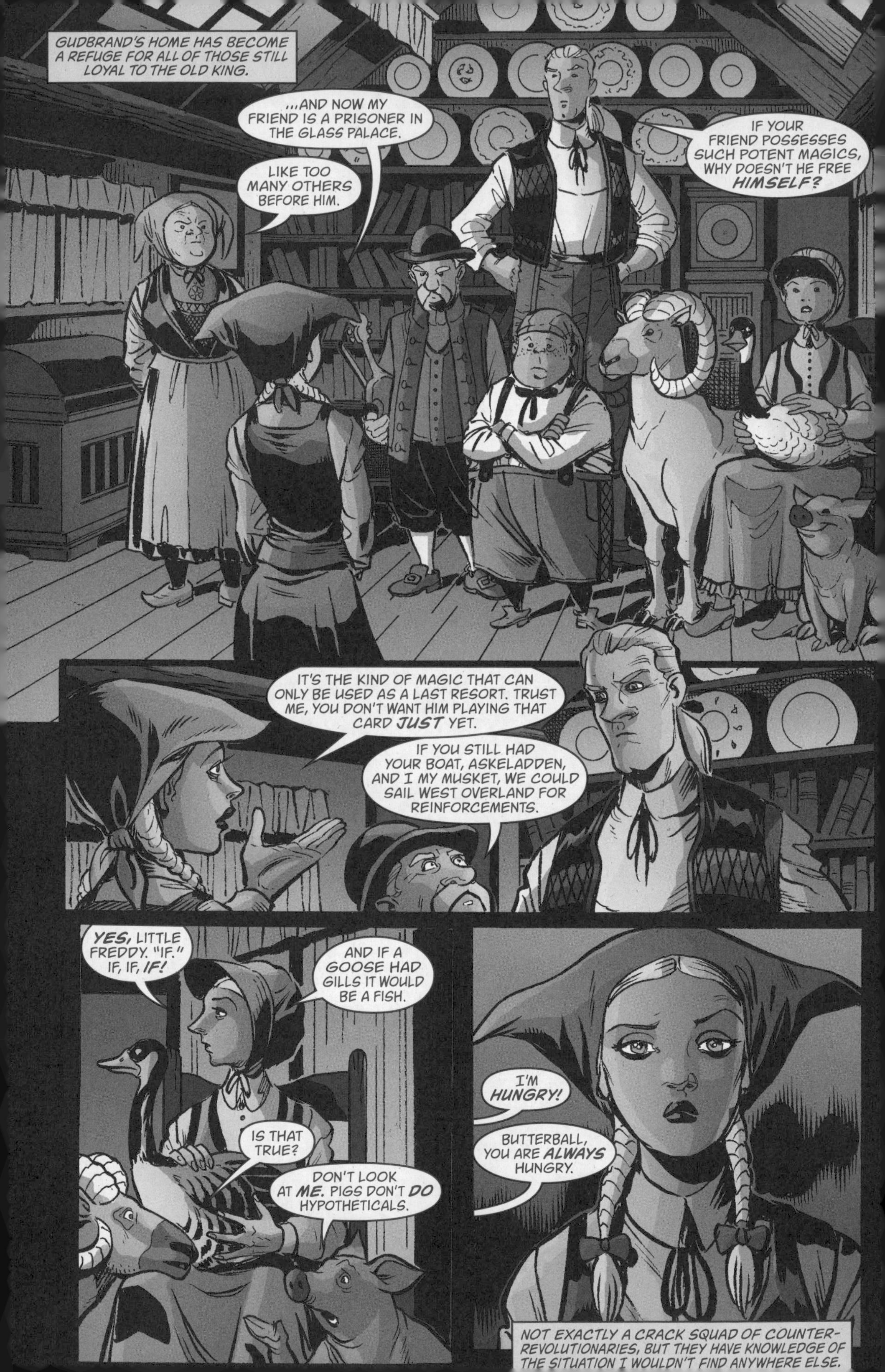
GUDBRAND'S HOME HAS BECOME A REFUGE FOR ALL OF THOSE STILL LOYAL TO THE OLD KING.
...AND NOW MY FRIEND IS A PRISONER IN THE GLASS PALACE.
LIKE TOO MANY OTHERS BEFORE HIM.
IF YOUR FRIEND POSSESSES SUCH POTENT MAGICS, WHY DOESN'T HE FREE HIMSELF?
IT'S THE KIND OF MAGIC THAT CAN ONLY BE USED AS A LAST RESORT. TRUST ME, YOU DON'T WANT HIM PLAYING THAT CARD JUST YET.
IF YOU STILL HAD YOUR BOAT, ASKELADDEN, AND I MY MUSKET, WE COULD SAIL WEST OVERLAND FOR REINFORCEMENTS.
YES, LITTLE FREDDY. "IF." IF, IF, IF!
AND IF A GOOSE HAD GILLS IT WOULD BE A FISH.
IS THAT TRUE?
DON'T LOOK AT ME. PIGS DON'T DO HYPOTHETICALS.
I'M HUNGRY!
BUTTERBALL, YOU ARE ALWAYS HUNGRY.
NOT EXACTLY A CRACK SQUAD OF COUNTER-REVOLUTIONARIES, BUT THEY HAVE KNOWLEDGE OF THE SITUATION I WOULDN'T FIND ANYWHERE ELSE.

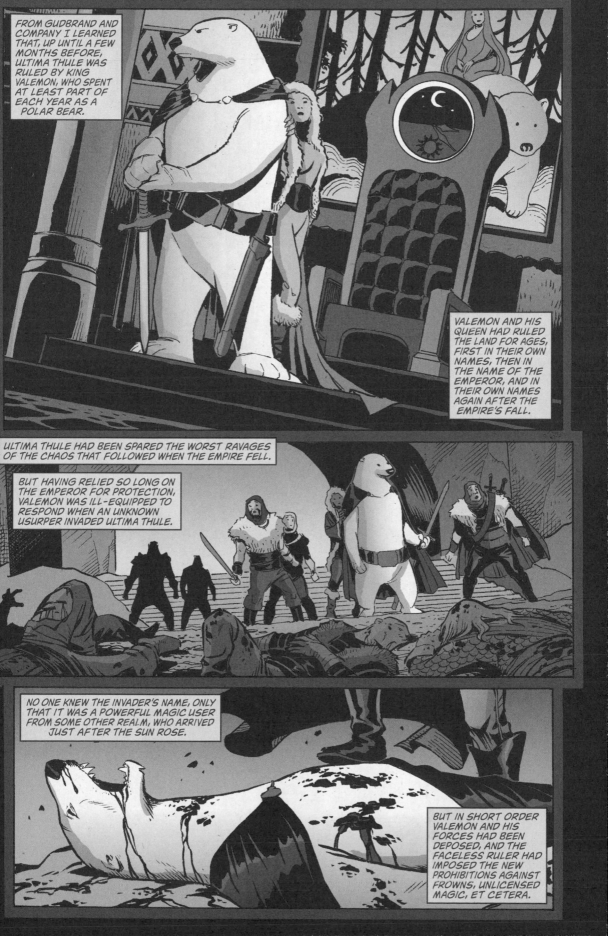

FROM GUDBRAND AND COMPANY I LEARNED THAT, UP UNTIL A FEW MONTHS BEFORE, ULTIMA THULE WAS RULED BY KING VALEMON, WHO SPENT AT LEAST PART OF EACH YEAR AS A POLAR BEAR.

VALEMON AND HIS QUEEN HAD RULED THE LAND FOR AGES, FIRST IN THEIR OWN NAMES, THEN IN THE NAME OF THE EMPEROR, AND IN THEIR OWN NAMES AGAIN AFTER THE EMPIRE'S FALL.

ULTIMA THULE HAD BEEN SPARED THE WORST RAVAGES OF THE CHAOS THAT FOLLOWED WHEN THE EMPIRE FELL.

BUT HAVING RELIED SO LONG ON THE EMPEROR FOR PROTECTION, VALEMON WAS ILL-EQUIPPED TO RESPOND WHEN AN UNKNOWN USURPER INVADED ULTIMA THULE.

NO ONE KNEW THE INVADER'S NAME, ONLY THAT IT WAS A POWERFUL MAGIC USER FROM SOME OTHER REALM, WHO ARRIVED JUST AFTER THE SUN ROSE.

BUT IN SHORT ORDER VALEMON AND HIS FORCES HAD BEEN DEPOSED, AND THE FACELESS RULER HAD IMPOSED THE NEW PROHIBITIONS AGAINST FROWNS, UNLICENSED MAGIC, ET CETERA.

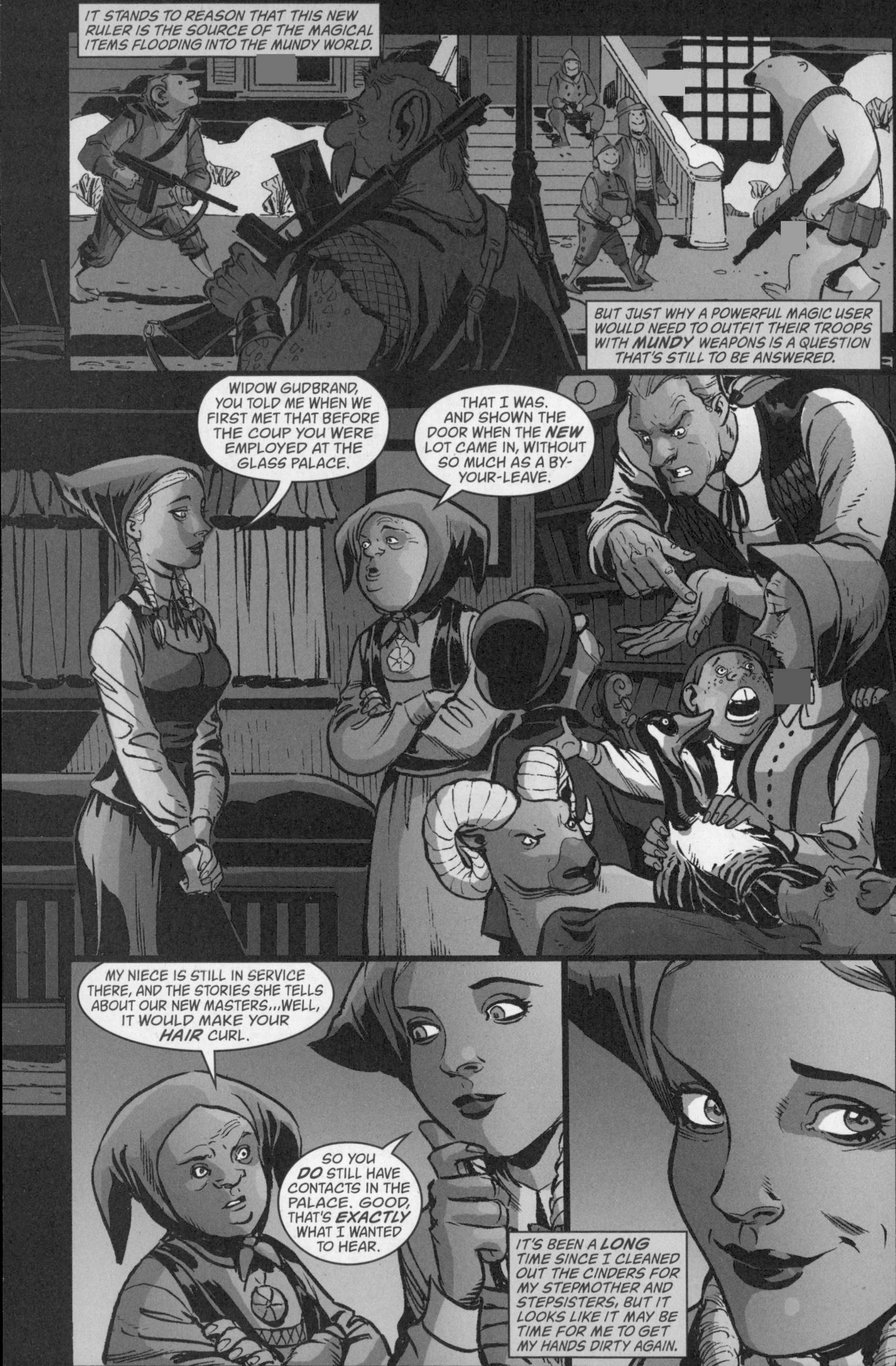
IT STANDS TO REASON THAT THIS NEW RULER IS THE SOURCE OF THE MAGICAL ITEMS FLOODING INTO THE MUNDY WORLD.
BUT JUST WHY A POWERFUL MAGIC USER WOULD NEED TO OUTFIT THEIR TROOPS WITH MUNDY WEAPONS IS A QUESTION THAT'S STILL TO BE ANSWERED.
WIDOW GUDBRAND, YOU TOLD ME WHEN WE FIRST MET THAT BEFORE THE COUP YOU WERE EMPLOYED AT THE GLASS PALACE.
THAT I WAS. AND SHOWN THE DOOR WHEN THE NEW LOT CAME IN, WITHOUT SO MUCH AS A BY-YOUR-LEAVE.
MY NIECE IS STILL IN SERVICE THERE, AND THE STORIES SHE TELLS ABOUT OUR NEW MASTERS...WELL, IT WOULD MAKE YOUR HAIR CURL.
SO YOU DO STILL HAVE CONTACTS IN THE PALACE. GOOD, THAT'S EXACTLY WHAT I WANTED TO HEAR.
IT'S BEEN A LONG TIME SINCE I CLEANED OUT THE CINDERS FOR MY STEPMOTHER AND STEPSISTERS, BUT IT LOOKS LIKE IT MAY BE TIME FOR ME TO GET MY HANDS DIRTY AGAIN.

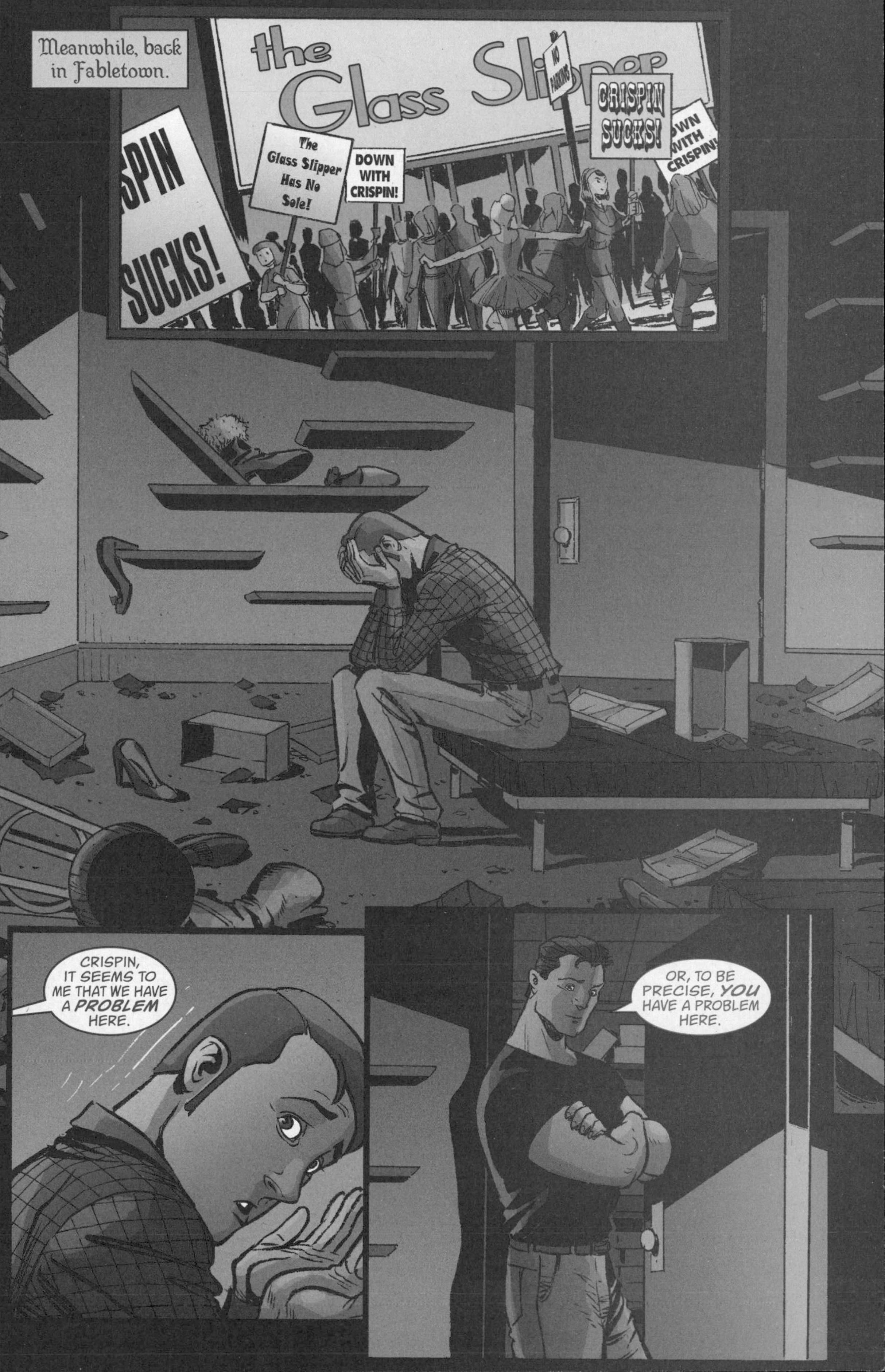

Meanwhile, back in Fabletown.
the Glass Slipper
NO PARKING
CRISPIN SUCKS!
The Glass Slipper Has No Sole!
DOWN WITH CRISPIN!
SPIN SUCKS!
CRISPIN, IT SEEMS TO ME THAT WE HAVE A *PROBLEM* HERE.
OR, TO BE PRECISE, *YOU* HAVE A PROBLEM HERE.

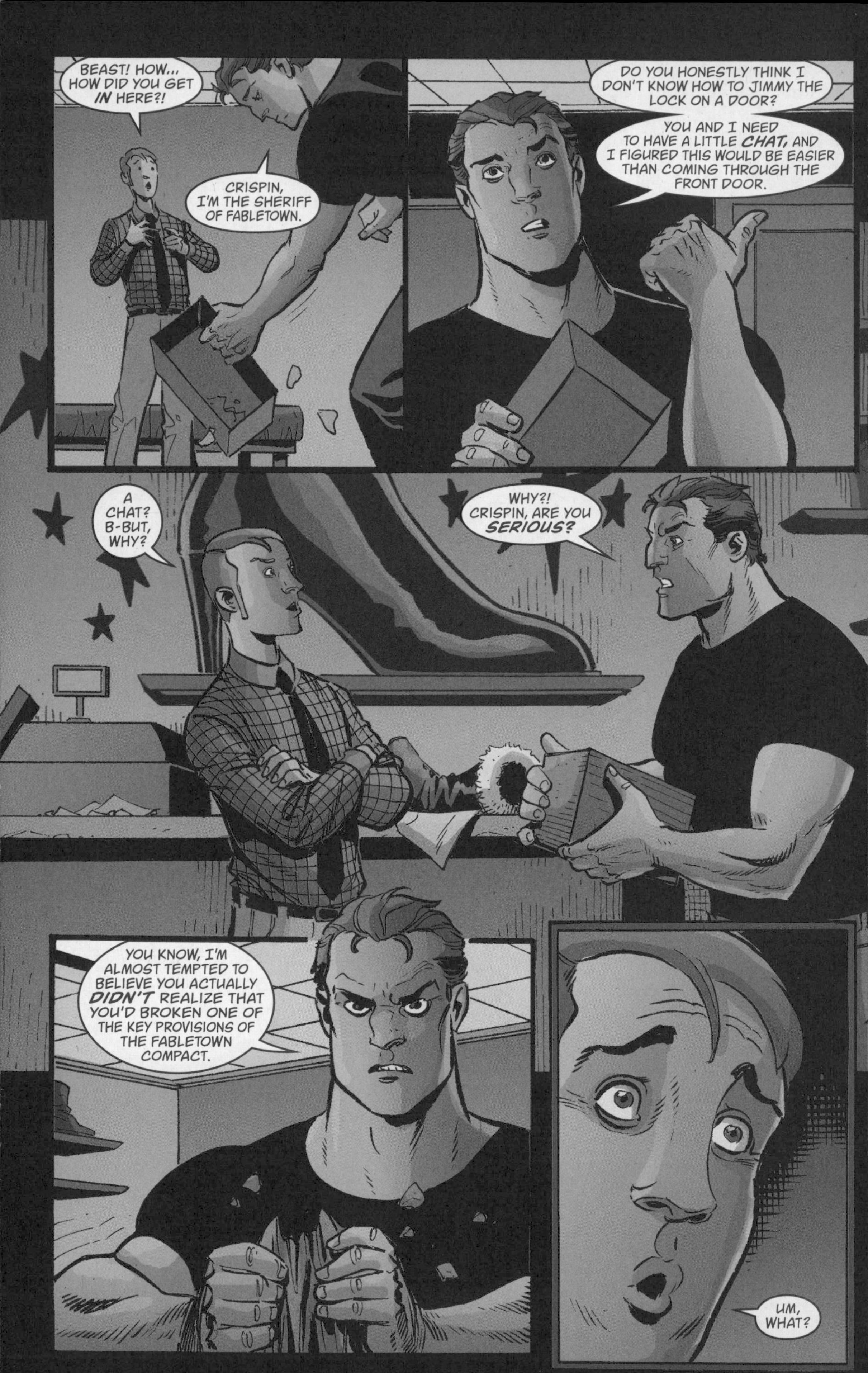
BEAST! HOW... HOW DID YOU GET IN HERE?!
CRISPIN, I'M THE SHERIFF OF FABLETOWN.
DO YOU HONESTLY THINK I DON'T KNOW HOW TO JIMMY THE LOCK ON A DOOR?
YOU AND I NEED TO HAVE A LITTLE CHAT, AND I FIGURED THIS WOULD BE EASIER THAN COMING THROUGH THE FRONT DOOR.
A CHAT? B-BUT, WHY?
WHY?! CRISPIN, ARE YOU SERIOUS?
YOU KNOW, I'M ALMOST TEMPTED TO BELIEVE YOU ACTUALLY DIDN'T REALIZE THAT YOU'D BROKEN ONE OF THE KEY PROVISIONS OF THE FABLETOWN COMPACT.
UM, WHAT?

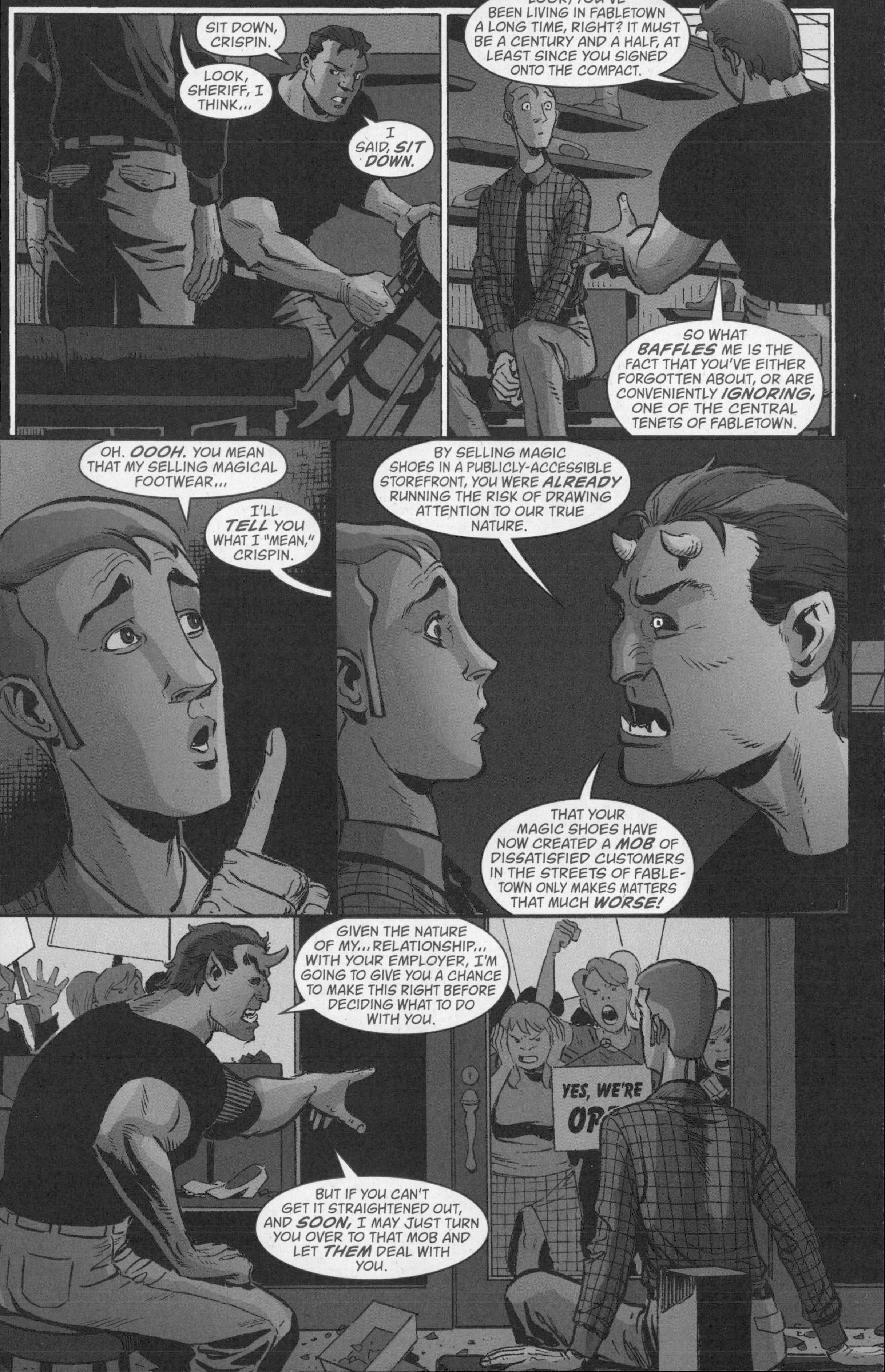
SIT DOWN, CRISPIN.
LOOK, SHERIFF, I THINK...
I SAID, SIT DOWN.
LOOK, YOU'VE BEEN LIVING IN FABLETOWN A LONG TIME, RIGHT? IT MUST BE A CENTURY AND A HALF, AT LEAST SINCE YOU SIGNED ONTO THE COMPACT.
SO WHAT BAFFLES ME IS THE FACT THAT YOU'VE EITHER FORGOTTEN ABOUT, OR ARE CONVENIENTLY IGNORING, ONE OF THE CENTRAL TENETS OF FABLETOWN.
OH. OOOH. YOU MEAN THAT MY SELLING MAGICAL FOOTWEAR...
I'LL TELL YOU WHAT I "MEAN," CRISPIN.
BY SELLING MAGIC SHOES IN A PUBLICLY-ACCESSIBLE STOREFRONT, YOU WERE ALREADY RUNNING THE RISK OF DRAWING ATTENTION TO OUR TRUE NATURE.
THAT YOUR MAGIC SHOES HAVE NOW CREATED A MOB OF DISSATISFIED CUSTOMERS IN THE STREETS OF FABLE-TOWN ONLY MAKES MATTERS THAT MUCH WORSE!
GIVEN THE NATURE OF MY...RELATIONSHIP... WITH YOUR EMPLOYER, I'M GOING TO GIVE YOU A CHANCE TO MAKE THIS RIGHT BEFORE DECIDING WHAT TO DO WITH YOU.
YES, WE'RE OP
BUT IF YOU CAN'T GET IT STRAIGHTENED OUT, AND SOON, I MAY JUST TURN YOU OVER TO THAT MOB AND LET THEM DEAL WITH YOU.

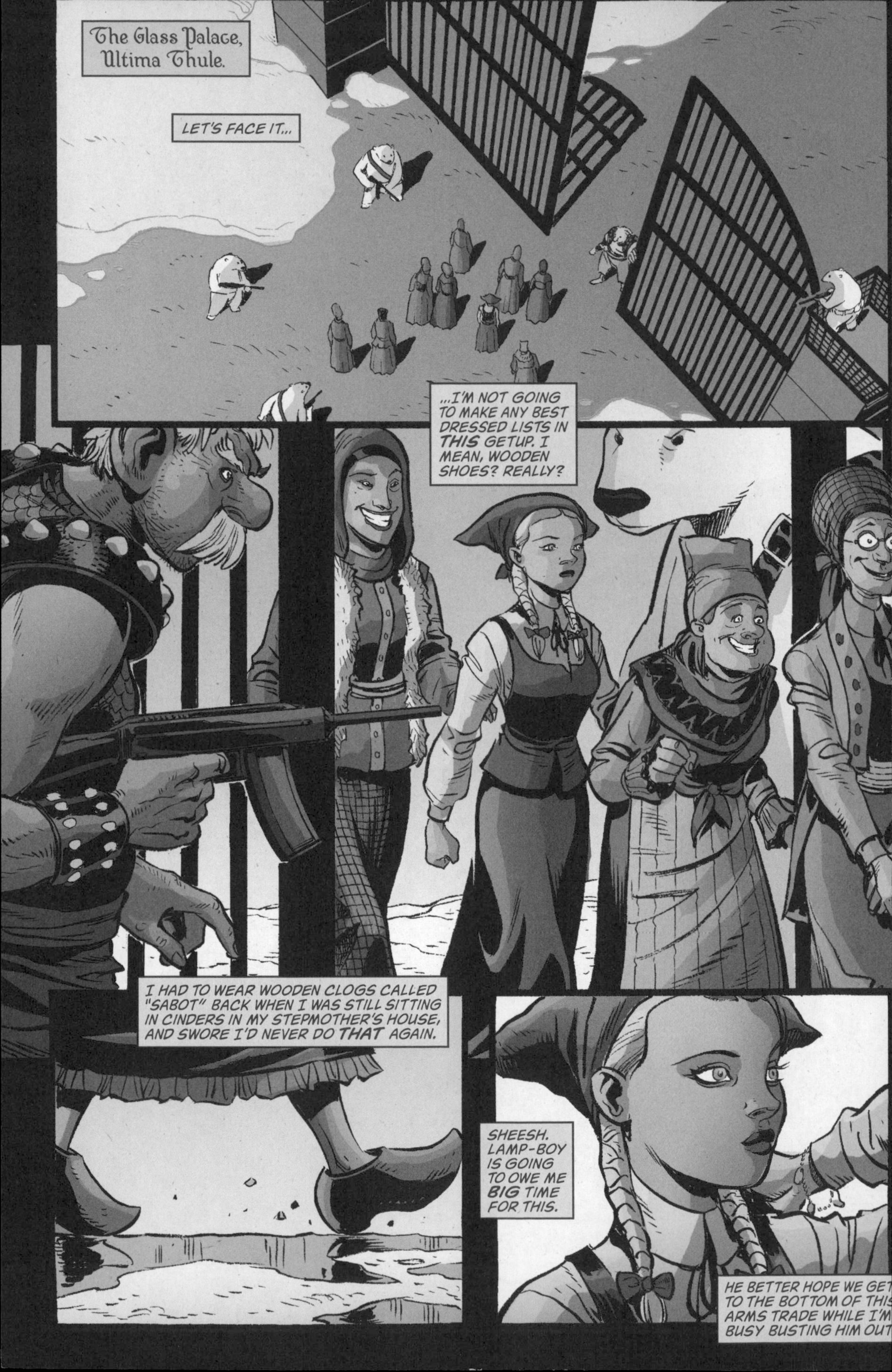
The Glass Palace, Ultima Thule.
LET'S FACE IT...
...I'M NOT GOING TO MAKE ANY BEST DRESSED LISTS IN THIS GETUP. I MEAN, WOODEN SHOES? REALLY?
I HAD TO WEAR WOODEN CLOGS CALLED "SABOT" BACK WHEN I WAS STILL SITTING IN CINDERS IN MY STEPMOTHER'S HOUSE, AND SWORE I'D NEVER DO THAT AGAIN.
SHEESH. LAMP-BOY IS GOING TO OWE ME BIG TIME FOR THIS.
HE BETTER HOPE WE GET TO THE BOTTOM OF THIS ARMS TRADE WHILE I'M BUSY BUSTING HIM OUT

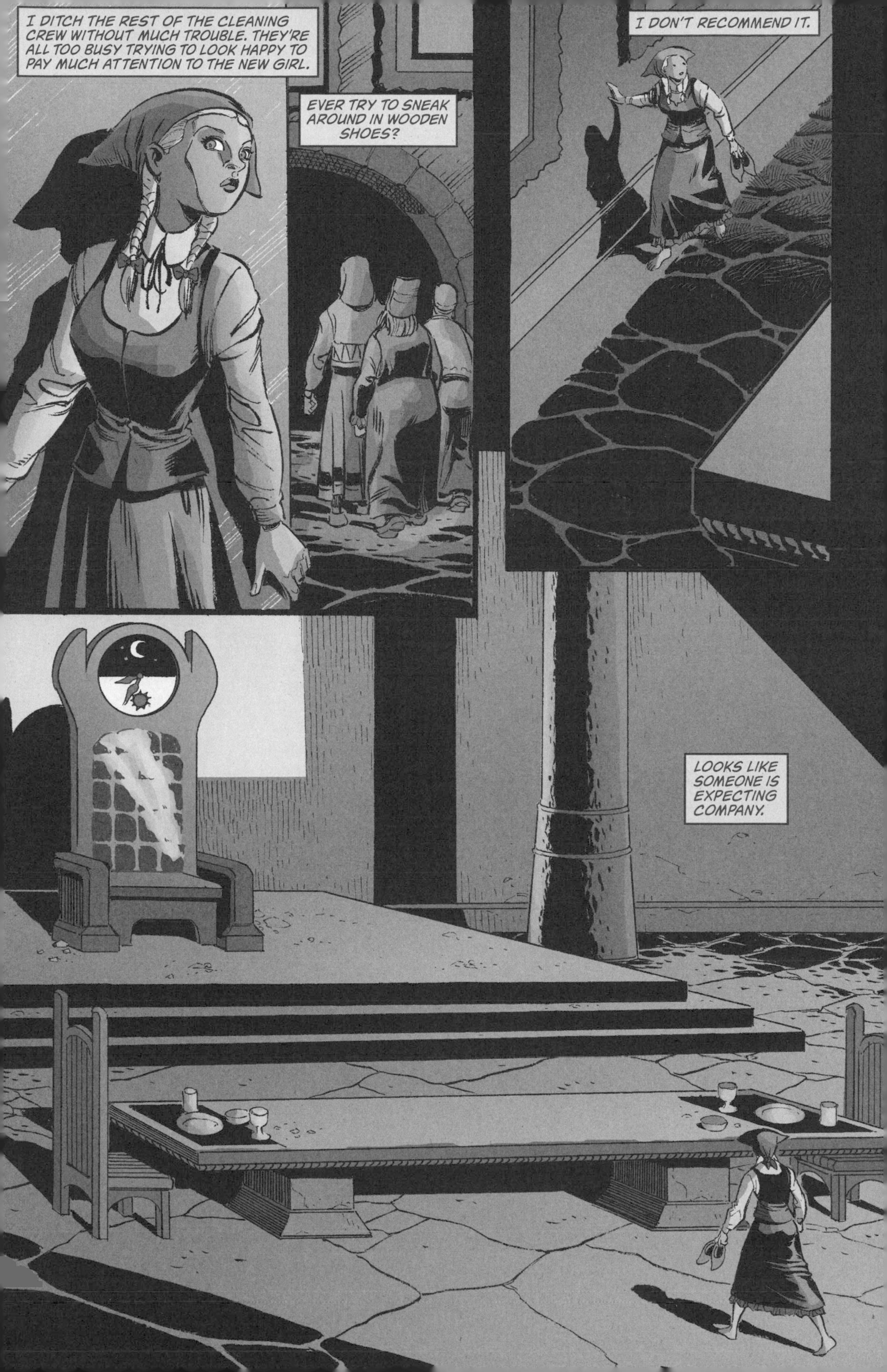
I DITCH THE REST OF THE CLEANING CREW WITHOUT MUCH TROUBLE. THEY'RE ALL TOO BUSY TRYING TO LOOK HAPPY TO PAY MUCH ATTENTION TO THE NEW GIRL.
EVER TRY TO SNEAK AROUND IN WOODEN SHOES?
I DON'T RECOMMEND IT.
LOOKS LIKE SOMEONE IS EXPECTING COMPANY.

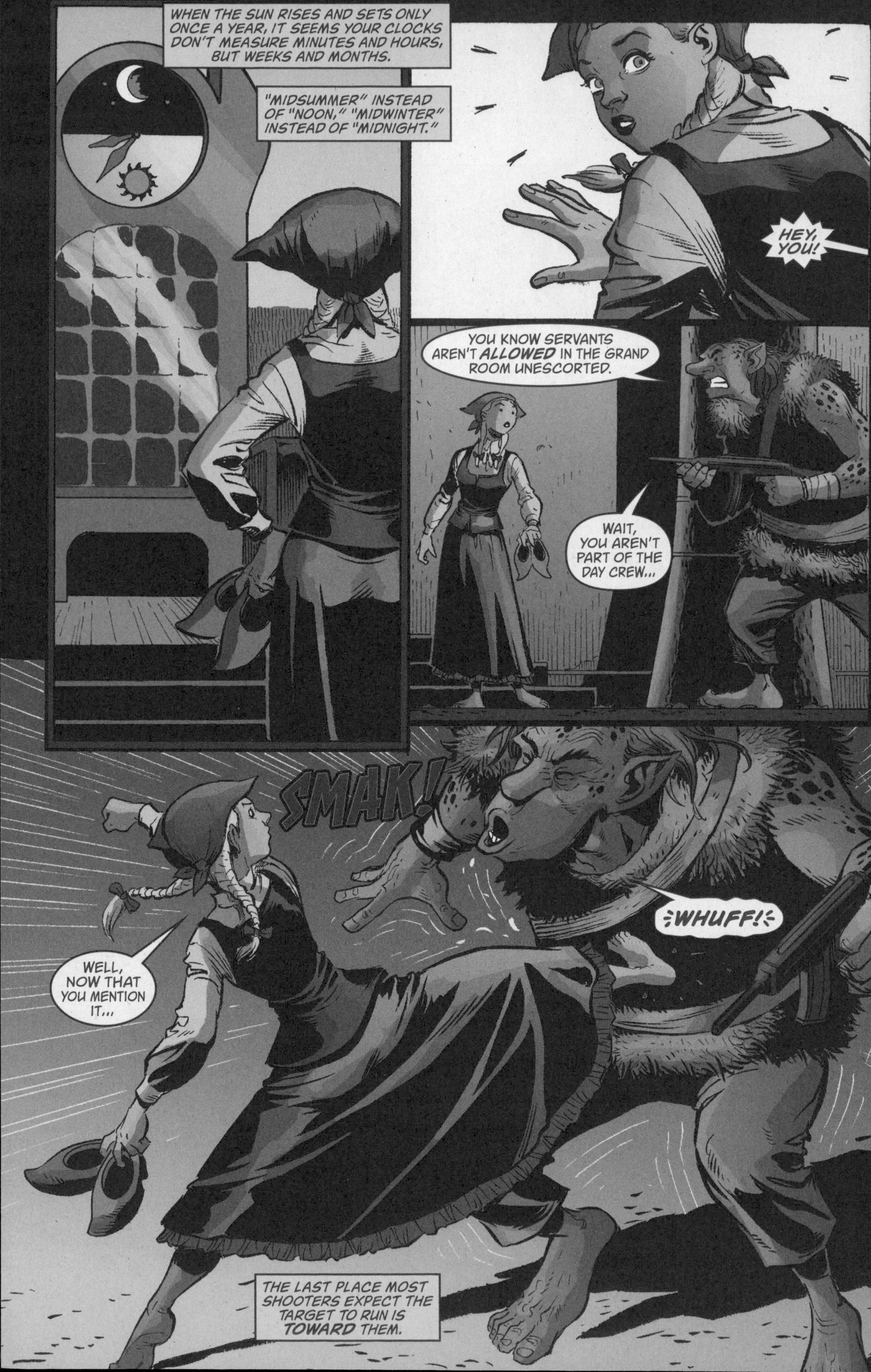

WHEN THE SUN RISES AND SETS ONLY ONCE A YEAR, IT SEEMS YOUR CLOCKS DON'T MEASURE MINUTES AND HOURS, BUT WEEKS AND MONTHS.
"MIDSUMMER" INSTEAD OF "NOON," "MIDWINTER" INSTEAD OF "MIDNIGHT."
HEY, YOU!
YOU KNOW SERVANTS AREN'T ALLOWED IN THE GRAND ROOM UNESCORTED.
WAIT, YOU AREN'T PART OF THE DAY CREW...
SMAK!
WHUFF!
WELL, NOW THAT YOU MENTION IT...
THE LAST PLACE MOST SHOOTERS EXPECT THE TARGET TO RUN IS TOWARD THEM.

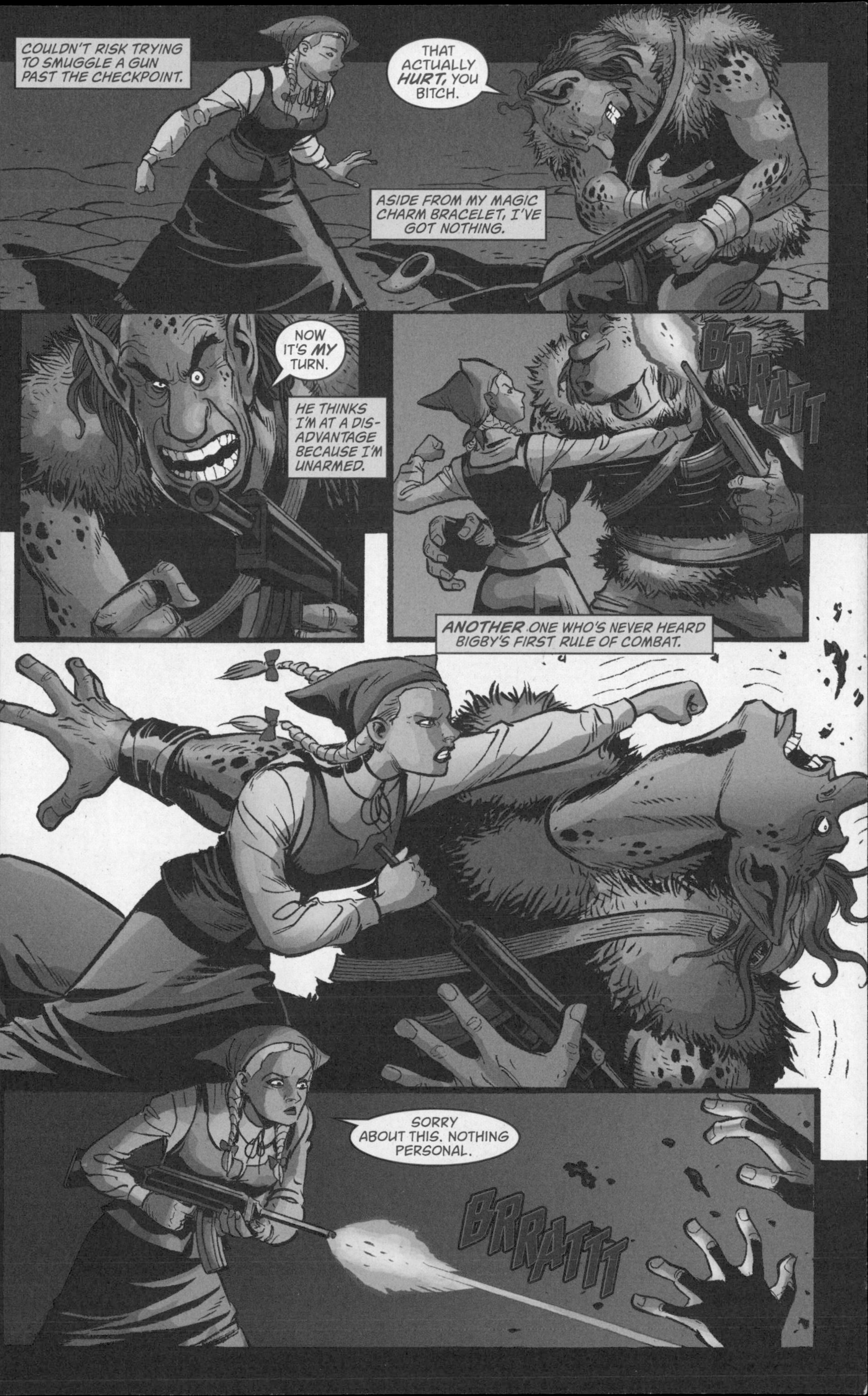
COULDN'T RISK TRYING TO SMUGGLE A GUN PAST THE CHECKPOINT.
THAT ACTUALLY HURT, YOU BITCH.
ASIDE FROM MY MAGIC CHARM BRACELET, I'VE GOT NOTHING.
NOW IT'S MY TURN.
HE THINKS I'M AT A DIS-ADVANTAGE BECAUSE I'M UNARMED.
BRRATT
ANOTHER ONE WHO'S NEVER HEARD BIGBY'S FIRST RULE OF COMBAT.
SORRY ABOUT THIS. NOTHING PERSONAL.
BRRATTT

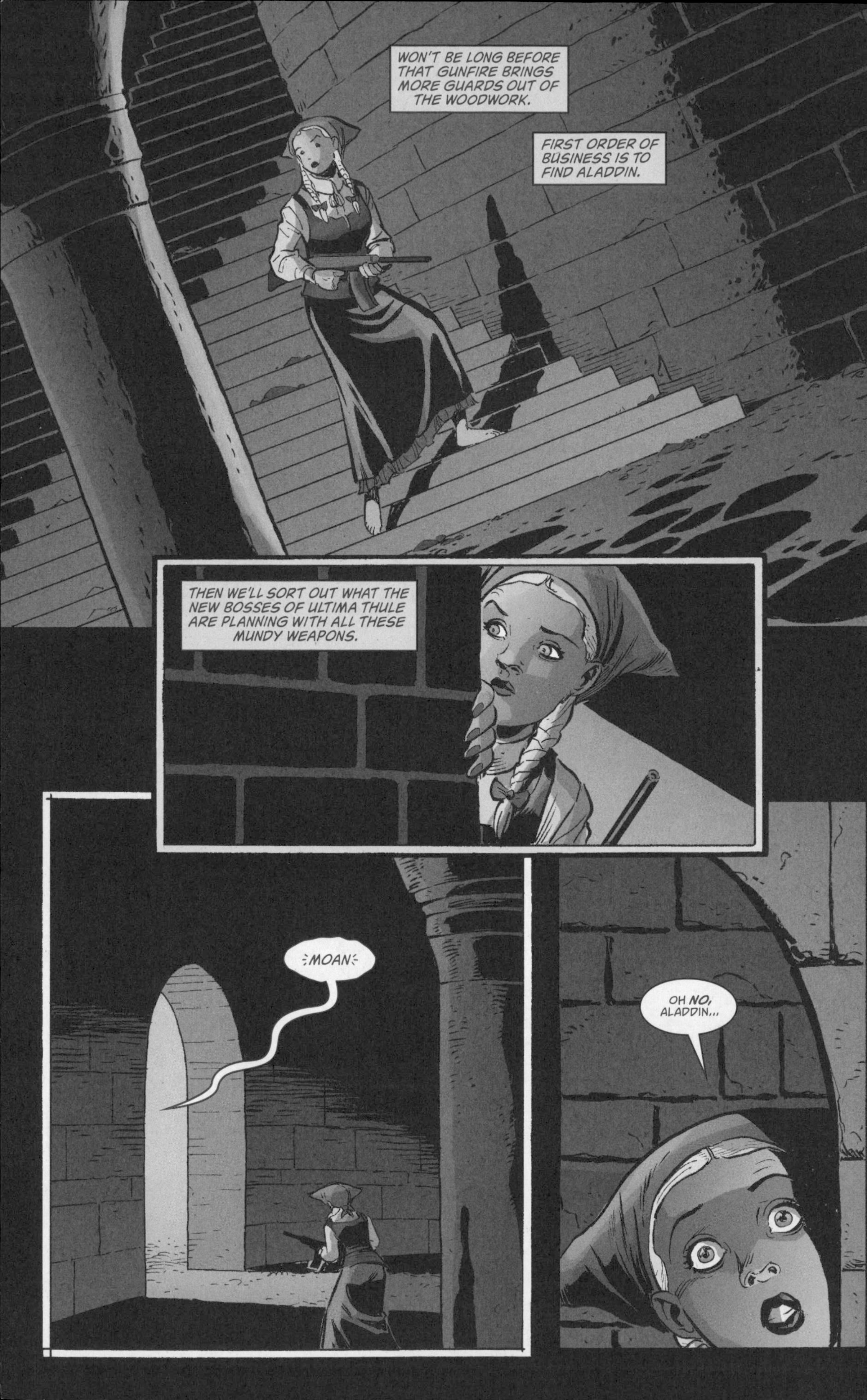
WON'T BE LONG BEFORE THAT GUNFIRE BRINGS MORE GUARDS OUT OF THE WOODWORK.
FIRST ORDER OF BUSINESS IS TO FIND ALADDIN.
THEN WE'LL SORT OUT WHAT THE NEW BOSSES OF ULTIMA THULE ARE PLANNING WITH ALL THESE MUNDY WEAPONS.
MOAN
OH NO, ALADDIN...

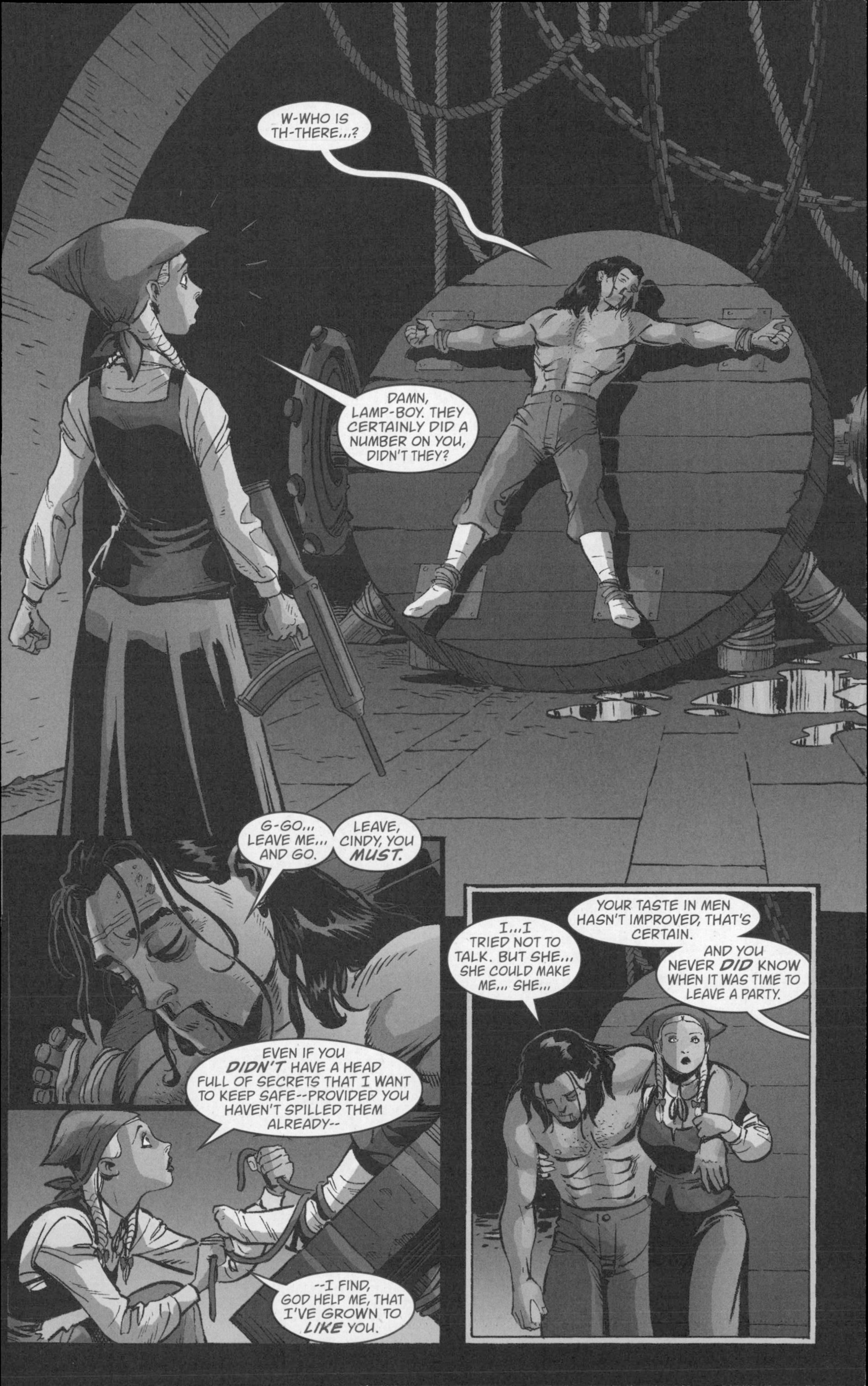
W-WHO IS TH-THERE...?
DAMN, LAMP-BOY. THEY CERTAINLY DID A NUMBER ON YOU, DIDN'T THEY?
G-GO... LEAVE ME... AND GO.
LEAVE, CINDY, YOU MUST.
EVEN IF YOU DIDN'T HAVE A HEAD FULL OF SECRETS THAT I WANT TO KEEP SAFE--PROVIDED YOU HAVEN'T SPILLED THEM ALREADY--
--I FIND, GOD HELP ME, THAT I'VE GROWN TO LIKE YOU.
I...I TRIED NOT TO TALK. BUT SHE... SHE COULD MAKE ME... SHE...
YOUR TASTE IN MEN HASN'T IMPROVED, THAT'S CERTAIN.
AND YOU NEVER DID KNOW WHEN IT WAS TIME TO LEAVE A PARTY.

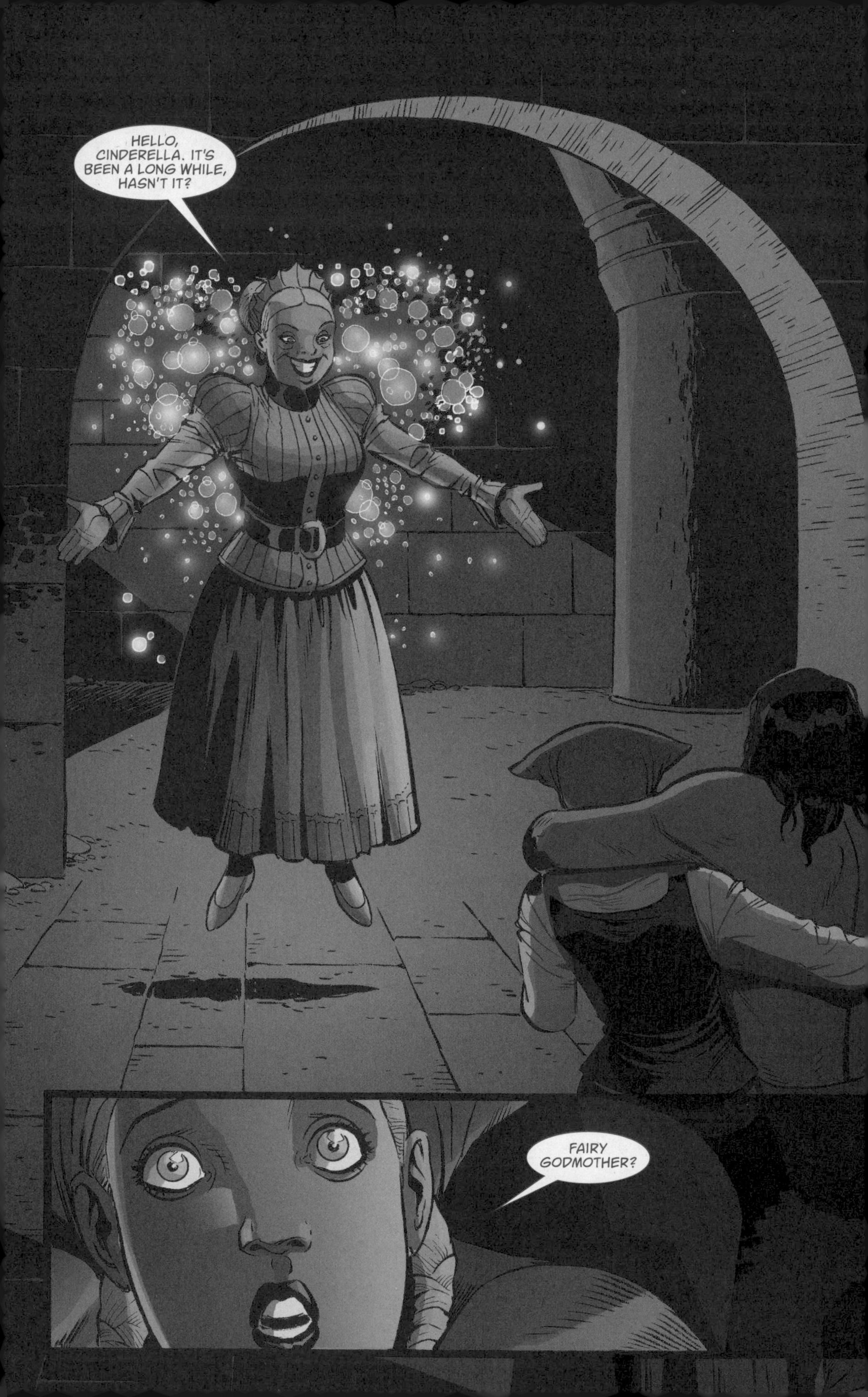
HELLO, CINDERELLA. IT'S BEEN A LONG WHILE, HASN'T IT?
FAIRY GODMOTHER?

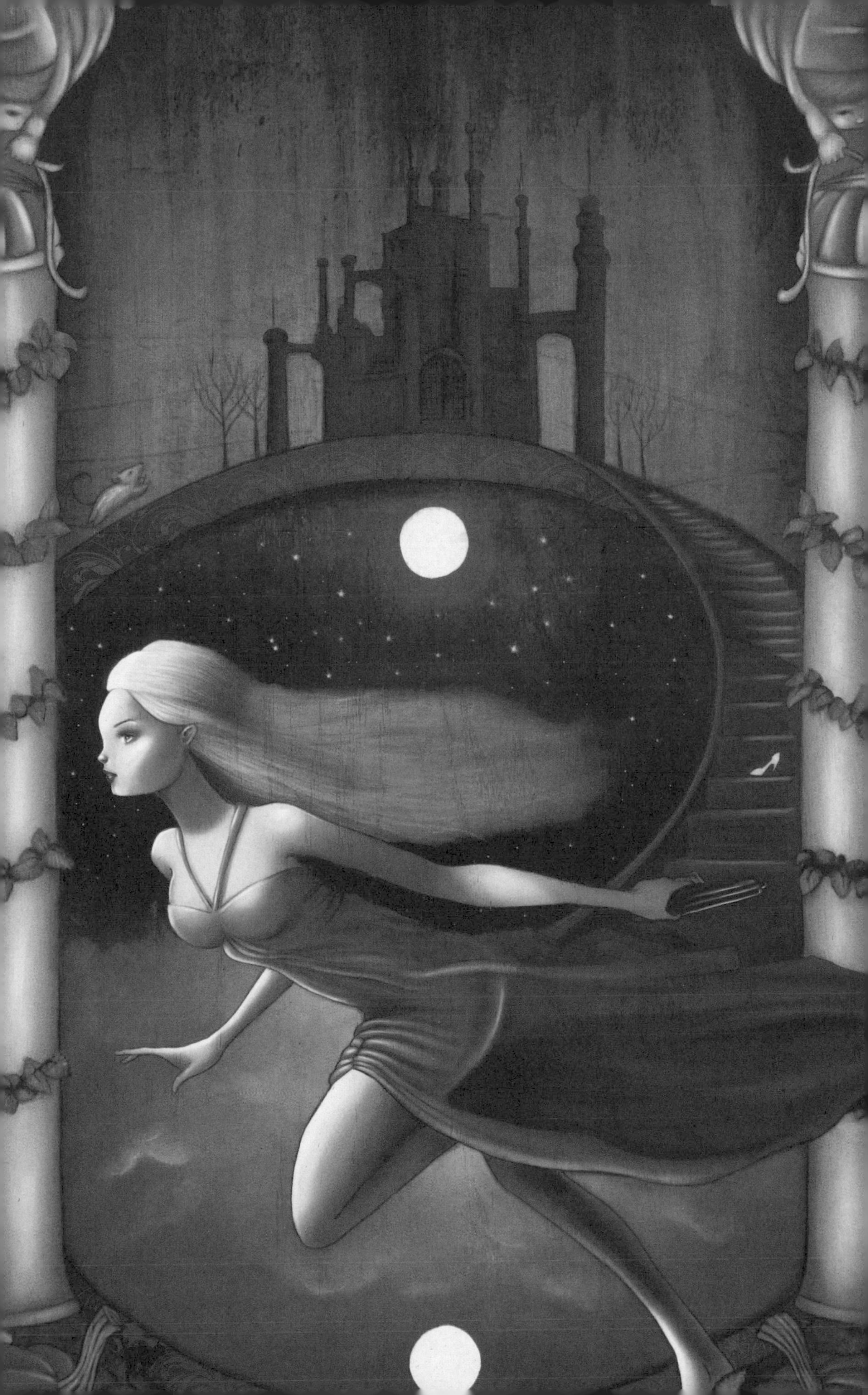

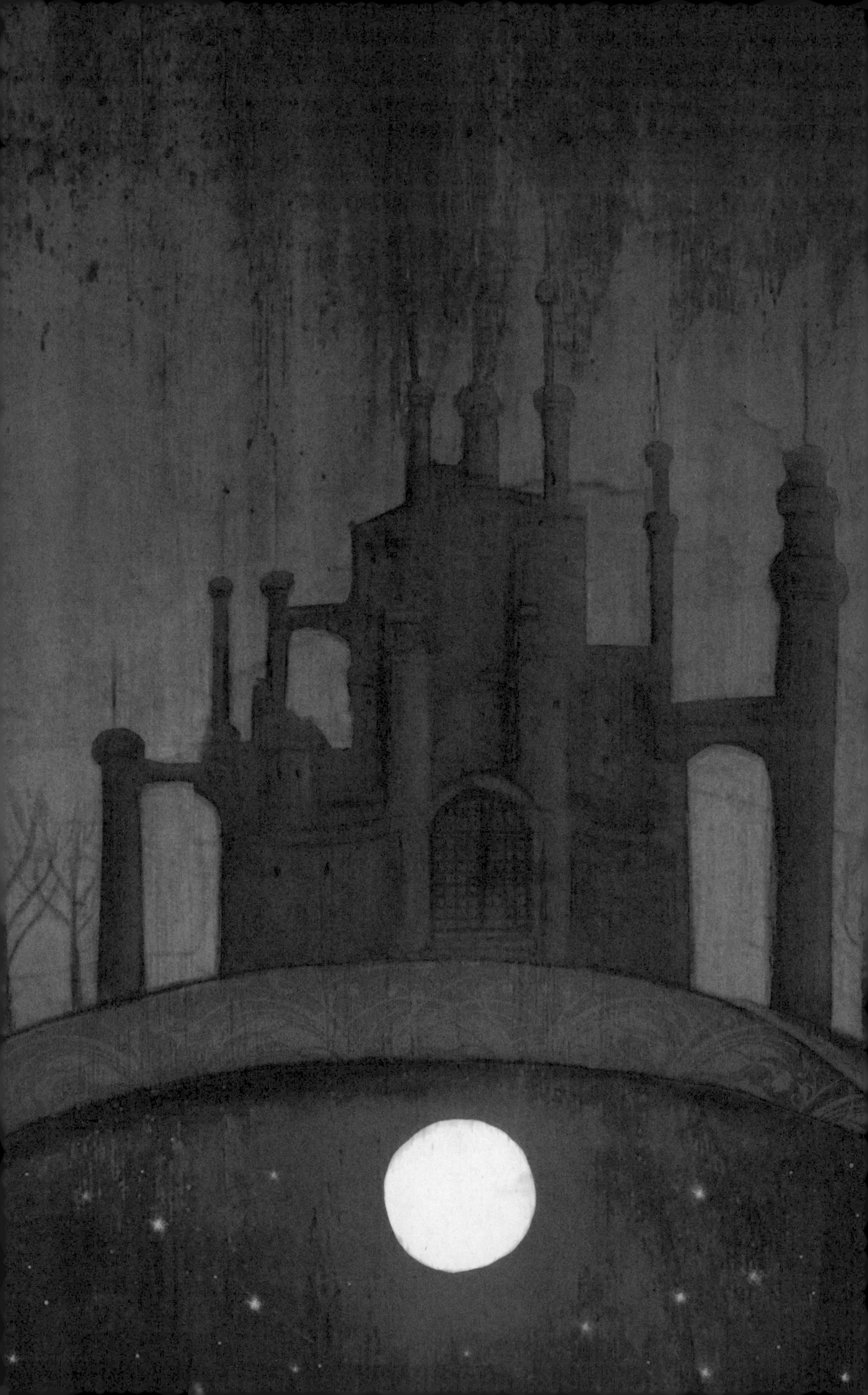

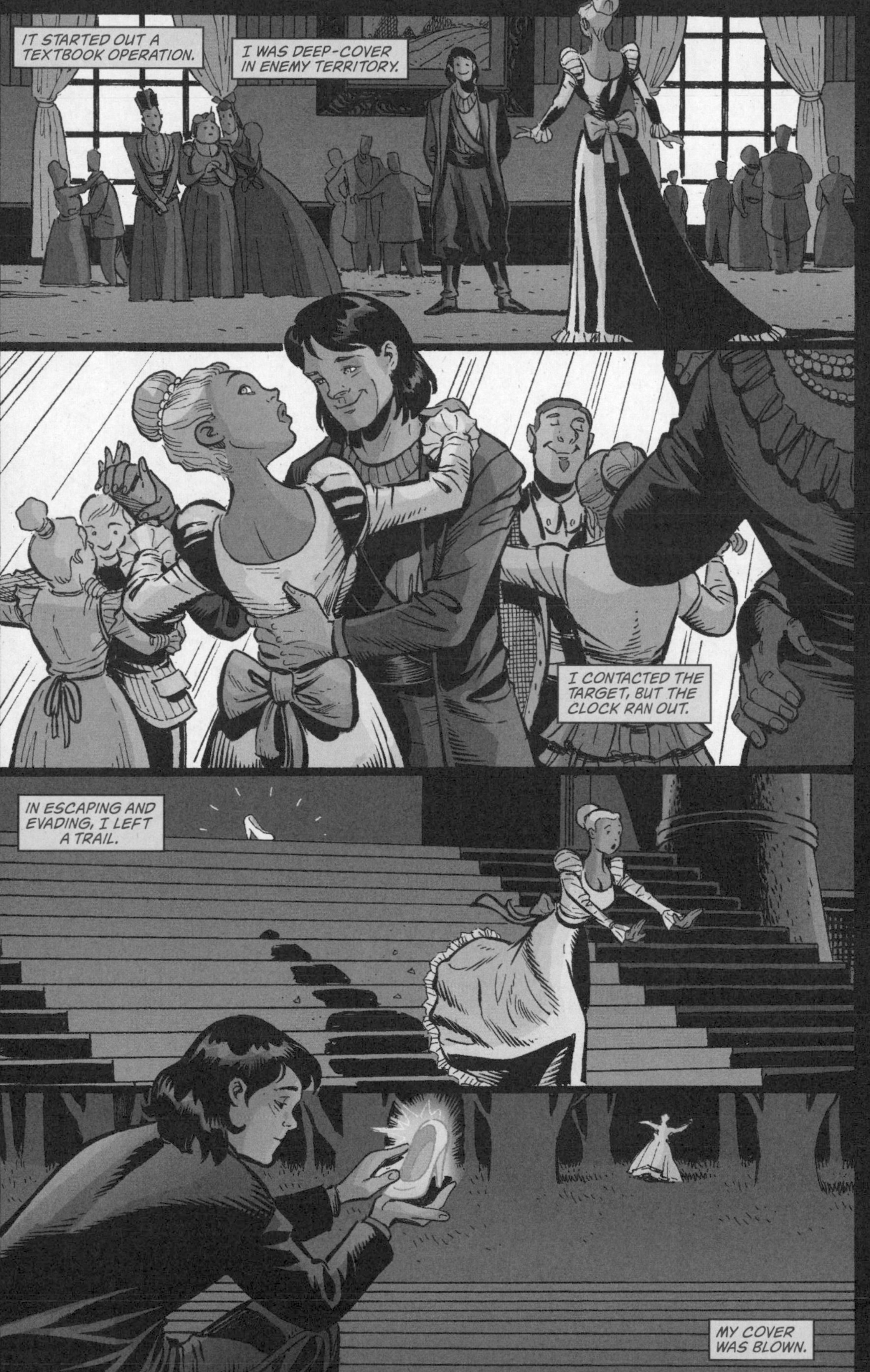
IT STARTED OUT A TEXTBOOK OPERATION.
I WAS DEEP-COVER IN ENEMY TERRITORY.
I CONTACTED THE TARGET, BUT THE CLOCK RAN OUT.
IN ESCAPING AND EVADING, I LEFT A TRAIL.
MY COVER WAS BLOWN.

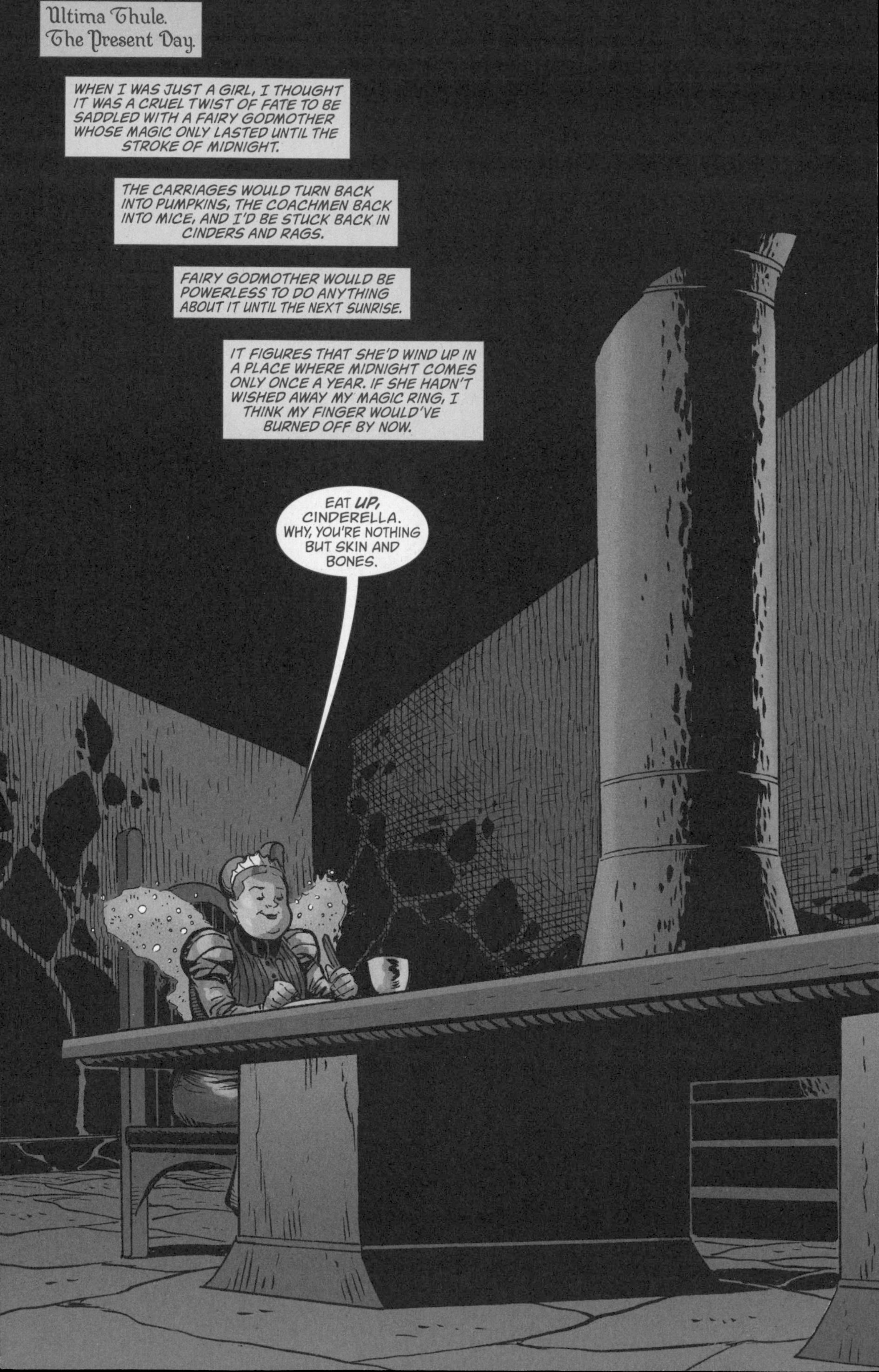
Ultima Thule.
The Present Day.
WHEN I WAS JUST A GIRL, I THOUGHT IT WAS A CRUEL TWIST OF FATE TO BE SADDLED WITH A FAIRY GODMOTHER WHOSE MAGIC ONLY LASTED UNTIL THE STROKE OF MIDNIGHT.
THE CARRIAGES WOULD TURN BACK INTO PUMPKINS, THE COACHMEN BACK INTO MICE, AND I'D BE STUCK BACK IN CINDERS AND RAGS.
FAIRY GODMOTHER WOULD BE POWERLESS TO DO ANYTHING ABOUT IT UNTIL THE NEXT SUNRISE.
IT FIGURES THAT SHE'D WIND UP IN A PLACE WHERE MIDNIGHT COMES ONLY ONCE A YEAR. IF SHE HADN'T WISHED AWAY MY MAGIC RING, I THINK MY FINGER WOULD'VE BURNED OFF BY NOW.
EAT UP, CINDERELLA. WHY, YOU'RE NOTHING BUT SKIN AND BONES.

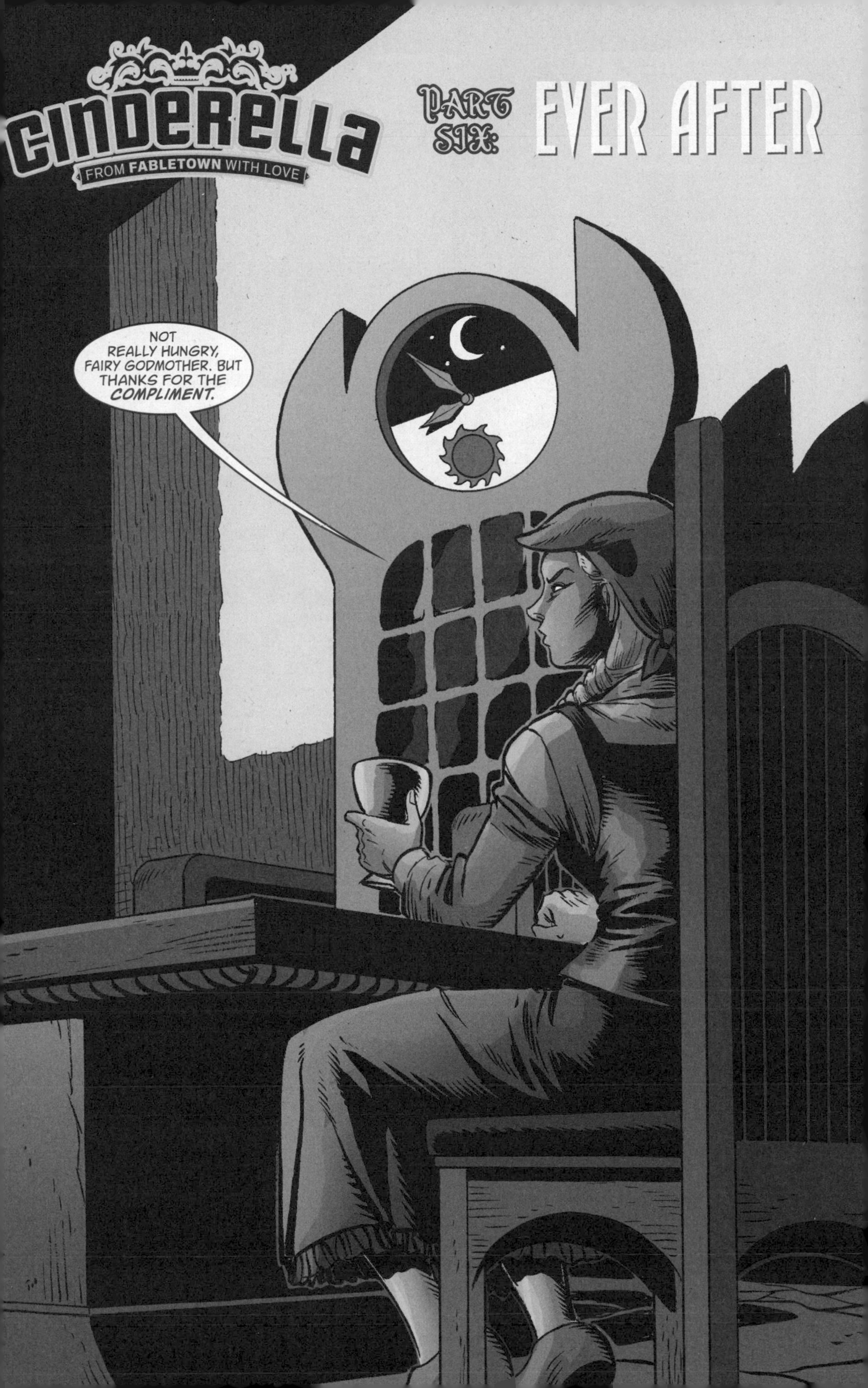
CINDERELLA
FROM FABLETOWN WITH LOVE
PART SIX: EVER AFTER
NOT REALLY HUNGRY, FAIRY GODMOTHER. BUT THANKS FOR THE *COMPLIMENT.*

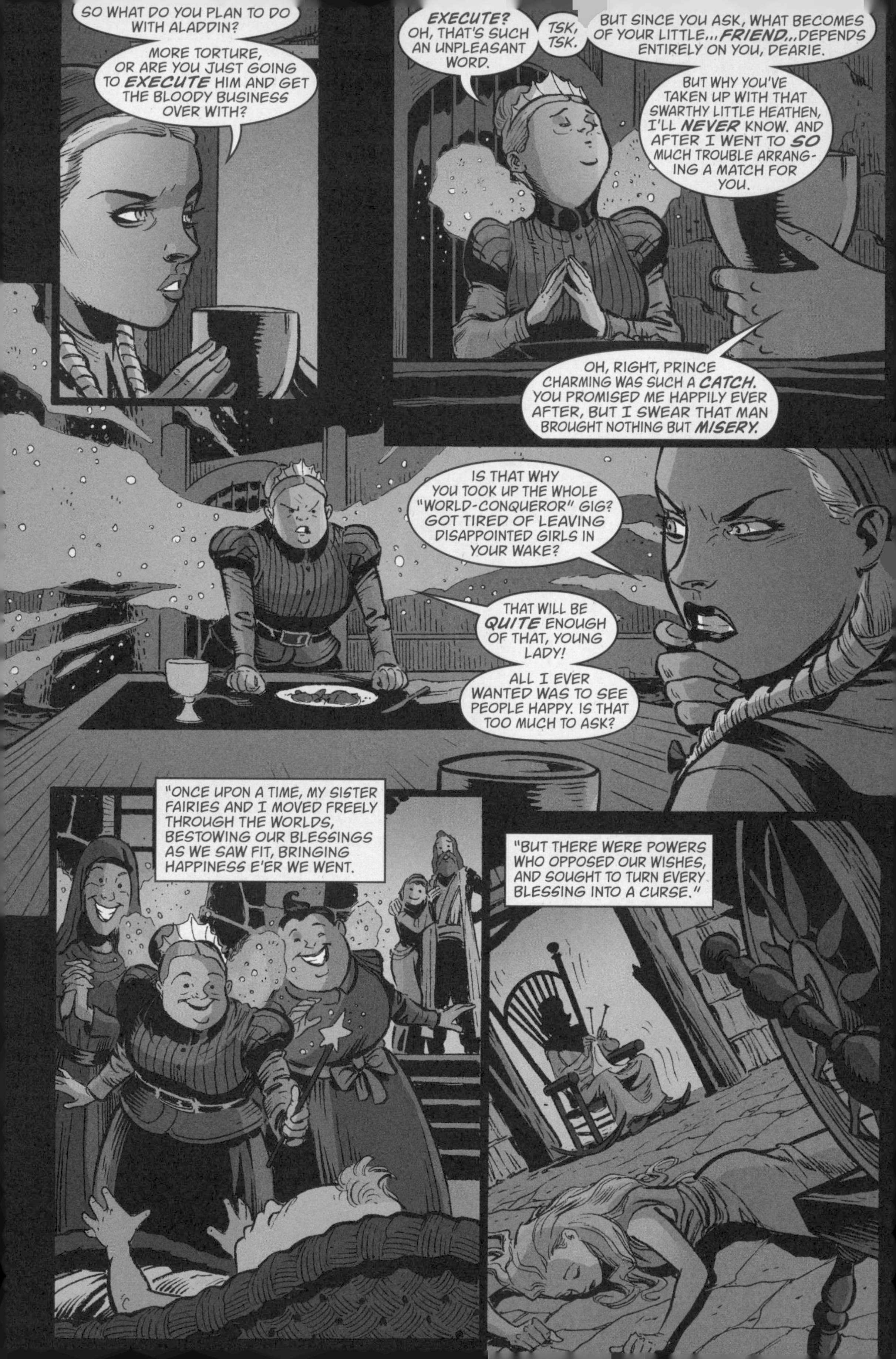
SO WHAT DO YOU PLAN TO DO WITH ALADDIN?
MORE TORTURE, OR ARE YOU JUST GOING TO EXECUTE HIM AND GET THE BLOODY BUSINESS OVER WITH?
EXECUTE? OH, THAT'S SUCH AN UNPLEASANT WORD.
TSK, TSK.
BUT SINCE YOU ASK, WHAT BECOMES OF YOUR LITTLE... FRIEND... DEPENDS ENTIRELY ON YOU, DEARIE.
BUT WHY YOU'VE TAKEN UP WITH THAT SWARTHY LITTLE HEATHEN, I'LL NEVER KNOW. AND AFTER I WENT TO SO MUCH TROUBLE ARRANGING A MATCH FOR YOU.
OH, RIGHT, PRINCE CHARMING WAS SUCH A CATCH. YOU PROMISED ME HAPPILY EVER AFTER, BUT I SWEAR THAT MAN BROUGHT NOTHING BUT MISERY.
IS THAT WHY YOU TOOK UP THE WHOLE "WORLD-CONQUEROR" GIG? GOT TIRED OF LEAVING DISAPPOINTED GIRLS IN YOUR WAKE?
THAT WILL BE QUITE ENOUGH OF THAT, YOUNG LADY!
ALL I EVER WANTED WAS TO SEE PEOPLE HAPPY. IS THAT TOO MUCH TO ASK?
"ONCE UPON A TIME, MY SISTER FAIRIES AND I MOVED FREELY THROUGH THE WORLDS, BESTOWING OUR BLESSINGS AS WE SAW FIT, BRINGING HAPPINESS E'ER WE WENT.
"BUT THERE WERE POWERS WHO OPPOSED OUR WISHES, AND SOUGHT TO TURN EVERY BLESSING INTO A CURSE."

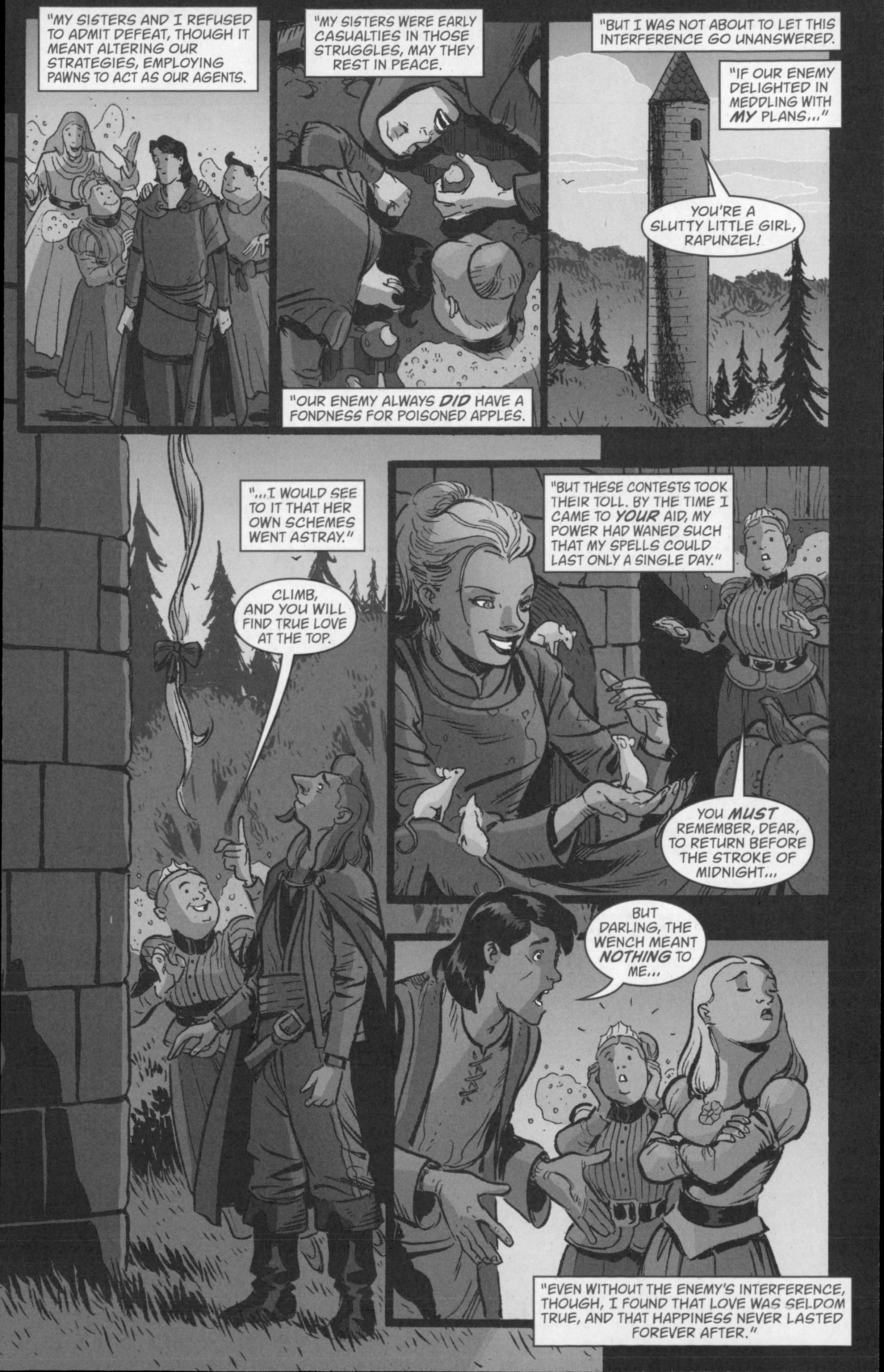
"MY SISTERS AND I REFUSED TO ADMIT DEFEAT, THOUGH IT MEANT ALTERING OUR STRATEGIES, EMPLOYING PAWNS TO ACT AS OUR AGENTS.
"MY SISTERS WERE EARLY CASUALTIES IN THOSE STRUGGLES, MAY THEY REST IN PEACE.
"OUR ENEMY ALWAYS DID HAVE A FONDNESS FOR POISONED APPLES.
"BUT I WAS NOT ABOUT TO LET THIS INTERFERENCE GO UNANSWERED.
"IF OUR ENEMY DELIGHTED IN MEDDLING WITH MY PLANS..."
YOU'RE A SLUTTY LITTLE GIRL, RAPUNZEL!
"...I WOULD SEE TO IT THAT HER OWN SCHEMES WENT ASTRAY."
CLIMB, AND YOU WILL FIND TRUE LOVE AT THE TOP.
"BUT THESE CONTESTS TOOK THEIR TOLL. BY THE TIME I CAME TO YOUR AID, MY POWER HAD WANED SUCH THAT MY SPELLS COULD LAST ONLY A SINGLE DAY."
YOU MUST REMEMBER, DEAR, TO RETURN BEFORE THE STROKE OF MIDNIGHT...
BUT DARLING, THE WENCH MEANT NOTHING TO ME...
"EVEN WITHOUT THE ENEMY'S INTERFERENCE, THOUGH, I FOUND THAT LOVE WAS SELDOM TRUE, AND THAT HAPPINESS NEVER LASTED FOREVER AFTER."

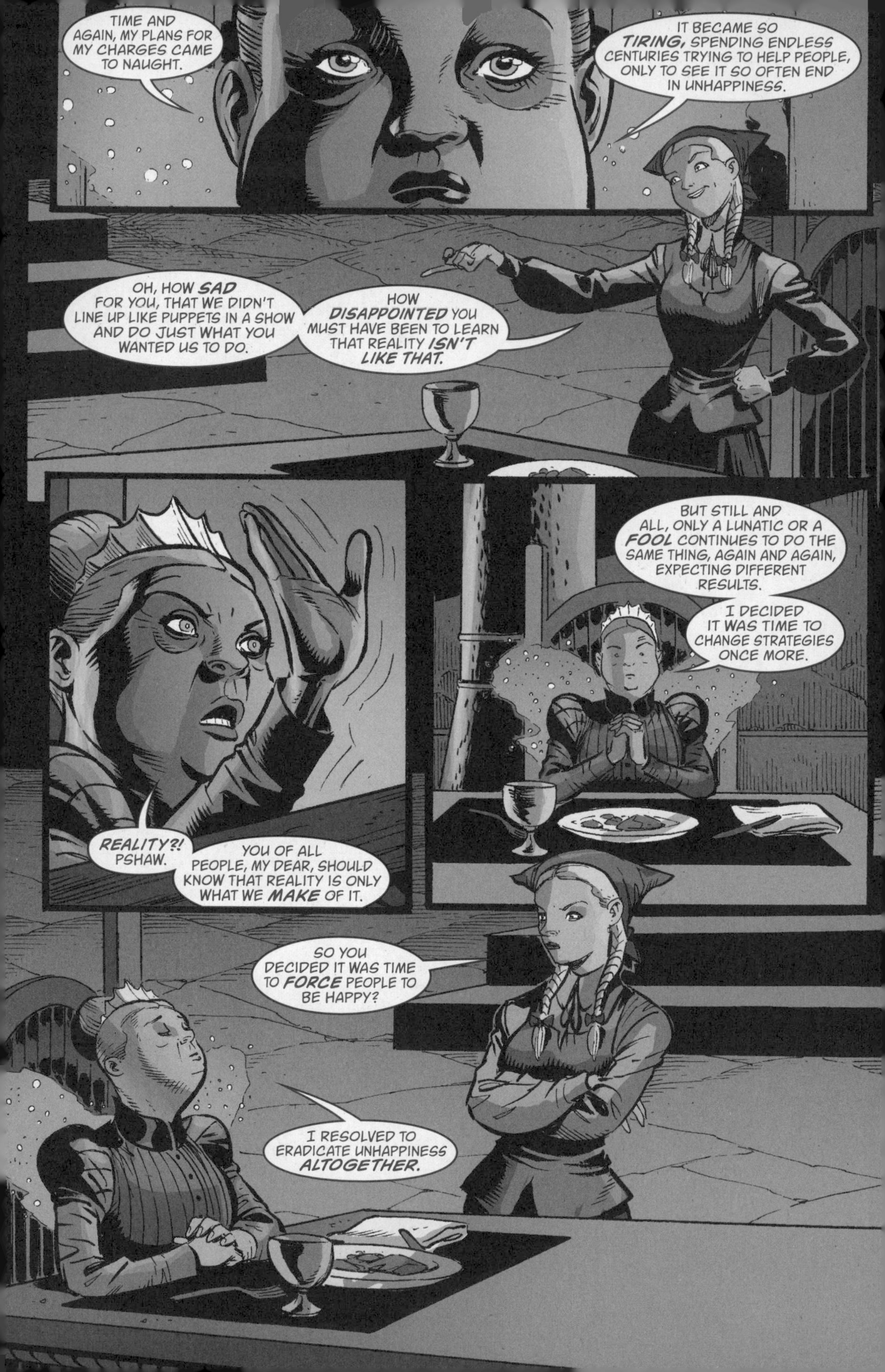

TIME AND AGAIN, MY PLANS FOR MY CHARGES CAME TO NAUGHT.
IT BECAME SO TIRING, SPENDING ENDLESS CENTURIES TRYING TO HELP PEOPLE, ONLY TO SEE IT SO OFTEN END IN UNHAPPINESS.
OH, HOW SAD FOR YOU, THAT WE DIDN'T LINE UP LIKE PUPPETS IN A SHOW AND DO JUST WHAT YOU WANTED US TO DO.
HOW DISAPPOINTED YOU MUST HAVE BEEN TO LEARN THAT REALITY ISN'T LIKE THAT.
REALITY?! PSHAW.
YOU OF ALL PEOPLE, MY DEAR, SHOULD KNOW THAT REALITY IS ONLY WHAT WE MAKE OF IT.
BUT STILL AND ALL, ONLY A LUNATIC OR A FOOL CONTINUES TO DO THE SAME THING, AGAIN AND AGAIN, EXPECTING DIFFERENT RESULTS.
I DECIDED IT WAS TIME TO CHANGE STRATEGIES ONCE MORE.
SO YOU DECIDED IT WAS TIME TO FORCE PEOPLE TO BE HAPPY?
I RESOLVED TO ERADICATE UNHAPPINESS ALTOGETHER.

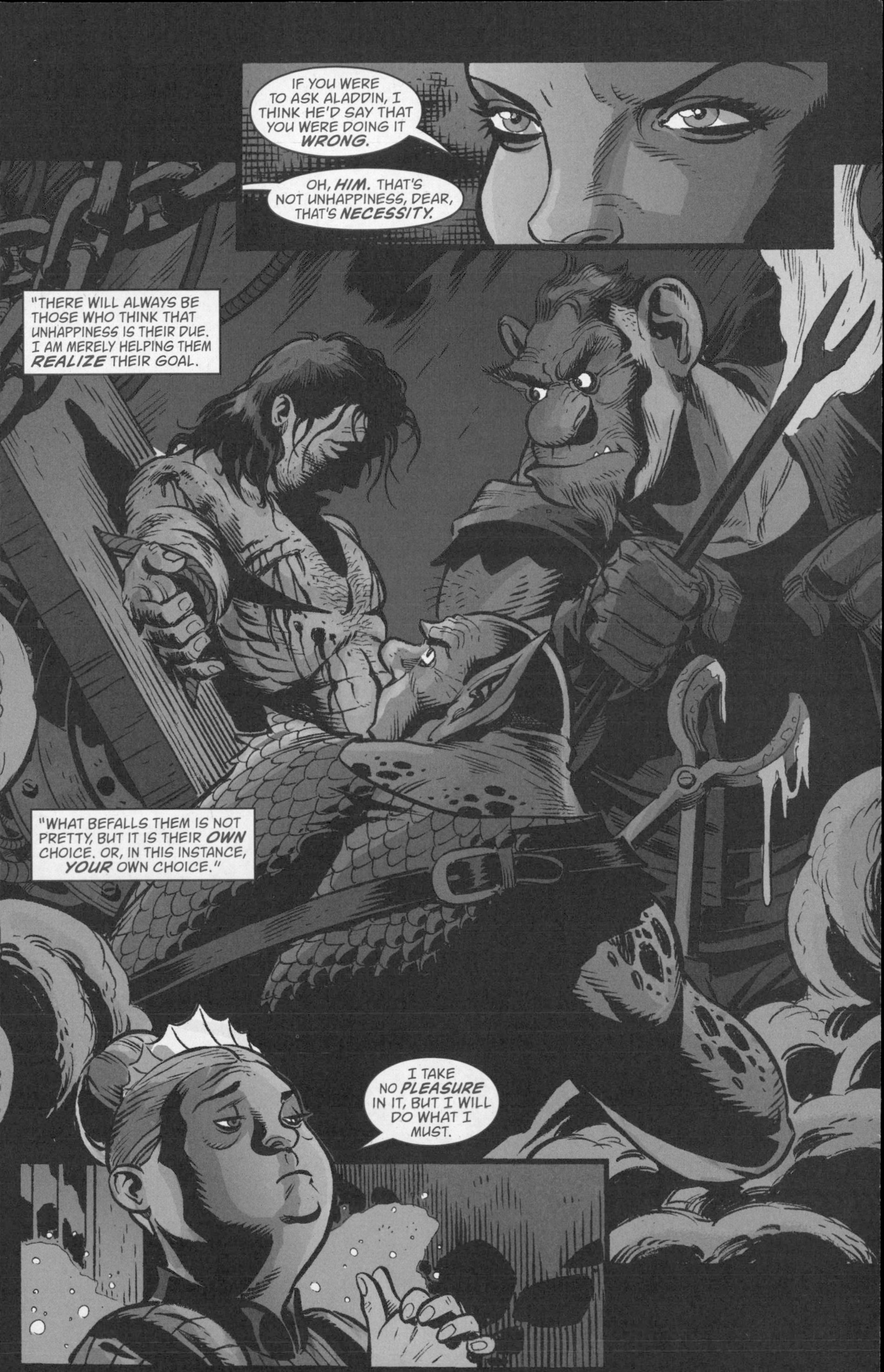
IF YOU WERE TO ASK ALADDIN, I THINK HE'D SAY THAT YOU WERE DOING IT WRONG.
OH, HIM. THAT'S NOT UNHAPPINESS, DEAR, THAT'S NECESSITY.
"THERE WILL ALWAYS BE THOSE WHO THINK THAT UNHAPPINESS IS THEIR DUE. I AM MERELY HELPING THEM REALIZE THEIR GOAL.
"WHAT BEFALLS THEM IS NOT PRETTY, BUT IT IS THEIR OWN CHOICE. OR, IN THIS INSTANCE, YOUR OWN CHOICE."
I TAKE NO PLEASURE IN IT, BUT I WILL DO WHAT I MUST.

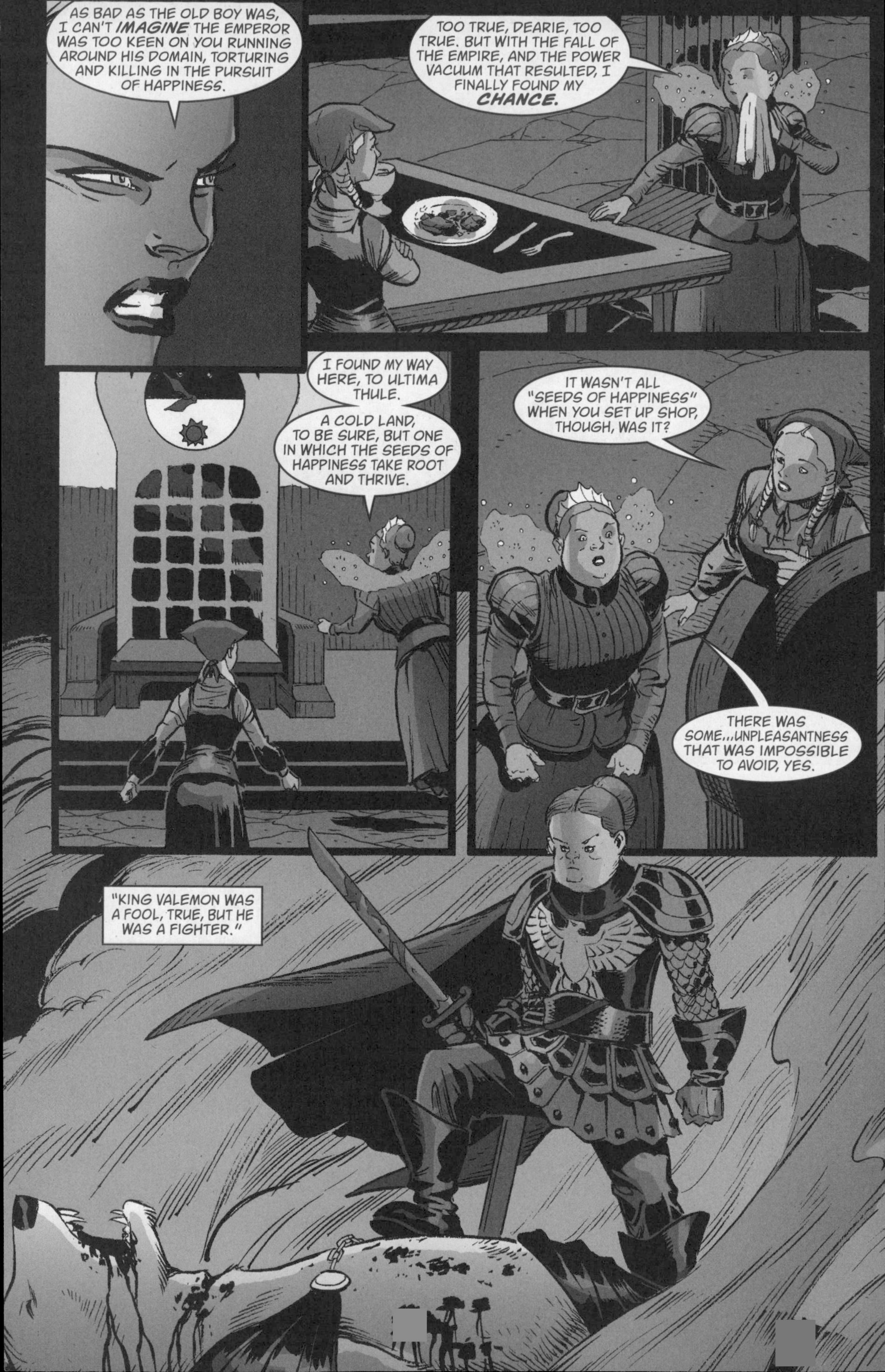

AS BAD AS THE OLD BOY WAS, I CAN'T *IMAGINE* THE EMPEROR WAS TOO KEEN ON YOU RUNNING AROUND HIS DOMAIN, TORTURING AND KILLING IN THE PURSUIT OF HAPPINESS.
TOO TRUE, DEARIE, TOO TRUE. BUT WITH THE FALL OF THE EMPIRE, AND THE POWER VACUUM THAT RESULTED, I FINALLY FOUND MY **CHANCE.**
I FOUND MY WAY HERE, TO ULTIMA THULE.
A COLD LAND, TO BE SURE, BUT ONE IN WHICH THE SEEDS OF HAPPINESS TAKE ROOT AND THRIVE.
IT WASN'T ALL "SEEDS OF HAPPINESS" WHEN YOU SET UP SHOP, THOUGH, WAS IT?
THERE WAS SOME...UNPLEASANTNESS THAT WAS IMPOSSIBLE TO AVOID, YES.
"KING VALEMON WAS A FOOL, TRUE, BUT HE WAS A FIGHTER."

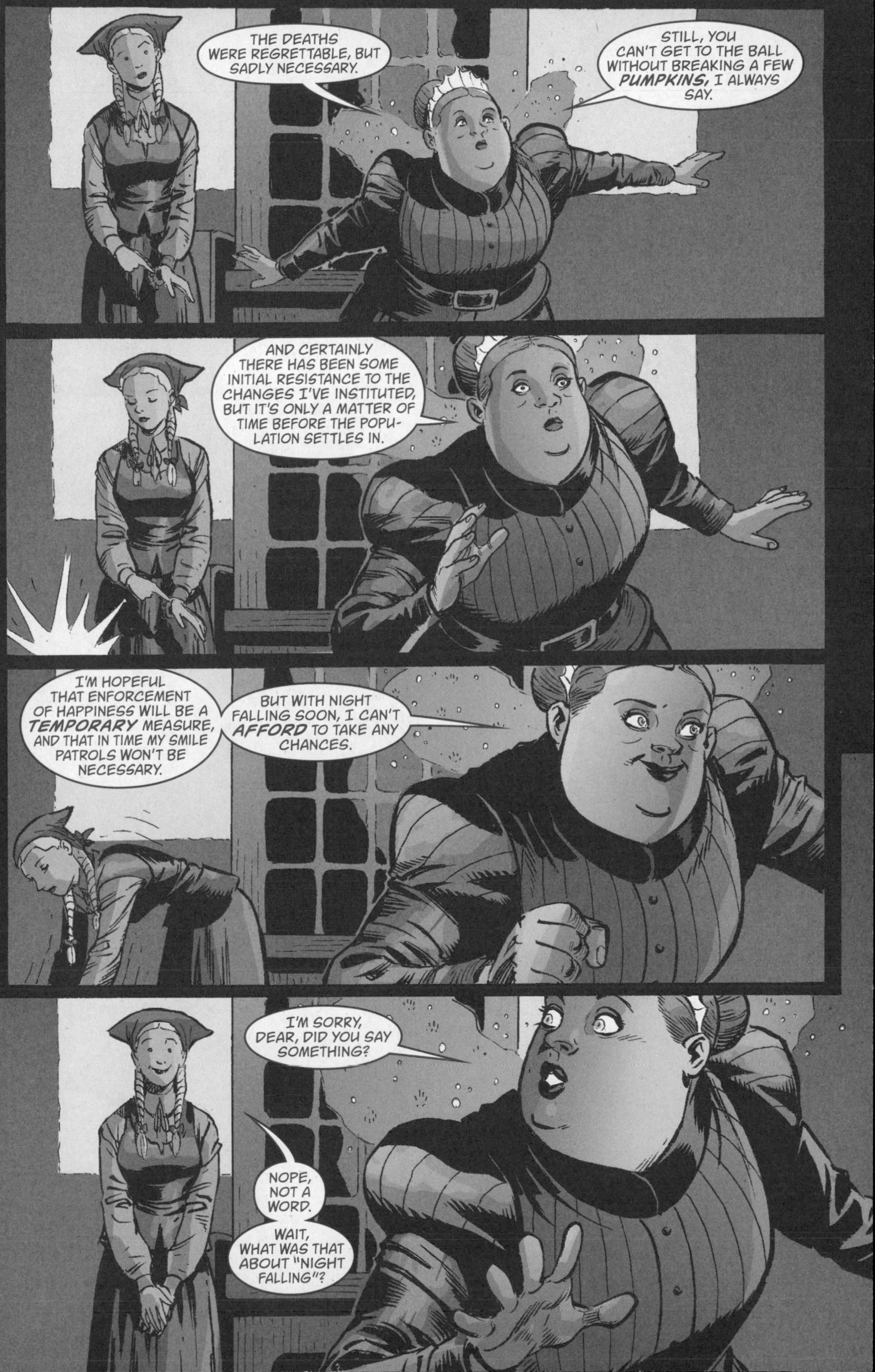
THE DEATHS WERE REGRETTABLE, BUT SADLY NECESSARY.
STILL, YOU CAN'T GET TO THE BALL WITHOUT BREAKING A FEW PUMPKINS, I ALWAYS SAY.
AND CERTAINLY THERE HAS BEEN SOME INITIAL RESISTANCE TO THE CHANGES I'VE INSTITUTED, BUT IT'S ONLY A MATTER OF TIME BEFORE THE POPULATION SETTLES IN.
I'M HOPEFUL THAT ENFORCEMENT OF HAPPINESS WILL BE A TEMPORARY MEASURE, AND THAT IN TIME MY SMILE PATROLS WON'T BE NECESSARY.
BUT WITH NIGHT FALLING SOON, I CAN'T AFFORD TO TAKE ANY CHANCES.
I'M SORRY, DEAR, DID YOU SAY SOMETHING?
NOPE, NOT A WORD.
WAIT, WHAT WAS THAT ABOUT "NIGHT FALLING"?

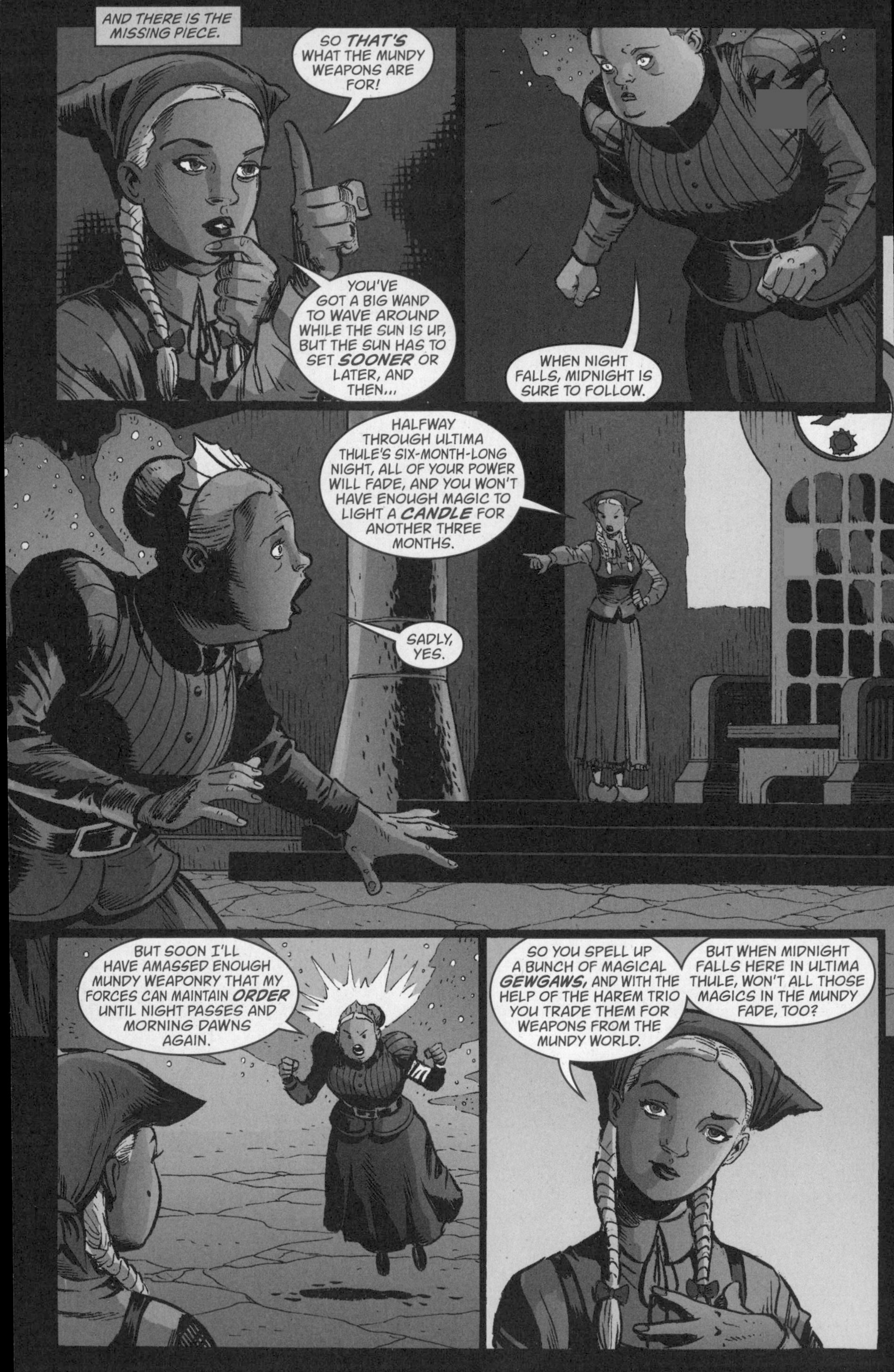
AND THERE IS THE MISSING PIECE.
SO THAT'S WHAT THE MUNDY WEAPONS ARE FOR!
YOU'VE GOT A BIG WAND TO WAVE AROUND WHILE THE SUN IS UP, BUT THE SUN HAS TO SET SOONER OR LATER, AND THEN...
WHEN NIGHT FALLS, MIDNIGHT IS SURE TO FOLLOW.
HALFWAY THROUGH ULTIMA THULE'S SIX-MONTH-LONG NIGHT, ALL OF YOUR POWER WILL FADE, AND YOU WON'T HAVE ENOUGH MAGIC TO LIGHT A CANDLE FOR ANOTHER THREE MONTHS.
SADLY, YES.
BUT SOON I'LL HAVE AMASSED ENOUGH MUNDY WEAPONRY THAT MY FORCES CAN MAINTAIN ORDER UNTIL NIGHT PASSES AND MORNING DAWNS AGAIN.
SO YOU SPELL UP A BUNCH OF MAGICAL GEWGAWS, AND WITH THE HELP OF THE HAREM TRIO YOU TRADE THEM FOR WEAPONS FROM THE MUNDY WORLD.
BUT WHEN MIDNIGHT FALLS HERE IN ULTIMA THULE, WON'T ALL THOSE MAGICS IN THE MUNDY FADE, TOO?

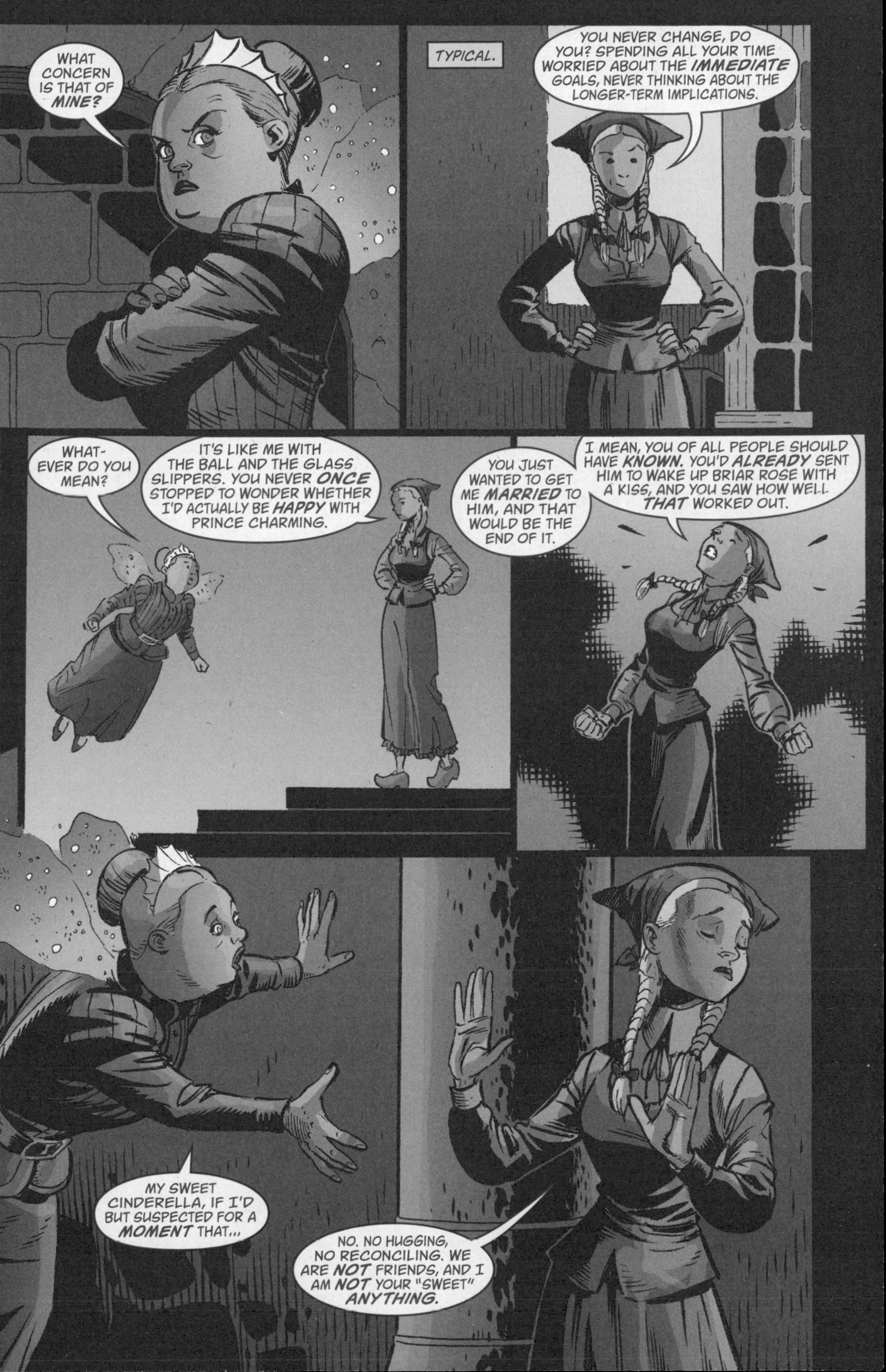
WHAT CONCERN IS THAT OF MINE?
TYPICAL.
YOU NEVER CHANGE, DO YOU? SPENDING ALL YOUR TIME WORRIED ABOUT THE IMMEDIATE GOALS, NEVER THINKING ABOUT THE LONGER-TERM IMPLICATIONS.
WHAT-EVER DO YOU MEAN?
IT'S LIKE ME WITH THE BALL AND THE GLASS SLIPPERS. YOU NEVER ONCE STOPPED TO WONDER WHETHER I'D ACTUALLY BE HAPPY WITH PRINCE CHARMING.
YOU JUST WANTED TO GET ME MARRIED TO HIM, AND THAT WOULD BE THE END OF IT.
I MEAN, YOU OF ALL PEOPLE SHOULD HAVE KNOWN. YOU'D ALREADY SENT HIM TO WAKE UP BRIAR ROSE WITH A KISS, AND YOU SAW HOW WELL THAT WORKED OUT.
MY SWEET CINDERELLA, IF I'D BUT SUSPECTED FOR A MOMENT THAT...
NO. NO HUGGING, NO RECONCILING. WE ARE NOT FRIENDS, AND I AM NOT YOUR "SWEET" ANYTHING.

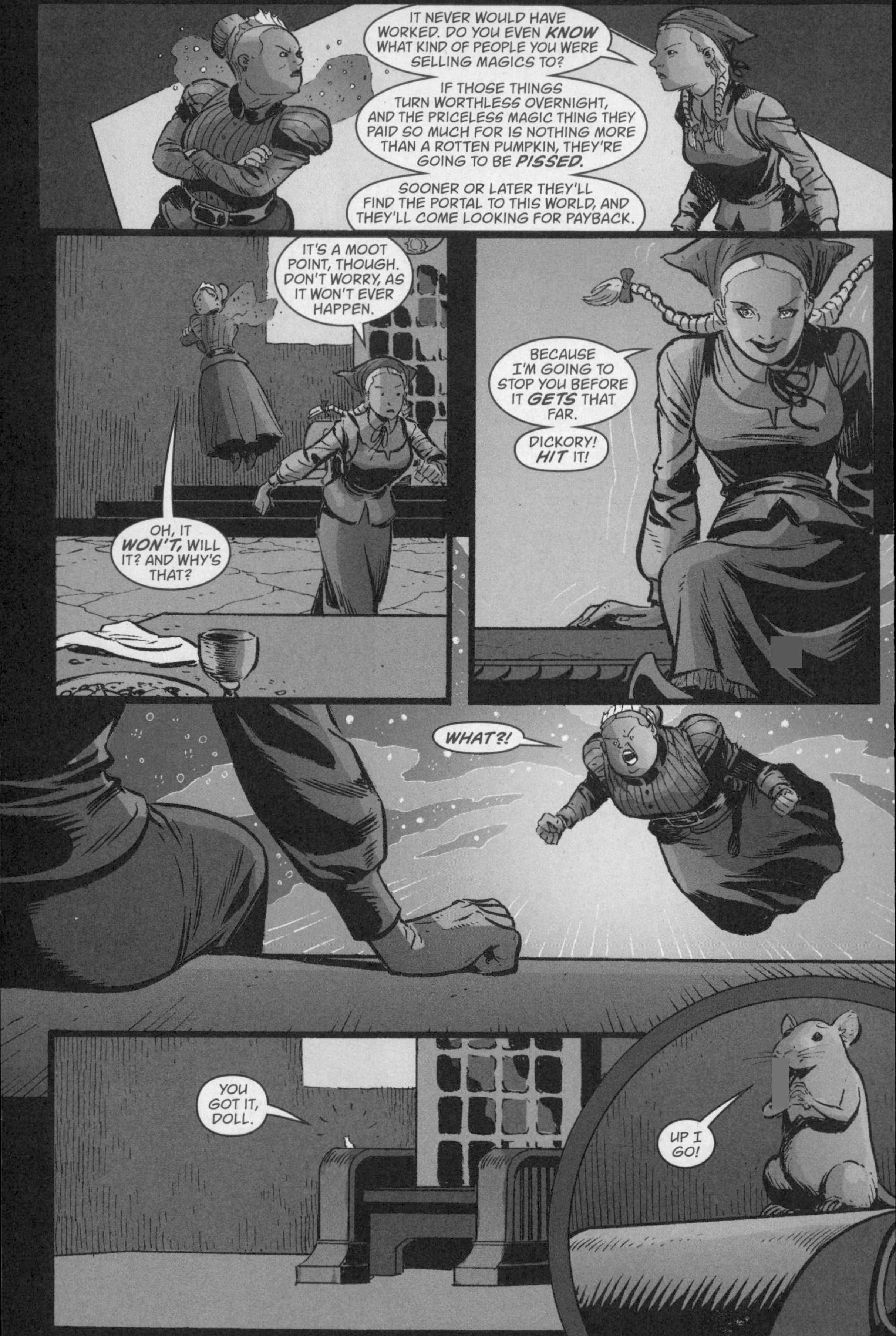
IT NEVER WOULD HAVE WORKED. DO YOU EVEN KNOW WHAT KIND OF PEOPLE YOU WERE SELLING MAGICS TO?
IF THOSE THINGS TURN WORTHLESS OVERNIGHT, AND THE PRICELESS MAGIC THING THEY PAID SO MUCH FOR IS NOTHING MORE THAN A ROTTEN PUMPKIN, THEY'RE GOING TO BE PISSED.
SOONER OR LATER THEY'LL FIND THE PORTAL TO THIS WORLD, AND THEY'LL COME LOOKING FOR PAYBACK.
IT'S A MOOT POINT, THOUGH. DON'T WORRY, AS IT WON'T EVER HAPPEN.
OH, IT WON'T, WILL IT? AND WHY'S THAT?
BECAUSE I'M GOING TO STOP YOU BEFORE IT GETS THAT FAR.
DICKORY! HIT IT!
WHAT?!
YOU GOT IT, DOLL.
UP I GO!

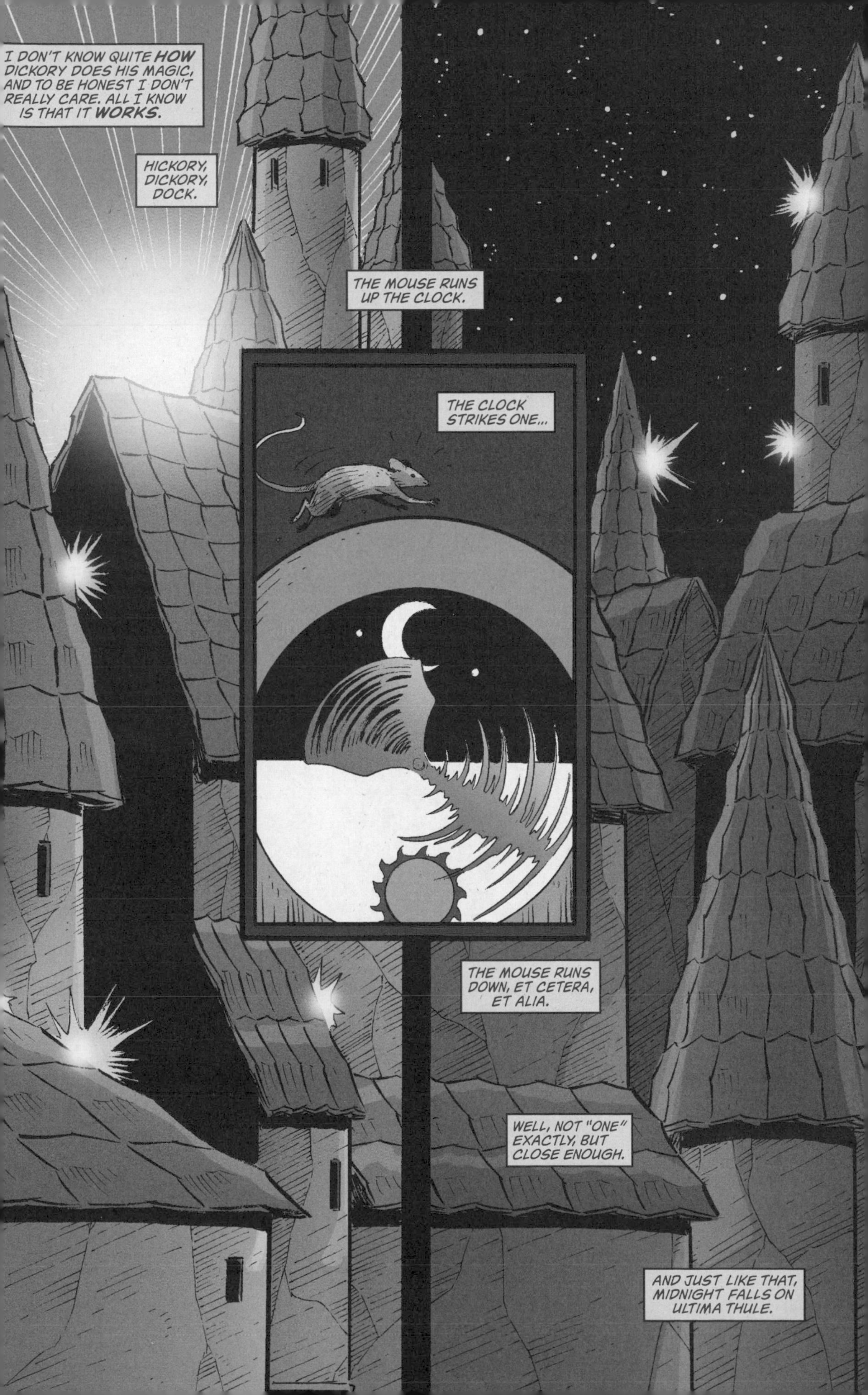
I DON'T KNOW QUITE HOW DICKORY DOES HIS MAGIC, AND TO BE HONEST I DON'T REALLY CARE. ALL I KNOW IS THAT IT WORKS.
HICKORY, DICKORY, DOCK.
THE MOUSE RUNS UP THE CLOCK.
THE CLOCK STRIKES ONE...
THE MOUSE RUNS DOWN, ET CETERA, ET ALIA.
WELL, NOT "ONE" EXACTLY, BUT CLOSE ENOUGH.
AND JUST LIKE THAT, MIDNIGHT FALLS ON ULTIMA THULE.

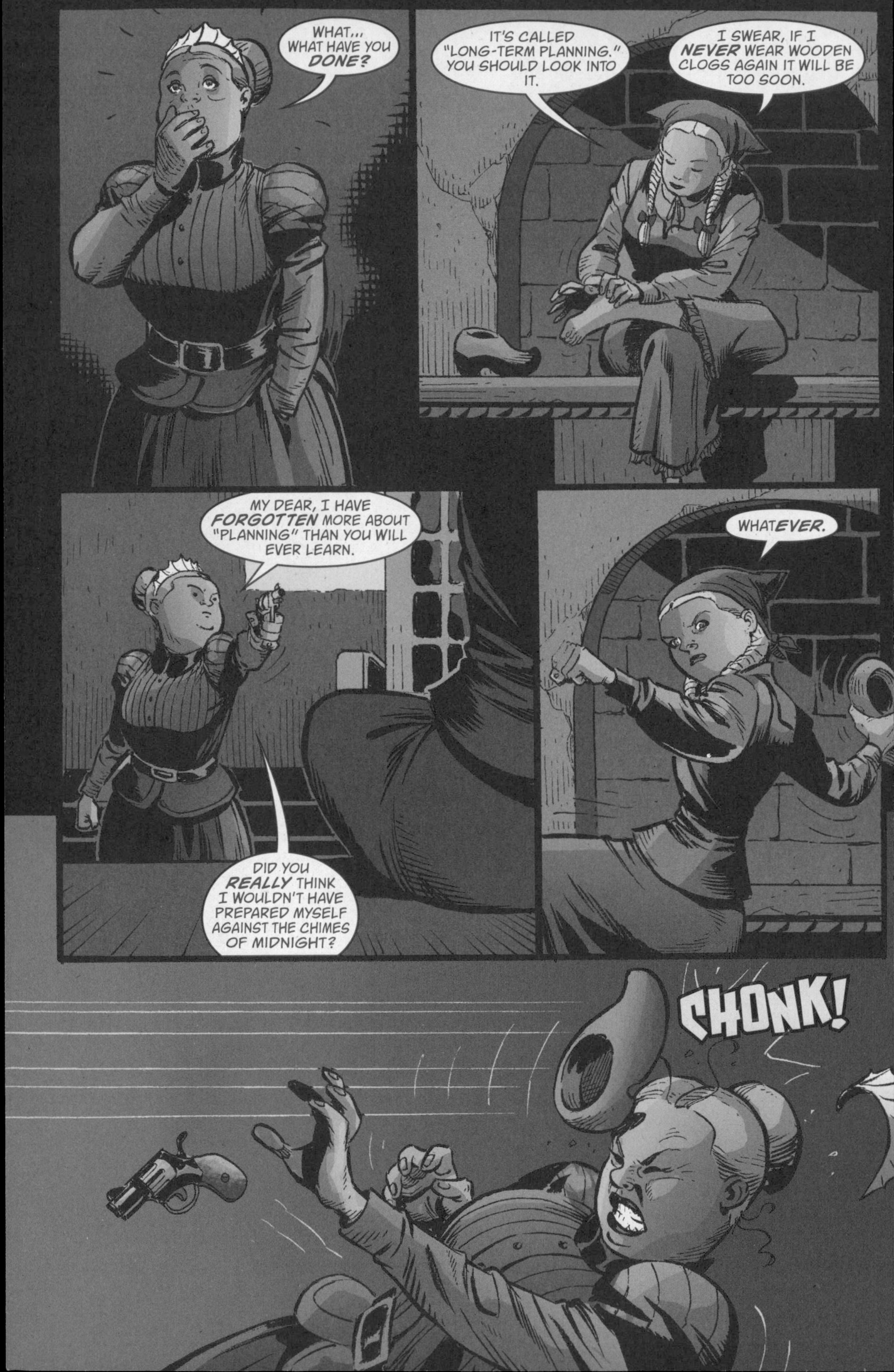
WHAT... WHAT HAVE YOU DONE?
IT'S CALLED "LONG-TERM PLANNING." YOU SHOULD LOOK INTO IT.
I SWEAR, IF I NEVER WEAR WOODEN CLOGS AGAIN IT WILL BE TOO SOON.
MY DEAR, I HAVE FORGOTTEN MORE ABOUT "PLANNING" THAN YOU WILL EVER LEARN.
DID YOU REALLY THINK I WOULDN'T HAVE PREPARED MYSELF AGAINST THE CHIMES OF MIDNIGHT?
WHATEVER.
CHONK!

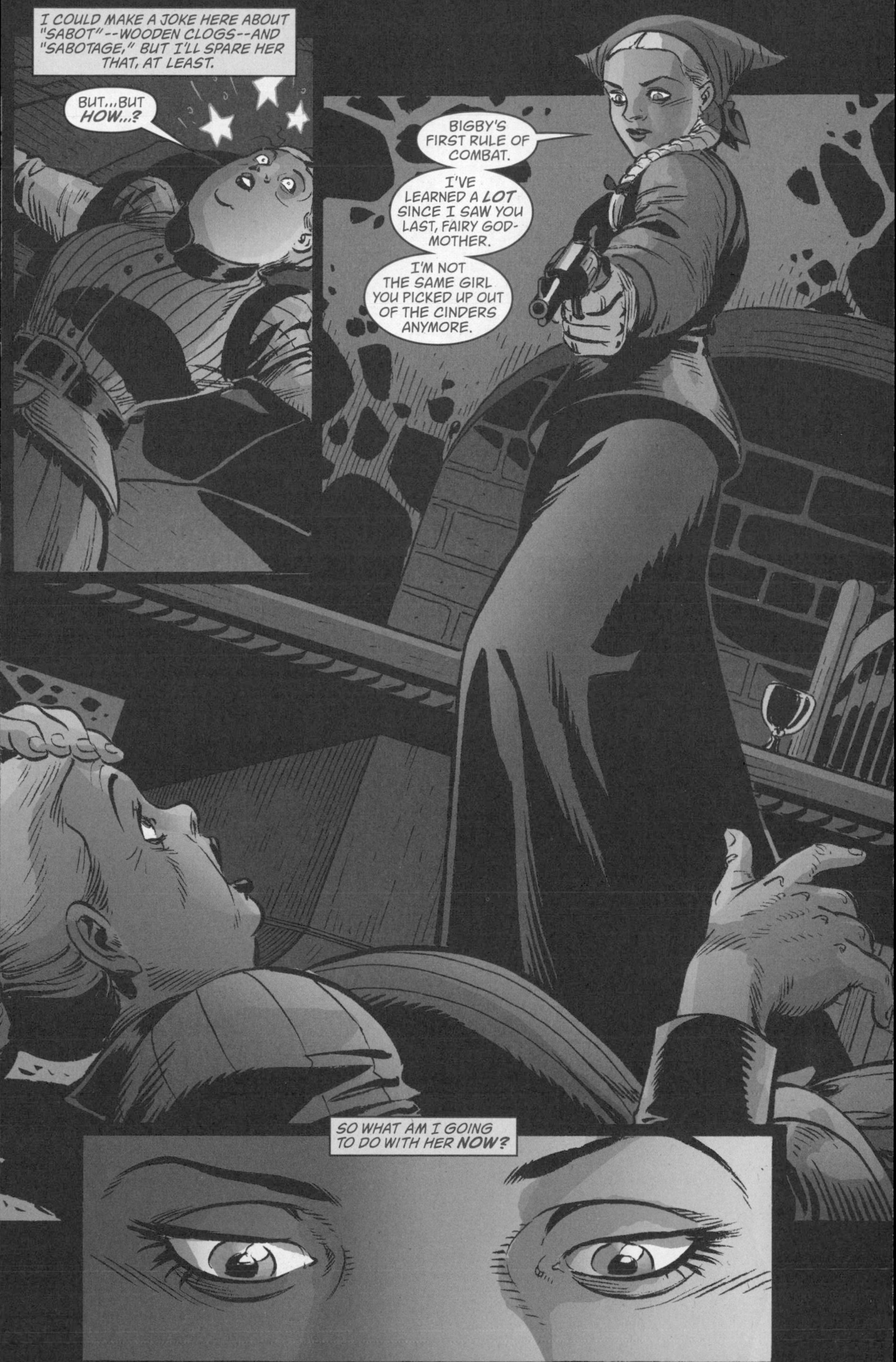
I COULD MAKE A JOKE HERE ABOUT "SABOT"--WOODEN CLOGS--AND "SABOTAGE," BUT I'LL SPARE HER THAT, AT LEAST.
BUT...BUT **HOW...?**
BIGBY'S FIRST RULE OF COMBAT.
I'VE LEARNED A **LOT** SINCE I SAW YOU LAST, FAIRY GOD-MOTHER.
I'M NOT THE SAME GIRL YOU PICKED UP OUT OF THE CINDERS ANYMORE.
SO WHAT AM I GOING TO DO WITH HER **NOW?**

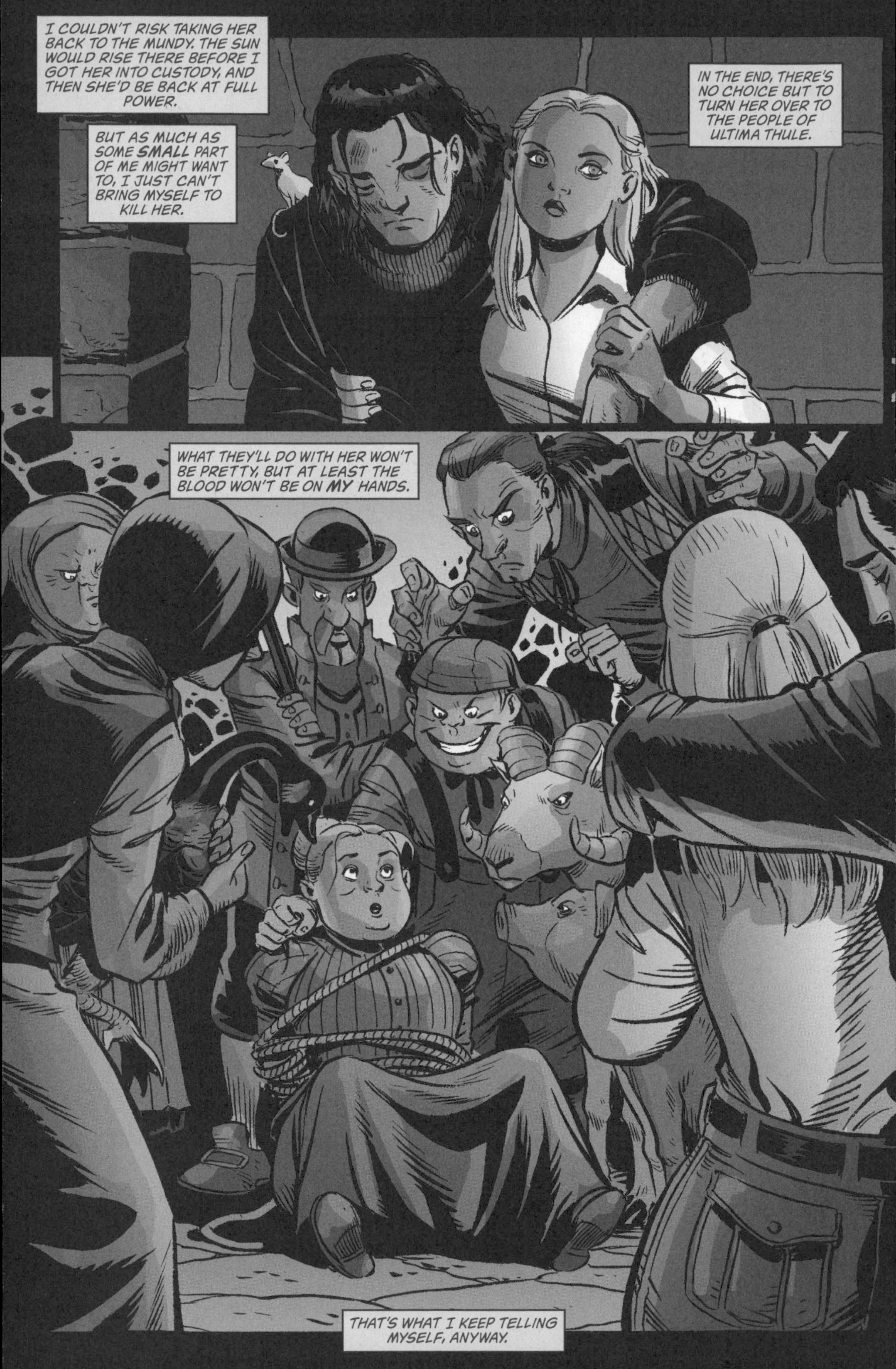
I COULDN'T RISK TAKING HER BACK TO THE MUNDY. THE SUN WOULD RISE THERE BEFORE I GOT HER INTO CUSTODY, AND THEN SHE'D BE BACK AT FULL POWER.
BUT AS MUCH AS SOME SMALL PART OF ME MIGHT WANT TO, I JUST CAN'T BRING MYSELF TO KILL HER.
IN THE END, THERE'S NO CHOICE BUT TO TURN HER OVER TO THE PEOPLE OF ULTIMA THULE.
WHAT THEY'LL DO WITH HER WON'T BE PRETTY, BUT AT LEAST THE BLOOD WON'T BE ON MY HANDS.
THAT'S WHAT I KEEP TELLING MYSELF, ANYWAY.

Fabletown.

A LONG BOAT-RIDE LATER, AND AFTER A QUICK SIDE TRIP TO THE FARM TO DROP OFF DICKORY, I'M BACK HOME.

AND LUCKY ME, LOOK AT THIS! A MOB OF FABLES STORMING MY STORE LIKE IT'S CASTLE FRANKENSTEIN.

the Glass Slipper

The Glass Slipper Has No Sole

CRISPIN SUCKS!

The Glass Slipper Has No Sole

Crispin Is A Fool!

spin s A fool!

CLEARLY, MY FAITHFUL SHOP ASSISTANT HAS GOTTEN UP TO SOME MISCHIEF IN MY ABSENCE.

IS THERE A PROBLEM?

NOT IN A MINUTE, THERE ISN'T.

IT TAKES A BIT OF NEGOTIATION...

...NO, *YOU* LISTEN. OUR AGREEMENT CLEARLY STATES THAT YOU'LL ACCEPT RETURNS ON "ANY DEFECTIVE MERCHANDISE," AND IF *THIS* DOESN'T QUALIFY I DON'T KNOW WHAT *DOES*...

...BUT IN THE END I'M ABLE TO CONVINCE THE ELVES TO TAKE BACK THE SHOES.

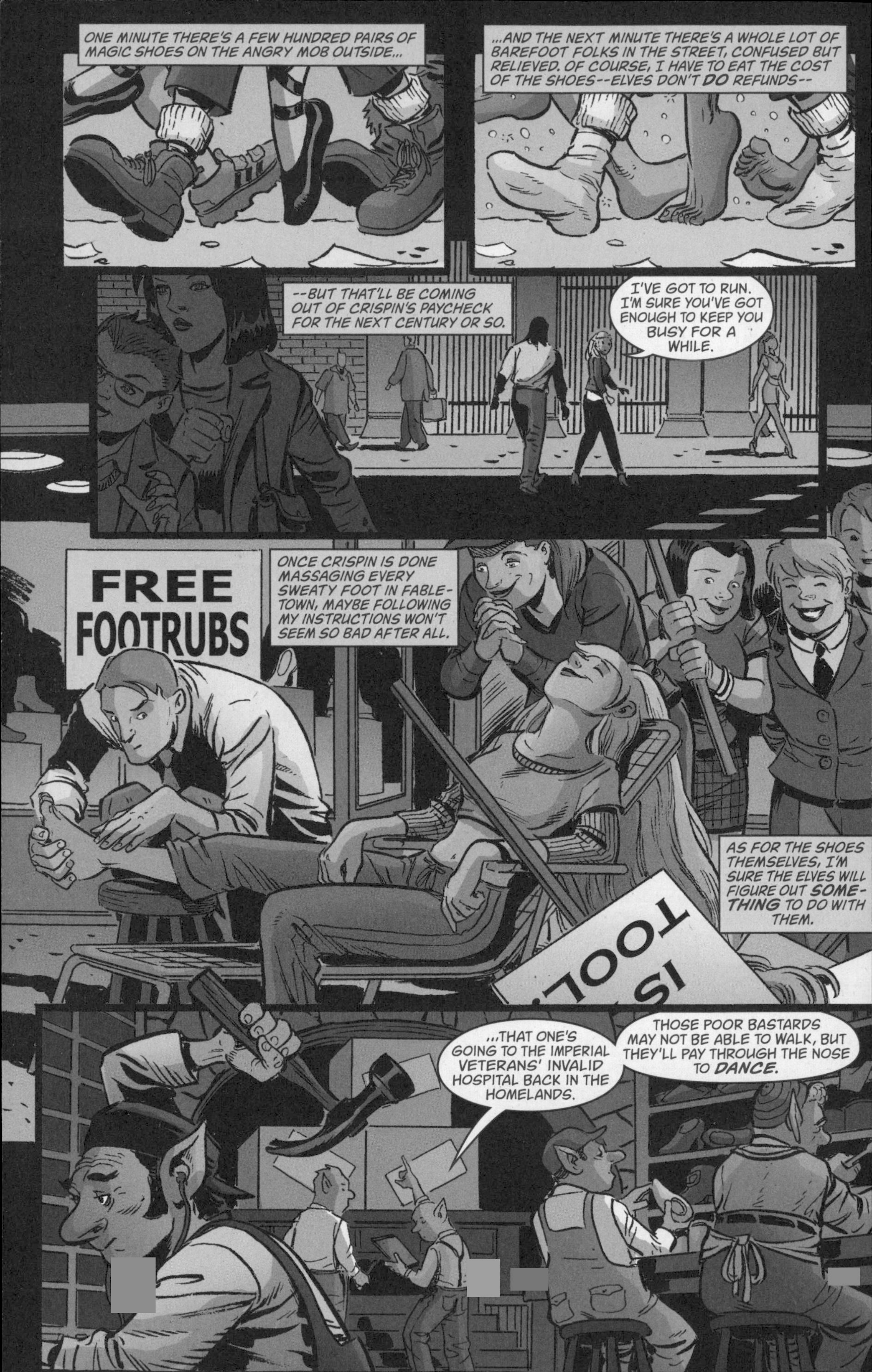
ONE MINUTE THERE'S A FEW HUNDRED PAIRS OF MAGIC SHOES ON THE ANGRY MOB OUTSIDE...
...AND THE NEXT MINUTE THERE'S A WHOLE LOT OF BAREFOOT FOLKS IN THE STREET, CONFUSED BUT RELIEVED. OF COURSE, I HAVE TO EAT THE COST OF THE SHOES--ELVES DON'T DO REFUNDS--
--BUT THAT'LL BE COMING OUT OF CRISPIN'S PAYCHECK FOR THE NEXT CENTURY OR SO.
I'VE GOT TO RUN. I'M SURE YOU'VE GOT ENOUGH TO KEEP YOU BUSY FOR A WHILE.
FREE FOOTRUBS
ONCE CRISPIN IS DONE MASSAGING EVERY SWEATY FOOT IN FABLE-TOWN, MAYBE FOLLOWING MY INSTRUCTIONS WON'T SEEM SO BAD AFTER ALL.
AS FOR THE SHOES THEMSELVES, I'M SURE THE ELVES WILL FIGURE OUT SOME-THING TO DO WITH THEM.
IS TOOL
...THAT ONE'S GOING TO THE IMPERIAL VETERANS' INVALID HOSPITAL BACK IN THE HOMELANDS.
THOSE POOR BASTARDS MAY NOT BE ABLE TO WALK, BUT THEY'LL PAY THROUGH THE NOSE TO DANCE.

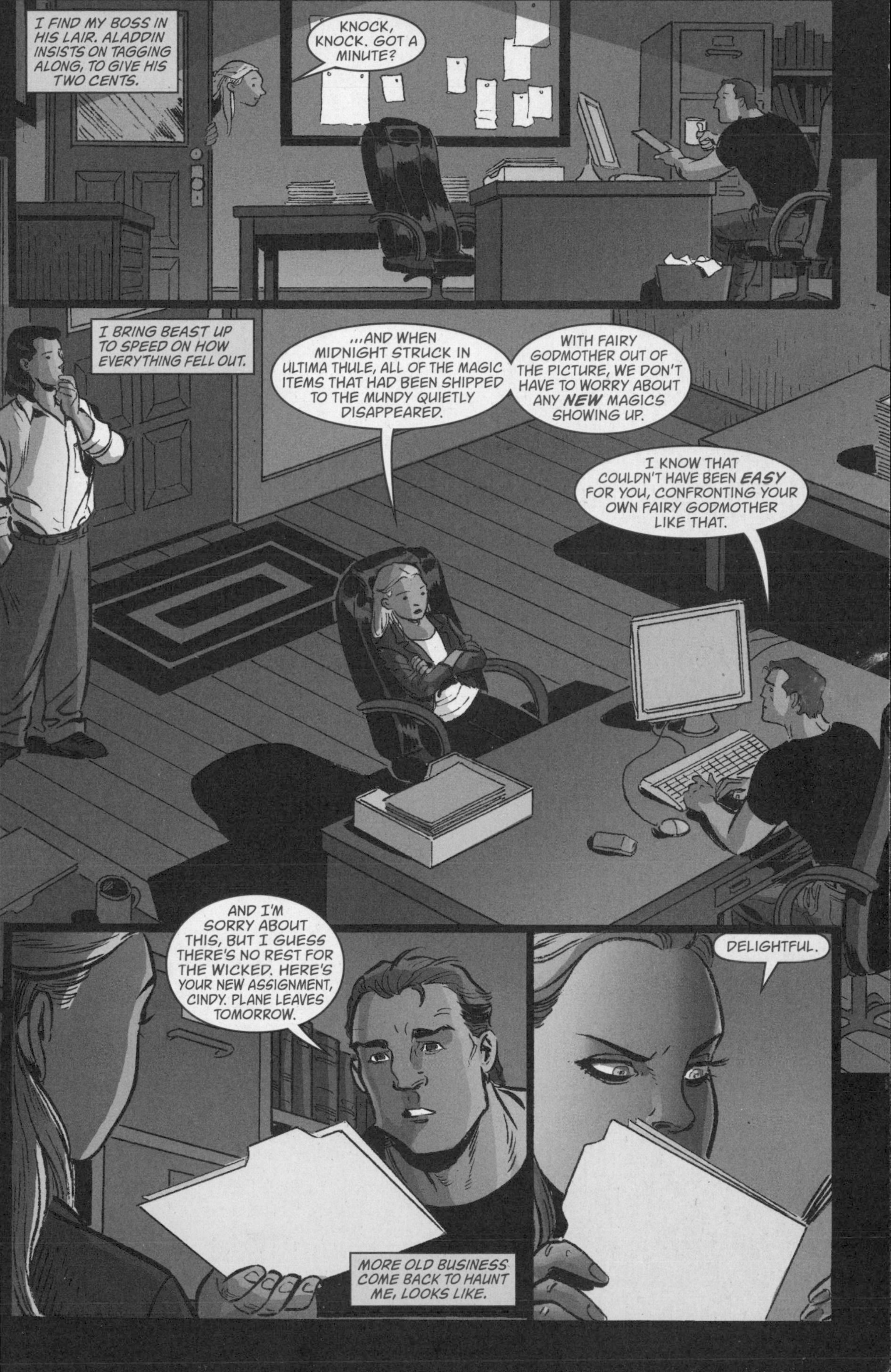
I FIND MY BOSS IN HIS LAIR. ALADDIN INSISTS ON TAGGING ALONG, TO GIVE HIS TWO CENTS.
KNOCK, KNOCK. GOT A MINUTE?
I BRING BEAST UP TO SPEED ON HOW EVERYTHING FELL OUT.
...AND WHEN MIDNIGHT STRUCK IN ULTIMA THULE, ALL OF THE MAGIC ITEMS THAT HAD BEEN SHIPPED TO THE MUNDY QUIETLY DISAPPEARED.
WITH FAIRY GODMOTHER OUT OF THE PICTURE, WE DON'T HAVE TO WORRY ABOUT ANY NEW MAGICS SHOWING UP.
I KNOW THAT COULDN'T HAVE BEEN EASY FOR YOU, CONFRONTING YOUR OWN FAIRY GODMOTHER LIKE THAT.
AND I'M SORRY ABOUT THIS, BUT I GUESS THERE'S NO REST FOR THE WICKED. HERE'S YOUR NEW ASSIGNMENT, CINDY. PLANE LEAVES TOMORROW.
MORE OLD BUSINESS COME BACK TO HAUNT ME, LOOKS LIKE.
DELIGHTFUL.

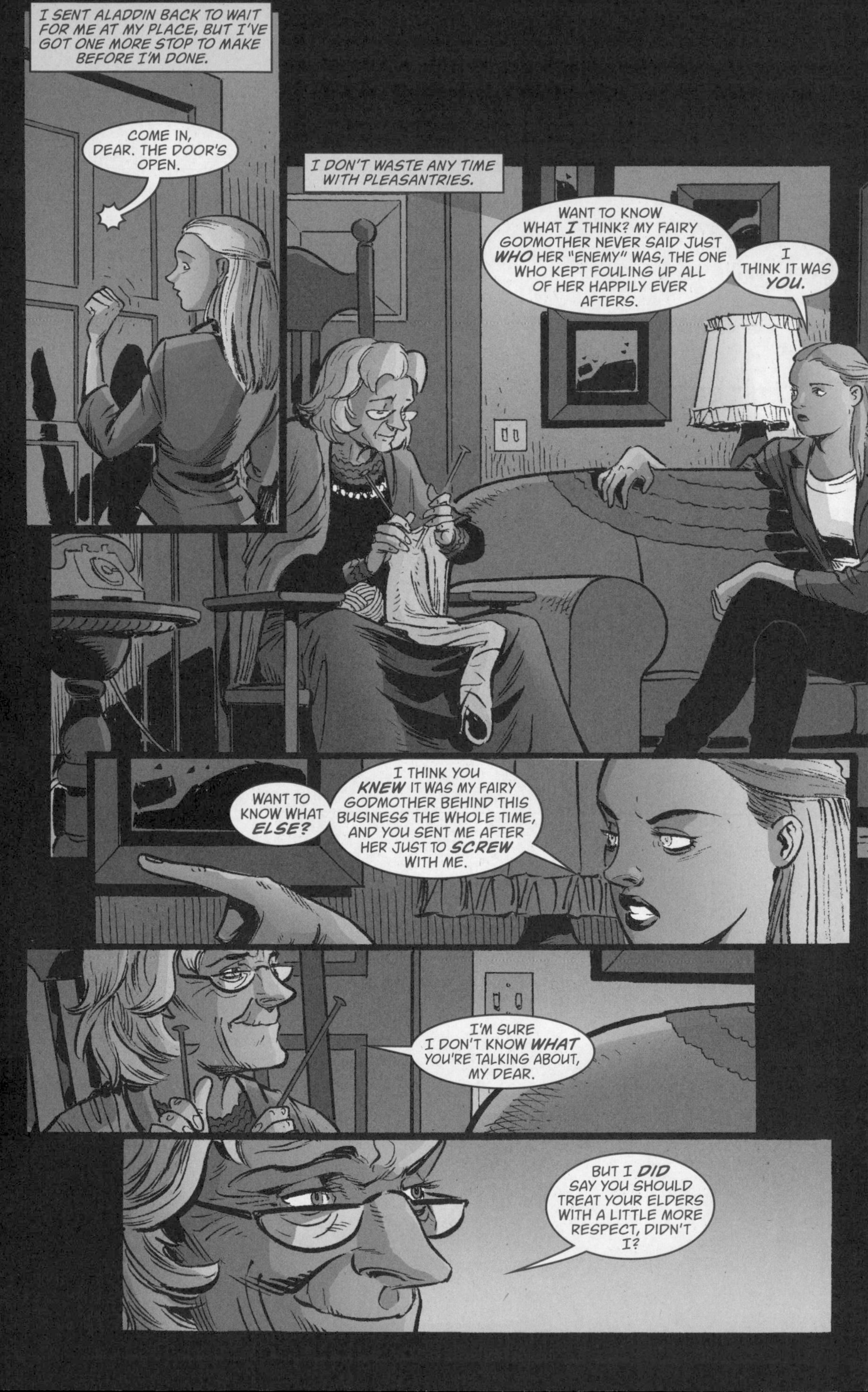
I SENT ALADDIN BACK TO WAIT FOR ME AT MY PLACE, BUT I'VE GOT ONE MORE STOP TO MAKE BEFORE I'M DONE.
COME IN, DEAR. THE DOOR'S OPEN.
I DON'T WASTE ANY TIME WITH PLEASANTRIES.
WANT TO KNOW WHAT I THINK? MY FAIRY GODMOTHER NEVER SAID JUST WHO HER "ENEMY" WAS, THE ONE WHO KEPT FOULING UP ALL OF HER HAPPILY EVER AFTERS.
I THINK IT WAS YOU.
WANT TO KNOW WHAT ELSE?
I THINK YOU KNEW IT WAS MY FAIRY GODMOTHER BEHIND THIS BUSINESS THE WHOLE TIME, AND YOU SENT ME AFTER HER JUST TO SCREW WITH ME.
I'M SURE I DON'T KNOW WHAT YOU'RE TALKING ABOUT, MY DEAR.
BUT I DID SAY YOU SHOULD TREAT YOUR ELDERS WITH A LITTLE MORE RESPECT, DIDN'T I?

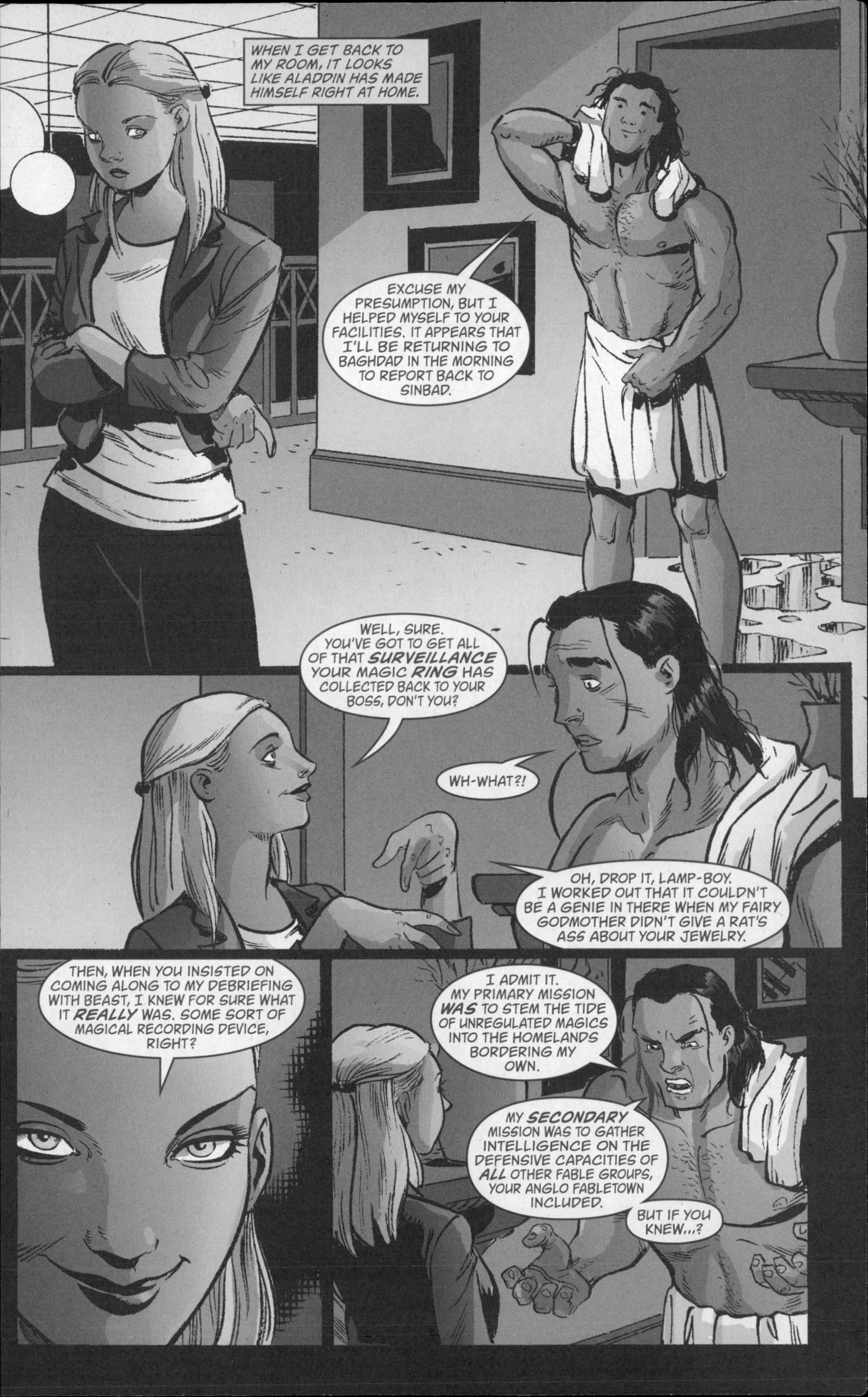
WHEN I GET BACK TO MY ROOM, IT LOOKS LIKE ALADDIN HAS MADE HIMSELF RIGHT AT HOME.
EXCUSE MY PRESUMPTION, BUT I HELPED MYSELF TO YOUR FACILITIES. IT APPEARS THAT I'LL BE RETURNING TO BAGHDAD IN THE MORNING TO REPORT BACK TO SINBAD.
WELL, SURE. YOU'VE GOT TO GET ALL OF THAT SURVEILLANCE YOUR MAGIC RING HAS COLLECTED BACK TO YOUR BOSS, DON'T YOU?
WH-WHAT?!
OH, DROP IT, LAMP-BOY. I WORKED OUT THAT IT COULDN'T BE A GENIE IN THERE WHEN MY FAIRY GODMOTHER DIDN'T GIVE A RAT'S ASS ABOUT YOUR JEWELRY.
THEN, WHEN YOU INSISTED ON COMING ALONG TO MY DEBRIEFING WITH BEAST, I KNEW FOR SURE WHAT IT REALLY WAS. SOME SORT OF MAGICAL RECORDING DEVICE, RIGHT?
I ADMIT IT. MY PRIMARY MISSION WAS TO STEM THE TIDE OF UNREGULATED MAGICS INTO THE HOMELANDS BORDERING MY OWN.
MY SECONDARY MISSION WAS TO GATHER INTELLIGENCE ON THE DEFENSIVE CAPACITIES OF ALL OTHER FABLE GROUPS, YOUR ANGLO FABLETOWN INCLUDED.
BUT IF YOU KNEW...?

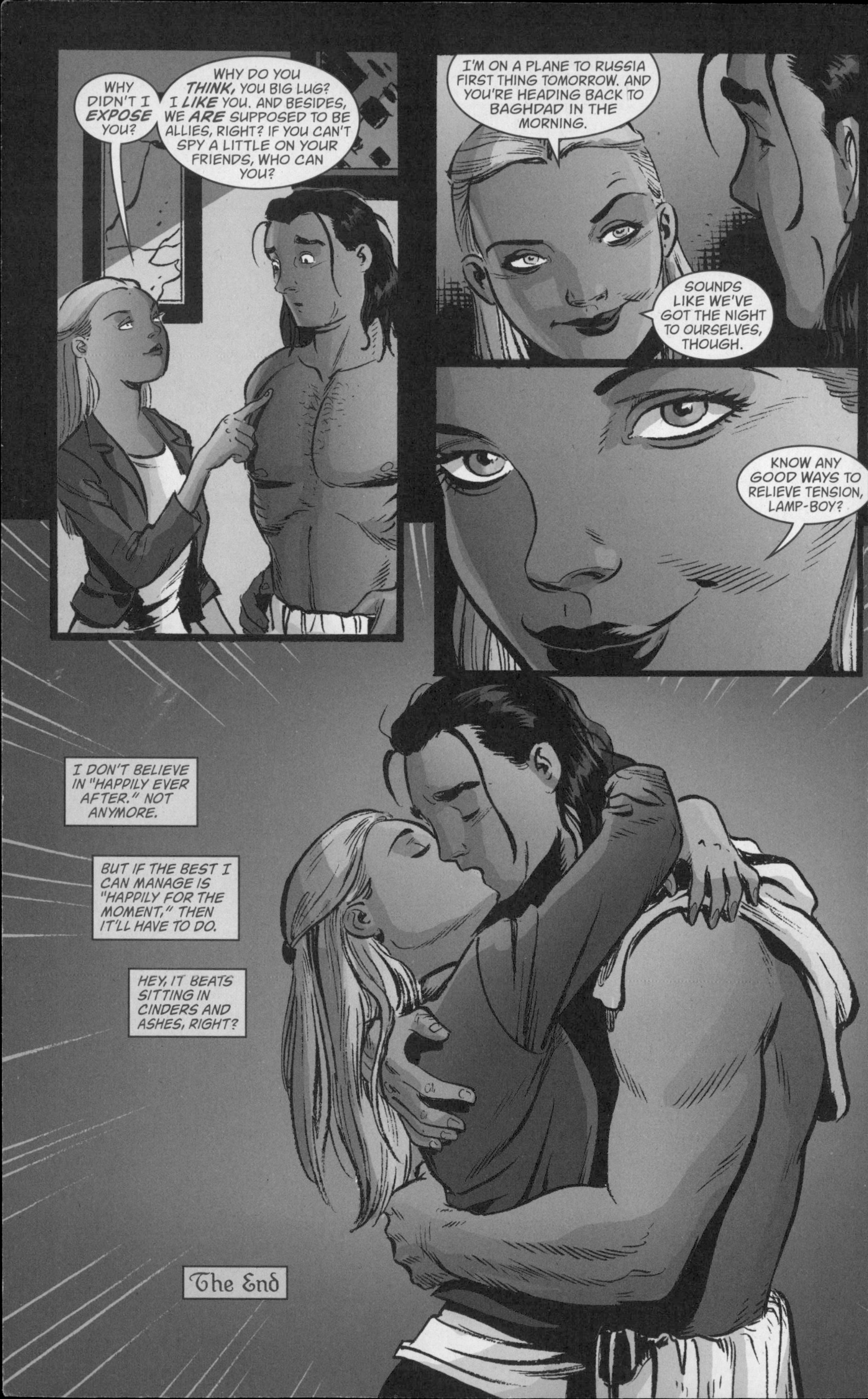
WHY DIDN'T I EXPOSE YOU?
WHY DO YOU THINK, YOU BIG LUG? I LIKE YOU. AND BESIDES, WE ARE SUPPOSED TO BE ALLIES, RIGHT? IF YOU CAN'T SPY A LITTLE ON YOUR FRIENDS, WHO CAN YOU?
I'M ON A PLANE TO RUSSIA FIRST THING TOMORROW. AND YOU'RE HEADING BACK TO BAGHDAD IN THE MORNING.
SOUNDS LIKE WE'VE GOT THE NIGHT TO OURSELVES, THOUGH.
KNOW ANY GOOD WAYS TO RELIEVE TENSION, LAMP-BOY?
I DON'T BELIEVE IN "HAPPILY EVER AFTER." NOT ANYMORE.
BUT IF THE BEST I CAN MANAGE IS "HAPPILY FOR THE MOMENT," THEN IT'LL HAVE TO DO.
HEY, IT BEATS SITTING IN CINDERS AND ASHES, RIGHT?
The End